Trial of the Century

People of the State of California
vs.
Orenthal James Simpson

Frank Schmalleger, Ph.D.

Prentice Hall
Upper Saddle River, New Jersey 07458

Library of Congress Cataloging-in-Publication Data

Schmalleger, Frank,
    Trial of the Century: people of the state of California
vs. Orenthal James Simpson / Frank Schmalleger
        p.   cm..
    ISBN 0-13-235953-7
    1. Simpson, O. J., 1947–   —Trials, litigation, etc.   2. Trials
(Murder)—California—Los Angeles.   I. Title
KF224.S485S35   1996
345.73 ' 02523 ' 09794—dc20
[347 .305252309794]

95–52152
CIP

Production Editor: *Adele Kupchik*
Managing Editor: *Mary Carnis*
Acquisitions Editor: *Neil Marquardt/R. Baliszewski*
Editorial Assistant: *Rose Mary Florio*
Director of Manufacturing & Production: *Bruce Johnson*
Manufacturing Buyer: *Ed O'Dougherty*
Marketing Manager: *Frank Mortimer, Jr.*
Formatting/page make-up: *Frank Schmalleger*
Printer/Binder: *R.R. Donnelley & Sons–Harrisonburg*
Cover Design: *Amy Rosen*
Cover Photos: *AP/Wide World Photos*

Printed in the United States of America

10 9 8 7 6 5 4 3 2 1

ISBN 0-13-235953-7

Prentice-Hall International (UK) Limited, London
Prentice-Hall of Australia Pty. Limited, Sydney
Prentice-Hall Canada Inc., Toronto
Prentice-Hall Hispanoamericana, S.A., Mexico
Prentice-Hall of India Private Limited, New Delhi
Prentice-Hall of Japan, Inc., Tokyo
Pearson Education Asia Pte. Ltd., Singapore
Editoria Prentice-Hall do Brasil, Ltda., Rio De Janeiro

For my mother,

MARGARETA "PEG" SCHMALLEGER

who taught me how to write.

Contents

Foreword

Putting the O.J. Simpson trial in perspective remains an important task for many in this country. A first step toward gaining a sense of perspective is to realize that the trial of O. J. Simpson represents the most recent addition to a long series of high interest, massively publicized, media-judicial events. Historically, "media-trials" occur with regularity. There have been at least a dozen trials called the "trial of the century" in this century alone. Interest in such trials by both the media and the marketplace has grown steadily. Following their allotted period of intense public and media scrutiny, such trials generally pass into folklore and relative obscurity. Public recognition of names such as Fatty Arbuckle, Sacco and Vanzetti, Bruno Hauptmann, the Rosenbergs, Patty Hearst and others has faded today, after one time mesmerizing public interest and media attention.

Media trials are thus judicial proceedings that have been co-opted by the mass media and repackaged and presented in entertainment style formats. The three most common types of media trials are: 1.) Abuse of Power, 2.) Evil Strangers, and 3.) Sinful Rich trials. The first type involves corruption and malfeasance by officials and authority figures, and is exemplified by cases involving government bribery and police brutality. The second involves murderous or brutal assaults by strangers on innocents and is exemplified by serial killers and child abuse cases. The third involves deviance and crime committed by the wealthy and famous. All three media trial themes are replicated in popular storylines consistently found in the entertainment media.

The Simpson trial is of the Sinful Rich genre. The trial's storyline can be found in numerous novels and Hollywood films: handsome, rich, successful ex-athlete is accused of murdering his ex-wife in a jealous rage amid a sea of rumored drug abuse, sexual deviance and fascinating sub-characters — racist cops, beautiful women, off-beat friends and acquaintances. Indeed, a large part of the reason for the interest in and for the ultimate social impact of this trial was that it became a long running, mass media entertainment vehicle — a drama-in-real-life. Emotions associated with the trial rose as spectators realized that this media story's ending might not be the one they expected or desired. And, unlike a Hollywood movie, this story could not have a happy ending for everyone.

The social impact and importance of media trials, including Simpson's trial, is seldom connected to the extent of harm directly resulting from the crimes they reflect. Their cultural significance is generated by the massive attention they receive and the intense public debate they engender. Their social importance lies not so much in what happened during crime commission, but in the perception and interpretation of what happened during trial proceedings. The coverage and marketing of these trials colors social perceptions of the criminal justice system, and of the larger society in which the justice system is imbedded. These trials are significant because they often impact public attitudes and views regarding crime, justice, and society for years to come.

It is therefore important for these media trials to be recognized as symbolic events and to simultaneously have accurate, objective accounts of them available for scrutiny. Frank Schmalleger's book, *Trial of the Century*, meets both of these needs, and does so in very readable fashion. While placing the trial in its social and legal contexts, his book is a refreshing exception to the plethora of O.J. works that are more akin to disposable tabloid productions than informative, intelligent considerations. This work is an unbiased summation of the trial based on the trial record. The book relates what was actually said and done, rather than what was reported. It utilizes the trial record to explain underlying legal standards and procedural steps. Concepts like courtroom work groups, preliminary hearings, factual versus legal guilt, and the adversarial system, to name a few, are clearly and concisely interwoven into a chronological review of the Simpson trial. As always, Schmalleger delivers a well written, quality text.

As such, the book will be interesting to students and citizens, and useful both in and out of the classroom. In contrast to the exploitative works and media "info-tainment" coverage, this book is indeed instructional. Many who watched and followed the trial will be fascinated to learn more about what they watched — and what they didn't have the opportunity to see. This book will help past spectators and future students understand this trial, its role, and its place in American culture. *Trial of the Century* provides a quality standard against which to measure other published versions of the Simpson trial.

Ray Surette, Ph.D.
Professor of Criminal Justice
  and Legal Studies
University of Central Florida

Preface

Few events in the history of this great country, aside from wars and massive natural disasters have captured American attention as did the O.J. Simpson double murder trial. Almost anyone reading this book will remember the tragic deaths of Nicole Brown Simpson and Ronald Goldman—murders for which former football superstar and media personality O.J. Simpson was tried, but acquitted. The trial splashed its way across television screens, radio dials, newspapers and magazines throughout much of 1995, with media interest in the drama's key personalities and events extending well into the following year.

While the "Simpson trial," as the event has come to be known, is noteworthy for the media coverage it received, the trial also provided an intense and informative look into the psyche of American society—highlighting divergent attitudes between racial and ethnic groups, the depths of which few had previously suspected.

The Simpson trial, however, is important for another reason, as well: it may have been the best documented criminal proceeding in the history of the United States (the trial produced more than 40,000 pages of transcribed materials, and countless other pages of commentary and analysis were associated with the event). As such, it provides an unprecedented opportunity for anyone to become more familiar with the workings of our nation's criminal justice system, especially 1.) trial practice, 2.) law enforcement investigative activities, 3.) scientific evidence gathering and analysis, 4.) tactics available to criminal defense attorneys, 5.) challenges facing prosecutors and district attorneys, and 6.) the everyday realities of American criminal justice practice.

A word of caution is in order, however—because the Simpson trial was so unusual in some respects (i.e., the "dream team" of defense attorneys assembled to defend Simpson, the intense media interest in the proceedings, the personality and reputation of O.J. Simpson himself, and the alleged interracial nature of the crimes) it is not necessarily a study in "typical" criminal justice procedures. Even so, the extensive documentation publicly available on the Simpson trial will insure that the event remains intellectual fodder for years to come.

The Simpson trial has already shaped perceptions of the justice system, and it will likely provide ammunition for critical thinking about that system for years to come. Ultimately, many hope, a careful consideration of the trial and its ramifications will feed the intellectual movement leading to continued improvements in the American way of justice.

The well-known British philosopher and statesman Benjamin Disraeli (1804-81) once defined justice as "truth in action." It is my hope that this book can serve at least some small, but positive, part in the process by which the practice of criminal justice in this country continues to evolve toward the "truth in action" ideal.

Frank Schmalleger, Ph.D.
Director
The Justice Research Association

Note: If you are a teacher and are planning to use this book in a classroom setting, an instructor's manual is available to help you. The manual includes useful discussion and test questions, as well as chapter summaries and learning objectives. Please contact your local Prentice Hall representative or call 800-526-0485 for further information.

Acknowledgments and Sources

No book is written in a vacuum. I wish to thank my family for their support during the time it took to write this volume. Thanks also to Denise Brown, copyeditor at Prentice Hall who laboriously read and corrected the manuscript as it developed; my Prentice Hall editors Robin Baliszewski and Neil Marquardt; Adele Kupchik, who headed production; photo researcher Chris Pullo; cover designer Marianne Frasco; and everyone else who contributed to this book — whether named or not. A special "thank you" goes to my good friend and legal scholar Terry Hutchins. Thanks also to "pool" photographers who shot the images used in this book, to *USA Today* and the *USA Today* Library for the graphic art they provided, to Bill Robles for his excellent drawings of the jury, and to the American Bar Association and Fraternal Order of Police for reprint permissions.

Much of the information contained between these covers came from or through various on-line sources, and I am grateful to those resources and to the people who run them for making my research both efficient and enjoyable. Transcripts, autopsy reports, and daily trial information were assembled from a variety of on-line areas, most of them through the Internet's World Wide Web. The following electronic sources deserve special recognition for the quantity and quality of the information they provided: *Dimitri's O.J. Simpson Trial Center*, Cable News Network's *O.J. Simpson Main Page*, Court TV's *Law Center*, Pathfinder's *O.J. Files*, *The News Tribune*, *The 'Lectric Law Library*, KNBC's *O.J. Simpson: The Trial* page, Jack Walraven's *The O.J. Simpson Trial Court Transcripts* site, as well as discussion and court document areas on CompuServe and America On Line which were devoted to the "O.J. Simpson case."

Given the reputable nature of most of these sources, I believe that the materials available through them are accurate even though their route to me may have sometimes been less than direct. Likewise, I have attempted to relate on-line transcribed materials as accurately as possible. However, any book is only as accurate as its sources. While I believe the sources used in preparing this book to be generally accurate, and while they have generally represented themselves to be so, I cannot absolutely warrant them to be correct. Should the reader have a question concerning the original source of any information contained herein, please contact the author.

About the Author

Frank Schmalleger, Ph.D. is Director of the Justice Research Association, a private consulting firm and "think-tank" focusing on issues of crime and justice. The Justice Research Association, which is based in Hilton Head Island, South Carolina, serves the needs of the nation's civil and criminal justice planners and administrators through workshops, conferences, and grant-writing and program evaluation support.

Dr. Schmalleger holds degrees from the University of Notre Dame and the Ohio State University, having earned both a master's (1970) and doctorate in sociology (1974) from Ohio State University with a special emphasis in criminology. From 1976-1994 he taught criminal justice courses at Pembroke State University, a campus of the University of North Carolina. For the last 16 of those years he chaired the university's Department of Sociology, Social Work, and Criminal Justice. As an adjunct professor with Webster University in St. Louis, Missouri, Schmalleger helped develop the university's graduate program in security administration and loss prevention. He taught courses in that curriculum for more than a decade. Schmalleger has also taught in the New School for Social Research's on-line graduate program, helping to build the world's first electronic classrooms in support of distance learning through computer telecommunications.

Frank Schmalleger is the author of numerous articles and many books, including the widely used *Criminal Justice Today* (Prentice Hall, 1997); *Criminology Today* (Prentice Hall, 1996); *Computers in Criminal Justice* (Wyndham Hall Press, 1991); *Career Paths: A Guide to Jobs in Federal Law Enforcement* (Regents/Prentice Hall, 1994); *Criminal Justice Ethics* (Greenwood Press, 1991); *Finding Criminal Justice in the Library* (Wyndham Hall Press, 1991); *Ethics in Criminal Justice* (Wyndham Hall Press, 1990); *A History of Corrections* (Foundations Press of Notre Dame, 1983); and *The Social Basis of Criminal Justice* (University Press of America, 1981).

Schmalleger is also founding editor of the journal *The Justice Professional.* He serves as editor for the Prentice Hall series *Criminal Justice in the Twenty-First Century*, and as Imprint Advisor for Greenwood Publishing Group's criminal justice reference series. His most recent project involves development of an encyclopedia on crime and justice for the Greenwood Publishing Group, for which he serves as editor-in-chief.

Schmalleger's philosophy of both teaching and writing can be summed up in these words: "In order to communicate knowledge we must first catch, then hold, a person's interest—be it a student, colleague, or policy-maker. Our writing, our speaking, and our teaching must be relevant to the problems facing people today, and they must — in some way — help solve those problems."

Chapter 1
Trial Background
and Court Procedure

Nicole Brown Simpson and O.J. Simpson in happier times.
Photo: AP/Wide World Photos.

TRIAL BACKGROUND

In the early morning hours of June 13, 1994 a man whose attention was attracted by a barking dog discovered two bodies in West Los Angeles. Dead was the beautiful white wife of black Heisman Trophy winner and football great Orenthal James Simpson. Killed along with her, in a savage knife attack, was handsome Ronald Goldman, a waiter and aspiring young actor. The murders occurred at 875 South Bundy Drive, in the exclusive Brentwood section of Los Angeles. Police investigators quickly found enough evidence, including what appeared to be matching blood stains at the murder scene and in Simpson's vehicle and in his nearby mansion for them to focus quickly on Simpson as their only suspect. Nineteen previous incidents of spouse abuse involving Simpson convinced them that they "had their man."

The Early Years

Orenthal James Simpson was born on July 9, 1947 at Stanford University Hospital to Simmie and Eunice Durden Simpson. Simpson had a brother, Melvin, and two sisters, Shirley and Carmelita. His teenage years were not without their problems. In 1960 Simpson, then 13-years-old, joined the Persian Warriors, a black San Francisco gang, and in 1962 spent a short time incarcerated at the San Francisco Youth Guidance Center. In 1965 Simpson graduated from San Francisco's Galileo High School, then entered San Francisco City College. On June 24, 1967, while still a student, he married eighteen-year-old Marquerite Whitley. From 1967 until 1969 he played football at the University of Southern California, dropping out in 1969 after winning the Heisman Trophy. He became the Buffalo Bills' first round draft pick in 1969.

He rose to football fame as a Heisman Trophy-winning running back for the University of Southern California Trojans, went on to an outstanding professional career in the National Football League with the Buffalo Bills and the San Francisco 49ers, and was inducted into the Pro Football Hall of Fame in 1985 — six months after his marriage to Nicole Brown.

Simpson met Nicole soon after she graduated from Dana Hills High School in Los Angeles in 1977. At the time he was in the throes of a failing first marriage.

After two decades on the football field, O.J. signed a contract with Hertz rental cars, becoming a national spokesman for the company. He also made promotional appearances for Nabisco Brands, Wilson Sporting Goods, Treesweet, and Dingo Boots. His numerous television appearances as a sports commentator for ABC and NBC, advertiser, on talk shows, and bit roles in a number of movies, including *Towering Inferno*, the *Clansman*, *Killer Force*, *Capricorn I*, *Firepower*, and various episodes of *Naked Gun*, and the HBO series *First and Ten* made him something of a television mainstay.

Both on camera and in the public eye, O.J. Simpson was renowned for his good spirits and caring attitude. He signed autographs with consistently good humor, regularly visited the sick and terminally ill in hospitals, and joked with nervous youngsters who wanted to meet him.

Nicole Brown Simpson was born in Frankfurt, Germany, on May 19, 1959, to Lou and Judy Brown. Her mother was a native-born German, who married Lou Brown while he was stationed in West Germany as a correspondent for the armed forces newspaper *Stars and Stripes* in the

1950s. Returning to the United States, the Brown family settled in Garden Grove, California, where Nicole and her two sisters grew up surrounded by middle class activities in Brownies, Girl Scouts, dance lessons, and the Pep Club. Nicole was known to family and friends as a "kind of wild, free spirit who had a zest for life." She had a temper, but also won a crown as homecoming princess at Dana Hills High School. Friends who knew her said she liked to party and hang out on the beach.

A broadcasting friend of O.J.'s later described Nicole this way: "She was a dramatic person. A person with physical electricity. A dramatic physical presence. If you ask me whether she was beautiful, I'd say no, she was not beautiful. If you ask me whether she was elegant, I'd say not necessarily. She had an electric physical presence. As for her personality, she had some vivacity, some spirit about her that was just there. If you were in a roomful of people, your eye turned to Nicole. There was something unusual about her. She was a willful, spirited person — a party animal. She loved to say, 'I want to go dance all night.'"[1]

In 1977, while and working as a waitress at a posh Beverly Hills nightclub called the *Daisy*, she met O.J. Simpson. Though still married to his first wife, Simpson had a reputation as a lady's man — with a penchant for young, beautiful white women. Nicole had just turned 18. In 1985 she and O.J. were married in a splashy affair at his Tudor home in Brentwood.

After they were married, the two had all the trappings wealth could bring — including homes in Laguna Beach, California, and New York City, plus and a personal fleet of Rolls-Royces, Ferraris, and other luxury cars. They took frequent and expensive trips to Mexico and Aspen, and Nicole once said that O.J. regularly gave her $6,000 a month in spending money.

She related well to O.J.'s children from his first marriage, daughter Arnelle, and son Jason, both of whom were teenagers when O.J. and Nicole married. Soon, however, she gave birth to her own children, Sydney Brook Simpson (born October 17, 1985), and Justin Ryan Simpson (born August 6, 1988). Not long after the birth of their second child, however, the Simpson's marriage began to fray. In 1989, for example, Beverly Hills lunch goers at the La Scala restaurant watched as Nicole confronted her husband as he left the restaurant — hurling obscenities at him and accusing him of having an affair. One observer described it this way: "All of a sudden, out of the blue, came Nicole. She just flipped out. She was screaming obscenities at us from her car. She screamed at O.J., 'If you're going to cheat on me, why don't you at least pick someone pretty.' She was absolutely crazy with rage. It wasn't a pretty sight." When a Beverly Hills police officer drove up Nicole drove away.

As the marriage fell apart Simpson started beating Nicole. On January 1, 1989 Nicole called Los Angeles 911 dispatchers at 3:30 am saying Simpson was attacking her. He was allegedly screaming "I'll kill you," as he beat her. Simpson pled guilty to charges of spousal abuse, and was sentenced on May 24, 1989 to two years probation and 120 hours of community service. He was also fined $470, ordered to pay $500 to Sojourn Battered Women's Program, and assigned to counseling. On February 6, 1992 Nicole and O.J. officially separated, and on February 25, 1992 Nicole filed for divorce. Under terms of the divorce settlement Nicole received a $700,000 condominium in the exclusive Brentwood section of Los Angeles, one of the couple's Ferraris, jewelry, a lump sum of $433,000, tax-free, and $10,000 a month in child support. Nicole started dating after the divorce was finalized, but Simpson became wildly jealous, and in 1993 the two began dating again.

Crime Chronology: June 12-13, 1994

At 12:10 a.m. on the morning of June 13, 1994, the slashed and bloodied bodies of Nicole Brown Simpson and Ronald Goldman were discovered in the gated courtyard leading to Ms. Simpson's expensive townhome in the exclusive Brentwood section of Los Angeles. Although no one other than the killer and the victims is known to have seen the murders take place, the following chronology of those two days' events can be pieced together (all hours shown are based upon Los Angeles or "Pacific" time):

June 12, 1994: 9 a.m. On the morning before the murders, O.J. Simpson played golf at the Riviera Country Club outside Los Angeles.

2:30 p.m. Brian "Kato" Kaelin, a friend who is living temporarily in O.J. Simpson's guest house, sees Simpson at home for the first time that day. He and Simpson discuss Simpson's morning golf game.

4 p.m. O.J. and ex-wife Nicole attend daughter Sydney's dance recital at Paul Revere Junior High school in West Los Angeles, but sit apart.

6 p.m. Simpson and Nicole leave dance recital separately.

6:30 p.m. Nicole goes to the Mezzaluna restaurant with her children and a few friends for dinner. Waiter Ronald Goldman is working in the restaurant, but he doesn't serve the group. O.J. is not with the dinner party.

6:30 – 7 p.m. Kato Kaelin sees and talks with O.J. at the estate after a televised basketball game between the Houston Rockets and the New York Knicks.

8:30 p.m. Kaelin leaves the Jacuzzi located on the Simpson estate and walks to his room to place a telephone call.

8:30 – 9 p.m. Nicole Brown Simpson leaves the Mezzaluna restaurant.

9:15 – 9:45 p.m. Kaelin and Simpson visit a local McDonald's restaurant, driving there and returning in Simpson's Rolls-Royce.

9:30 p.m. Returning home, Nicole telephones the Mezzaluna to say that she had left a pair of prescription sunglasses on the table. Waiter Ronald Goldman offers to return them when he leaves work. Glasses are placed in an envelope by the restaurant's manager and given to Goldman.

9:33 p.m. Ronald Goldman clocks out of the Mezzaluna Restaurant, has a quick drink in the restaurant's bar, and leaves the Mezzaluna about 9:50 p.m., walking the few blocks to Ms. Simpson's condominium.

10:00 – 10:15 p.m. Somewhere around this time Nicole Brown Simpson and Ronald Goldman are stabbed to death in the courtyard outside of the front entrance to Ms. Simpson's home.

10:15 – 10:20 p.m. Ms. Simpson's neighbor hears a dog's "plaintive wail."

10:25 p.m. Limousine driver Allan Park arrives at the Simpson estate to take Simpson to the airport where he is to catch a flight to Chicago. He buzzes for Simpson, but there is no answer.

10:40 p.m. Still on the telephone in the guest house, Kaelin hears a thumping noise against the outside wall of his room. The limousine driver continues to buzz the house using the intercom, but receives no answer.

10:41 – 10:45 p.m. Kaelin walks outside the guest house to investigate the noise. It is dark, and he sees nothing nearby. He does, however, notice the limousine waiting outside the gate.

10:50 p.m. The limousine driver pages his boss for instructions. His boss returns his call five minutes later and tells him to keep waiting.

10:50 – 10:55 p.m. A neighbor who is out walking his dog encounters Ms. Simpson's unattended white Akita dog which is barking and seems to have blood on its paws.

10:56 – 10:57 p.m. At the Simpson estate the waiting limousine driver sees a white male carrying a flashlight. About the same time he sees a 6-foot tall, 200-pound black person wearing dark clothes quickly cross the driveway and enter the house through the front door. Park again buzzes the house and someone, apparently Simpson, answers to say that he will be coming out shortly.

About 11:01 p.m. Simpson comes out of his house, speaks with the limousine driver, and helps load luggage into the trunk.

About 11:15 p.m. Simpson leaves the estate in the limousine, headed for the Los Angeles airport.

11:35 p.m. Simpson arrives at the Los Angeles airport.

11:45 p.m. Chicago to Los Angeles flight leaves Chicago's O'Hare Airport with Simpson on-board.

June 13, 1994: 12:01 a.m. The neighbor who found Nicole's Akita "let the dog lead us."

12:10 a.m. The dog leads neighbors to Ms. Simpson's exclusive condominium on Bundy Drive, where the bodies of Ms. Simpson and Ronald Goldman are discovered.

12:20 a.m. Police are called to the murder scene.

4:15 a.m. Simpson checks into the O'Hare Plaza-Hotel.

4:35 a.m. Determining the identity of Nicole Brown Simpson, police investigators go to O.J. Simpson's estate in Brentwood, which is located two miles from the murder scene. They intend to advise him of the death of his ex-wife. Finding no one at home they scale the gates of the estate, later saying that they feared someone inside might be injured. They then discover a trail of blood leading from Simpson's Bronco to the front door. Investigators also find a sleeping Kato Kaelin and a bloody glove near Kaelin guest room which matches one found lying at Goldman's feet.

5 a.m. A Los Angeles police officer telephones Simpson telling him that his ex-wife has been murdered. Immediately afterward, O.J. makes

10 calls from his hotel room. At least one is placed to a woman whom he had recently been dating.

6:30 a.m.   An apparently frantic O.J. checks out of the hotel and rushes back to the Chicago airport.

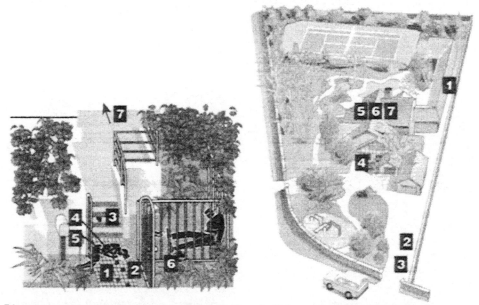

Diagram of the murder scene on South Bundy Drive. © 1995 *USA Today*.
Reprinted with permission.

Graphics Key, Left Diagram (Murder Scene)   Right Diagram (O.J.'s Estate)

1. O.J.'s blood (DNA testing)
2. O.J.'s blood (DNA testing)
3. Bloody shoeprint (size 12)
4. Nicole's body
5. Pool of blood (Nicole's)
6. Blood on Goldman's shoe (Nicole's)
7. O.J.'s blood on rear gate (DNA testing)

1. Bloody glove found
2. & 3. O.J.'s blood on drive
4. O.J.'s blood in foyer
5, 6 & 7. Spots of O.J.'s and Nicole's blood on socks found in bedroom.
Note location of Bronco.

7:41 a.m. Simpson begins the flight back to Los Angeles.

10:45 a.m. Police obtain a search warrant for Simpson's mansion. Shortly afterward they enter the home and find more blood in various areas of house and in the Bronco.

Post-Crime Chronology and Pre-Trial Activities

What follows is a listing of activities and significant events after Simpson's arrival back in Los Angeles on the morning of the murders, and up until the time his trial on double-murder charges began.

June 13, 1994: 11:30 a.m. Simpson arrives at Brentwood. By noon he been briefly questioned and is placed in handcuffs. Simpson's attorney, Howard Weitzman, arrives and persuades police to uncuff him.

12 noon. Simpson is taken to police headquarters and questioned for 3½ hours. The interrogation was conducted by detectives Philip Vannatter and Thomas Lange, the Los Angeles Police Department's chief investigators assigned to the case.

Excerpts from publically circulated versions of a transcript[2] of Simpson's June 13th police interrogation are reproduced below. Although the reported interrogation appears wide-ranging, detectives repeatedly questioned Simpson about a cut on his hand. At first Simpson alluded to cutting his hand in Los Angeles — before leaving on a flight to Chicago — but said that the wound was re-opened after arriving at his Chicago hotel:

Vannatter: How did you get the injury on your hand?

Simpson: I don't know. The first time, when I was in Chicago and all, but at the house I was just running around.

Vannatter: How did you do it in Chicago?

Simpson: I broke a glass. One of you guys had just called me, and I was in the bathroom, and I just kind of went bonkers for a little bit.

Lange: Is that how you cut it?

Simpson: Mmm, it was cut before, but I think I just opened it again, I'm not sure.

Lange: Do you recall bleeding at all in your truck, in the Bronco?

Simpson: I recall bleeding at my house and then I went to the Bronco.

The last thing I did before I left, when I was rushing, was went and got my phone out of the Bronco.

• • •

Lange: So do you recall bleeding at all?

Simpson: Yeah, I mean, I knew I was bleeding, but it was no big deal. I bleed all the time. I play golf and stuff, so there's always something, nicks and stuff here and there.

Lange: So did you do anything? When did you put the Band-Aid on it?

Simpson: Actually, I asked the girl this morning for it.

Lange: And she got it?

Simpson: Yeah, 'cause last night with Kato, when I was leaving, he was saying something to me, and I was rushing to get my phone, and I put a little thing on it, and it stopped.

After questioning Simpson about other matters, Detective Lange returns the focus of the interrogation to the cut on Simpson's hand:

Lange: ... We've got, of course, the cut on your finger that you aren't real clear on. Do you recall having that cut on your finger the last time you were at Nicole's house?

Simpson: A week ago?

Lange: Yeah.

Simpson: No. It was last night.

Lange: OK, so last night you cut it.

Vannatter: Somewhere after the recital?

Simpson: Somewhere when I was rushing to get out of my house.

Vannatter: OK, after the recital.

Simpson: Yeah.

Vannatter: What do you think happened? Do you have any idea?

Simpson: I have no idea, man. You guys haven't told me anything. I have no idea. When you said to my daughter, who said something to me today, that somebody else might have been involved, I have absolutely no idea what happened. I don't know how, why or what. But you guys haven't told me anything. Every time I ask you guys, you say you're going to tell me in a bit.

Vannatter: Well, we don't know a lot of answers to these questions yet ourselves, OJ, OK?

Near the conclusion of the interrogation, questioning again returns to the cut on Simpson's hand:

Lange: Understand, the reason we're talking to you is because you're the ex-husband.

Simpson: I know, I'm the number one target, and now you tell me I've got blood all over the place.

Lange: Well, there's blood at your house in the driveway, and we've got a search warrant, and we're going to go get the blood. We found some in your house. Is that your blood that's there?

Simpson: If it's dripped, it's what I dripped running around trying to leave.

Lange: Last night?

Simpson: Yeah, and I wasn't aware that it was...I was aware that I... You know, I was trying to get out of the house. I didn't even pay any attention to it, I saw it when I was in the kitchen, and I grabbed a napkin or something, and that was it. I didn't think about it after that.

Vannatter: That was last night after you got home from the recital, when you were rushing?

Simpson: That was last night when I was...I don't know what I was... I was in the car getting my junk out of the car. I was in the house throwing hangers and stuff in my suitcase. I was doing my little crazy what I do...I mean, I do it everywhere. Anybody who has ever picked me up says that O.J.'s a whirlwind, he's running, he's grabbing things, and that's what I was doing.

Vannatter: Well, I'm going to step out and I'm going to get a photographer to come down and photograph your hand there. And then here pretty soon we're going to take you downstairs and get some blood from you. OK? I'll be right back.

_____

June 14, 1994. Simpson returns to seclusion at his Brentwood estate.

June 15, 1994. Simpson attends private service for his ex-wife at Orange County funeral home as evidence against him continues to grow. Well-known criminal defense attorney Robert Shapiro replaces Simpson's personal attorney. Shapiro offers an alibi to the media reporters gathered to cover the story, saying that Simpson was at home waiting for a limousine to take him to the airport at the time of the murders.

June 16, 1994. Simpson accompanies his children to Nicole's funeral in Brentwood. A funeral is held for Goldman on the same day, but Simpson does not attend. Police announce they are searching a field next to the Chicago hotel where Simpson stayed, apparently trying to find the murder weapon.

June 17, 1994. Police lose track of Simpson — thrown off by a decoy dressed to look like Simpson. They later learn the man is an off-duty LAPD officer, working part-time for Simpson. Police investigators inform Shapiro that a warrant has been issued for Simpson's arrest, and Shapiro arranges with the police for Simpson to surrender at police headquarters. Simpson missed the surrender deadline and a officers are dispatched to bring him in. When officers arrive, however, they discover that Simpson and former teammate Al Cowlings have disappeared. Simpson is declared a fugitive and airport officials and border patrol officers are asked to watch for him. Shapiro then holds a press conference saying that Simpson had become suicidal before fleeing, and that he had drafted three letters: one to his mother, another to his children and a third to the public. One of the letters (reproduced in the appendix) was read to reporters. Simpson is spotted hours later in his white Bronco, driven by Al Cowlings on an Orange County freeway. A nationally-televised 60-mile long slow speed chase across Southern California ends at Simpson's mansion.   At 8:50 p.m., after a 50-minute standoff Simpson leaves the Bronco and surrenders. He is permitted to use the bathroom, call his mother and drink a glass of orange juice, before being taken to the police station for booking. In the Bronco detectives find a large amount of cash, a loaded handgun, and Simpson's passport.

The Warrant for O. J. Simpson's Arrest

Felony Complaint for Arrest Warrant, Case No. BA097211

The undersigned is informed and believes that:

COUNT 1

On or about June 12, 1994, in the county of Los Angeles, the crime of murder, in violation of Penal Code Section 187 (a), a felony, was committed by Orenthal James Simpson, who did willfully, unlawfully, and with malice aforethought murder Nicole Brown Simpson, a human being.

Notice: The above offense is a serious felony within the meaning of Penal Code Section 1192.7 (c) (1).

It is further alleged that in the commission and attempted commission of the above offense, the said defendant, Orenthal James Simpson, personally used a deadly and dangerous weapon, to wit, knife, said use not being an element of above offense, within the meaning of Penal code Section 12022 (b) and also causing the above offense to be serious felony within the meaning of Penal Code Section 1192.7 (c) (23).

COUNT 2

On or about June 12, 1994, in the county of Los Angeles, the crime of murder, in violation of Penal Code Section 187 (a), a Felony, was committed by Orenthal James Simpson, who did will willfully, unlawfully, and with malice aforethought murder Ronald Lyle Goldman, a human being.

Notice: The above offense is a serious felony within the meaning of Penal Code Section 1192.7 (c) (1).

It is further alleged that in the commission of above offense, the said defendant, Orenthal James Simpson, personally used a deadly and dangerous weapon, to wit, knife, said use not being an element of the above offense, within the meaning of Penal Code Section 12022 (b) and also causing the above offense to be a serious felony within the meaning of Penal Code Section 1192.7 (c) (23).

It is further alleged as to Counts 1 and 2 the defendant has in this proceeding been convicted of more than one offense of murder in the first or 2d degree within the meaning of Penal Code 190.2 (a) (3).

Further, attached hereto and incorporated herein are official reports and documents of a law enforcement agency which the undersigned believes establish probable cause for the arrest of defendant, Orenthal James Simpson, for the above-listed crimes. Wherefore, a warrant of arrest is requested for Orenthal James Simpson. I declare under penalty of perjury that the foregoing is true and correct and that this complaint, Case Number BA097211, consists of 2 counts.

Executed at Los Angeles, County of Los Angeles, on June 17, 1994.
Phillip Vannatter (LAPD Robbery-Homicide detective)
Declarant and Complainant.

June 30 – July 8, 1994. At the conclusion of a six-day preliminary hearing, Municipal Judge Kathleen Kennedy-Powell rules there is "ample evidence" to put Simpson on trial for the murders of Nicole Brown Simpson and Ronald Goldman. At 3:10 p.m. on July 8, 1994, the preliminary hearing comes to a close.

THE PRELIMINARY HEARING

*The purpose of a **preliminary hearing** is to establish whether or not sufficient evidence exists against a person to continue the justice process. At the preliminary hearing the hearing judge will seek to determine whether there is reason to believe that 1.) a crime has been committed, and 2.) the defendant committed it. Judge Kennedy-Powell's finding is excerpted from the transcript of the preliminary hearing and reproduced below:*

The Court: We're once again on the record in the case of People versus Simpson. The defendant is present with counsel, the people are represented.

The court has carefully considered the evidence in this case and the arguments of counsel. Keeping in mind that the proof in this matter is not proof beyond a reasonable doubt, the court feels that there is ample evidence to establish a strong suspicion of the guilt of the accused, and therefore the motion to dismiss is denied at this time.

• • •

The defendant will please stand. It appearing to me from the evidence presented that the following offenses have been committed, and there is sufficient cause to believe this defendant guilty of Count 1, a violation of Penal Code section 187(a), with a special allegation pursuant to Penal Code section 12022(b); and Count 2, a violation of Penal Code section 187(a), with a special allegation pursuant to Penal Code section 12022(b); and also that there is sufficient evidence of a special allegation pursuant to Penal Code section 190.2(a)(3), the court holds that the defendant be held to answer therefor, that there be no bail allowed in this case, and that the defendant be committed to the custody of the Sheriff of Los Angeles County.

Date of arraignment in Superior Court will be July the 22nd at 8:30 in Department 100. The defendant is remanded at this time, and this court is adjourned.

(PROCEEDINGS CONCLUDED AT 3:15 P.M.)
THE MUNICIPAL COURT OF LOS ANGELES JUDICIAL DISTRICT
COUNTY OF LOS ANGELES, STATE OF CALIFORNIA

July 20, 1994. Simpson and his lawyers offer a half-million dollar reward for information leading to the arrest of the "real killer or killers." Defense attorney Shapiro announces the creation of a national toll-free hotline for tips. As the hotline begins operation more than 100 calls per minute are received.

July 22, 1994. Judge Lance Ito is assigned to the case. In response to Ito's question "How do you plead?" Simpson answers "Absolutely 100% not guilty, your honor!" in Los Angeles County Superior Court.

July 27, 1994. Louis Brown petitions for custody of Justin and Sydney. Ronald Goldman's mother files a wrongful death lawsuit against Simpson, alleging that he "willfully, wantonly and maliciously" killed her son.

July 30, 1994. Judge Ito sets September 19, 1994 as the day trial is to begin. The defense claims to have a mystery witness — a burglar who, they say, was entering a house near Nicole Brown Simpson's around the time of the murders and reportedly heard a woman scream and saw two white men run from the murder scene. The witness was soon discredited, however, when authorities revealed that the man had previously provided police with false leads in two other murder cases.

August 11, 1994. Simpson undergoes minor surgery at Cedars-Sinai Medical Center in Los Angeles. Doctors remove a swollen lymph node in his armpit, suspecting cancer. None is found, and Simpson is returned to his cell.

August 22, 1994. Reporters learn from court papers that some recently completed DNA tests show that Simpson's blood was found at the murder scene.

August 31, 1994. Judge Ito delays the start of the trial for a week, declaring that jury selection will begin September 26, 1994.

September 9, 1994. Prosecutors announce they will not seek the death penalty for Simpson.

September 22, 1994. Judge Ito rules that most of the evidence seized from Simpson's estate on June 28, 1994 can be used during trial, and upholds the seizure of Simpson's Bronco.

September 26, 1994. Jury selection begins.

THE ADVERSARIAL NATURE
OF A CRIMINAL TRIAL

About halfway through the Simpson murder trial, the lead homicide investigator in the case, Detective Philip Vannatter, told CBS news that in 30 years of investigating crime scenes he had never seen more convincing evidence in a murder case. There could be no doubt in the mind of anyone who had access to all the evidence, said Vannatter, that O.J. Simpson was the killer.

Under the American system of justice, however, it is not enough that police investigators are convinced of who the perpetrator is. The system requires that police investigators convince prosecutors that sufficient evidence is at hand for a trial, and then it becomes the job of prosecuting attorneys, who work for the state or federal government, to take a case to trial, and to convince a jury that the defendant is guilty. If even one juror remains unconvinced, the defendant will go free.

In the next few pages we will describe the general structure and chronology of a criminal trial and comment on some widely accepted rules of criminal procedure. Before we begin the description, however, it is good to keep two points in mind. One is that *the primary purpose of any criminal trial is the determination of the defendant's guilt or innocence.* In this regard it is important to recognize the crucial distinction that scholars make between legal guilt and factual guilt. **Factual guilt** deals with the issue of whether or not the defendant is actually responsible for the crime of which he or she stands accused. If the defendant "did it," then he or she is, in fact, guilty. Legal guilt is not so clear. **Legal guilt** is established only when the prosecutor presents evidence which is sufficient to convince the judge (where the judge determines the verdict) or jury that the defendant is guilty as charged. The distinction between legal guilt and factual guilt is crucial, because it points to the fact that the burden of proof rests with the prosecution, and it indicates the possibility that guilty defendants may, nonetheless, be found "not guilty." Hence, the real question in the O. J. Simpson murder trial, as in any other, was not whether Simpson had "done it," but whether jurors could be made to think he had. Of course, if O. J. were actually guilty, but jurors could be convinced otherwise, a guilty man would go free. Even when factual guilt can seemingly be demonstrated (as is some spectacular cases where a video-tape of a crime being committed and which clearly identifies the suspect as the perpetrator is available), legal guilt may not accrue if a duly constituted jury returns a finding of "not guilty."

The second point to remember is that criminal trials under our system of justice are built around an **adversarial system**, and that central to such a system is the **advocacy model**. Participating in the adversarial system are advocates for the state (the prosecution or district attorney) and for the defendant (hired defense counsel or public defender). The philosophy behind the adversarial system holds that the greatest number of just resolutions in all foreseeable criminal trials will occur when both sides are allowed to effectively and vociferously argue their cases before a fair and impartial jury. The advocacy model requires that advocates for both sides (defense attorneys for the defendant, and prosecutors for the state or "the people") do their utmost, within the boundaries set by law and professional ethics, to protect and advance the interests of their clients. The advocacy model makes clear that it is not the job of the defense attorney or the prosecution to judge the guilt of any defendant. Hence, even defense attorneys who are convinced that their client is guilty are still exhorted to offer the best possible defense and to counsel their client as effectively as possible.

ACTORS IN A CRIMINAL TRIAL

To the public eye, criminal trials often appear to be well managed and even dramatic events. Like plays on a stage, they involve many participants playing a variety of roles. Parties to the event can be divided into two categories: "professionals" and "outsiders." The "professional" category includes official courtroom actors, well versed in criminal trial practice, who set the stage for and conduct the business of the court. Judges, prosecuting attorneys, defense attorneys, public defenders, court reporters, bailiffs, and others who earn a living serving the court fall into this category. Professional courtroom actors are sometimes called the **courtroom work group**, and some writers have pointed out that, aside from statutory requirements and ethical considerations, courtroom interaction between professionals involves an implicit recognition of informal rules of civility, cooperation, and shared goals. Hence, even within the adversarial framework of a criminal trial, the courtroom work group is traditionally committed to bringing the procedure to a successful close.[3]

In contrast, "outsiders" are generally unfamiliar with courtroom organization and trial procedure. Most outsiders visit the court temporarily to provide information, to serve as witnesses, or to serve as members of the jury. Similarly, because of their temporary involvement with the court, defendant and victim (or surviving family members of murdered victims) are also outsiders, even though they may have more of a personal investment in the outcome of the trial than anyone else. In the pages that follow we will briefly consider the roles played by both professional and non-professional courtroom participants.

The Judge

The trial judge is probably the figure most closely associated with a criminal trial. On all but a few days of the Simpson trial Judge Lance Ito presided over the courtroom in which the trial took place. The judge, who can be thought of as a kind of legal referee, has the primary duty of ensuring justice. In the courtroom the judge holds ultimate authority, ruling on matters of law, weighing objections from either side, deciding on the admissibility of evidence, and disciplining anyone who challenges the order of the court. In most jurisdictions judges also sentence offenders after a verdict has been returned, and in some states judges serve to decide guilt or innocence for defendants who waive a jury trial.

Biography: Judge Lance Ito

Born in 1951, Lance Ito grew up in the City Lake neighborhood of Los Angeles. His parents, who were both school teachers, met in a Japanese-American internment camp in Wyoming during World War II.

Ito received his undergraduate education at the University of California at Los Angeles (UCLA) and is a 1975 graduate of the University of California's Boalt Hall School of Law. Following graduation, Ito went into private practice for two years before joining the Los Angeles County District Attorney's Office. Ito was appointed to the Los Angeles County Municipal Court bench in 1987. In 1989 California Governor George Deukmejian appointed Ito a Superior Court judgeship.

At the time he was selected to oversee the O.J. Simpson murder trial, Judge Ito was an administrative judge, tasked with assigning trials rather than presiding over them. Even so, Ito has experience with other high-profile trials. His most famous trial (prior to the Simpson case) was probably the 1991 case of former savings and loan administrator Charles Keating. Keating was convicted of 17 counts of securities fraud, and Ito sentenced him to 10 years in prison — the maximum allowed by law.

Ito has a personal reputation for having a good sense of fairness and justice. He is also seen by friends and colleagues as a very stable and quiet person with no personal agenda. Ito is married to Los Angeles police Captain Margaret York, whom he met while working in the prosecutor's office. Captain York is the highest ranking woman in the LAPD.

Only two decades ago many states did not require any special training, education, or other qualifications for judges. Anyone (even someone without a law degree) who won election or was appointed could assume a judgeship. Today, however, almost all states require that judges in appellate and general jurisdiction courts hold a law degree, be licensed attorneys, and be members of their state bar associations. Many states also require newly elected judges to attend state-sponsored training sessions dealing with subjects such as courtroom procedure, evidence, dispute resolution, judicial writing, administrative record keeping, and ethics.

The Prosecuting Attorney

The prosecuting attorney, called variously the "solicitor," "district attorney," "state's attorney," "chief prosecutor," and so on, is responsible for presenting the state's case against the defendant. Technically speaking, the prosecuting attorney is the primary representative of the people by virtue of the belief that violations of the criminal law are an affront to the public. Except for federal prosecutors (called U.S. attorneys) and solicitors in five states, prosecutors are elected and generally serve four-year terms with the possibility of continuing re-election.[4]

In many jurisdictions, because the job of prosecutor entails too many duties for one person to handle, most prosecutors supervise a staff of assistant district attorneys who do most in-court work. Assistants are trained attorneys, usually hired directly by the chief prosecutor, and licensed to practice law in the states where they work. The prosecuting attorney under whose jurisdiction the Simpson case fell was Los Angeles County District Attorney Gil Garcetti. The Los Angeles County District Attorney's office, however, is a huge operation. Hundreds of assistant district attorneys, legal research assistants, secretaries, and clerical personnel serve under Garcetti. Two members of Garcetti's staff, Marcia Clark and Christopher Darden, were appointed to lead the Simpson prosecution.

In preparation for trial the prosecutor decides what charges are to be brought against the defendant, examines the strength of incriminating evidence, and decides what witnesses to call. One special decision the prosecutor makes concerns the filing of separate or multiple charges. The decision to try a defendant simultaneously on multiple charges can allow for the presentation of a considerable amount of evidence and permit an in-court demonstration of a complete sequence of criminal events. Such a strategy, which was used in the Simpson case when Simpson was tried for both the murder of Nicole Brown Simpson and Ronald Goldman, has a practical side as well: it saves time and money by substituting one trial for what might otherwise be any number of trials if each charge were to be brought separately. From the prosecutor's point of view, however, trying the charges one at a time may carry the advantage of allowing for another trial on a new charge if a "not guilty" verdict is returned the first time.

Prosecuting Attorney Biographies

Elected in 1992, **Gil Garcetti** (born August 5, 1941) is the Los Angeles District Attorney. He is a graduate of the University of Southern California, and UCLA Law School. Garcetti joined the District Attorney's Office in 1968 and served as chief deputy from 1984–1988. Garcetti and Johnnie Cochran once worked together in the D.A.'s office, and Cochran is reputed to have helped Garcetti win a substantial segment of the "black vote" in the 1992 election.

Marcia Clark was born on August 31, 1953. She is a graduate of the Southwestern University School of Law. Assigned to the Special Trials Division of the Los Angeles County District Attorney's Office, she was assigned by Gil Garcetti to be the lead prosecuting attorney in the Simpson case. Clark, who joined the District Attorney's Office in 1981, had previously prosecuted 20 murder cases.

Christopher Darden was born April 7, 1956. He is a graduate of San Jose State University and Hastings College of the Law. Darden joined the Los Angeles District Attorney's Office in 1980. He had prosecuted 19 homicide cases prior to the Simpson case.

Other members of the District Attorney's Office who helped with the prosecution were **Hank Goldberg** (31 years old) who had prosecuted about 30 felony trials including eight murder trials before the Simpson case; **William Hodgman** (born December 14, 1952) who is director of the Special Trials Division. A member of the District Attorney's Office since 1978, he has prosecuted about 130 trials, including 40 murder cases; **Lisa Kahn** (born December 28, 1957) who serves as the DNA coordinator for the district attorney's office; and **Cheri Lewis** (born August 8, 1952) who assisted with the research and preparation of prosecution motions.

It is the duty of prosecutors to, in effect, assist the defense in building its case, by making available any evidence in their possession. The U.S. Supreme Court has held that the prosecution is required to disclose to the defense any exculpatory evidence in its possession that directly relates to claims of either guilt or innocence.[5] The Court has also ruled that the prosecution must disclose any evidence that the defense requests,[6] reasoning that to withhold evidence, even when it does not relate directly to issues of guilt or innocence, may mislead the defense into thinking that such evidence does not exist.

Once trial begins, the job of the prosecutor is to vigorously present the state's case against the defendant. Prosecutors introduce evidence against the accused, steer the testimony of witnesses "for the people," and argue in favor of conviction. Since defendants are presumed innocent until proven guilty, the burden of demonstrating guilt beyond a reasonable doubt rests with the prosecutor. As members of the legal profession, prosecutors are subject to the American Bar Association's (ABA) Code of Professional Responsibility. The ABA Standard for Criminal Justice 3–1.1 describes the prosecutor's duty this way: "The duty of the prosecutor is to seek justice, not merely to convict." Hence, a prosecutor is barred by the standards of the legal profession from advocating any fact or position which he or she knows is untrue.

The activities of the prosecutor do not end with a finding of guilt (although they do with a "not guilty" verdict unless other charges are pending). Following conviction prosecutors usually are usually allowed to make sentencing recommendations to the judge. When convicted defendants appeal, prosecutors may need to defend their own actions, and to argue, in briefs filed with appellate courts, that convictions were properly obtained. Most jurisdictions also allow prosecutors to make recommendations when defendants they have convicted are being considered for parole or early release from prison.

Defense Counsel

A defense counselor is a trained lawyer who may specialize in the practice of criminal law. The task of the defense attorney is to represent the accused as soon as possible after arrest and to ensure that the civil rights of the defendant are not violated through inappropriate or unfair processing by the criminal justice system. Other duties of the defense counsel include testing the strength of the prosecution's case, being involved in plea negotiations, and preparing an adequate defense to be used at trial. In the preparation of a defense, criminal lawyers may enlist private detectives, experts, witnesses to the crime, and character witnesses. Some attorneys may perform aspects of the role of private detective or of investigator themselves. They will also review relevant court precedents in order to determine what the best defense strategy might be.

Defense preparation may involve intense communications between lawyer and defendant. Such discussions are recognized as privileged communications which are protected under the umbrella of lawyer-client confidentiality. In other words, lawyers cannot be compelled to reveal information which their client has confided in them.

If their client is found guilty, defense attorneys will be involved in arguments at sentencing, may be asked to file an appeal, and will probably counsel the defendant and the defendant's family as to what civil matters (payment of debts, release from contractual obligations, etc.) need to be arranged after sentence is imposed. Hence, the role of defense attorney encompasses many aspects, including attorney, negotiator, confidant, family and personal counselor, social worker, investigator, and, as we shall see, bill collector.

Within a day of Simpson's return from Chicago, and less than two days after the murders, his personal attorney, Howard Weitzman, who had built a reputation as a "lawyer to the stars," was replaced by what the media quickly dubbed a "dream team" of seasoned criminal defense attorneys. Included on the team were F. Lee Bailey, Johnnie Cochran, Alan Dershowitz, and Robert Shapiro. Brief biographies of each of Simpson's defense attorneys are provided in the box below.

Defense Attorney Biographies

F. Lee Bailey was born on June 10, 1933. He is a graduate of Harvard University and the Boston University School of Law. Bailey is a friend of Robert Shapiro, another Simpson attorney. Shapiro successfully defended Bailey against drunken driving charges in 1982. Bailey's name is a household word in the United States. He has been involved in numerous high-profile case, beginning with his famous defense of Albert De Salvo, the so-called "Boston Strangler." As he rose to fame, Bailey represented publishing heiress and 1960s radical Patricia Hearst. He was also instrumental in overturning the conviction of Sam Sheppard, a Cleveland doctor accused of murdering his wife.

Born on October 2, 1937, **Johnnie Cochran** grew up in Los Angeles, California, and graduated from the University of California at Los Angeles in 1959. Cochran went on to attended Loyola Marymount University School of Law, selling insurance part time to help pay tuition. After graduating from law school, Cochran became a deputy city attorney, and was given the job of prosecuting misdemeanors of all kinds. Three years later, Cochran entered private practice, working for Gerald Lenoir, a seasoned and well-regarded criminal defense attorney. A few years later he formed his own law firm, Cochran, Atkins & Evans — specializing in criminal law. Cochran rose to fame in Los Angeles legal circles when, in 1966, he represented the family of Leonard Deadwyler, a young black man, who was shot and killed by the police as he was rushing his pregnant wife to the hospital. Since then he has had many other clients, many of them famous. A few years ago, Cochran successfully defended actor Todd Bridges, the former star of *Different Strokes*, winning an acquittal for Bridges on charges of attempted murder, attempted involuntary manslaughter, and assault with a deadly weapon, even though four eyewitnesses testified that Bridges had committed the crimes. In 1992 Cochran won a $9.4 million jury award against the LAPD on behalf of Patricia Diaz, a 13-year-old girl molested by an off-duty L.A. police officer who entered her home on a pretext of official duty and threatened to hurt the girl and her family if she didn't comply. Those damages still stand as the largest verdict ever against the city of Los Angeles in a police misconduct matter. In 1993 Cochran was hired by Sean Abrams, an acquaintance of rap singer Snoop Doggy Dogg, after the two were charged with murder. In what was his most famous case prior to defending Simpson, Cochran was retained by Michael Jackson in 1993 to rebut charges that Jackson had sexually abused a 13-year-old boy. Jackson settled the case out of court for an undisclosed amount of money (but estimated to be in the range of $13-16 million), and criminal charges against him were dropped. Denzel Washington is reported to have consulted Cochran for his role as a plaintiffs lawyer in the movie *Philadelphia*. Cochran also represents Reginald Denny, the white truck driver who was pulled from his cab and beaten by a crowd of black men during the riots which followed the first "Rodney King trial." A self-made man and an aggressive defense attorney, Johnnie

Cochran drives a Rolls-Royce, lives in an exclusive neighborhood, and serves as a model of success within Los Angeles' black community.

Robert Shapiro was born on September 2, 1942. He is a graduate of UCLA and Loyola University School of Law. Following law school Shapiro worked for a time as a deputy district attorney. Shapiro's many famous clients have included Johnny Carson and John DeLorean. A few years ago Shapiro succeeded in getting a murder charge against Christian Brando, son of Marlon Brando, reduced to voluntary manslaughter after Brando was accused of killing his sister's Tahitian lover.

Alan Dershowitz was born on September 1, 1938. He is a Harvard University Law School professor and well-known author. Dershowitz is best known for winning a reversal of the conviction of Claus Von Bulow, who was charged with trying to murder his socialite wife via insulin injection. Von Bulow's wife was left in a comma. The case was made into the movie, *Reversal of Fortune*. Dershowitz client list has included Leona Helmsley, Mike Tyson and convicted evangelist Jim Bakker.

Other defense attorneys in the Simpson case included: **Carl Douglas** (born May 8, 1955) who is the managing attorney at the Law Offices of Johnnie Cochran, Jr., and is in charge of the firm's 12 lawyers; **Peter Neufeld** who, along with Barry Scheck, directs "The Innocence Project," representing more than 200 inmates seeking post-conviction release through DNA testing. Neufeld is also co-chairman of the National Association of Criminal Defense Lawyers DNA Task Force; **Barry Scheck**, (born September 19, 1949), a law professor and director of clinical education at the Cardoza Law School in New York City; and **Gerald Uelmen** (born October 8, 1940) who is a specialist on constitutional law, and professor at the Santa Clara University School of Law.

The Ethics of Defense

As mentioned above, at trial the job of defense counsel is to prepare and offer as vigorous a defense as possible on behalf of the accused. A proper defense often involves the presentation of evidence and the examination of witnesses, all of which requires careful thought and planning. Good attorneys, like quality craftspeople everywhere, may find themselves emotionally committed to the outcome of trials in which they are involved. Beyond the immediacy of a given trial, attorneys also realize that their reputations can be influenced by lay perceptions of their performance, and that their careers and personal financial success depend upon consistently "winning" in the courtroom.

The nature of the adversarial process, fed by the emotions of the participants, conspires with the often privileged and extensive knowledge that defense attorneys have about a case, to tempt the professional ethics of some counselors. Because defense counsel may often know more about the guilt or innocence of the defendant than anyone else prior to trial, the defense role is one which is carefully prescribed by ethical and procedural considerations. Attorneys violate both law and the standards of their own profession if they knowingly misrepresent themselves or their clients.

To help attorneys know what is expected of them, ethical standards abound. A portion of what may be the most significant source of ethical standards for trial lawyers — the American Bar Association's Standards of Professional Responsibility — is reproduced in the box below.

American Bar Association Standards of Professional Responsibility

In his representation of a client, a lawyer shall not:

- File a suit, assert a position, conduct a defense, delay a trial, or take other action on behalf of his client when he knows or when it is obvious that such action would serve merely to harass or maliciously injure another.
- Knowingly advance a claim or defense that is unwarranted under existing law...
- Conceal or knowingly fail to disclose that which he is required by law to reveal.
- Knowingly use perjured testimony or false evidence.
- Knowingly make a false statement of law or fact.
- Participate in the creation or preservation of evidence when he knows or it is obvious that the evidence is false.
- Counsel or assist his client in conduct that the lawyer knows to be illegal or fraudulent.

Source: Excerpted from ABA *Code of Professional Responsibility*, Disciplinary Rule 7–102. Reprinted by permission of the American Bar Association. Copyright © American Bar Association. Copies of this publication are available from Service Center, American Bar Association, 750 North Lake Shore Drive, Chicago, IL 60611.

Some years ago, the U.S. Court, recounting the development of ethical codes in the legal profession, held that a lawyer's duty to a client "is limited to legitimate, lawful conduct compatible with the very nature of a trial as a search for truth.... Counsel is precluded from taking steps or in any way assisting the client in presenting false evidence or otherwise violating the law."[7]

The Bailiff

Also called a "court officer," the bailiff, another member of the professional courtroom work group, is usually an armed law enforcement officer. The job of the bailiff is to ensure order in the courtroom, oversee members of the press and spectators, announce the judge's entry into the courtroom, call witnesses, and prevent escape of the defendant. Bailiffs also supervise the jury when it is sequestered and control public and media access to the jury. Because of the inordinate amount of interest in the Simpson trial, a number of bailiffs (usually three or four) were present in the court when it was in session.

The Court Recorder

Also called the "court stenographer" and "court reporter," the role of the recorder is to create a record of all that occurs during trial. Accurate records are very important in criminal trail courts, because appeals may be based entirely upon what went on in the courtroom. Especially significant are all verbal comments made in the courtroom, including testimony, objections, the rulings of the judge, the judge's instructions to the jury, arguments made by attorneys, and the results of conferences between the attorneys and the judge. Occasionally, the judge will rule that a statement should be "stricken from the record" because it is inappropriate or unfounded. The official trial record, often taken on a stenotype machine or audio recorder, may later be transcribed in manuscript form and will become the basis for any appellate review of the trial. Today's court stenographers often employ computer-aided transcription software (CAT), which translates typed stenographic shorthand into complete and readable transcripts. Court reporters may be members of the National Court Reporters Association, the United States Court Reporters Association, and the Association of Legal Administrators — all of which support the activities of these professionals. The O.J. Simpson trial benefited from the efforts of Janet M. Moxham and Christine M. Olson (who transcribed much of the official materials in this volume as testimony was presented), and other seasoned court reporters.

Clerk of Court

The duties of the clerk of court (sometimes also known as the "county clerk") extend beyond the courtroom. The clerk maintains all records of criminal cases, including all pleas and motions made both before and after the actual trial. The clerk also prepares a jury pool and issues jury summonses and subpoenas witnesses for both the prosecution and defense. During the trial the clerk (or an assistant) marks physical evidence for identification as instructed by the judge and maintains custody of such evidence. The clerk also swears in witnesses and performs other functions as the judge directs. Some states allow the clerk limited judicial duties such as the power to issue warrants and to serve as judge of probate—overseeing wills and the administration of estates and handling certain matters relating to persons declared mentally incompetent.[8]

Expert Witnesses

Most of the "insiders" we've discussed so far are either employees of the state or have ongoing professional relationships with the court (as in the case of defense counsel). Expert witnesses, however, may or may not have that kind of status, although some do. Expert witnesses are recognized for specialized skills and knowledge in an established profession or technical area. They must demonstrate their expertise through education, work experience, publications, and awards. By testifying at a trial they provide an effective way of introducing scientific evidence in such areas as medicine, psychology, ballistics, crime scene analysis, photography, and many other disciplines. An expert witness, like the other courtroom "actors" described in this chapter, is generally a paid professional. And, like all other witnesses, they are subject to cross examination. Unlike other ("lay") witnesses, they are allowed to express opinions and draw conclusions, but only within their particular area of expertise. Expert witnesses may be veterans of many trials. Some well-known expert witnesses traverse the country and earn very high fees by testifying at one trial after another. DNA specialist John Gerdes, for example, was paid $100 per hour for his work in support of the defense in the Simpson trial; and New York forensic pathologist Michael Baden charged $1,500 per day for time spent working for Simpson in Los Angeles. Baden billed Simpson more than $100,000, and the laboratory for which Gerdes works received more than $30,000 from Simpson's defense attorneys.[9]

One of the difficulties with expert testimony is that it can be confusing to the jury. Sometimes the trouble is due to the nature of the subject matter, and sometimes to disagreements between the experts themselves. Often, however, it arises from the strict interpretation given to expert testimony by procedural requirements. Sometimes experts may find it necessary to speak in the terminology of their discipline instead of in judicial jargon. Legal requirements, however, because of the uncertainties they create, may pit experts against one another and confuse the jury.

Even so, most authorities agree that expert testimony is usually interpreted by jurors as more trustworthy than other forms of evidence. In a study of scientific evidence, one prosecutor commented that if he had to choose between presenting a fingerprint or an eyewitness at trial, he would always go with the fingerprint.[10] As a consequence of the effectiveness of scientific evidence, the National Institute of Justice recommends that "prosecutors consider the potential utility of such information in all cases where such evidence is available."[11] Some authors have called attention to the difficulties surrounding expert testimony. Procedural limitations often severely curtail the kinds of information which experts can provide.

Lay Witnesses

A number of people find themselves either unwilling or unwitting participants in criminal trials. Into this category fall defendants, victims, and most witnesses. Although they are "outsiders" who lack the status of paid professional participants, these are precisely the people who provide the "grist" for the judicial mill. Without them, trials could not occur, and the professional roles described earlier would be rendered meaningless. The first category of non-professional courtroom participants is that of lay witness.

Nonexpert witnesses, otherwise known as **lay witnesses**, may be called by either the prosecution or defense. Lay witnesses may be eye witnesses, who saw the crime being committed or who came upon the crime scene shortly after the crime had occurred. The first lay witness called in the Simpson trial, for example, was Ronald Shipp, a self-described friend of O.J. Simpson. Shipp testified that the football legend told him on the day following Nicole's death that he had previously dreamed about killing his former wife. Shipp testified that guilt and the thought that he might have prevented Nicole's death drove him to reveal Simpson's statement. Although Shipp had been an LAPD officer some years before, he testified in the capacity of a lay witness in the Simpson trial since his expertise as a police officer was not called upon during testimony.

Another type of lay witness is the character witness, who provides information about the personality, family life, business acumen, and so on of the defendant in an effort to show that this is not the kind of person who would commit the crime he or she is charged with. Of course, victims who survive may also be witnesses, sometimes providing detailed and even lengthy testimony about the defendant and the event in question.

Witnesses are officially notified that they are to appear in court to testify by a written document called a **subpoena**. Subpoenas are generally "served" by an officer of the court or by a police officer, although they are sometimes mailed. Both sides in a criminal case may subpoena witnesses and might ask that persons called to testify bring with them books, papers, photographs, videotapes, or other forms of physical evidence. Witnesses who fail to appear when summoned may face contempt of court charges. Subpoenas issued by the courts of one state, however, are not necessarily recognized in other states, sometimes leading to lengthy court hearings when evidence is sought from someone residing in a state other than the one in which the trial takes place.

The job of a witness is to provide accurate testimony concerning only those things of which he or she has direct knowledge. Normally witnesses will not be allowed to repeat things told to them by others, unless it is necessary to do so in order to account for certain actions of their own. Since few witnesses are familiar with courtroom procedure, the task of testifying is fraught with uncertainty and can be traumatizing.

Anyone who testifies in a criminal trial must do so under oath, in which some reference to God is made, or after affirmation,[12] where a pledge to tell the truth is used by those who find either "swearing" or a reference to God objectionable. All witnesses are subject to cross-examination, a process that will be discussed in detail later in this chapter. Lay witnesses may be surprised to find that cross-examination can force them to defend their personal and moral integrity. A cross-examiner may question a witness about past vicious, criminal, or immoral acts, even where such matters have never been the subject of a criminal proceeding.[13] As long as the intent of such questions is to demonstrate to the jury that the witness may not be a person who is worthy of belief, they will generally be permitted by the judge.

Jurors

Article III of the U.S. Constitution requires that "[t]he trial of all crimes...shall be by jury...". States have the authority to determine the size of criminal trial juries. Most states use juries composed of 12 persons and 1 or 2 alternates designated to fill in for jurors who are unable to continue due to accident, illness, or personal emergency. Some states allow for juries smaller than 12, and juries with as few as 6 members have survived Supreme Court scrutiny.[14] The jury initially selected in the Simpson case, following California's laws of criminal procedure, consisted of 12 jurors and 8 alternates. As the trial progressed, a number of jurors were dismissed for a variety of reasons, leading to fears that an insufficient number of jurors would remain for the trial to conclude.

Jury duty is regarded as a responsibility of citizenship. Other than juveniles and certain job occupants such as police personnel, physicians, members of the armed services on active duty, and emergency services workers, persons called for jury duty must serve unless they can convince a judge that they should be excused for overriding reasons. Aliens, those convicted of a felony, and citizens who have served on a jury within the past two years are excluded from jury service in most jurisdictions.

The names of prospective jurors are gathered from the tax register, DMV records, or voter registration rolls of a county or municipality and are entered into a pool from which the jurors are selected for a given court session. Minimum qualifications for jury service include adulthood, a basic command of spoken English, citizenship, "ordinary intelligence," and local residency. Jurors are also expected to possess their "natural faculties," meaning that they should be able to hear, speak, see, move, and so forth. Some jurisdictions have recently allowed handicapped persons to serve as jurors, although the nature of the evidence to be presented in a case may preclude persons with certain kinds of handicaps from serving.

Ideally the jury is to be a microcosm of society, reflecting the values, rationality, and common sense of the average person. The U.S. Supreme Court has held that criminal defendants have a right to have their cases heard before a jury of their peers.[15] Peer juries are those composed of a representative cross section of the community in which the alleged crime has occurred and where the trial is to be held.

In a 1945 case, *Thiel* v. *Southern Pacific Company*,[16] the U.S. Supreme Court clarified the concept of a "jury of one's peers" by noting that while it is not necessary for every jury to contain representatives of every conceivable racial, ethnic, religious, gender, and economic group in the community, court officials may not systematically and intentionally exclude any juror solely because of his or her social characteristics.

The idea of a peer jury stems from the Magna Carta's original guarantee of jury trials for "freemen." "Freemen" in England during the thirteenth century, however, were more likely to be of similar mind than is a cross section of Americans today. Hence, although the duty of the jury is to follow the laws of the relevant jurisdiction and, ultimately, determine guilt or innocence based solely upon an objective consideration of the evidence presented to it, social dynamics may play just as great a role in jury verdicts as do the facts of a case. Hence, juries which are not carefully chosen may become fertile ground for hidden political agendas, personal biases, and prejudices of all sorts.

Some people, however, suggest that the jury can be a powerful tool — righting wrongs inherent in the law and American social structure. A rather radical "Jury Duty Handbook" making the rounds on electronic bulletin boards and the Internet around the time of the Simpson trial, for example, exhorted jurors everywhere to follow their consciences rather than the law — especially in cases where they thought the law improper. A passage from that handbook is reproduced on the following page.

Defense attorney Johnnie Cochran echoed such sentiments in the Simpson trial, when he told reporters near the close of proceedings that African Americans shouldn't avoid jury summonses because their voices are needed to combat racism at all levels of the criminal justice system.[17] "You go and you serve on jury duty," Cochran, told a nearly all-black audience. "Nobody is going to save us but us."

YOU ARE NOT A RUBBER STAMP!

By what logic do we send our youth to battle tyranny on foreign soil, while we refuse to do so in our courts? Did you know that many of the planks of the <u>Communist Manifesto</u> are now represented by law in the U.S.? How is it possible for Americans to denounce communism and practice it simultaneously?

The JURY judges the Spirit, Motive and Intent of both the law and the Accused, whereas the prosecutor only represents the letter of the law.

Therein lies the opportunity for the accomplishment of LIBERTY and JUSTICE for ALL. If you, and numerous other JURORS throughout the State and Nation begin and continue to bring in verdicts of NOT GUILTY in such cases where a man-made statute is defective or oppressive, these statutes will become as ineffective as if they had never been written.

Source: *Jury Duty Handbook*, Patriot Press, San Antonio, Texas, no date.

The Role of the Victim in a Criminal Trial

Not all crimes have clearly identifiable victims. Some, like murder, do not have victims who survive. Where there is an identifiable surviving victim, however, he or she is often one of the most forgotten people in the courtroom. Although the victim may have been profoundly affected by the crime itself, and is often emotionally committed to the proceedings and trial outcome, they may not even be permitted to participate directly in the trial process. Victims, like witnesses, experience many hardships as they participate in the criminal court process. Some of the rigors they endure are:

1. Uncertainties as to their role in the criminal justice process
2. A general lack of knowledge about the criminal justice system, courtroom procedure, and legal issues
3. Trial delays which result in frequent travel, missed work, and wasted time
4. Fear of the defendant or retaliation from the defendant's associates
5. The trauma of testifying and of cross-examination.

The trial process itself can make for a bitter experience. If victims take the stand, defense attorneys may test their memory, challenge their veracity, or even suggest that they were somehow responsible for their own victimization. After enduring cross-examination, some victims report feeling as though they, and not the alleged offender, have been portrayed as the criminal to the jury. The difficulties encountered by victims have been compared to a second victimization at the hands of the criminal justice system.

The Role of the Defendant in a Criminal Trial

The majority of criminal defendants in the United States are poor, uneducated, and often alienated from the philosophy which undergirds the American justice system. A common view of the defendant in a criminal trial is that of a relatively powerless person at the mercy of judicial mechanisms. Many defendants are just that. As the trial of O.J. Simpson demonstrates, however, such an image is often far from the truth. Defendants, especially those who seek an active role in their own defense, choreograph many courtroom activities. Experienced defendants, notably those who are career offenders, or well-educated defendants may be quite knowledgeable of courtroom procedure.

Defendants in criminal trials have a right to represent themselves, and need not retain counsel nor accept the assistance of court-appointed attorneys. Such a choice, however, may not be in their best interests. Even without self-representation, every defendant who chooses to do so can substantially influence events in the courtroom. Defendants exercise choice in (1) selecting and retaining counsel, (2) planning a defense strategy in coordination with their attorney, (3) deciding what information to provide to (or withhold from) the defense team, (4) deciding whether or not to testify personally, (5) deciding what plea to enter, and (6) determining whether or not to file an appeal, if convicted.

Nevertheless, even the most active defendants suffer from a number of disadvantages. One is the tendency of others to assume that anyone on trial must be guilty. Although a person is "innocent until proven guilty," the very fact that he or she is accused of an offense casts a shadow of suspicion that may foster biases in the minds of jurors and other courtroom actors. Another disadvantage lies in the often-substantial social and cultural differences which separate the offender from the professional courtroom staff. While lawyers and judges tend to identify with upper-middle-class values and life-styles, few offenders do. The consequences of such a gap (which, if anything, was reversed in the Simpson case) between defendant and courtroom staff may be insidious and far reaching.

The Press in the Courtroom

Often overlooked, because they do not have an "official" role in courtroom proceedings, are spectators and the press. At the Simpson trial both spectators and media representatives were present in large numbers. Spectators included members of the families of both victims and the defendant, friends of either side, and curious onlookers—some of whom were avocational court watchers.

Newswriters, TV reporters, other members of the press, and even screen writers, are apt to be present at "spectacular" trials (those involving some especially gruesome aspect, or famous personality) and at those in which there is a great deal of community interest. The right of reporters and spectators to be present at a criminal trial is supported by the Sixth Amendment's insistence upon a public trial. Coverage of the Simpson trial was provided by all of the major television networks, including Court TV (which operated video cameras in the courtroom) and the Cable News Network. Wire services set up special bureaus to handle daily reports emanating from the courtroom, and continuously fed the information they collected to newsrooms, newspapers and on-line services across the country.

Press reports at all stages of a criminal investigation and trial often create problems for the justice system. Significant pretrial publicity about a case may make it difficult to find jurors who have not already formed an opinion as to the guilt or innocence of the defendant. News reports from the courtroom may influence nonsequestered jurors who hear them, especially when they contain information brought to the bench, but not heard by the jury. After the Simpson jury was selected, Judge Ito issued an order barring jurors from exposure to certain kinds of media. The judge's order is reproduced below.

SUPERIOR COURT OF THE STATE OF CALIFORNIA
IN AND FOR THE COUNTY OF LOS ANGELES

Date: 12 December 1994
Department 103
Hon. Lance A. Ito, Judge
Deirdre Robertson, Deputy Clerk
People v. Orenthal James Simpson
Case #BA097211

COURT ORDER

During the course of this trial, and until further order of the court, the trial jurors and alternates in this case shall NOT read any newspaper article or other written account including magazines or books or watch any television programs dealing with this case, the defendant or his family, the victims or their families, the attorneys or any other matter concerning this case. The court will distribute to the jurors and alternates the local daily newspaper of their choice, edited to remove any coverage of this case.

Jurors and alternates shall NOT listen to any radio programming. Each juror and alternate may listen to audio tapes and compact discs, including books on tape that do not concern this case. Jurors and alternates who need current weather and traffic information may get this information by dialing (213) 962-3279.

Jurors and alternates shall NOT watch:

1) ANY television news program or news break.

2) ANY television "tabloid" program such as Hardcopy, A Current Affair, Inside Edition, American Journal or Premiere Story.

3) ANY television talk show such as Marilu, Leeza, Jenny Jones, Sally Jesse Raphael, Oprah!, Donahue, Good Morning America, Today, This Morning, The Montiel Williams Show, The Maury Povich Show, Rikki Lake, Rolanda, Rush Limbaugh and Geraldo.

4) ANY television news magazine program such as 60 Minutes, 20/20, Dateline, Eye To Eye, 48 Hours or Prime Time Live.

5) ANY entertainment news magazine such as Entertainment Tonight and EXTRA.

6) CNN, CNN Headline News, CNBC, The E! Channel, Sports Center on ESPN, Press Box on Prime Ticket, The News on MTV, any news or talk show on BET and Dennis Miller Live on HBO.

7) The Tonight Show (Jay Leno) and The Late Show With David Letterman

Jurors and alternates MAY watch:

1) Normal television entertainment programming, including sports and home shopping channels, not excluded above, however, jurors are strongly cautioned to avoid watching advertisements for upcoming news broadcasts known as "teasers."

2) Cable or satellite television channels: American Movie Classics, Showtime, Cinemax, The Disney Channel, The Movie Channel, The Shopping Channel, The Family Channel, The Cartoon Channel, Turner Classic Movies, MTV, Discovery Channel, Arts and Entertainment (A&E), Bravo, Lifetime, Nashville, Nickelodeon and Home Box Office.

3) Movies and other programming on video tape that do not involve this case, the defendant or his family, the victims or their families, or the attorneys and their families.

Any questions regarding this order shall be directed to Clerk of the Court, Mrs. Deirdre Robertson at (213) 974-5726.

IT IS SO ORDERED.

STAGES IN A CRIMINAL TRIAL

We turn now to a discussion of the steps in a criminal trial. As Figure 1-1 shows, trial chronology consists of 10 stages:

- Trial initiation
- Jury selection
- Judge's instructions to the jury
- Opening statements
- Presentation of evidence
- (Prosecution) rebuttal and (defense) rejoinder
- Closing arguments
- The judge's charge to the jury
- Jury deliberations
- The verdict

Sentencing, an eleventh stage, is not a part of the criminal trial per se, but follows a finding of guilt. Sentencing may occur at a later time, after attorneys and others have had the opportunity to provide the sentencing judge with additional information about the defendant.

Stages in a
Criminal Trial

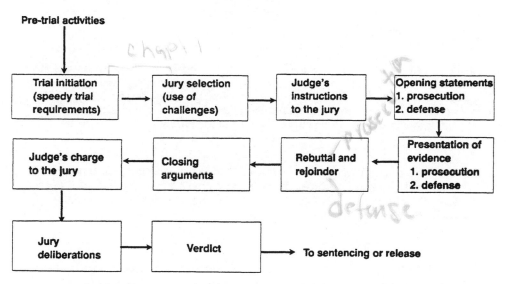

Figure 1-1. Stages in a Criminal Trial.

In what remains of this chapter, we will discuss the first two stages — trial initiation and jury selection — in some detail. In Chapter 2, we will summarize the opening statements made by opposing counsel. Chapter 3 reviews the presentation of evidence by the prosecution, and

Chapter 4 provides a condensed version of the defense's case. Chapter 5 provides an overview of the prosecution's rebuttal of defense contentions as well as a condensed defense rejoinder. Chapter 6 reviews the closing arguments of the prosecution, while the closing arguments of the defense are the subject of Chapter 7. Finally, Chapter 8 describes the jury's verdict, the conclusion of the Simpson trial, and reactions to it.

Trial Initiation: Speedy Trial Requirements

The Sixth Amendment to the U.S. Constitution guarantees that "In all criminal prosecutions, the accused shall enjoy the right to a speedy and public trial." California speedy trial provisions are contained in Article I, Section 29 of the California state constitution, which reads, "In a criminal case, the people of the State of California have the right to due process of law and to a speedy and public trial." They are also found in Section 1382 of the California Penal Code, which is excerpted below.

California Penal Code
Section 1382

(a) The court, unless good cause to the contrary is shown, shall order the action to be dismissed in the following cases: (1) When a person has been held to answer for a public offense and an information is not filed against that person within 15 days thereafter. (2) When a defendant is not brought to trial in a superior court within 60 days after the finding of the indictment or filing of the information

. . .

However, an action shall not be dismissed under this paragraph if either of the following circumstances exist: (A) The defendant enters a general waiver of the 60-day trial requirement . . . (B) The defendant requests or consents to the setting of a trial date beyond the 60-day period.

Clogged court calendars, limited judicial resources, and general inefficiency, however, often combine to produce what appears to many to be unreasonable delays in trial initiation. The attention of the Supreme Court was brought to bear on trial delays in *Strunk* v. *United States* (1973).[18] In *Strunk*, as in some previous cases, the Court asserted that the right to a speedy trial is a fundamental guarantee of the Constitution, and added that denial of a speedy trial should result in a dismissal of all charges.

In 1974, against the advice of the Justice Department, the U.S. Congress passed the federal Speedy Trial Act.[19] The act, which was phased in gradually, and became fully effective in 1980, allows for the dismissal of federal criminal charges in cases where the prosecution does not seek an indictment or information within 30 days of arrest (a 30-day extension is granted when the grand jury is not in session) or where a trial does not begin within 70 working days after indictment for defendants who plead not guilty. If a defendant is not available for trial, or witnesses cannot be called within the 70-day limit, the period may be extended to 180 days. Delays brought about by the defendant, through requests for a continuance, or because of escape, are not counted in the specified time periods. The Speedy Trial Act has been condemned by some as shortsighted. One federal trial court judge, for example, wrote: "The ability of the criminal justice system to operate effectively and efficiently has been severely impeded by the Speedy Trial Act. Resources are misdirected, unnecessary severances required, cases proceed to trial inadequately prepared, and in some indeterminate number of cases, indictments against guilty persons are dismissed."[20]

The federal Speedy Trial Act is applicable only to federal courts. However, in keeping with the trend toward reduced delays, many states have since enacted their own speedy trial legislation. Typical state legislation sets limits of 120 or 90 days as a reasonable period of time for a trial to commence.

Jury Selection

The Sixth Amendment guarantees every criminal defendant the right to an impartial jury — this is, a jury which is free from biases of any kind that might preclude its members from objectively considering the evidence presented to it, or from fairly deciding matters of fact. Some people interpret "impartiality" to mean that jurors selected to serve in a given trial should have no advance knowledge of the case they are about to try. An impartial jury, however, is not necessarily an ignorant one. In the Simpson trial it is likely that, because of extensive media coverage of the events, every person called for jury duty had some knowledge of the circumstances surrounding the deaths of Nicole Brown Simpson and Ronald Goldman. Although jurors will not always be excused from service on a jury if they have some knowledge of the case,[21] jurors who have already formed an opinion as to the guilt or innocence of a defendant are the most likely to be excused.

Anyone who has ever been called as a juror knows that some prospective jurors try to get excused and others who would like to serve are excused because they are not thought suitable. Prosecution and defense attorneys use challenges to help ensure the impartiality of the jury which is being empaneled. Three types of challenges are recognized in criminal courts: (1) challenges to the array, (2) challenges for cause, and (3) peremptory challenges.

Challenges to the array signify the belief, generally by the defense attorney, that the pool from which potential jurors are to be selected is not representative of the community, or is biased in some significant way. A challenge to the array is argued before the hearing judge before jury selection begins.

A second kind of challenge, the **peremptory challenge**, effectively removes potential jurors without the need to give a reason. Peremptory challenges, used by both the prosecution and defense, are limited in number. Federal courts allow each side up to 20 peremptory challenges in capital cases and as few as 3 in minor criminal cases.[22] States vary as to the number of peremptory challenges they permit. In California, 10 peremptory challenges are generally available to each side in a felony trial, while in cases punishable by death or life in prison (as in the Simpson case), each side is permitted 20 challenges.

A developing field, which seeks to take advantage of peremptory challenges, is scientific jury selection. Scientific jury selection uses correlational techniques from the social sciences to gauge the likelihood that potential jurors will vote for conviction or acquittal. It makes predictions based on the economic, ethnic, and other personal and social characteristics of each member of the juror pool. Sometimes prosecutors or defense attorneys, especially those using scientific jury selection techniques, intentionally select juries that are racially or economically imbalanced — hoping that proclivities to vote for guilt or innocence may be inherent in a jury which is so composed. The Simpson defense team hired nationally-known jury consultant Jo-Ellan Dimitrius to advise them on jury selection strategies. Dimitrius, who has an M.A. in government and a Ph.D. in criminal justice from California's Claremont Graduate School, assisted the defense with jury selection in the state trial of police officers accused of the beating of black motorist Rodney King, helped the defense choose the jury in the McMartin preschool case (California's longest-ever criminal prosecution), and worked with Miami defense attorney Roy Black, who successfully defended William Kennedy Smith against rape charges in late 1991.

During the jury selection process, both prosecution and defense attorneys question potential jurors in a process known as *voir dire* examination. Jurors are expected to be unbiased and free of preconceived notions of guilt or innocence, and the purpose of *voir dire* examination is to insure that each individual juror is not prejudiced about the case in any way. **Challenges for cause**, which may arise during *voir dire* examination, make the claim that an individual juror cannot be fair or impartial. This is called "challenging a juror." Typical grounds for challenging a juror are that the juror: 1.) is related to one of the parties (i.e., the defendant or someone on the prosecution or defense team, or an arresting or investigating officer), 2.) is prejudiced against the defendant, 3.) is prejudiced against the law (i.e., he or she may not believe that the activity of which the defendant stands accused should be illegal), 4.) has already formed an opinion as to the guilt or innocence of the defendant (from hearsay, news stories, etc.), 5.) may not agree with the punishment which might be imposed upon the defendant were he or he to be found guilty (as is sometimes the case in death penalty cases).

There is no limit on the number of challenges for cause that either side may bring. Such challenges, however, are not automatic grounds for dismissal, which is a decision made by the judge hearing the case. Attorneys in the Simpson case facilitated the *voir dire* process by creating a juror questionnaire which all potential jurors were asked to complete. Prospective jurors were asked 294 questions covering a broad range of subjects, including their attitudes on religion, race, domestic violence, the media and Simpson himself. The questionnaire contained 20 questions on domestic violence, 30 questions about Simpson, and 10 on ethnic prejudices. The questionnaire helped identify individuals who might have already formed opinions about Simpson's guilt or innocence, allowing them to be excluded from further consideration as jurors. Selected questions from the 80 page Simpson trial juror questionnaire, broken down by section, are reproduced below:

Employment

1. Are you currently employed outside the home? Yes? No?
2. If so, by whom are you employed? Full or part-time? If part-time, how many hours per week?
3. How long have you been so employed?
4. What are your specific duties and responsibilities on the job?
5. Does your job involve management or supervisory duties?
6. Do you have the authority to hire and fire employees. Yes? No? If yes, is this a difficult decision to make? Yes? No? Please explain.
7. Please list your work experience over the past ten years, and state when and for how long you were employed at each job. Please give a brief description of each job and the name of each employer.
8. Have you ever worked in the entertainment industry in any capacity? Yes? No? If yes, please explain.
9. Have you ever worked in journalism or the news industry in any capacity? Yes? No? If yes, please state where and when you were so employed and give a brief description of your duties.

Military

1. Have you ever served in the military? Yes? No?
2. If yes, please list: Branch of service: Rank: Dates of service:
3. Combat experience? Yes? No?

---

4. While serving in the military, did you ever see someone being killed or who had been killed? Yes? No? If yes, please describe.

DNA

The ability of DNA analysis to prove the identity of the person (s) whose blood or hair is found at a crime scene has been the subject of some television and radio shows, and magazine and newspaper articles. The following questions pertain to the subject.

1. Before the Simpson case, did you read any book, articles or magazines concerning DNA analysis? Yes? No? If yes, please name the book, magazine, newspaper or other periodical where you read about it and briefly describe what you recall having read?
2. Are you aware of any other court cases involving DNA analysis? Yes? No?
3. What is your view concerning the reliability of the DNA analysis to accurately identify a person as the possible source of blood or hair found at a crime scene? Very reliable? Not very reliable? Somewhat reliable? Unreliable? Don't know? Please explain your answer.
4. Have you followed any of the court hearings concerning DNA analysis in the Simpson case? Yes? No?
5. What are your views concerning what you have heard and or read about the DNA hearings in the Simpson case?

Ethnic Prejudice

1. How big a problem do you think racial discrimination against African-Americans is in Southern California? A very serious problems? A somewhat serious problem? Not too serious? Not at all serious? Not a problem?
2. Have you ever experienced fear of a person of another race? Yes? No? If yes, please explain the circumstances.
3. Is there any racial or ethnic group that you do not feel comfortable being around? Yes? No? If yes, please explain.

Violence and Domestic Violence

1. Have you ever experienced domestic violence in your home, either growing up or as an adult? Yes? No?
2. Please describe the circumstances and what impact it had on you.
3. Have you ever had a relative or close friend experience domestic violence? Yes? No? If yes, please explain the circumstances and what effect it had on you.
4. Have you ever known anyone who had problems leaving an abusive relationship? Yes? No? If yes, who was involved? Please explain the circumstances.
5. Why do you think she/he had problems leaving the relationship?
6. When is violence an appropriate response to domestic trouble?
7. Have you ever felt sufficiently frustrated with a domestic relationship that you considered violence?
8. Do you think using physical force on a fellow family member is sometimes justified? Please explain.

9. Do you believe people with professional lives that involve physical confrontation or the use of violence are more susceptible to imposing violent solutions in their personal lives? Please explain your answer.

10. Have you ever had occasion to use a knife against another person (whether cutting or just brandishing), including in self-defense? Yes? No? If yes, please explain.

11. Male professional athletes who participate in contact sports are more aggressive in their personal lives than other people. Strongly agree? Agree? No opinion? Disagree? Strongly disagree?

12. Male professional athletes who participate in contact sports are more aggressive towards women. Strongly agree? Agree? No opinion? Disagree? Strongly disagree?

Familiarity with O.J. Simpson

1. Have you ever seen O.J. Simpson in any form of advertising, such as television commercials for Hertz or in orange juice commercials? Yes? No?

2. Did you see O.J. Simpson play football in college or as a professional football player? Yes? No? If yes, describe the circumstances and your feelings towards O.J. Simpson as a football player.

3. Have you ever seen O.J. Simpson as he appeared in movies such as Roots or Naked Gun 2½? Yes? No? If yes, describe your feelings towards O.J. Simpson based upon your observations of him as an actor.

4. Will you hold the prosecution to a higher standard than is legally required because the defendant is : African-American? Yes? No? Wealthy? Yes? No? Famous? Yes? No?

5. Does the fact that O.J. Simpson excelled at football make it unlikely in your mind that he could commit murder? Why or why not?

6. Have you purchased or otherwise obtained any commercial item related to this case? Yes? No?

Victim or Witness to Crime

1. Are you or have you been a member of Neighborhood Watch? Yes? No? If yes, what was the nature of your involvement?

2. Do you have (please check) Security bars? Alarms? Guard Dog? Weapons for self-protection?

3. Have you ever been a victim of a crime? Yes? No? If yes, how many times? What kind of crime(s)? Do you feel the job the police did on it was: Satisfactory? Why? Unsatisfactory? Why?

A total of 304 prospective jurors completed the questionnaire, and juror selection entered the next stage — *voir dire* questioning of individuals jurors to determine whether any should be dismissed for cause — on October 12, 1994. A final panel of 12 jurors and eight alternates had been selected by the conclusion of the *voir dire* process on November 3, 1994.

The demographic profile of the 900 prospective jurors initially selected for screening in the Simpson case is as follows: 37.9% were white; 28.1% were African-American; 17% were Hispanic; with the remainder listed as Native-American, Chinese, Filipino, Hawaiian, Japanese-American, Korean-American, Vietnamese-American, Asian-Indian and Aleut. Males comprised approximately 50% of the pool, as did females. Even so, when jury selection was complete, and final selections had been made, the Simpson jury was predominantly African-American, and contained twice as many women as men. The original 12 jurors, based upon information supplied in questionnaires filled out by the jurors were as follows:

- Black female, 50. Occupation: vendor.
- Black female, 25. Occupation: flight attendant.
- Male of Native-American and white heritage, 52. Occupation: high school teacher.
- Hispanic male, 32. Occupation: drives a soft drink delivery truck.
- Black female, 37. Occupation: post office mail sorter.
- Black male, 48. Occupation: works for Hertz rental car company.
- Black female, 38. Occupation: employment interviewer.
- Black female, 38. Occupation: environmental health specialist.
- Black female, 52. Occupation: clerk.
- Hispanic female, 38. Occupation: letter carrier.
- White female, 22. Occupation: insurance claims adjuster.
- Black male, 46. Occupation: courier.

After wrangling over jury selection had run its course, the Simpson jury was sworn in. Judge Ito ruled that members of the jury were to remain sequestered at state expense for the duration of the trial. Members of **sequestered juries** are not permitted to have contact with the public and are typically housed in a motel or hotel until completion of the trial. Anyone who attempts to contact a sequestered jury or to influence members of a sequestered juror may be held accountable for jury tampering.

Judge Ito's Instructions to the Jury at the Start of The Trial

Following jury selection, the stage is set for opening arguments[23] to begin. Judge Lance Ito read instructions to the Simpson trial jury, as required by California law, shortly after jury selection was complete and the jurors had been impaneled. Because Ito's instructions provide a concise course in legal terminology, legal procedure and California law, they are worth including here almost in their entirety. We have boldfaced a number of terms that are especially important, or which will appear again later in this book.

━━━

Judge Ito (addressing the jury): Good afternoon, ladies and gentlemen. First of all, I hope this will be the last time that I have to apologize to you for keeping you waiting for so long, but I suspect that won't be true in this case. ...Now, what will happen today is I am going to give you some preliminary instructions on the law that applies to this case. Now what we are going to do as soon as I finish doing that is we will recess for the day, and then tomorrow morning at 10 o'clock, we will start with the opening statements by the lawyers and then proceed to the presentation of evidence.

Now, what I'm going to give you today are preliminary instructions. This is sort of my effort to give you a gauge or rule by which you should look at the evidence as it is presented to you. I'm required by the law to state to you the law that applies to this case here in open court. However, it's also my personal policy to make these instructions available to you in the jury room when you do your deliberations in written form. So I encourage you each to listen very carefully to my instructions on the law. However, you need not take any detailed notes as to their content since they will be available to you in their exact written form in the jury room.

Ladies and gentlemen of the jury, it is my duty to instruct you on the law that applies to this case. The law requires that I read these instructions to you. You will have these instructions in written form in the jury room to refer to during your deliberations. You must base your decisions on the facts and the law. You have two duties to perform. First, you must determine the facts from the evidence received in the trial, and not from any other source. A **fact** is something proved directly or circumstantially by the evidence, or by stipulation. A **stipulation** is an agreement between the attorneys regarding the facts. Second, you must apply the law that I state to you to the facts as you determine then, and in this way arrive at your verdict and any finding you are instructed to include with your verdict. You must accept and follow the law as I state it to you, whether or not you agree with the law. If anything concerning the law said by the attorneys and their arguments or at any other time during the trial conflicts with my instructions on the law, you must follow my instructions. You must not be influenced by pity for a defendant or by prejudice against him. You must not be biased against the defendant because he has been arrested to this defense, charged with a crime, or brought to trial. None of these circumstances is evidence of guilt, and you must not infer or assume from any or all of them that he is more likely to be guilty than innocent. You must not be influenced by mere sentiment, conjecture, sympathy, passion, prejudice, public opinion, or public feeling.

Both the prosecution and the defendant have a right to expect that you will conscientiously consider and weigh the evidence, apply the law, and reach a just verdict, regardless of the circumstances. You must decide this case solely upon the evidence presented here in the courtroom. You must completely disregard any press, television, radio, or other media reports that you may have read, seen, or heard, concerning this case or the defendant. These reports are not evidence, and you must not be influenced in any manner by such publicity.

You are not to discuss among yourselves, or with anyone else, any subject connected with this trial. You are not to form or express any opinion on the case until the case is submitted to you for your deliberations in the jury room. You must completely disregard any press, television, radio, or any other media reports you may have read, seen, or heard, concerning this case or the defendant. You must not read or listen to any accounts or discussions of the case reported by newspapers or other news media.

You must not make any independent investigation of the facts or the law or consider or discuss facts as to which there is no evidence. This means, for example, that you must not on your own visit the scene, conduct experiments, or consult reference works of persons for additional information.

Prior to, and within 90 days of your discharge, you must not request, accept, agree to accept, or discuss, with any person receiving or accepting any payment or benefit in consideration for supplying any information concerning the trial.

You have a duty to immediately report to the court any act of juror misconduct that you see, hear, or learn. Your failure to do so is misconduct in and of itself. If you are uncertain whether a particular act is misconduct, you should report the act and allow the court to make the determination. You must promptly report to the court any incident within your knowledge involving any attempt by any person to improperly influence any member of the jury.

If any rule, direction, or idea, is repeated or stated in different ways in these instructions, no emphasis is intended, and you must not draw any inference because of its repetition. Do not single out any particular sentence or any individual point or instruction and ignore the others. Consider the instructions as a whole, and each in light of the others. The order in which the instructions are given has no significance as to their relative importance.

Statements made by the attorneys during the trial are not evidence, although if the attorneys have stipulated or agreed to a fact, you must regard that fact as conclusively proved. If an objection is sustained to a question, do not guess what the answer might have been. Do not speculate as to the reason for the objection. Do not assume to be true any insinuation suggested by a question asked a witness. A question is not evidence, and may be considered only as it enables you to understand the answer. Do not consider, for any purpose, any offer of evidence that was rejected or will be rejected, or any evidence that will be stricken by the court. You must treat it as though you had never heard it. You must decide all questions of fact in this case from the evidence received in this trial, and not from any other source. You must not make any independent investigation of the facts or the law, or consider or discuss facts as to which there is no evidence. This means, for example, that you must not, on your own, as I indicated, visit the crime scene, conduct experiments, or consult reference works or other persons for additional information. You must not discuss this case with any other person except a fellow juror, and you must not discuss the case with a fellow juror until the case is submitted to you for a decision, and then only when all jurors are present in the jury room.

Evidence consists of the testimony of witnesses, writings, material objects, or anything presented to the census and offered to prove the existence or non-existence of a fact. Evidence is either direct or circumstantial. **Direct evidence** is evidence that directly proves a fact without the necessity of an inference. It is evidence which, by itself, if found to be true, establishes that fact. **Circumstantial evidence** is evidence that, if found to be true, proves a fact from which an inference of the existence of another fact may be drawn. An inference is a deduction of fact that may logically and reasonably be drawn from another fact or group of facts established by the evidence.

It is not necessary that facts be proved by direct evidence. They may be proved also by circumstantial evidence, or by a combination of direct evidence and circumstantial evidence. Both direct evidence and circumstantial evidence are acceptable as a means of proof. Neither is entitled to any greater weight than the other. However, a finding of guilt as to any crime may not be based on circumstantial evidence unless the proved circumstances are not only, one, consistent with the theory that the defendant is guilty of the crime, but two, cannot be reconciled with any other rational conclusion. Further, each fact which is essential to complete a set of circumstances necessary to establish the defendant's guilt must be proved beyond a reasonable doubt. In other words, before an inference essential to established guilt may be found to have been proved beyond a reasonable doubt, each fact or circumstance upon which such inference necessarily rests must be proved beyond a reasonable doubt. Also, if the circumstantial evidence as to any particular count is susceptible of two reasonable interpretations, one of which points to the defendant's guilt and the other to his innocence, you must adopt that interpretation which points to the defendant's innocence and reject that interpretation which points to his guilt. If, on the other hand, one interpretation of such evidence appears to you to be reasonable, and the other interpretation to be unreasonable, you must accept the reasonable interpretation and reject the unreasonable.

Certain evidence will be admitted for a limited purpose. At the time this evidence is admitted, you will be admonished that it cannot be considered by you for any purpose other than the limited purpose for which it is admitted. Do not consider such evidence for any purpose except the limited purpose for which it is admitted. Neither side is required to call as a witness all persons who may have been present at any of the events disclosed by the evidence, or who may appear to have some knowledge of these events, or to produce all objects or documents mentioned or suggested by the evidence. Every person who testifies under oath is a witness. You are the sole judges of the believability of a witness and the weight to be given the testimony of each witness. In determining the believability of a witness, you may consider anything that has a tendency and reason to prove or disprove the truthfulness of the testimony of the witness, including, but not limited to, any of the following; the extent of the opportunity or the ability of the witness to hear, see, or otherwise become aware of any matter about which the witness has testified; the ability of the witness to remember or communicate any matter about which the witness has testified. the character and quality of that testimony, the demeanor and manner of the witness while testifying; the existence or non-existence of a bias, interest, or other motive; evidence of the existence or non-existence of any fact testified to by the witness, the attitude of the witness toward this action or toward the giving of testimony; a statement previously made by the witness that is consistent or inconsistent with the testimony of the witness; the character of the witness for honesty or truthfulness or their opposites, and admission by the witness of any untruthfulness.

Discrepancies in a witness' testimony, or between his or her testimony and that of others, if there are any, do not necessarily mean the witness should be discredited. Failure of recollection is a common experience. Innocent mis-recollection is not uncommon. It is also a fact that two persons witnessing an incident or transaction often will see or hear it differently. Whether a discrepancy pertains to a fact of importance or only to a trivial detail should be considered in weighing its significance. A witness who is willfully false in one material part of his or her testimony is to be distrusted in others. You may reject the whole testimony of a witness who has willfully testified falsely as to a material point, unless, from all the evidence, you believe the probability of truth favors his or her testimony in other particulars.

You are not bound to decide an issue of fact in accordance with the testimony of a number of witnesses which does not convince you as against a testimony of a lesser number or other evidence which appeals to your mind with more convincing force. You may not disregard the testimony of the greater number of witnesses merely from caprice, whim, or prejudice, or from a desire to favor one side against the other. You must not decide an issue by the simple process of counting the number of witnesses who have testified on the opposing sides. The final test is not in the relative number of witnesses, but in the convincing force of the evidence. You should give the testimony of a single witness whatever weight you think it deserves. However, the testimony by one witness which you believe concerning any fact is sufficient for the proof of that fact, you should carefully review all the evidence upon which the proof of such fact depends.

Evidence will be introduced for the purpose of showing that the defendant committed acts other than that for which he is on trial. Such evidence, if believed, will not be received and may not be considered by you to prove that the defendant is a person of bad character or that he has a disposition to commit crimes. Such evidence will be received and may be considered by you only for the limited purpose of determining if it tends to show the existence of the intent which is necessary — which is a necessary **element** of the crime charge, the identity of the person who committed the crime, if any, of which the defendant is accused, a motive for the commission of the crime charge, or a characteristic method, plan, or scheme, in the commission of acts similar to the method, plan, or scheme, used in the commission of the offense in this case, which would further tend to show the existence of the intent which is a necessary element of the crime charge, the identity of the person who committed the crime, if any, of which the defendant is accused; or a clear connection between the other act and the one which the defendant is accused so that it may be inferred that if the defendant committed the other acts, the defendant also committed the acts — excuse me, also committed the crimes charged in this case. For the limited purpose for which you may consider such evidence, you must weigh it in the same manner as you do all other evidence in the case. You are not permitted to consider such evidence for any other purpose. Within the meaning of the preceding instructions, such other acts purportedly committed by the defendant must be proved by a preponderance of the evidence. You must not consider such evidence for any purpose unless you are satisfied the defendant committed such other acts.

The prosecution has the burden of proving these facts by a preponderance of the evidence. **Preponderance of the evidence** means evidence that has more convincing force and the greater probability of truth than that opposed to it. If the evidence is so evenly balanced that you are unable to find that the evidence on either side of an issue preponderates, your finding on that issue must be against the party who has the burden of proving it. You should consider all the evidence bearing upon every issue, regardless of who produced it.

Motive is not an element of the crime charge and need not be shown. However, you may consider motive or lack of motive as a circumstance in this case. Presence of motive may tend to establish guilt. Absence of motive may tend to establish innocence. You will, therefore, give its presence or absence, as the case may be, the weight to which you find it to be entitled.

An **admission** is a statement made by the defendant other than at his trial which does not by itself acknowledge his guilt of the crimes for which such defendant is on trial, but which statement tends to prove his guilt when considered with the rest of the evidence. You are the exclusive judges as to whether the defendant made an admission, and, if so, whether such statement is true, in whole or in part. If you should find that the defendant did not make the statement, you must reject it. If you find that it is true, in whole or in part, you may consider that part which you find to be true. Evidence of an oral admission of the defendant should be viewed with caution.

No person may be convicted of a criminal offense unless there is some proof of each element of the crime, independent of any admission made by him outside of this trial. The identity of the person who is alleged to have committed a crime is not an element of the crime. Such identity may be established by an admission. In determining the weight to be given an opinion expressed by any witness, you should consider his or her credibility, the extent of his or her opportunity to perceive the matters upon which his or her opinion is based, and the reasons, if any, given for it. You are not required to accept such opinion, but should give it the weight, if any, to which you find it to be entitled.

A person is qualified to testify as an **expert** if he or she has special knowledge, skill, experience, training, or education, sufficient to qualify him or her as an expert on the subject to which his or her testimony relates. A duly qualified expert may give an opinion on questions and controversy at a trial. To assist you in deciding such questions, you may consider the opinion, with the reasons given for it, if any, by the expert who gives the opinion. You may also consider the qualifications and credibility of the expert. You are not bound to accept an expert opinion as conclusive, but should give to it the weight to which you find it to be entitled. You may disregard any such opinion if you find it to be unreasonable.

In examining an expert witness, counsel may propound to him or her a type of question known in the law as a "hypothetical question." By such question, the witness is asked to assume to be true a set of facts, and to give an opinion based upon that assumption. In permitting such a question, the court does not rule and does not necessarily find that all the assumed facts have been proved. It only determines that those assumed facts are within the probable or possible range of the evidence. It is for you, the jury, to find, from all the evidence, whether or not the facts assumed in a hypothetical question have been proved. If you should find that any assumption in such question has not been proved, you are to determine the effect of that failure of proof on the value and weight of the expert opinion based upon the assumed facts.

In resolving any conflict that may exist in the testimony of expert witnesses, you should weigh the opinion of one expert against that of another. In doing this, you should consider the relative qualifications and credibility of the expert witnesses as well as the reasons for each opinion and the facts or other matters upon which it was based.

A defendant in a criminal action is presumed to be innocent until the contrary is proved, and, in case of a reasonable doubt, whether his guilt is satisfactorily shown, he is entitled to a verdict of not guilty. This presumption places upon the prosecution the burden of proving him guilty beyond a reasonable doubt. Reasonable doubt is defined as follows — it is not a mere possible doubt, because everything relating to human affairs is open to some possible or imaginary doubt. It is that state of the case which, after the entire comparison and consideration of all the evidence, leaves the minds of the jurors in that condition that they cannot say they feel abiding conviction of the truth of the charge.

In the crimes charged in counts one and two, there must exist a union or joint operation of act or conduct, and a certain mental state in the mind of the perpetrator. Unless such mental state exists, the crime to which it relates is not committed. The mental state required is included in the definition of the crime set forth elsewhere in my instructions. The defendant in this case will introduce evidence for the purpose of showing that he was not present at the time and place of the commission of the alleged crime for which he is here on trial. If, after consideration of all the evidence, you have a reasonable doubt that the defendant was present at the time the crime was committed, you must find him not guilty.

The defendant is accused in counts one and two of having committed the crime of murder, a violation of Penal Code section 187. Every person who unlawfully kills a human being with malice aforethought is guilty of the crime of murder in violation of section 187 of the penal code. In order to prove such crime, each of the following elements must be proved. One, a human being was killed; two, the killing was unlawful; three, the killing was done with **malice aforethought**. Malice may be either expressed, or implied. Malice is expressed when there is manifested an intention unlawfully to kill a human being. Malice is implied when, one, the killing resulted from an intentional act; two, the natural consequences of the act are dangerous to human life; and three, the act was deliberately performed with knowledge of the danger to and with conscious disregard for human life. When it is shown that a killing resulted from the intentional doing of an act with expressed or implied malice, no other mental state need be shown to establish the mental state of malice aforethought. The mental state constituting malice aforethought does not necessarily require any ill will or hatred of the person killed.

The word "aforethought" does not imply deliberation or the lapse of considerable time. It only means the required mental state must precede, rather than follow, the act. All murder which is perpetrated by any kind of willful, deliberate, and premeditated killing with express malice aforethought is murder of the first degree. The word "willful," as used in this instruction, means intentional. The word "deliberate" means formed or arrived at, or determined upon as a result of a careful thought and weighing of considerations for and against the proposed course of action. The word "premeditated" means considered beforehand. If you find that the killing was preceded and accompanied by a clear, deliberate intent on the part of the defendant to kill, which was the result of deliberation and premeditation, so that it must have been formed upon pre-existing reflection and not under a sudden heat of passion or other condition precluding the idea of deliberation, it is murder of the first degree. The law does not undertake to measuring units of time, the length of the period during which the thought must be pondered before it can ripen into an intent to kill which is truly deliberate and premeditated. The time will vary with different individuals and under varying circumstances. The true test is not duration of time, but rather the extent of the reflection. A cold, calculated judgment and decision may be arrived at in a short period of time, but a mere unconsidered and rash impulse, even though it includes an intent to kill, is not such deliberation and premeditation as will fix an unlawful killing as murder of the first degree. To constitute a deliberate and premeditated killing, the slayer must weigh and consider the question of killing, and the reasons for and against such choice, and having in mind the consequences, he decides to and does kill.

Murder of the second degree is the unlawful killing of a human being with malice aforethought when there is manifested an intention unlawfully to kill a human being, but the evidence is insufficient to establish deliberation and premeditation. Murder is classified into two degrees, and if you should find the defendant guilty of murder, you must determine whether you find the murder to be of the first or second degree. If you find the defendant in this case guilty of murder of the first degree, you must then decide if the following special circumstance is true or not true: the defendant has, in this proceeding, been convicted of more than one offense of murder in the first or second degree. The prosecution has the burden of proving the truth of a special circumstance. If you have a reasonable doubt as to whether a special circumstance is true, you must find it to be not true. To find the special circumstance as referred to in these instructions as multiple murder and convictions is true, it must be proved the defendant has in this case been convicted of at least one crime of murder of the first degree, and one or more crimes of murder of the first or second degree.

In your deliberations, the subject of penalty or punishment is not to be discussed or considered by you. This is a matter which must not in any way affect your verdict or affect your finding as to the special circumstance alleged in this case. It is alleged in counts one and two that in the commission of the crime charged, the defendant personally used a deadly or dangerous weapon. If you find such defendant guilty of the crime thus charged, you must determine whether or not such defendant personally used a dangerous or deadly weapon in the commission of such crimes. A **deadly or dangerous weapon** means any weapon, instrument, or object, that is capable of being used to inflict great bodily injury or death. The term "used a deadly or dangerous weapon," as used in this instruction, means to display such weapon in an intentionally menacing manner, or intentionally to strike or hit a human being with it.

The prosecution has the burden of proving the truth of this allegation. If you have a reasonable doubt that it is true, you must find it to be not true.

The attitude and conduct of jurors at all times is very important. You are not to discuss, amongst yourselves, or with any other person, any subject connected with this trial. You are not to form or express any opinion on the case until the case is submitted to you for deliberations in the jury room. Remember that you are not partisans or advocates in this matter. You are the impartial judges of the facts. You will be given notebooks and pencils for your use during the course of the trial. You are to leave them on your seat when you leave each day, and at each recess. You will be able to take them into the jury room for your deliberations. A word of caution about note-taking; you may take notes, however, you should not permit note-taking to distract you from the ongoing proceedings. Remember, you are the judges of the credibility of the witnesses. Further, notes are only an aid to memory and should not take precedence of independent recollection. A juror who does not take notes should rely upon his or her independent recollection of the evidence, and not be influenced by the fact that other jurors do take notes. Notes are for the note-taker's own personal use in refreshing his or her recollection of the evidence. Finally, should any discrepancy exist between a juror's recollection of the evidence and his or her notes, he or she may request that the reporter read back the relevant proceedings, and the trial transcript must prevail over the notes.

The purpose of the court's instructions is to provide you with the applicable law so that you may arrive at a just and lawful verdict. Whether some of the instructions apply will depend upon what you find to be the facts. Disregard any instruction which applies to facts determined by you not to exist. Do not conclude that because an instruction has been given, that I am expressing an opinion as to the facts. I do not intend, by anything that I say or do or by any questions that I may ask, or by any ruling that I may make during the course of this trial, to intimate or to suggest to you what you should find to be the facts, or that I believe or disbelieve any of the witnesses who testify here in court. If anything that I do or say seems to so indicate, you will disregard it and form your own opinion.

All right. Ladies and gentlemen, this concludes my preliminary instructions to you on the law as it applies to this case. You are going to stand and recess now until tomorrow morning at ten o'clock when we will proceed to the opening statements by the attorneys. All right.

Notes

[1] Richard Hoffer, "O.J.Simpson Stands Accused of Brutally Killing Two People, One of Them the Woman He Loved," *Time*, June 27, 1994

[2] Readers should be aware that although the information contained in this "transcript" appears consistent with news reports and in-court evidence, the "transcript" itself was never introduced into evidence. The "transcript" was originally published in the November 29, 1994 issue of *Star*, and became available through various internet sites, including "alt.fan.oj-simpson" to which it was uploaded from an e-mail address at "onramp.net." The "transcript" eventually made its way to *Dimitri's O.J. Simpson Trial Center* home page on the World Wide Web, from which these segments are reproduced. Neither the source, the accuracy, nor the authenticity of the "transcript" have been verified.

[3] See, for example, Edward J. Clynch and David W. Neubauer, "Trial Courts as Organizations," *Law and Policy Quarterly*, Vol. 3 (1981), pp. 69–94.

[4] Bureau of Justice Statistics, *Report to the Nation on Crime and Justice: The Data* (Washington, D.C.: U.S. Department of Justice, 1983).

[5] *Brady* v. *Maryland*, 373 U.S. 83 (1963).

[6] *U.S.* v. *Bagley*, 473 U.S. 667 (1985).

[7] *Nix* v. *Whiteside*, 475 U.S. 157 (1986).

[8] See, for example, Joan G. Brannon, *The Judicial System in North Carolina* (Raleigh, NC: The Administrative Office of the Courts, 1984), p. 14.

[9] Jennifer Bowles, "Simpson-Paid Experts," The Associated Press on-line, August 12, 1995.

[10] Joseph L. Peterson, "Use of Forensic Evidence by the Police and Courts," a National Institute of Justice, *Research in Brief* (Washington, D.C.: NIJ, 1987), p. 3.

[11] Ibid., p. 6.

[12] *California* v. *Green*, 399 U.S. 149 (1970).

[13] Patrick L. McCloskey and Ronald L. Schoenberg, *Criminal Law Deskbook* (New York: Matthew Bender, 1988), Section 17, p. 123.

[14] *Williams* v. *Florida*, 399 U.S. 78, 90 S.Ct. 1893, 26 L.Ed. 2d 446 (1970).

[15] *Smith* v. *Texas*, 311 U.S. 128 (1940).

[16] *Thiel* v. *Southern Pacific Co.*, 328 U.S. 217 (1945).

[17] "Cochran," The Associated Press on-line, September 23, 1995.

[18] *Strunk* v. *U.S.*, 412 U.S. 434 (1973).

[19] The Federal Speedy Trial Act, 18 U.S.C., Section 3161 (1974).

[20] *U.S.* v. *Brainer*, 515 F. Supp. 627 (D.Md.1981).

[21] See, for example, the U.S. Supreme Court's decision in the case of *Murphy* v. *Florida*, 410 U.S. 525 (1973).

[22] Rule 24(6) of the *Federal Rules of Criminal Procedure*.

[23] Although the words "argument" and "statement" are sometimes used interchangeably in alluding to opening remarks, defense attorneys and prosecutors are enjoined from drawing conclusions or "arguing" to the jury at this stage in the trial. Their task is simply to provide information to the jury as to how their case will be presented.

Chapter 2
Opening Statements

The prosecution team. Left to right: co-counselors Christopher Darden, Marcia Clark, and William "Bill" Hodgman. AP/Wide World Photos.

INTRODUCTON

On January 24, 1994 the murder trial of O.J. Simpson got into full swing as Deputy District Attorney Christopher Darden presented the prosecution's opening statement to the jury in open court. Darden, an African-American, was added to the all-white prosecution team seemingly at the last minute, in what some interpreted as an attempt by the district attorney's office to appease racial sensitivities possibly harbored by members of the jury.

   An **opening statement** is not an argument — that is, it is not intended to prove anything to the jury. Similarly, it is not evidence, nor does it provide evidence. It's purpose is to provide an outline or summary of the case about to be heard. An opening statement gives members of the jury a general sense of how the trial will proceed and informs them of what the attorney making the statement intends to prove. Opening statements are not permitted to be argumentative — that is, they must consist of a straightforward presentation of claims and may not build inappropriately upon those claims. While opening statements provide a powerful tool for attorneys on both sides to use to set the tone for the remainder of a trial, claims made in opening statements must be "backed up" by later evidence, or such claims may eventually be used against the side making them.

Criminal procedure generally allows for an opening statement by the prosecution, followed by the defense's opening statement. A transcript of Deputy District Attorney Christopher Darden's opening statement follows.

(Editor's note: Simpson's home address was 360 Rockingham Avenue in the Brentwood section of Los Angeles. Nicole lived in a duplex condominium located at 875 South Bundy Drive, also in Brentwood. Her address is referred to in courtroom proceedings as the "Bundy Location," while Simpson's house is called the "Rockingham address.")

THE PROSECUTION'S OPENING STATEMENT

(The following proceedings were held in open court, out of the presence of the jury):

The Court: All right. Back on the record in the Simpson matter. Mr. Simpson is again present before the court with his counsel, Mr. Shapiro, Mr. Uelmen, Mr. Cochran, Mr. Douglas, Mr. Bailey — people represented by Miss Clark, Mr. Darden and Mr. Hodgman. The jury is not present. Deputy Magnera, may we have the jury, please.

The Bailiff: Yes, your honor.

(The following proceedings were held in open court, in the presence of the jury):

The Court: All right. Counsel and the audience, please be seated. All right. Good morning, ladies and gentlemen.

The Jury: good morning.

The Court: We are going to begin with the opening statements made by the lawyers in the case. Let me remind you from my instructions to you yesterday that any statements made to you by the attorneys during the course of their opening statements are not evidence and should not be considered as such by you.

These opening statements are normally given by the attorneys to sort of give you an overall view of the evidence that they intend to present. It's to give you a road map so to speak as to how to evaluate the evidence.

This case, as you know, will be relatively long. And by necessity, some of this evidence will be presented to you out of chronological or logical order. So they'll need to explain to you the case that they intend to present.

All right. Are both sides prepared to go forward? Mr. Cochran?

Mr. Cochran: We are, your honor.

The Court: Miss Clark?

Ms. Clark: Yes, we are, your honor.

The Court: Do the people wish to make an opening statement?

Ms. Clark: Yes, we do, thank you.

The Court: You may proceed. Mr. Darden.

Mr. Darden: Thank you, your honor.

The Court: Thank you.

Mr. Darden: Your honor, Judge Ito, Mr. Cochran and Mr. Shapiro and Dean Uelmen, to my colleagues seated here today in front of you and to the real parties in interest in this case, the Brown family, the Goldman family and the Simpson family and to you, ladies and gentlemen of the jury, good morning.

The Jury: Good morning.

Mr. Darden: I think it's fair to say that I have the toughest job in town today except for the job that you have. Your job may just be a little bit tougher. It's your job — like my job, we both have a central focus, a single objective, and that objective is justice obviously.

It's going to be a long trial and I want you to know how much we appreciate your being on the panel. We appreciate the personal sacrifices you're making by being sequestered. We understand that can be difficult.

And I would like to thank you in advance for keeping the promises you made to us when you were selected for the jury initially.

You promised to be fair and you promised to be open-minded and you promised to hear and see and carefully consider all the evidence in the case and you promised to find this case — to come to a verdict in this case solely on the basis of the evidence and the law given to you by Judge Ito.

And you promised to do that based on the law, based on the facts and the evidence and nothing else. You promised us that you had no hidden agenda, that you only wanted to see justice done and you promised us that you would do everything you could under the law to see that justice was done.

And so I thank you for that and I thank you in advance for the verdict you will at some point render in this case.

Now, we're here today obviously to resolve an issue, to settle a question, a question that has been on the minds of people throughout the country these last seven months. It certainly has been on the minds of my people up in Richmond, California and friends in Fayetteville, Georgia and all across the country.

Everybody wants to know and everybody I know often poses a question to me: "Did O.J. Simpson really kill Nicole Brown and Ronald Goldman?"

Well, finally, ladies and gentlemen, I am here in front of you this morning to answer that question. And we'll answer that question from the witness stand and from the exhibits you'll see in this case and from the evidence.

And when you see the evidence and when you hear the witnesses and when you put it all together and consider the totality of circumstances in this case, the answer will be clear to you as well.

The answer to the question is yes. The evidence will show that the answer to the question is yes, O.J. Simpson murdered Nicole Brown and Ronald Goldman. And I'm sure you will be wondering why as the trial proceeds on and I'm sure you are wondering why right now.

As the judge instructed you already, opening statements are not evidence. Opening statements are given by lawyers. And in an opening statement, we inform the jury of what we think the evidence will show in this case, what we believe the evidence will show.

But we're lawyers. We're not witnesses. We're not under oath. Nothing we say is evidence. The things we say to you today are not the things that you should carry into the jury room and into deliberations.

You should carry into the jury room and into your deliberations the evidence in the case, the testimony from the witness stand, the exhibits admitted at trial, the instructions given to you by the court. And when you look at all of that, when you go back and reflect on the testimony and the exhibits and everything you heard and saw in this case, you will know why he killed Nicole Brown and Ronald Goldman.

• • •

What we've been seeing, ladies and gentlemen, is the public face, the public persona, the face of the athlete, the face of the actor.

It is not the actor who is on trial here today, ladies and gentlemen. It is not that public face. It is his other face like many men in public. Like many public men, they have a public image, a public persona, a public side, a public life and they also have a private side, a private life, a private face. And that is the face we will expose to you in this trial, the other side of O.J. Simpson, the side you never met before.

We will expose in this trial and show to you in this trial that other face, the face he wore behind the locks and the gates and the wall at Rockingham, that other face, the one that Nicole Brown encountered almost every day of her adult life, the one she encountered during the last moments of her adult life; the same face Ronald Goldman encountered during the last moments of his life.

When we look upon and look behind that public face, the public face of the man who sits here in court today, you'll see a different face. And the evidence will show that the face you will see and the man that you will see will be the face of a batterer, a wife beater, an abuser, a controller. You'll see the face of Ron — of Ron's and Nicole's murderer.

To understand what happened at Bundy, we need to examine this defendant's relationship with Nicole. Because when we do, we can discern from that, we can see a motive, we can see his motive for killing his ex-wife.

And I submit to you, ladies and gentlemen, that as the trial proceeds on and as you hear the evidence in this case, that motive will become clear.

He killed Nicole for a single reason. Not because he hated her. He didn't hate Nicole. He didn't kill her because he didn't love her anymore, because in his mind, in his mind, he did. He killed her for a reason almost as old as mankind itself. He killed her out of jealousy. He killed her because he couldn't have her; and if he couldn't have her, he didn't want anybody else to have her.

He killed her to control her. Control is a continuing thing. It was a continuing thing, the central focus of their entire relationship.

By killing Nicole, this defendant assumed total control over her. By killing her, he committed the ultimate act of control. By killing her, no one else could have her, no one but him.

And he killed Ron Goldman. And he killed Ron Goldman for another reason. He killed Ron Goldman because he got in the way.

He killed Nicole because he had a problem with her as men and women sometimes do have in a relationship. They have a problem.

And this defendant's problem, the man in the courtroom — I think he stated his problem rather eloquently at her wake as he stood over her body at her wake, and he said then and he said on other occasions, and I quote, he said while standing over that casket, while standing over Nicole's body, "my problem was that I loved you too much."

• • •

Let me proceed on. The evidence will show in this case that he abused her mentally. He stripped her of her self esteem.

This defendant dictated the way Nicole would dress. He dictated the way she would wear her hair. And when he didn't like her appearance, he would criticize her, he would humiliate her to the point where she would cry. If he didn't like her shoes, he would go out and buy shoes. "This is what I want you to wear. Wear this. Look like this."

She was not a Barbie doll, ladies and gentlemen.

The evidence will show that he was so controlling that he attempted to define her identity. He attempted to define who she was.

When she was pregnant and put on weight, the evidence will show that this defendant was so abusive that he called her names.   He called her fat. He called her a pig. And he did this in the presence of her family and in the presence of her friends and he humiliated her.

That is the face we intend to expose in this trial. That's the other side of this defendant we're going to show you in this trial.

And by doing these things and by hurtling these insults, he stripped her of her self esteem.

And when you're controlling someone financially and when they have no self esteem and when they have no identity, you have them, you control them.

The evidence will show that this defendant, this man in the courtroom was a very controlling and possessive man and that the dominant thing throughout their relationship was his control of Nicole Brown.

• • •

By demeaning her and controlling the purse strings and isolating her and defining who she would see and who she wouldn't see and who her friends would be and who they would not be wasn't all this defendant did to control this woman.

There are more powerful forms of control.   There's force, there's violence, there's fear, there's intimidation.

And you will hear testimony, you will see evidence that in his quest to control Nicole, this defendant used all these things.   He used fear, he used intimidation and he used violence.

• • •

I mentioned earlier that they met when she was around 18 years old back in 1977, and they dated for eight years and they eventually married in 1985. And the marriage was a stormy marriage and it was a marriage punctuated by acts of violence.

And that violence would always be followed by an apology. He would apologize, give her jewelry, buy her flowers.

He would promise to do better, promise, promise to maintain control of himself and he would promise not to do it again. And then those acts of violence would be followed by additional acts of violence, and it became a cycle; violence, apologies, a period of quiet and calm, then violence and apologies, quiet and calm, violence, apologies, quiet, calm.

A cycle of violence characterized their relationship. It characterized their marriage.

And domestic violence, ladies and gentlemen, that's — that's a difficult topic because domestic violence is something that happens behind the gates and the walls. It happens in the bedroom and inside the home and places where the public can't see.

Domestic violence is a private affair generally while it's occurring, and so it makes it difficult to obtain evidence, to gain proof that the violence occurred and it makes it difficult to obtain evidence and gain proof that the relationship is a violent relationship.

But we do have that proof. We do have proof. We do have evidence. You will hear testimony from witnesses in this case, and they will discuss the violent relationship, the violent marriage this defendant had with Nicole Brown.

In 1985, the police responded to the defendant's home on Rockingham in response to a call. And when they arrived, they were met by Nicole. She was crying, she was upset and her face was puffy and she was near hysterics.

She told these people, she said, "we had a fight. After the fight, I was trying to leave. And when I tried to leave, the defendant grabbed a baseball bat, and he took that baseball bat and he smashed the windshield to my car." This is 1985.

• • •

You will be hearing evidence, you will be hearing testimony, you will be seeing witnesses in this case regarding an incident that happened on January 1, 1989.

It was almost 4:00 o'clock in the morning on January 1st when the 911 operator received a telephone call from Rockingham. And that operator will be here to testify in court and that operator will be here to authenticate the tape of that 911 call from Rockingham.

And when the operator appears and when the tape is played, listen very carefully, because if you listen carefully, in the background, you will hear a woman screaming and you will hear something else. You will hear the sound of this defendant, this man beating this woman. You will hear the sound of his hand smacking across her face. You will hear the sound of this defendant beating his wife.

When the police arrived, they arrived at Rockingham in response to that telephone call. And Nicole never got to tell the 911 operator that, "come and help me," or anything like that. All she did was scream.

And the operator could hear her screaming and the operator could hear her being beaten, and she advised LAPD units to respond to 360 north Rockingham. "We can hear the sound of a woman being beaten now, right now."

And the officers arrived at Rockingham a short time later.   And when they did, they rang the buzzer to the security gate. And as they did so, they saw someone run from the bushes, run from the darkness in their direction.

And the person that they saw was Nicole. And Nicole came run- ning out of the darkness wearing nothing but sweat pants and a bra running towards the officers, and she was covered with mud and she was dirty, she was filthy.

And she ran towards the officers. And as she ran towards the officers, she was shouting and yelling, "he's going to kill me. He's going to kill me."

And the officers stood there. They didn't know what to do.

• • •

I'm not suggesting and the evidence won't suggest that every day of their marriage or their relationship was stormy, rocky and filled with violence. That's not what we're suggesting here.

What we are suggesting, and the evidence will show, that there was a cycle of violence, a cycle of violence; and the dominant theme in that relationship and in that cycle and the ultimate objective was always control, control.

• • •

And if you are the other person in Nicole's position as she was — and this will be reflected in the evidence — she wanted to believe, she wanted to believe that her marriage could survive.   She wanted to have hope, and he gave her hope for a while because this is a cycle.

And so he beat her up on January 1. He admitted to her privately in his letters that he was responsible, and he apologized and he gave her things and he tried to make it all better, and he gave her hope and he roped her back in, and she stayed.   She stayed because she had hope and because she wanted to believe that January 1, 1989 would be the last time that he would abuse her physically or mentally.

As you hear the evidence in this case, something very sad becomes very apparent. They met when she was 18 and he was almost 30, and in 1992, they divorced. She was only 33 years old and she died when she was almost 35.

Throughout her adult life, throughout most of her adult life, her concept of marriage and relationship was defined by this defendant. That was adult love. Her notion of adult love for 15 years was what this defendant gave her, and he abused her throughout that relationship.

As I said before, you know, sometimes you get roped in. People get roped in. Nicole got roped in by the defendant, and she stayed and she stayed. And people stay in those situations, those abusive relationships for years and years until one or two things happen; one, they just can't take it anymore, or, two, until they just can't take it anymore and they wake up to reality.

And finally, in 1992, Nicole woke up to the reality of her situation, and in January 1992, she moved from Rockingham, she left the defendant and she filed for divorce.

Well, this did not sit well with this defendant and this will be reflected in the evidence. He did not like this. He did not like the fact that Nicole was leaving his house going somewhere else to live in her own house away from him.

There is that issue of control. How could he control her? She wasn't right there with him.

• • •

But he couldn't deal with the loss of Nicole. He couldn't deal with not having her there. He couldn't deal with the loss of control and he couldn't help but pursue her.

You'll hear testimony in this case from Nicole's mother, and she'll tell you about some of the telephone conversations she had with the defendant in 1992 and some even more recent. And one conversation, he told her, he told her, he said, "all my friends tell me that I should just leave her alone, just forget about it, just go on with my own life."

And when Mrs. Brown said, "why don't you do that, let her go. If you let her go, then maybe she'll come back to you. Just let her go, and maybe she'll come back," and his response was, "I can't. You know I can't. You know I can't help myself. I can't let her go."

He couldn't let her go. He couldn't help but pursue her. He couldn't leave her alone. He couldn't handle the loss of control. And because she had left his house and moved somewhere else and established her own home, her own house and began establishing her own relationships, he did the only thing he could do to gain control, to try to gain control, to try to find out what was going on with her, and so he stalked her. He stalked her.

When she left Rockingham in January of '92 and set up a new household on Gretna Green also in Brentwood, she began dating a man named Keith, Keith Zlomsowitch, and she got a baby-sitter for their two children.

Whenever Keith and Nicole would go out, not every time, but enough, he would show up. If they went to a nightclub — and Keith will tell you about this. He will be here to testify — defendant showed up.

• • •

And there's more, and you'll hear about the other incidents. There's more evidence of stalking in this case and you'll hear about that.

There was one evening when Keith and Nicole, they went to a comedy show, and after the show, they went to Nicole's house on Gretna Green. It was about 3:00 in the morning. And they were seated on the sofa in her living room. The kids, the kids were upstairs asleep. It's 3:00 o'clock in the morning. And Keith and Nicole made love on the couch.

But they weren't alone. There was somebody watching. There was someone watching through the window. It was the defendant. At 3:00 o'clock in the morning, he was looking through Nicole's window watching her make love to another man.

And the next day, when Keith and Nicole were together, he walked right into her house, and he was beside himself and he was angry and he said some very naughty things. But one of the things that he said to Keith and Nicole was that, he said, "I watched you last night. I watched you and I saw everything."

The evidence will show that that is somewhat unusual behavior to say the least. The evidence will show also that this is all part of this cycle. It's all part of this dominant theme in their relationship. This is all part of his need to know everything about her, to know where she is, to know who she's with, to know what she's doing, to control her.

It's control. It's all about control.

• • •

And Nicole was as much a party to that as the defendant was. But there was a situation in October of 1993, an incident, another control incident.

He forced his way through the back door of her place on Gretna Green. He forced her door in. He entered her house without her permission, without her knowledge and he confronted her and he scared her, he frightened her. And he scared her so badly that she telephoned 911, and she asked for police assistance.

And you will hear the tape of that 911 call and you will see the 911 operator and you will hear the defendant in the background. This is October 1993.

He watched Keith and Nicole have sex in April of 1992. And when you listen to the October 1993 911 tape, you can hear him in the background still yelling and shouting about what happened in April of 1992.

But that 911 tape is a telling glimpse into their relationship that's for sure, and it's also an example of this defendant's private side, his private face, the other man, the man in the courtroom, the man that's on trial here today.

And you will hear Nicole on the telephone talking to the operator. And as you listen to her, you can't help but discern from the tone of her voice and the things that she says that she is a tough woman, but that she's also afraid and intimidated. And not only that, but that she feels that her situation is hopeless.

The evidence will show that by October of 1993, Nicole, her situation was hopeless and she was helpless.

Way back in 1989, the defendant said that the police had been to the house eight times before and never done anything. Nicole said the same thing on the telephone to the 911 operator in 1993.

Her situation was hopeless and she was helpless. And you can infer from the evidence that Nicole Brown expected or had no expectation that anyone would ever do anything to this defendant because he beat her. There was no help coming and she didn't expect any help.

• • •

She woke up to the true reality of her situation. She couldn't be balked anymore. She couldn't live like that. And the evidence will show that she let the defendant know that it was over. This is it, hasta la vista.

And this was significant in the mind of this defendant, ladies and gentlemen. It was something that had never happened before.

He would do things to her and he would try to appease her by giving her things, and she would accept those things and they would reconcile. But not this day. This day, she couldn't be appeased. She couldn't be bought. She couldn't be bribed. She had had enough.

And the evidence will show that she let the defendant know that. And the evidence will show that finally, after 17 years, he finally got the message. It finally became clear that she wanted to live her own life and that in her life, that he was not going to be a part of it.

She couldn't handle it. She woke up to reality. She wanted to live and have her own identity. She no longer wanted to be under his control, under his thumb. She let him know that it was over, that it was over, it was over and it was final, but this defendant's private side, the other man, not the one on TV, the defendant, he couldn't take that. He couldn't accept that. He could not accept that loss of control, and he wouldn't and he didn't.

On June 12, a dance recital was held in Brentwood for the defendant's daughter Sidney. The entire Brown family went to the recital as did some friends, Candice Garvey for instance.

The auditorium was crowded. So not everyone could sit, you know, next to a family member. And so their party was, you know — there were people between them. They were separated somewhat and different people had to sit in different rows and not all together.

Well, the defendant arrived late and he arrived carrying a bouquet of flowers, flowers he had bought for his daughter.

Well, when he walked into the auditorium, he greeted just about everyone in the party in the Brown family. He said hello to them, he kissed Denise on the cheek, "how are you, how you doing," whatever, and he pretty much addressed everybody except Nicole.

He sat behind the Brown's for a few moments. And then he got up and he grabbed a chair and he dragged it in the corner of the auditorium and he turned that chair around and he sat in it, and he sat there facing Nicole and he just stared at her. He just sat there staring at her.

And you'll hear testimony about this, and the evidence will show that this was a menacing stare, a penetrating stare, it was an angry stare, and it made everyone very uncomfortable.

When the recital was over, there was a little issue whether or not the defendant was allowed to give Sidney some flowers, and he gave her some flowers. But the Brown family had decided to go over to the Mezzaluna restaurant for dinner. And as they left, they made it clear to the defendant that he was not invited, and he wasn't invited.

And by not inviting him, it was a reaffirmation of what he had already been told, and that is that it was over. He was no longer being treated as a part of the family. He was no longer the central centerpiece of every family outing. Nicole was getting on with her own life.

And as the Brown family left, they looked toward the defendant and they saw him, and he was angry and he was depressed and they were concerned and everyone wondered what is he up to now. Miss Clark will tell you exactly what the defendant was up to as the day proceeded on.

But there's some things you should know about this evidence as you hear it.

This is not character assassination. This is evidence of a controlling personality, of a controlling relationship, this proof of jealousy.

And as Miss Clark talks and the evidence develops in this case and as you hear it and see it and process it, you will see that cycle of violence. You will see how things escalated. You'll see how controlling he is and you'll see why he would kill on June 12.

This is not character assassination. This is not some tabloid prosecution. The evidence you hear in this case will be evidence of this defendant's life, of his conduct, the things he did.

You will hear evidence of his relationship with one of the victims. And as you hear it, you will — as you hear the evidence and as you listen to Miss Clark, you'll see how it is that Ron Goldman happened to be at the wrong place at the wrong time.

As you listen to the evidence, you will see that his decision to kill finally was merely a final link in a progressive chain of abusive and controlling conduct, and it was a chain that consisted of fear and intimidation and battery and emotional and mental abuse and economic abuse and control and stalking.

And you'll see that there was a common scheme and common plan in all of this, and that was to control, to control her. It was all designed just to control her. And in controlling her, it was the private man, private O.J. Simpson, it was the defendant who committed that final ultimate act of control.

She left him. She was no longer in his control. He was obsessed with her. He could not stand to lose her, and so he murdered her.

And as you hear the evidence in this case, it will become clear that in his mind, she belonged to him; and if he couldn't have her, then nobody could.

Thank you.

The opening remarks of Prosecutor Darden were followed by those of his co-counsel Marcia Clark. Ms. Clark described for the jury what the prosecution believed to have been the course of events on the night of June 12, 1994 — the night Nicole Brown Simpson and Ronald Goldman were murdered. The descriptions were lengthy and built around a time-line focusing on the alleged activities of the defendant, the victims, and possible witnesses.

Ms. Clark described what witnesses are thought to have seen and heard at O.J. Simpson's Rockingham home. She also described the barking of a dog at Nicole's condominium and provided detailed descriptions of the physical layout of both locations.

Photographs of both victims were presented to the jury, showing that Nicole's throat had been "hideously slashed," leaving her head almost severed from her body.

Clark also introduced the concept of DNA fingerprinting, which she called "a very powerful tool to pinpoint the identify of the person who left blood or hair or bodily fluid in an area." She told the jury that DNA evidence would show that some of the blood at the crime scene matched that of the defendant, and that other drops of blood, later shown to belong to O.J. Simpson, Ronald Goldman, and Nicole Brown Simpson, formed "a trail of blood from Bundy drive to Rockingham Avenue and into the defendant's very bedroom linked by the defendant's white Ford Bronco." Only the start and the conclusion of Clark's remarks (along with numerous defense objections) are reproduced here.

(The following proceedings were held in open court, in the presence of the jury):

The Court: Miss Clark.

Ms. Clark: Thank you, your honor. Good morning, ladies and gentlemen.

The Jury: Good morning.

Ms. Clark: You've all seen me for quite a while, but you haven't seen Mr. Darden. He was busy with other matters. And he is an integral part of this case.

Let me introduce some of the lawyers you haven't met, but you will be seeing throughout the course of this trial. Mr. Hank Goldberg.

Mr. Goldberg: Good morning.

Ms. Clark: Mr. Woody Clark and Mr. Rochmond Harmon. They will all be presenting the scientific evidence in this case that relates to the blood analysis and DNA testing.

When you hear the amount of evidence that we have, you'll understand why I need the help. And I thank them very much for their able assistance thus far.

• • •

Apart from the test results, ladies and gentlemen, the mere fact that we find blood where there should be no blood in the defendant's car, in his house, in the driveway and even on the socks in his very bedroom at the foot of his bed, that trail of blood from Bundy through his own Ford Bronco and into his house in Rockingham is devastating proof of his guilt.

And the results of the analysis of that blood confirms what the rest of the evidence will show that on June the 12th, 1994, after a violent relationship in which the defendant beat her, humiliated her and controlled her, after he took her youth, her freedom and her self respect, just as she tried to break free Orenthal James Simpson, took her very life in what amounted to his final and his ultimate act of control.

And in that final and terrible act Ronald Goldman, an innocent bystander, was viciously and senselessly murdered.

Remember that in *voir dire* we asked you if you could use your common sense and reason to fairly and to objectively evaluate this evidence as neutral impartial judges of the facts. You all promised that you could and you would and we believe that you will.

We have every faith and belief in the fact that you will all keep that promise, but it will not be easy. You will be tested and tempted throughout this case to accept the unreasonable and be distracted by the irrelevant.

The defense will talk to you about possibilities and they will insinuate many sinister things based on those possibilities, possibilities of contamination, possibilities of set-up, all in an effort to explain away all of the physical evidence, but possibilities alone do not equal proof.

You've heard the instruction that says that all matters subject to human affairs are capable of some possible doubt. That is why the standard is reasonable doubt. And you will hear the word "reasonable" more than once in the jury instructions and you already have, because if the proof standard was beyond all possible doubt, there could never be a conviction, there can always be a possible doubt about something.

The question is whether you have a doubt that is founded in reason, so beware of the efforts to get you to accept the unreasonable, be distracted by the irrelevant and to base your decision on speculation, on mere possibilities with no hard evidence to show that any of them really occurred.

Listen carefully to all the possibilities and the hints raised by the defendants and ask yourselves is there any proof that any of these possibilities actually occurred? Listen carefully for the defense to explain how the defendant's blood got on 875 South Bundy walkway.

It is going to be up to you, ladies and gentlemen. You are going to have to be ever vigilant in acting as the judges in this case. Each one of you is a judge. Each one of you is a trier of fact.

You have to examine all the evidence very carefully and ask you — do ask yourselves — is this reasonable? Is this logical? Does this make sense? Would I look at this evidence the same way —

Mr. Cochran: Your honor, she is starting to argue now.

The Court: Sounds like argument to me.

Ms. Clark: Look at the evidence the same way you would for any other case.

Now, winning is not what this is about. This is not a game. This is about justice and seeing that justice is done. Two people have been brutally murdered and the evidence consistently will point to the guilt of only one person as the murderer.

Mr. Cochran: Objection as argument.

Ms. Clark: Talking about what the evidence will show.

The Court: Are you about to conclude?

Ms. Clark: Uh-huh. Thank you.

There was no rush to judgment in this case. It was very carefully considered before it was filed.

The evidence will show, ladies and gentlemen, that as of June the 15th many DNA results had already been returned. As of June the 15th there had already been a match between the defendant and the blood found at Bundy drive. There had already been a match between the victims and the blood found on the glove at his house.

Many things were known and yet it was examined carefully, the entire case examined very carefully, and was not filed until two days after those results were obtained.

My job is to seek justice. I've had cases before this one, there will be cases after it.

This case is not about the lawyers, myself, Mr. Hodgman, Mr. Darden or Mr. Cochran.

You will have to remember what this case is about; justice for all.

Ladies and gentlemen, if those words are to mean anything, we must all be equal in the eyes of the law and we cannot use a sliding scale to judge guilt or innocence based on a defendant or a victim's popularity. We live in very, very strange times.

Mr. Cochran: Your honor, she is arguing.

The Court: Counsel, this has all been argument for the last five minutes.

Ms. Clark: I will wrap up, your honor.

The Court: Please.

Ms. Clark: We cannot succumb to the temptation to thwart justice and throw truth out the window.

The Court: Counsel, I'm going to have to stop you right here. I have warned you three times now.

Ms. Clark: All we are asking is that —

The Court: Counsel, I'm warning you. I have warned you three times now.

Ms. Clark: I am concluding right now, your honor.

The Court: Please.

Ms. Clark: May I?

The Court: Please.

Ms. Clark: Thank you. All we ask is that you stay focused on what the case is about, about the murder of Ron Goldman.

The Court: Counsel, will you approach, please.

Ms. Clark: Thank you.

THE DEFENSE'S OPENING STATEMENT

On January 25, 1994 defense attorney Johnnie Cochran, Jr. began delivering opening arguments for the defense. When he concluded, days later, Cochran called his remarks "very possibly the longest opening argument in the history of this building." An abbreviated transcript of his remarks follows:

Defense Attorney Johnnie Cochran Jr.: Judge Ito, my colleagues on the right — the prosecutors — my colleagues on the defense side, to the Brown family, the Simpson family, to the Goldman family — ladies and gentlemen, good morning to you.

As the court indicated yesterday, I would have liked to have had this opportunity at about 3:30 to address you, and it's my opportunity, it's my honor and privilege, on behalf of the defense, and our defense team, as it were, to stand before you now and address you in what is called an opening statement.

Now, the opening statement is not an opening argument, but it's just that: an opening statement. If you want to go to a movie, there's something called the previews or coming attractions, and that's what this is supposed to be. It's supposed to be a guide, our road map, if you will, of what we expect the evidence to show.

As an officer of this court, and in the course of my remarks this morning, maybe this afternoon, I would expect to tell you as honestly, as forthrightly as I can what I expect the evidence to be. As the court so appropriately indicated, what I say is not evidence. It's just to aid you and guide you.

I hope you remember something else the judge said to you last night. You've heard the prosecutors' opening statement yesterday, that the same admonition would apply to them, is that you keep an open mind, that you promise to do that throughout.

We started this process of trial back on September 26, 1994, on the first day we all met, when we came down the jury room up on the 11th floor. And here we are now, several months later, in this search for justice. You've heard a lot about this talk of justice. I guess Dr. Martin Luther King said it best when he said that 'Injustice anywhere is a threat to justice everywhere.' So we are now embarked upon a search for justice, this search for truth, this search for the facts.

Each of you made a number of promises in the course of the *voir dire* examination, which is basically unprecedented and due mainly to the largess of Judge Ito in understanding the possibility of media taint associated with this case. So we know a lot about you at this point and we, of course — all sides are very, very pleased with the fact you agreed to serve as jurors, to give us your time to leave your lives, to be sequestered, as it were. That's a remarkable sacrifice. Abraham Lincoln said it best when he said that, 'The highest act of citizenship is jury service.' And you embarked on that jury service.

And it doesn't stop with just coming down and taking notes. It doesn't stop with the inconvenience of being away from your families. It stops when you can render a verdict in this case, and whether or not that verdict reflects the evidence in this case. A verdict void of sympathy for or passion against Mr. Simpson or any side in this case. You made these promises on both sides and we know you're going to keep those promises. Cicero said that 'He who violates his oath profanes the faith of divinity itself.' And, of course, we know that you will live up to your promises, and be fair, and keep an open mind and decide this case not on speculation, not on conjecture, not on surmise, but based upon the facts.

You, as jurors, are the conscience of this community. Your verdicts set the standards of what we should have and what should happen in this community. You have this rare opportunity, it seems to me, to be participants in this search for justice and for truth. In the final analysis, hopefully by April of this year — I'm optimistic still — you'll be able to render perhaps the most important decision of your lives. So we want to keep your minds open and fresh so you can render that decision impartially on both sides, so that people all across the world can say, 'This system works. This was a fair trial. These were fair people.' So thank you in advance for your service, for the verdict you're likely to render and for all the things you're doing here for us.

Prosecutor William Hodgman: Your Honor, the court knows me and I know Mr. Cochran knows me. I have to inject, at this point, that this is...

The Court: They are introductory remarks that were similar in nature to the prosecution's opening remarks. I think Mr. Cochran has just concluded his opening remarks.

Cochran: I trust so, Your Honor.

Hodgman: Again, I hesitate to interrupt another lawyer's opening statements, but I simply wanted to make sure that this type of statement (inaudible). Thank you, Mr. Cochran.

Cochran: Thank you, Mr. Hodgman. I was just about to compliment the District Attorney's office on their opening statement yesterday. Maybe I'll take that out now. I was about to say they did a thorough job, as far as they went. But they're advocates, and all of us, as you will see today, have an obligation to tell you the whole truth of these facts. So in the course of my statement today, let me tell you some of the things they didn't tell you yesterday, and we'll have to wonder why they didn't do that.

The evidence in this case we believe will show that O.J. Simpson is an innocent man wrongfully accused. Mr. Darden said yesterday that in Richmond, Calif., and someplace in Georgia people were asking questions. Well, I'd like to think in my hometown of Shreveport, La., my mother-in-law in New Orleans, La., and other places throughout this country, today they're asking why did Mr. Darden spend all that time on domestic violence? This is a murder case. Why'd he do that? He was going to give me an answer. He was going to answer the question for all of America. It's a little presumptuous, don't you think, because the answer of O.J. Simpson's guilt or innocence can only be determined by you if you're able to do it.

None of us were out there on June 12, 1994. You can only deal with the witnesses as they were. It seems to me that this case, the prosecution's case, based on what we heard from the evidence, will show this case is about a rush to judgment, an obsession to win at any cost and by any means necessary. The evidence will show that the prosecution in this case has enlisted the services of many, many police agencies across the United States, the FBI, many local police agencies. They have gone around the world talking to witnesses. But the evidence will show they failed to go next door to Mr. Simpson's house and talk to a witness that they knew about who provided him with an alibi, and there are other witnesses like that and we will have to only ask ourselves why.

Let me just briefly talk about the witnesses they didn't talk about yesterday and they didn't tell you about. There's a lady who lives next door, that works next door to Mr. Simpson's home on Rockingham. This lady was interviewed, I think, as far back as July. She indicated, essentially, that on this night in question, she came out to walk her dog on several occasions. She knew Mr. Simpson, she knew his voice, she knew the Bronco. She'd seen it parked there many times. She will indicate that when she came out to walk her dog at about 8 o'clock, that Bronco was parked at the curb there. It was parked at kind of a unique angle so that she noticed it. The rear wheels were a little bit further from the curb. And when you go out there, and I think the court will probably share with you, that at some point you'll get a chance to go out — to see for yourself these areas. When you come out of Rockingham gate and you make your turn, the evidence will show it's a quick turn, so you can't line your car quite like you'd like to.

But this lady will testify that she was out with her dog and saw that Bronco parked at that particular angle at about 8:00, 8:30, on June 12, 1994, a Sunday evening. She will indicate to you that she heard Mr. Simpson's voice at or about the time he and Mr. Kato Kaelin went to McDonald's to get the hamburger and that she could hear, because her quarters are right across the fence there, that after he left, she heard something very strange. She heard a prowler, as she described, out there in the yard, with like hard-soled shoes. And she was concerned about this prowler is what her statement was. She relaxed when she heard Mr. Simpson return back, could hear his voice back over in the yard.

She was concerned because the people she works for were out of town at this time. She was concerned about this prowler. We'll talk about that more later. She went about her business. And then, she heard Mr. Simpson's voice again about 11:00. She could hear his voice at that time, as though he was leaving — we know that's correct because he's leaving to go on a trip to Chicago for a pre-planned trip. And then she didn't hear his voice anymore. Among the important things she tells me is that after Mr. Simpson had left, after 11 o'clock, she heard men's voices over on the Simpson property between 12 o'clock up 'til about 2:30 or 3 o'clock in the morning. She heard these men's voices over there talking. She didn't know what was going on. I hope I told you that when she came out to walk her dog at 10:15 that same night — the Bronco was parked exactly the same way at that curb. When she saw the Bronco the next morning, it was parked at that same spot at that same place. And one of the most unique things about this lady is the fact that the morning of June 13th, that Monday morning, a police officer came over to her residence, asked her what she heard and to put her on alert that if she found any weapons or the gardeners found any weapons, let them know. And she can identify that officer as Detective Mark Fuhrman. Detective Mark Fuhrman will play an integral part in this case for a number of reasons.

It's very interesting that the prosecution never once mentioned his name yesterday. It's like they want to hide him, but they can't hide him. He's very much a part of this case. And we ask ourselves, 'Why didn't they mention him?' I think that answer will become very clear to you as the case progresses.

And she will identify Detective Fuhrman as the person who spoke with her, and she told him that time about her observations, about hearing this prowler, and about the fact she heard these voices that went on to about 3 o'clock because she couldn't go to sleep until about 4:00. When she woke up it was around 7:30 or 8:00 and he was there, showing his (inaudible) through the door. She saw him on television at the preliminary hearing, so that's how she can identify him. He said that somebody from the LAPD will get back to you. But they never came back. They never came back at all because there's a rush to judgment here.

There's another witness, Marianne Gerjus. Very interestingly, has her own business. On this particular night on June of 1994, she wanted to find a place in the West Los Angeles-Brentwood area. She drove her car — she closed up her business Sunday evening and went to Catholic church, went to Mass, went to park her car, she over there on Bundy. Very interesting. Let me tell you what she has to say. Let me tell you her contact with law enforcement. The evidence will show that Marianne Gerjus, had she became aware of what she had seen, had some great relevance to this case. She started calling the police, she kept being transferred and transferred around, couldn't get anybody really to talk to her. Finally, when she finally reached a police officer, they told her 'We've got that case wrapped up.' They didn't want to hear from anybody else.

And then, lo and behold, she called the District Attorney's office, spoke to a person whose name will be reviewed during the testimony and she didn't feel she was treated quite appropriately. In fact, she will say the person put her on hold and said, 'Excuse me, I'm talking to a psychic right now and I'll get back to you.' I guess it was a part of that hotline that they had. So it seems they were more interested in talking to a psychic than talking to her. So ultimately she called the defense and we talked to her, walked with her out at the scene. Here's what she will testify about, that on June 12th, 1994, sometime after 10:30 in the evening, she's walking down Bundy Street. She's looking, it was a warm night, she says, she's looking for a place with signs on them for rent or to lease.

That Nicole Brown Simpson's condo, you recall, is on one side of the street, that's the west side, and she's on the east side of the street. And at about 10:45 p.m., she sees four men who come within 10 feet of her, two of which — gentlemen — appear to be Hispanic and the others are Caucasian, several of which, I believe, have knit caps on their heads. The two who are behind apparently have something in their hands they are carrying. She thinks they may be undercover police. She doesn't know. They get into an unmarked car and they speed away and she sees them. And that's what this lady was trying to tell the police, trying to tell the District Attorney, trying to tell anybody who will listen. They didn't want to listen because they made that decision and this rush to judgment.

There are other witnesses I won't bother you with right now because we'll talk about them later on during the opening statement that bear upon that evening because it sets the stage for many of the remarks Miss Clark made yesterday. You will recall that in her opening statement — quite well done — Miss Clark kept telling you that she fixed the time of death in this case at about 10:15. She made it based upon a dog's wail. It's the first case you'll ever hear the prosecution's theory is that you've got to determine the time of death by a dog's wail, this most scientific of all cases. But there's a reason why she wants that. She wants to give enough time for her theory on O.J. Simpson to work. But we will produce for you — hopefully all of these witnesses will be available. As you're well aware, these witnesses are afraid because of all the media attention, but we're going to try to get them. What I say to you is what these witnesses said to us at this point.

Two people who have been to Mezzaluna restaurant — Mr. Dan Mandel and Miss (inaudible). They've been on a blind date, it's like their first date. And they're walking home. They walk home and they come right down Bundy Street also. It's very interesting as they walk down Bundy, they walk on the west side of the street right past 875, Mrs. Nicole Brown Simpson's residence. They walk past there — and it's interesting because, as you saw from those pictures — and we all apologize to her for you to look at those pictures, certainly for the family we want to be as careful as we can with those pictures.

As you saw those pictures, you could see with the gate open, you walk right past, the sidewalk is very visible with the gate open. They didn't see any gate open or any bodies or anything. It was like 10:25, 10:25 at that point. So what's that do to their theory about 10:15, when the dogs (inaudible). Well, I don't want to be argumentative. At any rate, there will be evidence that at 10:25, that people will walk past, who have no ax to grind, have nothing to do with this case, who they know about and we know about, don't see any crime having been committed. There are other witnesses who are going to testify they don't hear any barking at 10:15 or no plaintive wail, whatever that means.

• • •

So I use those examples early on to talk about our contention that there is this rush to judgment in this case, that when Miss Clark said yesterday that they did everything they could to exclude Mr. Simpson, we're going to talk to you about the trails that they didn't pursue or go down today. We can also talk to you about this evidence, what we call the lack of integrity of much of the prosecution's evidence.

You saw yesterday some pictures of this crime scene, and the crime scene was certainly bloody. We all noticed that. But I think you'll find the evidence will show that the LAPD, in its infinite wisdom in this case, assigned a trainee named Mazzola, who was the officer in charge of collecting this evidence. This was her third crime scene, and, contrary to what you heard yesterday from Miss Clark, our experts — and we have a number of experts who'll be called to testify.

In fact, one of our experts is named Dr. Carrie Mullus. Let me tell you who Dr. Carrie Mullus is. Dr. Carrie Mullus is a DNA expert. He is the man who invented PCR, polymerase chain reaction. He's the man who received the Nobel Peace Prize (sic) for this invention. And he will come in here and tell you about this evidence, how sensitive it is and how these police departments are not trained in the collection and use of it. But this is, by all accounts, 21st-century, cyberspace technology that is being used by these police departments with covered-wagon technology.

And so when Miss Clark tells you yesterday that it's possibly just like cooking or doing something like that — she said she wasn't an expert, and I agree now on that, at least. She's an expert lawyer, but not in this area.

Experts will say that's just not true. And so the collection of the evidence becomes very, very, very important in this case. And so, you know, when they were trying to hide Fuhrman yesterday, there were a couple of pictures yesterday of an officer leaning down, pointing at the glove and the cap and everything, and you noticed that, as they talked about it — that was Officer Fuhrman — never bothered to mention his name, never bothered with that.

And so we have then this concept of the prosecution's theories. We heard Mr. Darden stand up and tell you his theory of how this happened, but a theory is only good until the facts come along. It makes clear to you what actually took place. And so we think that, if you keep an open mind, you will be able to deal with these theories and then apply the facts, which is your job as the sole and exclusive judges of the evidence in this case.

• • •

With regard to Mr. Darden's statements yesterday, you recall Mr. Darden said that Nicole Brown Simpson never held a job, and he wanted to paint this picture for us of being totally under control and being controlled by O.J. Simpson and under his thumb and that sort of thing. Well, I think that some of us would feel that somebody who raises two children, who's an excellent mother, that's a pretty major job, being a homemaker. And we'll talk about whether or not Nicole Simpson was a Barbie doll that one could just make in their own mode. Because even in Darden's statement, he said, 'This was a strong, tough lady.' I think you'll find that's what the evidence is going to be.

But with regard to this whole aspect of battering, in this case, let me say up front that Mr. Simpson is not proud at all of the fact that he and his wife got into an altercation and she was struck on Jan. 1st, 1989. He's not proud of that. In fact, in the course of this evidence, you're going to see perhaps three letters that he wrote apologizing to his wife.

What Mr. Darden and what the evidence hasn't shown you so far was that from 1989, Jan. 1st, 1989, they made a big thing out of that. From that day forward to the present day, there's no evidence that O.J. Simpson ever struck his wife again. Now, you should never strike your wife. But even when he made a mistake on January 1st, '89, he paid his debt for that. He went to court and he pled *nolo contendre*. He pled no contest for that. He was sentenced to community service, and he paid his debt. Now they want to retry that, I suppose.

They don't tell you that there was not any touching after that. In fact, O.J. Simpson did something else. After that incident, he was so contrite that he had a prenuptial agreement with Nicole Brown Simpson, so if they got a divorce, what her share would be. And he went and he had his lawyer put in writing, which was later signed by her, that 'If I ever strike you again, the prenuptial agreement is voidable.' Until the date of her death, that agreement was never made void or voidable.

Now, those are the facts. And so when Dr. Walker comes and testifies to you, she will talk about the fact that life-threatening violence usually proceeds a homicide incident, and she does not find that in this case. She will, I believe, testify that according to the National Institute of Justice, approximately two and one-half million women are battered in this country every year, an intolerable situation. But statistics indicate, however, that between 1,200 and 4,000 of those women are killed. That's 1,200 to 4,000 of the two and one-half million battered. Dr. Walker will testify that it is impossible to use these statistics to prove that anybody who allegedly batters becomes a murderer.

You might liken it to an example of smoking. Somebody may get lung cancer. The fact that they get lung cancer may mean they smoke, and may not. But if you smoke, I cannot automatically predict you're going to get lung cancer. So that this is not a predictable science, according to the lady who's the mother of this particular area. Although domestic violence is a very, very serious problem in this country, the level of violence in this case and the pattern is atypical. Atypical, means 'untypical' of those relationships where a lethal incident often occurs.

For instance, stalkers don't go all across the United States working, doing commercials, shooting movies, having a new girlfriend, going on with their life, doing all the things you're going to find this evidence is about. They don't have a new girlfriend by the name of Paula Barbieri, who you've been very serious about from the time, from April of 1992 'til April of 1993, till Nicole Brown Simpson asked to reconcile and get back together.

She did it in this way. She sent to Mr. Simpson, among other things, a video of their marriage, a video of the birth of their children, accompanied by a long letter spelling out how much she wanted to get back with his family. I think you'll find that's not stalking. Mr. Simpson's response was, 'We've had problems in the past. I have a girlfriend now. I'm happy. Let's take our time about this.'

But she pursued. She followed up on that. She pursued. She wanted to move back to Rockingham. She didn't like the housekeeper there. She wanted him to fire her. Michelle was her name. And ultimately she got into an altercation and struck Michelle. He didn't want to fire Michelle. Ultimately Michelle did leave, after being struck. It was her who pursued this, in May of 1993 to May of 1994. When Darden talked to you yesterday, he didn't mention that. We will conclusively prove that to you, so that when Dr. Walker talks to you about stalkers demonstrate obsessive behavior that concentrates on controlling their woman at all times is inconsistent with making a new life, beginning a new relationship with a woman such as Paula Barbieri, traveling away from home on business assignments, all of those things go against any idea of stalking that they would have you believe in this case.

Dr. Walker will also tell you that there is a major, major, major difference between a wealthy person who gives gifts and someone who uses material possessions to gain power and control. And so the prosecution would have you believe that if Mr. Simpson gives Nicole Brown Simpson a gift, that she can be bought and paid for. Nothing could be further from the truth. Let me give you an example of the testimony that will come out in this case. Before Mr. Simpson ever got married to his wife, he bought her a condominium in San Francisco and paid $500,000 for it and gave it to her free and clear, in her name, so she could have money, up to $3,000 a month. He never, ever saw any of that money or wanted any of that money. There were no strings attached. This was before they got married.

And later on in this discussion, I'm going to talk to you about what I call his circle of benevolence, those who have come within the gambit and sphere of O.J. Simpson, and his philanthropic largess, what he's done for 'em. And there are many other things. This $500,000 condo free and clear, he then gave her some more money to buy the condo on Bundy. These are all her own separate things, while they're still separated. He asked for no control. She had her own bank accounts. He gave her $4,000 a month for food at the house. And he paid all of the bills when they were together.

Let me talk about this circle of benevolence while we're on it right now. It extended not just to Miss Nicole Brown Simpson, but to her family, to Mr. Lou Brown. He helped him become a Hertz licensee at the Ritz-Carlton in Laguna Beach for seven years. The sisters, Dominique, he paid the tuition for Dominique for a couple of years at USC until she dropped out. Paid the tuition for Tanya, the other sister, at San Diego State for a year or so, 'til she dropped out. There's a cousin, Ralph Bauer, who worked for seven years at Mr. O.J. Simpson's chicken franchise, Pioneer Chicken franchise. The mother, Juditha, is a travel agent. He gave her his business and encouraged his friends to do likewise.

This man had a great relationship with his in-laws. He did wonderful things for 'em. Took 'em all on trips, paid their way. Took 'em all out to dinner. They'd go to Hawaii and Cabo San Lucas. This is the same man that Mr. Darden was talking to you about.

Mr. Darden says that she never worked. O.J. Simpson encouraged her to become a decorator. She became a decorator. He helped her get jobs from his friends. She redecorated the Rockingham house to the tune of one-half million dollars. And he paid her. He paid his own wife a fee to decorate the house. This man that Darden was talking about, this man gives $5,000 every year to the Angel City Links, the inner-city black organization. And the condition of his gift every year is it has to be anonymous. He doesn't want them to know that he does that.

The thing that he's perhaps proudest about are these next two things I'm going to tell you about. Number one is his mother, Eunice Simpson there. As soon as he was able, he bought her a house. She still lives in that house in San Francisco. This is a man, 47 years old, who grew up in the poor areas of San Francisco, in Portrero Hill. But he never forgot. He became rich and famous, but he didn't forget. So that, to this day, he buys the uniforms for the kids at the Portrero Hill gymnasium, where the kids go to work out. He still does that, even right now, even while in his jail cell. He bought his mother's house. You'll hear about those kinds of things.

And the second thing he's most important — proud about is that he had a child who drowned at a young age. That's always a tragedy and you'll hear evidence about that, and the pronounced effect that it had upon him. And after that he became involved in all these kind of pediatric endeavors. And he has participated in raising hundreds of thousands of dollars for Camp Good Time, for kids who have cancer. He's very proud about that. There's testimony and evidence about that. People who know him, not people who speculate about him, will come in and testify about those things. And so when Dr. Walker tells you that for a wealthy person to give gifts doesn't mean that you're exercising any control, one of the sisters needed some money, up to $5,000, and he gave it to the sister and her boyfriend. And the condition was, 'Don't tell Nicole.' That's a lot of control, isn't it?

So when you hear about theories, I'm going to tell you about the facts. So you'll hear from Dr. Walker and you'll hear ultimately about the battery of tests. And I think you'll find that she will say that in looking at O.J. Simpson and in interviewing him and looking at him at this point, she finds no evidence of anti-social personality disorder. I think you'll find that becomes very important in this case. And understand that this is no Janie-come-lately. This is the leading lady in America who testifies in these kind of cases where a battered woman shoots and kills her husband. So this is an area where obviously you'll get a chance to see her qualifications and her abilities as she goes about this.

• • •

And so he (Darden) tried to paint O.J. Simpson as a jealous man. Let me tell you what the evidence is going to be about that. You heard about this incident of Keith Zlomsowitch. I'm sure as a witness he's going to be called. Mr. Darden described it, remember yesterday he said, 'Well, he didn't punch out Nicole and he didn't punch out Keith,' or words to that effect. He certainly didn't. What happened was, Mr. Simpson, in one of these incidents, had seen his ex-wife out. They went out dancing afterward, and he stopped by her house afterward to try to talk to her. He would go by and woo her on occasion.

And the evidence will be that when they first broke up, he was advised in January of 1992 that she wanted a divorce. In January and April of 1992, it was hard on him. You go with somebody for 17 years, he didn't want to lose her. He likes family. He learned that from his mother and he's got this close-knit family. He likes that. He loved his children. He didn't want to lose his wife. But something happened in April of 1992. As soon as he became aware that she had a boyfriend, from that point on, his interest changed, and he went on.

• • •

The evidence will show and will be relevant to you, is that on or about June 3rd of 1994, Faye Resnick, who had had a long-time relationship with a Dr. Christian Reichardt, whom we will definitely be calling. They'd been living together for a long time. And because of her drug uses, usage, because of the fact she was free-basing cocaine, he put her out, literally.

They broke up. She's one of these parties, who they ran in this circle out there in Brentwood. And when she was put out on June 3rd, which I think was a Friday, she then moved over and lived with Nicole Brown Simpson because they were friends — they would go out at night. These were all friends. The evidence will be these ladies would go out, two, three, four nights a week and stay out till five o'clock in the morning. Nobody was controlling these women. There's group of them and you'll hear about it. They'd go out dancing. They'd do whatever they would do. And we know Faye Resnick was using drugs in this period of time. It got so bad, the evidence will be that on June 8, 1994 they had what we call an intervention — that Nicole and Christian Reichardt, and her former husband Paul Resnick, all got together to try and convince her she had to go into a drug treatment facility called Exodus.

• • •

She goes into a drug treatment facility on June 8th. She remains there, and she's there on June 12th. I think you'll hear from the evidence that she is one of the people who calls Miss Nicole Brown Simpson on the night of June 12th, perhaps after nine o'clock that particular night from this drug treatment facility. We'll be talking about that and her role in this whole drama.

To conclude then, what I've tried to do in this opening statement is to lay out for you the fact that in almost everything you hear in this case, there are two sides. But as jurors, I'm sure you're not going to rush to judgment. That this should not be a case about character assassination. I hope you'll keep an open mind until you hear all of the evidence as it relates to who Mr. Simpson is.

• • •

Just before we wrap up for lunch, I think the evidence will show you that in order to believe that O.J. Simpson committed these horrible murders, you'd have to believe that he came back from back East, where he'd been working, to come to his daughter's recital, attended that recital — you see his picture there — and was home getting ready for a trip to Chicago that had been long pre-planned; that he was hungry — and the evidence will be that he didn't have any dollar bills or $20 bills — and he asked to borrow some money from Kato Kaelin.

Kato Kaelin gave him this money, and went and had a Big Mac. You'd have to believe he was planning to kill his wife either before he got this Big Mac, or then went and got the Big Mac — that Kato Kaelin will describe he was dressed in some kind of sweat clothes and some tennis shoes. That if you follow the People's case, you'd have to believe that he then came home and said, 'Gee, I think what I'll do is I'll go over and kill my wife now, and I think I'll take these tennis shoes off and put on some dress shoes — some hard-soled shoes and change clothes,' knowing he's going to be leaving shortly to go to the airport. And then — you'd have to believe that to believe their theory. And to make their theory work, they spent all this time talking about the plaintive wail of a dog, because they've got to make this as early as possible — at 10:15. We know that that's not correct, based upon the facts that you've heard.

To conclude, isn't it interesting that in all of the discussion yesterday by these two very excellent lawyers, they never once mentioned their coroner, Dr. Golden. He's another mysterious mystery witness they don't want to talk about. When we come back this afternoon, let's talk about why the prosecution doesn't want you to know about Dr. Golden. Let's talk about when Miss Clark says, well, you can't really fix the time of death here with any precision. We will have testimony from one of the leading pathologists in the United States, Michael Baden, who's also worked for the L.A. County District Attorney's Office, who's written a book about the John Belushi death. He was able to pinpoint the time of death to within one hour. And yet, in this case, because the coroner was not called for 10 hours after these bodies were found — or eight hours, and they got out there about 10 hours, violating the state law — we are precluded from pinpointing this. And they have to tell you that it's about a dog's wail when a man's life is at stake. We'll pick up after lunch, Your Honor.

The Court: Thank you, Mr. Cochran. All right, ladies and gentlemen, we will stand in recess for the jury until 1:30 p.m. Let me speak to counsel after the jury has departed. All right, let's clear the courtroom please.

When court resumed that day, defense attorney Johnnie Cochran, Jr., continued offering the defense's opening statement, a portion of which is reproduced below:

Cochran: We expect, as we indicated last week, to show that based at this particular crime scene at Bundy could be a number of things that we expect the evidence to show, that one of which is this crime scene and the patterns of the crime scene are consistent with a major struggle.

Mr. Ron Goldman's blood, as I told you, should be all over the perpetrator, especially in the upper and middle parts of the perpetrator's body. You will recall that Detective Fuhrman's description this morning, we described this rather small area where Mr. Goldman's body was found. You recall he talked about a fence. You've seen, I think, some pictures. You'll see a tree in the area. It's a very (small) area. Like he had to go outside to look outside the fence to see where the body was. And I think that you'll find if there was this major confrontation, and you'll recall last week Mr. Goldman's hand. I indicated to you I expect there'll be testimony that hand came in blunt force trauma with one of his perpetrators or one of the perpetrators there. And there would be some marks, some injuries, it would seem. Plus there are trees. There's this fence, and there was a violent struggle. So that if you recall the pictures of Mr. O.J. Simpson last week, you understand that it will be important evidence as to the lack of any marks, bruises or anything of that nature.

In the area we expect the scene to also show that in the area where these murders took place, there are a number footprints in a very small area, which means that most likely the perpetrator had to be there for a period of time that there was this pattern of fighting. I think the evidence will be in this case that Mr. Goldman's blood is on different areas of the location, which means that he too was moving around. So there was this kind of a confrontation or this fight that went on over a period of time. As one is fighting for one's life and as you know it was a violent struggle in which he ultimately was stabbed some 31 times — 30 times.

The prosecutor indicated to you all this happened very fast. I think that you will see from the evidence that's not exactly correct given the situation when one is fighting valiantly for their life.

There was some testimony last week about certain blood drops I think by the prosecutors that were at or near the many footprints, and I think that you will find that it will be unusual and it will be a remarkable occurrence that there are only four drops of blood that they talk about and so many footprints.

Further, we'll look very closely during the course of this trial at the glove, both gloves. We'll look at the glove found at Rockingham, the right glove. We'll look at the glove found at Bundy, and we'll be looking to see whether or not there are any cuts on those gloves consistent with any cuts or anything on Mr. O.J. Simpson's hands.

Expect that, as I mentioned to you last week, there will be fingerprints on the railings that are fresh at Bundy, and we think those fingerprints are not O.J. Simpson's fingerprints. That there are hairs on the cap and the glove at Bundy that are not O.J. Simpson's. That there is at the crime scene — I believe you recall when the prosecutors were making their case last week — there is a triangular piece of paper shown in the photograph near Nicole Brown Simpson's head which was never saved apparently by the police. We don't have that. And of course you've already seen, and there will be a number of other photographs of unprotected shoes standing in and about the crime scene.

There will of course be photographs of criminalists without proper head covering and gloves actually involved in collecting evidence.

• • •

So I hope this gives you kind of a preview of how these detectives collected evidence and how they dealt with this particular scene, a scene that would be best videotaped so you could see everything that took place other than just still photographs, a scene that would be best preserved where only people who have their real business are there, not people just walking around and traipsing through the evidence. You'll hear a lot about that during the course of this trial.

• • •

Cochran: Now — we will now with your permission turn our attention now to this whole concept of the discussion of DNA evidence and the Los Angeles police department.

I suppose that there is a saying that you have garbage in, you get garbage out, and we have several charts that we think will be illustrative of this whole concept of DNA evidence and what it actually is.

Mr. Douglas is placing a chart on the board . . .

• • •

Nowhere, I think, will you find in this case is the problem of the evidence being contaminated, compromised and corrupted, more important than the area of DNA testing.

This is, the evidence will show, is a very new and powerful technology. In the past five years police departments and crime labs have tried to transfer this DNA test that has been used for research and medical diagnosis and apply it to crime scene samples.

We expect all of you will hear in the course of this, the evidence, this transfer of technology has not been simple or easy, and so I want to share with you in the course of my opening statement now some differences between DNA testing for medical purposes and forensic DNA testing on crime scene samples.

Remembering as we — in the graphic, that all evidence passes through first the LAPD's hands. If it is compromised when it starts, it is compromised when it comes out.

If the evidence was contaminated at the scene or mishandled by the Los Angeles police department, it doesn't matter what DNA tests are done afterwards, how many times they are done or which laboratories did them, the results will not be reliable we can expect the evidence to show.

Now, to understand the problem of contamination, one must understand, first of all, how small these samples are, and Mr. Douglas has gotten ahead of me just a little bit.

Let's go back to the small amounts of DNA for illustrative purposes to illustrate this for you. This is a chart that is entitled "small amounts of DNA from specks of blood," and what we have is a regular size penny here at the far left, and I want you to be able to compromise — strike that.

I want you to be able to compare a regular size penny with 20 nanograms of DNA and that amounts to — those of you who can see very well, I am pointing to it, almost like a pin prick, 20 nanograms. Much of the evidence in this case you will be asked to make decisions regarding is one/tenth of that amount, one/tenth of the 20 nanograms or two nanograms, an amount so small that you can't even see it.

That is the what — what we are trying to demonstrate with this chart. The penny, 20 nanograms, the two nanograms, an amount that you could not even see with the naked eye.

• • •

We think the evidence will show, and including the last chart that was taken down, that these small minuscule amounts of DNA are very easy to spread around. They can get on your clothes, in your hair, tweezers, scissors, other tools, be moved from one place to the other without anyone seeing or knowing what is happening.

The — this of course is how you get contamination.

Now, during the course of my remarks today and then last week, and before that the remarks of the prosecutors, we have all stood at this particular podium. If I sneezed or if any saliva came out or if I scratch my hair and any dandruff was there or if I touch this and I had any blood on my finger or a splinter there, if Miss Clark did likewise, if Mr. Darden did likewise, then our DNA would be on this area.

And if I took a handkerchief out and wiped this, this is what they do in labs, that would pick up the various DNA that is here. You can't see it, that is how small it is under these circumstances.

So that gives you an idea. If we were to wipe it across here, our handkerchief could now be taken to the lab and allegedly taken. In fact, some medical labs do in fact do this and it is done in a lab to determine whether or not there is any contamination. That is how they test it to see if there is any contamination.

If you are trying to see if someone is going to be compatible for a particular organ transplant, they check to see, because you can't see this.

If I had been the only one here, you might expect to find only my DNA, but if Mr. Darden and Miss Clark were here, you might expect to find their DNA. If Mr. Vannatter here sneezed, you might find his DNA, so there is all kind of ways in which we have this possible contamination.

And one of the problems with the test is that it cannot tell one person's DNA from another. This is what we call — and I think the evidence will be a mixed sample. There is quite a controversy, we think the evidence will show, about whether small mixed samples can be tested reliably even if everything else is done properly and there is no contamination, so if you add contamination to it, then you can see what the problems are.

● ● ●

This is, as I indicated to you last week, cyberspace or 21st century technology, and I think you will find the evidence will be that the collection procedures are 19th century or covered wagon collection procedures and that is why it is such a problem.

And so if you looked at this medical research area, in general you could expect that in the medical field that there are clean samples, more than likely in a clean medical lab, the blood is carefully taken under antiseptic conditions in hospitals, and in a forensic setting DNA testing is done by definition generally and dirty samples are taken from crime scenes, from sidewalks, from carpets and they are exposed to all sorts of contamination, that there are many different sources, that these — as you know already, these are minute specks of blood, there may be saliva, there may be skin, cells, dandruff, as I indicated to you, even a spray of a sneeze can contaminate the forensic sample.

So what I want to do in this sample, we have these charts here, is that in comparing the medical research, compare the medical research with the forensic and see which one is more likely to be reliable under the circumstances.

Well, I think that the evidence will show that as opposed to the clean sample and the dirty samples, in this instance the clean sample in the medical lab will be far more reliable, something that you can rely upon.

The next area we will be talking about is generally in a medical lab you have a generous sample size, the doctor can have whatever sample size he usually wants or needs.

In forensics the sample comes generally in very, very limited minute amounts and in working with such small amounts often the test can only be done once.

And of course we think the evidence will show that is — it is harder to produce reliable results under those circumstances.

In fact, you will hear we think in this case, that most of the important DNA tests performed by the prosecution were done with amounts of DNA that were actually below the preferred amounts for reliable testing.

• • •

I mentioned the wipe test. In labs they do that because they are concerned about contamination in the labs when you go to the doctor. You want to have the doctor make sure his lab is contamination free as near as possible. That brings about confidence and that is what we have done, a whole industry based upon.

Transferring this technology to the forensics area, the error rates are not nearly as well known, as I think you can see, so again there is a higher risk of contamination and error in this area also.

I think you will find that in the course of the testimony that the labs have a higher standard for doing DNA testing in medical laboratories, they are much stricter on themselves than the standard that forensics and the police departments and laboratories are using.

• • •

And finally, with regard to statistical controversy in this area, in medical testing, usually you are just trying to see if someone has inherited a copy of the diseased gene from their parent or whatever, has the correct genetic types for transplantation of an organ, has been infected with a harmful bacteria or virus. That is what you are looking for, and there is no elaborate statistical estimates are needed to get reliable test results for that.

In forensics we think you will hear testimony that there is a bitter and complicated statistical controversy regarding this entire area, DNA, specifically PCR, about a DNA match and what a match means.

And while we are about it, I think the evidence will show, when you hear the prosecutor talking about it is a match, it is a match, it is a match, what she really means to say is that it is consistent with — these are not fingerprints — consistent with someone else's genotype or with their blood type.

So with regard to this whole area of statistical controversy, again the forensics area, the higher risk of contamination error in this area again.

So as you look at this — this chart, you look at blood on both sides of that, you can see clearly, and I expect the evidence to be that because of the dirty samples, the minuscule sample size, the mixed sample from unknown sources, the multiple handling, the error rates not well-known, the low lab standards, the easy proficiency testing, and the major statistical controversy, that in all those areas in seeking to transfer this technology to forensics is fraught with all kind of problems and this is a much higher risk of contamination and error.

• • •

These are not fingerprints. And the numbers that you will hear, if you hear them in this case, have nothing to do with the issue of contamination that we have been talking about. They do not have anything to do with the issue of laboratory errors. They don't have anything to do with the issue of tampering, whether the sample was tampered with, and they have nothing to do with other important DNA issues which you will hear about in the course of this case.

Specifically under the DNA testing aspect, we think that you will hear testimony in this case about polymerase chain reaction, so-called PCR testing, and I think you will find out in here that the very best medical and research labs that do PCR have contamination problems.

And as I mentioned to you last week, I think that you will hear that this is an area that presents a real problem.

We expect during the course of our evidence in this case to show that from their own studies the LAPD's laboratory is a cesspool of contamination. Looking at their own records and the tests they have run we will demonstrate for you what those records show.

We expect then in this entire area the evidence will show that the careless, slipshod negligent collection, handling and processing of samples by basically poorly trained personnel from LAPD has contaminated, compromised and corrupted the DNA evidence in this case.

And your honor, this may be a good spot, unless you want me to go further.

The Court: All right. Thank you, counsel. All right. Ladies and gentlemen, we are going to take our recess for the noon hour. Please remember my admonition to you. Do not discuss this case amongst yourselves, form any opinions about the case. Don't allow anybody to talk to you about the case. And you are not to perform any deliberations on the case until the matter has been submitted to you after the completion of the case. And we will resume again at 1:30.

All right. We will stand in recess. Thank you, counsel.

In concluding his opening statement, defense attorney Johnnie Cochran, Jr., reminded members of the jury that American criminal justice is based upon a presumption of innocence. Cochran also described the concept of reasonable doubt, and advised jurors that if any reasonable doubt as to Simpson's guilt remains in their minds at the end of the trial, the law requires them to return a finding of "innocent."

Mr. Cochran: In the final analysis, this is a case that will rest primarily on circumstantial evidence. And you know what that evidence is.

And there's a jury instruction that applies to that that's extremely appropriate, and I think — I applaud judge Ito for having given you this instruction early on because I think it's very, very important for you to be aware of this as you consider this evidence, especially circumstantial evidence and how it will be applied at the very end of this particular case.

This is part of that instruction, and the relevant portions would be as follows, that: "A finding of guilt as to any crime may not be based on circumstantial evidence unless the proved circumstances are not only, 1.) consistent with the theory that the defendant is guilty of the crime, but cannot be reconciled with any other rational conclusion.

Further, "each fact which is essential to complete a set of circumstances necessary to establish the defendant's guilt must be proved beyond a reasonable doubt." In other words, before an inference essential to establish guilt may be found to have been proved beyond a reasonable doubt, each fact or circumstance upon which such inference necessarily rests must be proved beyond a reasonable doubt.

Also, "if the circumstantial evidence as to any particular count" — there are two counts here, susceptible to two reasonable interpretations, one of which points to the defendant's guilt and the other to his innocence, "you must adopt that interpretation which points to the defendant's innocence and reject that interpretation which points to his guilt."

• • •

If after you've heard all the evidence — and you know what circumstantial evidence is — you will then be in a position to make a judgment as to whether it applies to this particular point, without arguing what it is now. We'll have a chance to argue it at a later time.

The point I wanted to make at this point is for you to understand what this instruction would be as the court has.

And lastly, as Miss Clark pointed out: "If on the other hand, one interpretation of such evidence appears to you to be reasonable and the other interpretation to be unreasonable, you must accept the reasonable interpretation and reject the unreasonable."

It seems reasonable, doesn't it?

The point is that you, no one else, will be the sole and exclusive judges of the facts and the weight of the evidence. That's a determination that you must make, and no one can tell you what to make in that regard. And each of you in *voir dire* has promised to give us your individual opinion in doing that.

And the last jury instruction . . . is the so-called presumption of innocence, reasonable doubt, burden of proof instruction. It's the last instruction I want to leave with you today.

"A defendant in a criminal action is presumed to be innocent until the contrary is proved and in a case of reasonable doubt whether his guilt is satisfactorily shown, he is entitled to a verdict of not guilty. This presumption of course," as you know, "places upon the people the burden of proving him guilty beyond a reasonable doubt."

And: "Reasonable doubt has been defined as follows: it is not a mere possible or imaginary doubt because everything relating to human affairs depending upon — that everything related to human affairs is open to some possible or imaginary doubt. It is that state of the case where, after the entire comparison and consideration of all the evidence, leaves the minds of the jurors in that condition that they cannot say they feel an abiding conviction of the truth of the charge.

Now, that's what reasonable doubt is in this case, in every case. And I wanted to make sure that you again were aware of that as you listen to this case.

• • •

In summary, as you then look at all of the evidence in this case, we expect the evidence will show that O.J. Simpson, as you see him there, is not a perfect human being. He, like all of us, has made mistakes. Of course, we know there's only one perfect person who ever walked the earth.

We think the evidence will show he's not guilty of these horrible crimes, that he has been blessed bountifully by God and he's shared his largess and blessings with many, many people; that in this instance, the prosecutor's theory that there was only one murderer is just a theory. We expect to introduce evidence to show there was more than one killer, that the prosecutor's theory will be overcome by the facts which we present.

We also expect that the evidence will show that the reason the prosecution maintains there's only one killer is that Mr. Simpson — who they want to portray as a stalker, and stalkers don't come in pairs. It could only be one person under that scenario. That ex-husbands who are stalkers don't come in pairs and that's why they're wedded to this one murderer theory, even contrary to what their own coroner may very well indicate.

You know the circumstances. You know there are generally two sides to every situation. We cannot call our witnesses until we get our time in the part of the case when it's our time to put the witnesses on.

That's why I've spent so much time in this opening statement to try to detail for you what we expect the evidence to be and what we expect to show. You understand that the fact that someone has an altercation with one's wife in 1989 is not capable of being predicted whether that person would kill her or be involved in any other fights or whatever.

And so I started off by indicating to you that I thought this case would be a case where we would establish there was a rush to judgment by the prosecution, and they would have theories and speculation and we would have the facts.

In this instance, in this case, both sides are interested in the search for truth. That's what a trial really is. It's a journey for truth, for you to determine the true facts of what happened on June 12th, 1994. We spent a great amount of time in selecting each of you for this task because it will be a very significant task.

And in truth, I'm always reminded of something that James Russell Lowell said, that: "truth forever on the scaffold wrong forever on the throne, yet that scaffold sways the future and beyond the dim unknown standeth God within the shadows keeping watch above his own."

In this case, God knows what happened on June 12th. And we hope after you've heard all the evidence in this case, you can make a rational decision and you too will know what happened, and you will know that . . . . The evidence will show that O. J. Simpson, that man pictured over there, on June 12th did not kill his wife, did not kill Ronald Goldman, and he is entitled to an acquittal.

Thank you very much for your attention.

(This) may be the longest opening statement in the history of this building. I appreciate your patience and the fact that you took the time to listen.

Thank you.

The Court: All right. Thank you, counsel. Deputy Magnera, we're going to take a break.

Because attorney Cochran's opening statement alluded to witnesses to be called which the prosecution had not been informed of, Judge Ito took the highly unusual step of allowing the prosecution to make a second, but limited, opening statement addressing certain points raised by the defense. Judge Ito called this opportunity for the prosecution "virtually unprecedented in any criminal case I have ever seen . . .," but placed a ten minute time limit on prosecutors. The prosecution's second opening statement is partially reproduced in the next few pages.

(The following proceedings were held in open court, in the presence of the jury):

The Court: All right, ladies and gentlemen, please be seated . . . . All right. Ladies and gentlemen, good morning.

The Jury: Good morning.

The Court: The court has granted a prosecution request to reopen their opening statement to address defense counsel's comments in his opening statement regarding three witnesses who had not previously been disclosed or whose statements had not been previously disclosed to the prosecution before trial, as is required by the law.

You are reminded, however, that any statements by the attorneys in this case are not evidence and should not be considered by you as such. Miss Clark, you have ten minutes.

Ms. Clark: Good morning, ladies and gentlemen.

The Jury: Good morning.

Ms. Clark: Mr. Cochran made some comments about — first of all, I'm going to talk about a videotape that has outtakes of the defendant making an exercise video, and Mr. Cochran made some comments to you about the defendant's alleged arthritic condition.

According to him the defendant's arthritic condition became acute sometime after he had played golf and after he had been swinging the golf club on the evening of June the 12th at 10:00 p.m. He said at that point, after that, the arthritic condition became acute.

Mr. Cochran told you that the defendant's physical capabilities are very limited as a result of that condition. The prosecution will show you evidence to the contrary.

We will show you outtakes of an exercise videotape which was made by the defendant only two weeks before the murders. We will show you a portion of that videotape to demonstrate just what the defendant's physical capabilities really were on the evening of June the 12th, 1994.

In it you will see the defendant, just two weeks before the murders, that he weighed 215 pounds, which is what he weighed fifteen years ago, that the defendant prided himself in that tape on being in good physical condition. You will see him doing push-ups. You will see him lifting his arms overhead, you will see him stretching, reaching, throwing jabs and uppercuts and he does that for several minutes in this tape. You will see him doing trunk twists.

And this tape took hours to make and that he came back after that day, went back the next day and spent a lot more time doing that very same thing. We are going to show you that tape during the course of this trial.

Second of all, counsel made reference to the fact that — to a statement that Howard Weitzman, who was then the defendant's attorney, was not permitted to be present during the interview with the police officers on June the 13th.

And you were told by counsel that they refused, the police officers actually refused to allow Mr. Weitzman to remain with the defendant during that interview. That is completely wrong.

And in fact what the evidence will show is that the detectives asked Mr. Weitzman to stay for the interview, but that he declined to do so, stating that he would prefer to go out to lunch and that prior to that interview he had had approximately half an hour alone with Mr. Simpson to talk to him, after which he said, "go ahead," went out to lunch, and that is what the evidence will show.

And that was after the detectives invited him to come in and sit during the interview with him.

Now, lastly, you heard Mr. Cochran talk to you about a witness named Mary Anne Gerchas. Now, he told you about this witness, he said it was a very important witness, he discussed at some length what she would testify to, telling you that she claimed to have seen four men on the night of the murders, at least two of whom were Hispanic, at least one or two of whom were wearing a knit cap, that she stated she saw them possibly running from the area of Nicole Simpson's condo on the night of the murders.

Now, you will be hearing a lot more about Miss Gerchas during the course of this trial, but right now I am just going to address a few points that the evidence will show that Mr. Cochran didn't tell you about.

For example, she spoke to her friend Sheila Carter the day after the murders of Ron and Nicole. She told her friend, Sheila Carter, that she was not even at Bundy on the night of the murders.

Mary Anne Gerchas had planned to go and look for an apartment on Brentwood on the night of the murders on June the 12th. The next day she spoke to Sheila Carter and said she did not go to Brentwood on that night and she was glad because there had been murders committed there the night before.

But Miss Carter is also going to tell you something else. In addition to the fact that she will tell you that Miss Gerchas told her she did not go to Brentwood on the night of the murders, she is also going to tell you something very important about Miss Gerchas' credibility. She will tell you about a statement which proves that Miss Gerchas is one of these people who comes out of the woodwork in high-profile cases so they can get involved.

And here is what Miss Carter will tell you: Miss Gerchas was obsessed with this case and she talked as if she knew the defendant personally. She said that Miss Carter would send her to the store to buy every *Enquirer*, every *Star* and every tabloid pertaining to this case, anything that talked about the Simpson case.

She would read it all and she would save it and talk about the case constantly. But she somehow never told anyone that she had been on Bundy on the night of the murders until the time that Robert Shapiro started the hotline requesting that anyone with information come forward and call that hotline number.

And it was right around that time that he put out the hotline number that Mary Anne Gerchas started to say, well, maybe I was driving by that area, maybe I did see something.

Mr. Cochran accused us of not telling you about her and we didn't because we didn't know about her. And if you believe her, she asked the defense attorneys if they would tell us about her and they said they would. She spoke to Robert Shapiro and Shapiro's people told her not to talk to anyone about her statement, and when they finished taking her statement, they told her they weren't going to use her as a witness. They spent hours interviewing her back on July 10th and July 12 of 1994 and they never told us about her.

Now that jury instruction counsel showed you about credibility of witnesses applies to all witnesses, ladies and gentlemen. The evidence will show that Mary Anne Gerchas is a known liar and a Simpson case groupie. Thank you for keeping an open mind and listening to all the evidence.

The Court: all right. Thank you, counsel . . . .

Chapter 3
Presentation of Evidence:
Witnesses for the
Prosecution

Prosecution witness, detective Mark Fuhrman, being cross-examined by defense attorney F. Lee Bailey.   Photo: Vince Bucci/APF/Bettman.

INTRODUCTION

Following the conclusion of opening statements the prosecution presents its case. The prosecution has the first opportunity to present evidence because it carries the burden of proof — that is, it is the responsibility of the prosecution to establish the truth of the facts claimed in the complaint or indictment against the defendant. Conviction in an American criminal court requires that the prosecution prove its case beyond a **reasonable doubt**. Reasonable doubt, which is defined a in later chapter by Judge Ito as he offers jury instructions near the close of the Simpson trial, has generally been understood to mean that if an objective and reasonable individual (practically speaking, a judge or juror) still entertains doubt about a person's guilt after hearing all of the evidence against that person, then the state has not proven its case. If the prosecution fails to offer reasonable proof of its case, the defense may successfully move for dismissal of all charges before presenting any of its own evidence.

Most evidence presented to a jury is introduced via the testimony of witnesses, and is called **testimonial evidence**. Witnesses generally begin their time on the stand during what is called direct examination. **Direction examination** occurs whenever the party (the prosecution or the defense) calling the witnesses first asks them to testify. **Cross-examination,** which can be defined as the examination of a witness by anyone other than the direct examiner, follows as opposing counsel questions the witnesses. Cross-examination may be followed by a **re-direct examination**, then a **re-cross examination**, and so on. Many, but not all, jurisdictions require that questions asked during cross-examination be limited to issues raised in the direct examination.

While **evidence** can be defined as anything presented to a judge or jury which is intended to prove or disprove a fact which is at issue, there are two general kinds of evidence: direct and indirect. **Direct evidence** is that which, if believed, directly proves a fact. So, for example, if a witness says "I saw the defendant pull the trigger and shoot the victim," then a form of direct evidence has been offered. If, on the other hand, a witness says "I heard a gunshot, and when I looked I saw the defendant standing with a gun in his hand," then the jury may infer that the defendant was indeed the one who fired the shot. In this second case, **indirect evidence** (or **circumstantial evidence**) has been offered and it requires members of the jury to reach a conclusion as to whether or not it was the defendant who fired the weapon. Circumstantial evidence is no less valuable than direct evidence, and many attorneys prefer to weave a web of incriminating circumstantial evidence in which the conclusion that the defendant committed the crime in question is inescapable. A third kind of evidence, **real evidence**, refers to physical evidence. Real evidence may be introduced during witness testimony, and it can consist (as it did in the Simpson case) of items of clothing (socks, shoes, and gloves), blood drops or blood stains, hair, fibers, tools, notepads, and handwritten or typed letters, (see the appendix for a list of 234 items of evidence removed from O.J. Simpson's Rockingham Estate).

A crucial question for any court centers on the **admissibility** of particular items of evidence. Jurisdictions vary somewhat as to the kinds of evidence they allow. Rules of evidence particular to each jurisdiction specify exactly what kinds of evidence can be used in court. Rules of evidence are determined by courts (through precedent setting decisions) and legislative bodies (i.e., via legislative decree). As we will later see, for example, the admissibility of certain kinds of DNA evidence became an issue for the Simpson court. DNA evidence, which relies upon the scientific analysis of human genetic material left at the crime scene, represents a new and emerging area for criminal courts throughout the nation, and California precedent at the time of the Simpson trial was less than clear on the use of such evidence. The admissibility of any evidence should be distinguished from its weight. Evidence has **weight** if it is likely to convince the jury of a fact which is at issue. Obviously, some evidence is more "weighty" than other evidence. Similarly, evidence may be **relevant** or irrelevant. If it is relevant to the case, then is it likely to be admissible. Non-relevant evidence will probably be barred. Similarly, most judges will allow evidence to be introduced only if it is **competent** — that is, if it is reliable and adequate to prove a fact which is at issue. Frequently the relevancy and competency of evidence must be demonstrated, through a practice referred to as **laying the foundation** for the evidence, before it can be introduced.

Sometimes not only is the evidence being offered controversial, but the witness offering it may lack believability. Hence, it is not unusual for the opposing side to attempt to cast doubt upon the testimony of witnesses who have been called to testify, and the memory, integrity, and believability of witnesses may all be challenged by opposing counsel. When the integrity of a witness has been impugned, then the credibility of the testimony offered by that witness may also be called into question in the minds of jurors. Because incompetent witnesses waste the court's time and resources, witnesses who have been proven incompetent (as in the case of chronic and known liars, or persons known to be insane) are not allowed to testify.

An example of defense attempts to discredit a prosecution witness can be seen at the start of this chapter, in which the testimony of police detective Mark Fuhrman is scrutinized under cross-examination. The tables are turned on Detective Fuhrman, who testified that he found a bloody glove at Simpson's residence which matched another found at the murder scene, when defense attorney F. Lee Bailey attempts to show that Fuhrman is a racist who may have had personal motivations for "framing" Simpson. Efforts during cross-examination appear intended to lead the jury to conclude that Fuhrman may have planted the bloody glove at the Simpson estate after removing it from the scene of the crime.

Such a defense strategy, in effect, attempts to put prosecution witnesses on trial. If even partially successful, this kind of strategy may shift attention away from the possible guilt of the defendant.

Various kinds of witnesses can be identified. For one thing, both the defendant and the victim (where the victim survives) can elect to take the stand, and testimony offered by these parties probably should be distinguished from testimony offered by other, less interested, persons. Generally, however, witnesses are classified into two types: expert and non-expert (also called "lay witnesses"). **Expert witnesses** have specialized knowledge or skill in a trade, craft, or profession, which they can bring to bear on questions of fact in a given case. A ballistics expert, for example, may be called upon to testify as to the likelihood that a given weapon fired a particular bullet. Similarly, a pathologist or coroner may be asked to testify as to the medical cause of death in murder cases. Both would be regarded as expert witnesses. A special feature of testimony offered by expert witnesses is that experts are permitted to offer opinions and draw conclusions based upon those opinions. **Lay witnesses**, on the other hand, are non-expert in the matter under review, and when called to the stand are required to testify to facts alone.

THE FIRST WITNESSES ARE CALLED

January 31, 1995

At the conclusion of prosecutor Clark's unusual ten-minute continuing opening statement, Judge Ito thanked her and allowed the prosecution to call its first witness. The first day of testimony began.

The prosecution called its first witnesses, Sharyn Gilbert, an LAPD emergency 911 dispatcher. Gilbert, who was on duty during the night of January 1, 1989, related details of a call made by Nicole Brown Simpson to 911 operators pleading for police protection from her husband. A second witness, police detective John Edwards, who responded to the 911 call, testified that he saw a severely beaten Nicole Brown Simpson run from a hiding place in bushes near the estate. Edwards said Nicole was screaming, "He's going to kill me, he's going to kill me!" When he asked "who is going to kill you?" she said, "O.J. ... O.J. Simpson."

The Court: All right. Thank you, counsel . . . . All right. Mr. Darden, Miss Clark, are you ready to call your first witness?

Ms. Clark: Yes, we are, your honor. Thank you.

The Court: All right. Call your first witness . . . . Mr. Darden, who is your first witness?

Ms. Clark: Sharyn Gilbert, your honor.

The Court: All right. Miss Gilbert, would you step over here by the witness stand, please, by the court reporter.

Sharyn Gilbert, called as a witness by the people, was sworn and testified as follows:

The Clerk: Please raise your right hand. Do you solemnly swear that the testimony you may give in the cause now pending before this court, shall be the truth, the whole truth and nothing but the truth, so help you God.

The Witness: I do.

The Clerk: Please be seated and state and spell your first and last names for the record.

The Witness: my first name is Sharyn, spelled S-h-a-r-y-n. Last name is Gilbert, G-i-l-b-e-r-t.

The Court: Mr. Darden.

Mr. Darden: Thank you, your honor.

Q **Good morning, Miss Gilbert.**
A Good morning.
Q **Miss Gilbert, who do you work for?**
A Los Angeles police department.
Q **And what is your job title?**
A I'm a police service representative.
Q **And are you also a 911 operator and dispatcher?**
A Yes.
Q **Okay. And were you a 911 operator and dispatcher on January 1, 1989?**
A Yes, I was.
Q **And were you on duty between 3:00 and four o'clock in the morning on that date?**
A Yes, I was.
Q **And on that date and during that time period did you receive a telephone call?**
A Yes, I did.

• • •

Q **Miss Gilbert, showing you what has been marked as people's 2 for identification, do you recognize that document?**
A Yes, I do.

Q   (By Mr. Darden): what is the document marked people's 2 for identification?

A   It is termed what we call an incident format.

Q   How is that form generated?

A   On my screen, which is the screen directly in front of me, we have a format which allows to us create an incident by the computer by inserting certain commands.

• • •

Q   Now, does the — does the form also provide a space for you to add comments?

A   Yes, it does.

Q   And did you add some comments to that form in this situation?

A   Yes, I did. That — that is where it shows . . . an update of my incident in the top example and that was after I entered the comments.

Q   Okay. And did you add those comments to this form?

A   Yes.

Q   And the comments that you added to this form, were these comments based on your perception, your hearing?

A   Yes, it was.

• • •

Q   I'm sorry, Miss Gilbert. What time did you say you received the telephone call?

A   3:58.

Q   3:58 in the morning?

A   Yes.

Q   And does the incident report indicate the origin of the telephone call?

A   No. It just shows — I have the ability to update it and I have the ability to update the incident type when I first got the call I had it as an unknown trouble.

Q   Okay. Okay. So the call came to you, right?

A   Right. It was an open line.

Q   Okay. Could you hear anything over the open line?

A   No. At the beginning, no.

Q   Okay. Did the line remain open?

A   Yes, it did.

Q   And while the line was opened, at any point in time could you hear anything?

A   Yes, I did.

Q   What did you hear?

A   At first I heard a female screaming and that is when I went back and changed my incident type from an unknown trouble to a screaming woman.

Q   **Okay. And did you hear anything else?**

A   Yes, I did.

Q   **What did you hear?**

A   I heard someone being hit.

Q   **You heard a noise that you associated with someone being hit?**

A   Yes.

Q   **And what did you do with that information?**

A   That is when I went back and updated it to — in the fact that I heard a female screaming and then I heard what I thought was a slap. I went back and updated it as a female being beaten at the location, to give the responding officer an indication of what was going on, that it was no longer an unknown trouble.

Q   **In fact, you indicated that a female being beaten at location could be heard over the telephone; is that right?**

A   Yes.

• • •

Q   **And the screams that you heard, you say that those screams were the screams of a woman?**

A   It sounded like a female to me.

Q   **It didn't sound like a man?**

A   No.

Q   **Are 911 calls recorded by the LAPD?**

A   Yes, they are.

Q   **And have you listened to the 911 call you received at 3:58 in the morning on January 1, 1989?**

A   Yes, I have.

Q   **And when was the last time you listened to that tape?**

A   Approximately a week and a half ago.

Q   **And when you listened to the tape a week and a half ago, could you hear slaps or strikes?**

• • •

A   I could in remembering the call. I could determine after the first scream, then I heard someone being hit.

Mr. Darden: Okay. Thank you. With the court's permission, your honor, I would like to play the 1989 911 tape.

The Court: All right. Do you have that identified as an exhibit?

Mr. Darden: Yes. It has been marked People's 1.

The Court: All right.

At 10:11 a.m. People's exhibit 1 for identification, an audiotape, was played. At 10:12 a.m. the playing of the audiotape ended.

Q (By Mr. Darden): Miss Gilbert, is that a tape-recording of the telephone call you received at 3:58 a.m. On January 1, 1989?
A   Yes, it is.
Q Okay. Now, we hear other voices, male voices, and apparently other dispatchers in this tape; is that correct?
A   Right.

• • •

Q So it is during the telephone call then that you typed in the comment about your hearing a woman being beaten?
A   Yes.
Q Okay. Did the caller ever speak to you directly?
A   No.

Mr. Darden: Thank you. That is all I have.

Cross-examination by Mr. Cochran:

After a series of preliminary questions, defense attorney Johnnie Cochran asks:

Q But what I'm asking you, you hadn't talked to anybody so you don't know what was taking place at that location, do you?
A   No, I do not.
Q You have no way of knowing that, do you?
A   Only what I heard. I have to create an incident according to what I hear. Either way, I was sending the police at the beginning as an unknown trouble. Something was going on at that location that someone dialed 911. Our procedure is anytime you get a call on 911, whether you hear anyone or not, you have to send the police on an unknown trouble.
Q I understand. And that is exactly the point. It was unknown trouble to you, right?
A   In the beginning.
Q Right. You are downtown at 150 north Los Angeles; is that correct?
A   Right.
Q And you don't know what is happening — between any two or three parties at the location; is that correct?
A   That's correct.

Q   All right. You hear certain things; is that right?
A   Right.
Q   And then based upon what you hear, you start to type into your computer; is that correct?
A   That's correct.
Q   Did I also hear a lot of static on that line?
A   The static that you heard was when I brought up the frequency to broadcast to the other units. That is the transmissions from the computer to the radio, not from the telephone.
Q   All right. So the static was something that was generated by what you did in broadcasting to the other unit on a police frequency; is that correct?
A   Yes.
Q   All right. So did you hear static, right?
A   Yes.
Q   We heard typing and we heard static and during this period of time you mentioned, I believe at some point, that you became excited as you heard this; is that correct?
A   Yes.
Q   And that is part of your job, to — to create under stress and pressure; is that correct?
A   That's correct.
Q   Because your job is to try to get a unit out there as fast as you can because you don't know what is going on, right?
A   Right.
Q   All right. So at the time this call had ended or by the time this call had ended, you had not talked with anybody at 360 north Rockingham, had you?
A   No.

· · ·

Q   All right. Now, at some point you type into and you described for us that you type into your computer "female being beaten at location could be heard over the phone," and that was what you concluded after you heard this woman screaming; is that right?
A   Yes.
Q   And you don't know whether there was a mutual fight or what was going on, do you, at that point?
A   No, I do not.
Q   All right. So you — what you wrote down was what you concluded at that particular time; is that correct?
A   What I concluded that I heard.
Q   That was back in January of 1989, right?
A   Yes.

Q You never at any time talked to any of the parties who were actually at that house?

A No.

Mr. Cochran: Thank you very kindly, your honor. Nothing further from Miss Gilbert at this point. Thank you, ma'am.

The Court: All right. Mr. Darden, do you wish to call your next witness?

Mr. Darden: Yes, your honor. Thank you. The people call Detective Edwards, your honor.

John Edwards, called as a witness by the people, was sworn and testified as follows:

The Clerk: Please raise your right hand. Do you solemnly swear that the testimony you may give in the cause now pending before this court, shall be the truth, the whole truth and nothing but the truth, so help you God?

The Witness: Yes, I do.

The Clerk: Please be seated. Please state and spell your first and last name for the record.

The Witness: John Edwards, E-d-w-a-r-d-s.

The Court: Mr. Darden.

Ms. Clark: Thank you, your honor.

Direct examination by Mr. Darden:

Q **Good morning, sir.**
A Good morning.
Q **Sir, on January 1, 1989, were you employed by the LAPD?**
A Yes, I was.
Q **What is your present rank today?**
A Detective, Van Nuys homicide.
Q **Okay. And what was your rank and assignment on January 1, 1989?**
A Training officer for West L.A. patrol.

• • •

Q **Were you on duty between 3:00 and 4:00 a.m. On that date?**
A Yes, I was.
Q **Were you in uniform?**
A Yes.
Q **Was your partner in uniform?**
A Yes, she was.
Q **Did you have a police vehicle?**
A Yes.
Q **Was that a plain clothes vehicle?**
A It was a black and white patrol car.
Q **So you had "LAPD, to protect and to serve" and all of that on the doors?**
A Yes, it did.
Q **On that date, around four o'clock in the morning, did you receive a radio call?**
A I believe it was around 3:30 in the morning.
Q **Okay. Do you know the exact time?**
A Not really, but I thought it was somewhere around 3:30, 3:40, somewhere in there.
Q **Okay. But you did receive a radio call?**
A Yes.
Q **And what was the nature of that call?**
A It was a 911 radio call at 360 north Rockingham, woman being beaten. The operator could overhear it, and according to the comment, the operator could overhear the woman being beaten on the phone.
Q **And did you proceed to 360 North Rockingham?**
A Yes, I did.

· · ·

Q **How long did it take you to get there, if you recall?**
A Less than ten minutes.

· · ·

Q **Had you ever been to 360 North Rockingham, that is, prior to January 1, 1989?**
A No, I had not.
Q **Had you ever met the defendant here seated at the end of counsel table?**
A No, I had not.
Q **So you and your partner proceeded to that address?**
A Yes.
Q **Tell the jury what happened next.**
A Well, when I arrived in the Sunset/Rockingham area and went into the hills on Rockingham, it was — it was dark, it was misty, it had

been raining earlier in the evening, and as I went by the first part of the estate, I was not aware that there was a gate on Rockingham. I passed it and I ended up on the next gate, which I believe is on Ashford, if I'm not mistaken, an electronic gate, and I stopped my black and white patrol car there and noted that it was a locked security gate with a little call box out front with a button.

Q Did you get out of the car at that time?

A Yes, I got out of the car and pressed the button and waited for someone to speak to me and a female came over the speaker, said she was the housekeeper, that her name was Michelle, and that she wanted to know what I wanted. And I said, well, I just responded there on a 911 call, a woman had been beaten —

Mr. Cochran: Your honor, object. This is hearsay.

The Court: Sustained.

Mr. Cochran: Move to strike and the jury admonished.

Mr. Darden: Timely objection, your honor.

The Court: All right. Ladies and gentlemen, you are to disregard the last statement regarding what the housekeeper said.
All right, Mr. Darden.

Q What was your response to the housekeeper?

A I told her that I was there on a 911 call, that a woman had placed a 911 call and said she was being beaten and the operator could hear her being beaten over the phone and I needed to see and talk to the person who made that call.

Q Okay. Did the person you spoke to, Michelle, did she allow you entry into the compound or estate at that point?

A No. On the contrary, she said that there was no problem there.

Q What did you do?

A I told her I was not leaving until I saw the person that made the 911 call.

Q What happened next?

A Then a woman came running out of the bushes to my left, across the driveway. She was a female Caucasian, blond hair. She was wearing a bra only as an upper garment and she had on dark — I believe it was a dark lightweight sweatpants or night pajama bottom and she ran across and collapsed on the speaker — the identical kind of a speaker post on the inside of the gate. She collapsed on it and started yelling, "he's going to kill me, he's going to kill me." Then she pressed the button which allowed the gate to open and then she ran out again yelling "he's going to kill me."

Q   Did you have a flashlight with you at that time?

· · ·

A   Yes, I did.
Q   **What was your reaction? How did you react when you saw this woman run out of the darkness in her bra and night clothes?**
A   Well, she — she seemed to be exhausted.

Mr. Cochran: Move to strike, your honor, as nonresponsive. What was his reaction?

The Court: Sustained. The jury is ordered to disregard the last question and answer. Mr. Darden, ask the question again, please.

Q   **What was your response when you saw this woman running toward you screaming, "he's going to kill me, he's going to kill me"?**
A   Illuminated her briefly with my flashlight and then illuminated the bushes around her or near her and as much of the house as I could.
Q   **Did you see anyone else at that time?**
A   No, I didn't.
Q   **What was her demeanor as she ran toward you shouting, "he's going to kill me, he's going to kill me"?**
A   She was hysterical.
Q   **And you say that she pushed the button to the gate?**
A   Well, she had pushed it more than once. She pushed it three or four times like she was panicking. Several times she kept pushing it.
Q   **Did the gate open?**
A   Yes, it opened, and she ran out to me. I didn't enter.
Q   **Okay. What happened when she ran out to you?**
A   She — she clung on to me and then made several statements to me at that time.
Q   **Now, you say that she ran to you and clung to you?**
A   Well, she collapsed on me.
Q   **She collapsed on you?**
A   Yes.
Q   **And what was her physical demeanor and physical appearance at that time?**
A   Well, she — she was wet. She was — she was shivering, she was cold. I could — I could feel her — her bones and she was real cold and she was beat up.
Q   **And at some point did you identify this woman?**
A   Yes.

Q   **Who was this woman that you . . . ?**
A   Nicole Simpson.
Q   **What, if anything, did she say to you after she collapsed?**
A   She said, "he's going to — he's going to kill me." I said "well, who is going to kill you?" She said, "O.J."
Q   **What did you say?**
A   I said . . . "O.J. Who? Do you mean the — the football player, O.J. the football player?" And she said, "yes, O.J. Simpson, the football player."

• • •

Q   **Did she say anything at that time, detective?**
A   Yes. She made a series of spontaneous statements prior to us attempting to ask her any questions.
Q   **What did she say?**
A   She said, "you guys never do anything" something to the effect, that "you never do anything about him. You come out. You have been out here eight times. You never do anything about him." And she says, "I want him arrested. I want my kids back. I want to go in the house."

• • •

Q   **What happened next?**
A   And then I turned my attention back to the gate as my partner was getting the rest of the details for the report, and I saw Mr. Simpson walking towards me from the house wearing a bathrobe.
Q   **When you say "Mr. Simpson," you are referring to the defendant seated here in front today?**
A   Yes, O.J. Simpson, wearing the gray jacket, suit jacket.

The Court: Indicating the defendant.

Q   **You could see the defendant's face?**
A   Yes. It was O.J. Simpson.
Q   **Were you still outside the gate?**
A   Yes, I was outside the gate.
Q   **And the defendant, which side of the gate was he on?**
A   He was on the — inside the gate on the driveway.
Q   **So the gate was between you and the defendant?**
A   Yes.
Q.   **What was his demeanor at the time?**
A   He seemed very furious.

• • •

Q **What happened next, detective?**
A The defendant approached directly to me at the gate where he was on one side and I was on the other. We were in close proximity. Then he peered towards the black and white police vehicle and he started making some statements.

. . .

Q **And what was his tone of voice as he said those things?**
A Extremely angry and loud and rapid.
Q **What did the defendant say at that time?**

. . .

A He said, "I don't want that woman in my bed anymore. I got two other women. I don't want that woman in my bed anymore."
Q **By Mr. Darden: now, did he say this or did he shout it or . . .**
A He shouted it I believe twice and he pointed at her — well, he pointed at my patrol vehicle while he was making the statement.
Q **Did you realize at that time that the woman in the patrol car, Nicole Brown, was the defendant's wife?**
A Yes.

Cross examination:

Q **Are you aware that with regard to these proceedings, that Mr. O.J. Simpson entered a no contest plea and resolved this incident in the criminal justice system? Are you aware of that?**
A Yes.
Q **And are you aware that he thereafter wrote letters of apology to his wife regarding this incident? Are you aware of that?**

Later testimony revealed that the defendant informed investigating officers that he "regretted the incident." As a result of the disturbance, however, Simpson was formally charged with one count of spousal battery under section 273(a) of the California penal code.

(At 4:25 p.m. an adjournment was taken until Wednesday, February 1, 1995, 9:00 a.m.)

February 1, 1995

Former LAPD police officer Ronald Shipp, who described himself as a friend of Simpson's, testified that Simpson told him that he had had many dreams about killing his wife, Nicole. The revelations came, said Shipp, a day after Nicole had been killed, as Simpson discussed his hesitancy about taking a lie detector test. Shipp implied that Simpson was concerned he might not pass a lie detector test because dreams might be confused with reality.

During cross-examination Shipp admitted that he had withheld information about his conversation with Simpson from police, and said that he was not a very close friend of Simpson's. Under questioning by defense attorney Carl Douglas Ronald Shipp admitted that he had a drinking problem and said that he had been disciplined as a police officer for alcohol abuse. He claimed that he had not been drinking on the night that Simpson talked to him about dreams. Prosecutors then played a 1993 recording of Nicole Brown Simpson pleading for help from an emergency operator. Simpson could be heard in the background yelling and cursing at her. The jury was shown Polaroid pictures of Nicole Brown Simpson's bruised and battered face, and newspaper clippings about the January 1, 1989 abuse incident.

(The following proceedings were held in open court, in the presence of the jury):

The Court: All right. Thank you, ladies and gentlemen. Be seated. All right. Good morning, ladies and gentlemen.

The Jury: Good morning.

The Court: . . . All right. Are the people ready to call their next witness?

Mr. Darden: Yes, your honor. We are. Good morning.

The Court: Mr. Darden.

Mr. Darden: Good morning, ladies and gentlemen.

The Jury: Good morning.

Mr. Darden: The people call Ron Shipp to the stand, your honor.

The Court: All right. Mr. Shipp.

Ronald Shipp, called as a witness by the people, was sworn and testified as follows:

The Clerk: Please raise your right hand. Do you solemnly swear that the testimony you may give in the cause now pending before this court, shall be the truth, the whole truth and nothing but the truth, so help you God?

The Witness: Yes, I do.

The Clerk: Please be seated and state and spell your first and last names for the record.

The Witness: RONALD Shipp, R-o-n-a-l-d S-h-i-p-p.

The Clerk: Thank you.

The Court: Mr. Darden.

Direct examination by Mr. Darden:

Q **Good morning, sir.**
A Good morning.
Q **Mr. Shipp, are you acquainted with the defendant in this case?**
A Yes, I am.
Q **How long have you known him?**
A Approximately 26 years.
Q **And do you recall the circumstances in which you first met him?**
A Yes, I do.
Q **What were those circumstances?**
A Umm, when I was about 16 years old my brother, Mike, played against O.J. In high school up in San Francisco, and he had come down to Los Angeles right after O.J. had won the Heisman trophy, and myself, Mike and my brother Skip went over to O.J.'s house and congratulated him and this is when I was 16 years old.
Q **And did you and the defendant develop a friendship after that initial meeting?**
A Umm, not — we weren't very close at that time. I had run into him from time to time and, umm, every time I would see him he would ask me how was Mike doing, and but we weren't really that close at that time.
Q **Okay. Well, as the years went on, did you develop a closer relationship?**
A I would say approximately from about 1978 on.
Q **Did you visit the defendant's home?**
A Yes, I did.
Q **On how many occasions?**
A How many occasions?
Q **Yes.**
A Gee, umm — let's see. In '78 I was a police officer at the time and I was assigned to West Los Angeles division and at that time I would

go up there on occasion, probably approximately maybe two times a week up until 1982.

Q **You were an LAPD officer?**
A Yes, I was.
Q **When did you join the LAPD?**
A 1974.
Q **And you are no longer an LAPD officer?**
A No, I'm not.
Q **When did you leave the LAPD?**
A I believe it was October of 1989.
Q **And you say that during the time that you were a police officer you were assigned to West L.A. station?**
A No. I was assigned to west L.A. from 1978 to '82.

• • •

Q **You said that O.J. or the defendant trusted you?**
A Yes, he did. I felt he did.
Q **What period of time are we talking about here?**
A ... Approximately from 1978 to '82.

• • •

Q **Well, did he ask you any questions, any questions about the investigation?**
A After he told me about what they found at his house, he asked me how long does it take DNA to come back.
Q **And at that time, did you know the correct answer to that question?**
A I did not know the correct answer, but what I did say, I just off the cuff say two months.
Q **And what did he say in response to your indication that it takes DNA two months to come back?**
A He kind of jokingly just said, you know, "to be honest, Shipp" — that's what he called me, Shipp. He said, "I've had some dreams of killing her."
Q **Did he say how many dreams he had had of killing her?**
A No, he did not.
Q **Did he say it was more than one?**
A He just said dreams, plural.

Cross-examination By Mr. Douglas:

Q **When you were there on this occasion, did you ask Mr. Simpson to go and bring you some wine?**
A That's correct.

Q   You drink a lot, don't you?
A   I used to.
Q   **You've had a drinking problem, haven't you?**
A   In the past I have.

February 3, 1995

Denise Brown, sister of Nicole Brown Simpson, took the witness stand and — in emotional testimony — told jurors how Nicole's husband had publicly humiliated and physically abused his wife, throwing her out of his mansion.

Out of the presence of the jury, a new witness, Leif Tilden, told prosecutors that he saw four men near Nicole Brown Simpson's home on the night of the murders at around 10 p.m. and 10:30 p.m.

The Court: Back on the record in the Simpson matter. Mr. Simpson is again present with counsel, Mr. Cochran, Mr. Blaiser, people represented by Mr. Harmon. All right. . . . Deputy Magnera, let's have the jury please.

The following proceedings were held in open court, in the presence of the jury:

The Court: Thank you, ladies and gentlemen. Be seated. All right. On the record in the Simpson matter. Mr. Simpson is again present with his counsel, Mr. Shapiro, Mr. Cochran, Mr. Douglas, people represented by Mr. Darden, Mr. Gordon. Mr. Darden, call your next witness.

Mr. Darden: Thank you, your honor. The people call Denise Brown.

Denise Brown, called as a witness by the people, was sworn and testified as follows:

The Clerk: Please have a seat on the witness stand and state and spell your first and last name for the record.

The Witness: Denise Brown, D-e-n-i-s-e B-r-o-w-n.

The Clerk: Thank you.

The Court: All right.

Direct examination by Mr. Darden:

Q   **Miss Brown, you are Nicole Brown's oldest — older sister?**

A   Yes, I am.

Q   **Do you have other sisters?**

A   Yes, I do.

Q   **How many?**

A   There's Dominique and Tanya and of course Nicole.

Q   **And you are the oldest of the sisters; is that correct?**

A   Yes, I am.

• • •

Q   **Do you know the defendant seated here at the end of counsel table?**

A   Yes, I do.

Q   **He's your former brother-in-law?**

A   Yes, he is.

Q   **When did you first meet the defendant?**

A   Back in 1977.

Q   **Miss Brown, your sister Nicole married the defendant in February 1985?**

A   Yes, she did.

Q   **Did you attend the wedding?**

A   Yes, I did. I was the maid of honor.

Q   **Do you have a half sister named Wendy?**

A   Yes, I do.

Q   **And where was she living in 1987 and 1988?**

A   Wendy?

Q   **Yes.**

A   In Arizona.

Q   **And was there an occasion during that time period in which she came from Arizona to your family's home in Laguna Beach on vacation?**

A   Yes, she did.

Q   **And did she bring someone with her?**

A   A girlfriend of hers who was also living there.

Q   **And what is the girlfriend's name?**

A   Julianne Hendricks.

Q   **And did you, your sister Wendy, your sister Nicole and Julianne Hendricks go out during that vacation period?**

A   Yes, we did.

Q   **Was there ever an occasion when the four of you and the defendant went out and went to the Red Onion in Santa Ana?**

A   Yes, we did.

Q   **Did anyone else go on that excursion or that trip that night?**

A   There was Dino Bucolla and Reggie MacKenzie.

Q   **And who is Dino Bucolla?**

A   He was my boyfriend at the time.

Q   **And who was Reggie MacKenzie?**
A   A friend of O.J.'s.
Q   **And he is a former —**
A   Football player.
Q   **Now, was there some plan or agreement amongst the group to meet at a certain location and at a certain time?**
A   We were going to go and meet them, meet O.J., and we were running a little late and we got there and he got upset. But that blew over and then we continued on, went to the club.
Q   **So when you arrived late, the defendant got a little upset you say?**
A   Yeah. He was annoyed with us, yeah, for being late.
Q   **And that was you, Nicole, Wendy —**
A   Wendy.
Q   **— and Julianne?**
A   Right.
Q   **And then the group went out; is that correct?**
A   Right.
Q   **Did you all go out in one car?**
A   No. There were a couple of cars.
Q   **And who owned the two cars that you used to go out in that night?**
A   I think — that night, it was O.J.'s car and I'm not sure who else was driving or who else's car it was.
Q   **Did you go to the Red Onion?**
A   Yes, we did.
Q   **Is there a bar in the Red Onion?**
A   Yes.
Q   **And did you have something to drink?**
A   Yes, I did.
Q   **Really. What did you drink?**
A   We were all — well, actually, we were all doing shots of tequila.
Q   **The defendant was doing shots of tequila?**
A   Yes.
Q   **Was Nicole doing shots of tequila?**
A   Yes.
Q   **Did Julianne drink tequila?**
A   I think she may have. I'm not sure, but I know that we were.
Q   **How about Reggie MacKenzie? Did he drink shots of tequila?**
A   Yeah. Yeah, he did too.
Q   **Now, were there other persons or patrons in the bar?**
A   Oh, it was packed. There were lots of people there.
Q   **And did some of those patrons recognize the defendant?**
A   Yeah. He always gets recognized wherever he goes.
Q   **And did the people walk up to the defendant and talk to him?**
A   Oh, sure.

Q **Did he sign autographs?**

A I don't know if he signed autographs that night, but, you know, he's friendly to people. He shakes hands.

Q **Did people in the bar buy him anything?**

A Oh, they could have. I think the bartenders, they had given him shots of tequila and things like that, sure. I mean, that happens when he goes out.

Q **So the drinks were free?**

A I'm not saying all of them were. I'm not sure, but people do tend to buy him drinks and buy us — and they were buying us drinks too because we were with him.

Q **And did you see the defendant drink shots of tequila?**

A Uh-huh. Yes.

Q **Did anything unusual happen that night in the Red Onion?**

A Yes.

Q **What was that?**

A Well, we all started — well, we were all drinking and goofing around and being loud and dancing and having a great time. And then at one point, O.J. grabbed Nicole's crotch and said, "this is where babies come from and this belongs to me." And Nicole just sort of wrote it off as if it was nothing, like — you know, like she was used to that kind of treatment and he was like — I thought it was really humiliating if you ask me.

Q **And when he grabbed your sister's crotch and said, "this is where babies come from" — is that what he said?**

A "This is where babies come from and this belongs to me," and, "This is mine."

Q **And when he said this and when he grabbed her in the crotch, were there people around?**

A Oh, yeah. The bar was packed.

Q **Strangers?**

A Yeah. Yeah. He was talking to the strangers.

Q **Did your sister Nicole react to this at all?**

A She just kind of wrote it off and just, you know, shrugged her shoulders, you know, stop it or whatever. I mean it was — I don't know. She didn't really react.

Q **Did the defendant appear mad or angry or upset when he grabbed your sister's crotch and made these statements in front of these strangers?**

A No. No. He wasn't angry. It was his. That's the way he — he — just the way he acted, the way — it was like, "this belongs to me. This is mine." He wasn't angry when he said it. He just made it a point. He wanted it to be known that that was his.

Q **Was she wearing a dress or was she wearing pants, if you recall?**

A Ahh, I don't remember.

Q And during the time that these strangers were approaching him and shaking hands and things like that, did he appear to shy away from the attention at all?

A Oh, no. No, not at all. He loves the attention. He loves it. He's got a big ego. It feeds his ego.

• • •

Q Let me direct your attention to the La Cantina restaurant, okay?

A Okay.

Q Are you acquainted with someone by the name of Ed McCabe?

A Yes, I was.

Q This is someone you've known over the last decade or so?

A I've known Ed for a while. I used to date him.

Q And when did you stop dating Ed McCabe?

A Oh, I think we may have gone out for a year or two, maybe two years.

Q Do you still speak to Ed McCabe?

A Not too often.

Q And in what city and state does he live?

A He's in New York.

Q Do you recall an occasion when you and Ed McCabe and Nicole and the defendant went out to dinner?

A Yes, I do.

Q And where did the four of you go after you left the La Cantina restaurant?

A We went to O.J.'s house, O.J. and Nicole's house.

Q On Rockingham?

A Yes.

Q Now, had you had something to drink at the restaurant before?

A Yeah. Margueritas.

Q And did the defendant have something to drink?

A Yeah. We all did.

Q All four of you?

A Yes.

Q And what did you do when you returned to the defendant's home on Rockingham?

A We were sitting at the bar talking, having some more drinks and talking.

Q Okay. While you were talking, did you say something to the defendant?

A Yes, I did.

Q What did you say to him?

A I told him he took Nicole for granted, and he blew up.

. . .

Q And what happened next?
A He started yelling at me, "I don't take her for granted. I do everything for her. I give her everything," and he continued, and then a whole fight broke out and pictures started flying off the walls, clothes started flying — he ran upstairs, got clothes, started flying down the stairs and grabbed Nicole, told her to get out of his house, wanted us all out of his house, picked her up, threw her against the wall, picked her up, threw her out of the house.

    She ended up on her — she ended up falling. She ended up on her elbows and on her butt. Then she — he threw Ed McCabe out. We were all sitting there screaming and crying, and then he grabbed me and threw me out of the house.

Q Are you okay, Miss Brown?
A Yeah. It's just so hard. I'll be fine.

The Court: Ladies and gentlemen, we are going to take our recess for the afternoon . . . . Please remember my admonition; don't discuss this case amongst yourselves, don't form any opinions about the case, don't allow anybody to speak to you about the case or speak to anybody else about it, do not conduct any deliberations until the matter has been submitted to you.

    I'll see you back here Monday morning 9:00 o'clock. Have a nice weekend.

At 3:00 p.m. an adjournment was taken until Monday, February 6, 1995, 9:00 a.m.

February 6, 1995

Testimony by Denise Brown continued. Brown told jurors that Simpson had a "frightening" look in his eye and stared at his ex-wife in a hostile fashion during a dance recital on the day she was killed.

    Defense attorney Robert Shapiro used the cross-examination to have Brown admit to a previously acknowledged drinking problem. She testified that she had been drinking on both of the nights she saw Simpson abuse his wife.

(The following proceedings were held in open court, out of the presence of the jury):

The Court: All right. Good morning, counsel. All right. Back on the record in the Simpson matter.

The record should reflect the defendant is again present before the court with counsel, Mr. Shapiro, Mr. Cochran, Mr. Douglas, Mr. Bailey. The people are represented by Miss Clark, Mr. Darden, Mr. Gordon. The jury is not present.

The Court: Deputy Magnera, let's have the jury, please.

(The following proceedings were held in open court, in the presence of the jury):

The Court: All right. Thank you, ladies and gentlemen. Be seated, please. All right. Let the record reflect that we have been rejoined by all the members of our jury panel. Good morning, ladies and gentlemen.

The Jury: Good morning.

The Court: ...All right. Let's resume with Denise Brown. Miss Brown, would you come forward, please.

Denise Brown, the witness on the stand at the time of the evening adjournment, resumed the stand and testified further as follows:

The Court: And would you resume the witness chair, please. Good morning, Miss Brown. You are reminded you are still under oath.

The Court: All right. Mr. Darden, do you wish to continue your direct examination?

Mr. Darden: Yes, I do, your honor. Thank you.

The Court: You are welcome.

Mr. Darden: Good morning. Good morning, ladies and gentlemen.

The Jury: Good morning.

Direct examination (resumed) by Mr. Darden:

Q **Miss Brown, when we left off last Friday you told us about the crotch grabbing incident at the Red Onion. Do you recall that?**
A Yes.
Q **And you also talked to us about an incident that occurred after you and your sister, Nicole, and Ed McCabe returned to the defendant's house after an evening at the La Cantina?**

A   Yes, I did.

• • •

Q   **The pictures that you mentioned last Friday, where were those pictures located?**

A   They were going up the stairs, up the staircase to the second story.

Q   **Okay. And had you seen those pictures before?**

A   Oh, sure, many times.

Q   **How many pictures were there?**

A   Oh, I think there is about three or four rows going up like this, (indicating), and all the way up the staircase.

Q   **And who was depicted in those photographs?**

A   It was family members.

Q   **Brown family members?**

A   Brown family, O.J.'s family, umm, a lot of different pictures.

Q   **Okay. And you mentioned that pictures began flying off the walls. How — how were those pictures removed or how did they come flying off the wall?**

A   O.J. Was walking up the hall or up the staircase and he started throwing them. He took them off the wall and started throwing them down.

Q   **And was he saying anything to — did the defendant say anything as he threw those —**

A   He wanted her out of his house.

Q   **That is what the defendant said?**

A   He wanted her out of his house and he continued going up the stairs and he grabbed the clothes out of her closet and started throwing them down onto the foyer where we were down on the bottom, and came back down and grabbed Nicole.

He threw her up against the wall and then he grabbed her. And the only thing I remember is that it was — he looked so — his whole facial structure changed. Everything about him changed.

• • •

Q   **Okay. Did you see the defendant's face immediately after you told him that he took your sister for granted?**

A   Yes, I did.

Q   **Okay. And what, if anything, unusual did you notice about his face at that time?**

A   At that time he got very upset and he started screaming.

Q   **Now, was his anger manifested in any way other than the fact that he became — other than the fact that he began screaming?**

A   Yeah. His whole facial structure changed. I mean, everything changed about him.

Q   **Okay. When you say his facial structure changed, what do you mean? Elaborate on that for us, please.**

A   It was calm, quiet, normal conversation, like we were sitting here right now, and then all of a sudden it turned into — the eyes got real angry. It was as — his whole jaw, everything started, you know — his whole face just changed completely when he got upset. Umm — it wasn't as if it was O.J. any more. He looked like a different person and that is what Nicole had always said when he gets angry.

. . .

Q   **Now, had you seen the defendant angry on other occasions?**

A   Not like this.

Q   **Okay. Well, this change in his facial structure that you just testified to, is that something that commonly happens when the defendant becomes angry?**

A   I had never seen it like this before, no.

Q   **So that was the first time you had ever seen him get that angry?**

A   Yes.

. . .

Q   **Miss Brown, you have a niece and a nephew by your sister Nicole; is that correct?**

A   Yes, I do.

Q   **That is Sydney and Justin?**

A   Yes.

Q   **Do you recall in which year each of your niece and nephew were born?**

A   Sydney was born in 1985 and Justin was born in 1988.

Q   **I take it that your sister gained weight while she was pregnant?**

A   Yes.

Q   **And after each of those pregnancies did she keep the weight on for a while? Did you ever hear the defendant comment about her weight?**

A   Yes, I did.

Q   **What did the defendant say about your sister's weight while she was pregnant?**

A   He used to call her a fat pig. He used to comment like this all the time.

Q   **Did he make hand gestures?**

A   Yes.

Q   **Holding both hands apart as you just indicated on the record?**

A   Yes.

Q   **Okay. Did you actually hear him call your sister a fat pig while she was pregnant?**

A   Yes.

Q   **And after she had had each of the children would he make similar comments about her weight?**

A   Yeah. He hated fat women.

Q   **He would tell your sister that he hated fat women?**

A   He would always comment about her weight.

Q   **And you would be present on occasion when he made these comments?**

A   Yes, I was.

Q   **Did your sister Nicole react in any way on those occasions when the defendant would call her a fat pig or say that he hated fat women?**

A   At one point she didn't care how much weight she gained, she just wanted him to leave her.

• • •

Q   **Miss Brown, you described for us the incident after you went to the La Cantina restaurant and you also described the incident at the Red Onion and you also testified that you consumed alcohol on each of those specific occasions; is that correct?**

A   Yes, I did.

Q   **And on those occasions, did you have a drinking problem?**

A   Yes, I did.

Q   **You're a recovering alcoholic?**

A   Yes, I am. Sober for over a year now.

• • •

Q   **Miss Brown, directing your attention to June 12, 1994, on that day, was a recital held for your niece Sidney?**

A   Yes, it was.

Q   **And where was that recital held, if you recall?**

A   Umm, Paul — I think Paul Revere School.

Q   **And that's a middle school in Brentwood?**

A   Yes, it is.

Q   **It was a dance recital, wasn't it?**

A   Uh-huh. Yes.

Q **And did you drive up from Laguna Beach to attend the recital?**
A Yes, I did.
Q **Did other members of your family also drive up from Laguna Beach to attend the recital?**
A My whole family did.
Q **That would include your sister, Dominique and Tanya?**
A No. Tanya wasn't there. Dominique was, my mom and dad, my son, Dominique's son.

• • •

Q **And when he greeted you and your sister Dominique and your parents, what was his demeanor?**
A Umm, he had a very bizarre look in his eyes. It was a very far-away look.
Q **You say he had a bizarre look, far-away look?**
A He had a very far-away look. It was actually really kind of spooky. It was a frightening look.
Q **Was he smiling?**
A Umm, no. No.
Q **Can you describe for us physically his physical demeanor at the time?**
A He just had a very different look about him. It wasn't — it wasn't like O.J. Just walking into a place and being, you know, hey, here I am, you know, kind of sure of himself type of attitude. It was more of a — of a — like a glazed over, kind of frightening, dark eyes. It just didn't look like the O.J. that we knew.

• • •

Q **Did the defendant go with you?**
A To Mezzaluna?
Q **Yes.**
A No.
Q **Did you have dinner?**
A Yes, we did.
Q **What did you do after dinner was over?**
A We got up and — we got up and we walked out, and Nicole was going to go get some ice cream with the kids. And we kissed each other good-bye. The last thing I told her was that I loved her. I'm sorry.

The Court: Miss Brown, do you want us to just take a few minutes now?

Mr. Darden: I have no further questions, your honor.

The Court: Thank you.

Cross-examination by Mr. Shapiro:

Q **Miss Brown, I, as you know, have to ask you some questions.**
A Yes.

. . .

Q **The incident that you were telling us about at the Red Onion —
and you told us a list of people that were there and I don't
want to go over it — but it was about five or six different
people?**
A Right.
Q **At that time, were you still drinking?**
A Oh, I was drinking at that time, yes.
Q **And how would you describe your consumption of alcohol?**
A I said I had a problem.
Q **That could mean different things to different people. And I
don't mean to embarrass you, but this particular evening,
could you tell us how much you had to drink, if you recall?**
A Oh, I don't recall how many drinks, no.

. . .

Q **Can you give us some type of approximation as to what your
drinking pattern would be like?**
A On that night?
Q **Yes.**
A We were doing shots of tequila.
Q **How many shots would you imagine that you would drink? I
know it would be impossible to remember precisely.**
A That night, I don't remember.
Q **Could you give us any idea?**
A I don't remember.
Q **How about, did you have any Margueritas there?**
A Yes, we did.
Q **Do you remember how many Margueritas you had?**
A No. It was in between dancing and going, having a drink.
Q **It was a party atmosphere; was it not?**
A Yes, it was.
Q **And the Red Onion was very crowded?**
A Yes, it was.
Q **A lot of noise?**
A Yes.

Q   A lot of loud music?
A   Yes.

. . .

Q   And would — how would you describe your state of sobriety
    when you were at the Red Onion?
A   Happy.
Q   In terms of intoxication, if we use the terms sober being one
    who had just consumed a minimum amount of alcohol but still
    would be able to drive and drunk and intoxicated in between,
    would you be able to put yourself on that scale?
A   Well, I would not have driven home.
Q   And isn't it a fact, Miss Brown, that your boyfriend at the time,
    Dino, was the designated driver for the evening and he was the
    only one who didn't have anything to drink?
A   Right.

February 7, 1995

*The prosecution began trying to establish the time that the murders
occurred — focusing on the time that Ronald Goldman left the Mezzaluna
restaurant (about 9:50 p.m.). A neighbor of Nicole Simpson's, Pablo
Fenjves, testified that a barking Akita-type dog wandered around the
neighborhood. The dog led neighbors to the murder scene and the
bodies. Fenjves said that the dog started barking about 10:15 p.m. The
defense argued that Simpson would not have had enough time to commit
the murders, dispose of the evidence and return to his home by 11 p.m.
— the time he caught a limousine to the airport.*

*A 63-year-old white female juror was dismissed, replaced by a 54-
year-old black man, leaving only 3 non-blacks on the 12-member jury
panel. Seven of the jurors were then women, five men.*

February 8, 1995

*Sukru Boztepe, Nicole Brown Simpson's neighbor testified that he was led
to the murder scene by the Akita dog, and found the bodies outside of
Nicole's townhome. Boztepe and neighbor Steven Schwab had found the
dog earlier in the evening with what appeared to be blood on its paws.*

*Defense attorney Johnnie Cochran tried to show that the witnesses
were unsure of the time events occurred. Schwab testified, however, that
he was sure of the times involved because he had been watching his
favorite television reruns, and went out at 10:30 p.m., at the end of the
Dick Van Dyke Show.*

February 9, 1995

LAPD Officer Robert Riske, the first police officer at the murder scene, described the evidence he found as well as the bodies of Nicole and Goldman. Riske said that the front door to Nicole Simpson's residence was open, and that he saw bloody shoe prints, a knit cap, a glove, and an envelope near the bodies. Riske found Nicole's two children asleep. He also said that he understood the need to preserve evidence at a crime scene, and that he attempted to avoid disturbing the scene. Defense attorney Cochran questioned Riske about police procedures at the crime scene.

February 12, 1995

Judge Ito ordered that jurors should view the murder scene, and they were driven to Nicole Brown Simpson's townhouse where they were allowed to familiarize themselves with the area's layout. They also toured O.J. Simpson's Brentwood mansion two miles away.

February 14, 1995

Cross-examination of Officer Riske continued, with attorney Cochran asking why he didn't inspect trash cans inside the townhome or measure the temperature of the water found in Nicole Brown Simpson's bathtub. Cochran appeared to be trying to show that police mishandled evidence at the scene, and ignored important details. During a re-direct examination by Marcia Clark Riske explained that he was only to preserve the integrity of the crime scene, leaving the investigation of the murders and the gathering of evidence up to detectives and criminalists.

February 15–17, 1995

During a hearing out of the jury's presence, the prosecution told the court that blood found on a rear gate of Nicole Brown Simpson's residence belonged to O.J. Simpson. When the jury returned, LAPD detective Ron Phillips testified that Simpson was not initially a suspect, and that police tried to break the news about his wife's death to him gently.

Phillips said that O.J. Simpson's first words on learning that his former wife had been killed were, "Oh my God, Nicole is killed. Oh my God, she's dead." Simpson sounded "very upset" when notified by telephone in Chicago of his ex-wife's death, said Phillips. Phillips also testified that Simpson did not ask any questions about the murders or the circumstances surrounding them.

On cross-examination by defense attorneys, Officer Phillips admitted that Simpson asked him, "What do you mean, she's been killed?" when he spoke with him in Chicago. He said Simpson became too upset on the phone for him to attempt to answer the question.

February 21–22, 1995

LAPD detective Tom Lange took the stand to testify that, based upon an observed lack of blood on the bottom of Nicole Brown Simpson's bare feet, she was killed first, then Ronald Goldman. Nicole "perhaps went down initially before a fight really ensued with the other victim," said Lange. She didn't walk through the blood he concluded. On the other hand, said Lange, blood was present on the soles of Goldman's white shoes. Goldman's hands also showed defensive wounds, resulting from an effort to grab the knife as he was attacked. Lange also described for the jury the activities of detective Mark Fuhrman at the crime scene. Fuhrman, said Lange, found a bloody glove at Simpson's estate. Under questioning by Marcia Clark, Lange explained that detectives climbed a wall into O.J. Simpson's estate without waiting for a search warrant to arrive because someone in the house might have been "bleeding or worse."

Defense attorneys cross-examined detective Lange in an effort to show that investigators were sloppy in their handling of evidence at the crime scene. Lange admitted that although he ordered a criminalist to take blood samples from the back gate at Nicole Brown Simpson's home on June 13, those samples were not taken until July 3.

February 24, 1995

Judge Ito ruled out that the defense could have what it claimed was a crucial alibi witness testify in the middle of the prosecution's case. Ito feared that Rosa Lopez, a maid at a home next door to Simpson's estate, might flea the country before the defense began presenting it's case.

February 27, 1995

Rosa Lopez testified that she saw the white Ford Bronco usually driven by Simpson parked in the street outside his home at around the time of the murders. She claimed to see the car as she walked her employers' golden retriever around 10:15 p.m. on June 12. Lopez's testimony was videotaped out of the presence of the jury, in order that it might later be played when the defense presents its case.

February 28, 1995

Out of the presence of the jury, prosecutor Clark cited "numerous" and "glaring" inconsistencies between statements made to investigators on a July 29 statement and a second statement made on August 18. Attorney Cochran defended Lopez, but conceded that she did not originally mention seeing the Bronco when first interviewed.

March 1, 1995

Judge Ito dismissed a 46-year-old black male juror, replacing him with a 38-year-old white female. Reporters said that the dismissed juror may have offered to bet money before the trial began that Simpson would be found innocent.

March 2–3, 1995

Rosa Lopez was cross-examined on videotape, and testified that she was not sure exactly what time she saw Simpson's Bronco outside of his mansion on the night the murders occurred. "All I said was that it was after 10," she said, failing to be more specific. Prosecutors questioned Lopez about a conversation in which she told a friend that she had been offered $5,000 to testify on Simpson's behalf — but she denied having said it. Defense attorneys said that they had not decided whether to show the video recording of Lopez to the jury. About the same time, Judge Ito imposed a $950 fine on defense attorneys for failing to turn over a previously tape-recorded interview with Lopez to the prosecution. Ito told the attorneys that he would instruct jurors that they had violated the law if they played Lopez's videotaped testimony to the jury.

March 6–7, 1995

LAPD detective Tom Lange testified that investigating officers never considered anyone other than O.J. Simpson a suspect in the murders. "I had absolutely no other evidence that would point me in any other direction," Lange replied to a question in the cross-examination. Lange admitted that investigators did not seriously consider the possibility that Ronald Goldman (and not Nicole Brown Simpson might have been the primary target in the murders; nor, he said, did they examine the relationship between Faye Resnick, who was Nicole Brown Simpson's roommate, (but who was in a drug rehabilitation center the night of the murders) and the killings. Lange testified that he believed Nicole Brown Simpson and Ronald Goldman were killed by the same individual. He pointed to various items of evidence, including the fact that there was only one set of bloody footprints leaving the murder scene. Blood found under Nicole Brown Simpson's fingernails was hers, Lange said, countering defense claims that it came from an unknown party.

March 9, 1995

LAPD Detective Mark Fuhrman took the witness stand and denied having met a woman named Kathleen Bell who claims he made racist remarks while speaking to her ten years earlier. Prosecutor Clark confronted prosecution claims directly by asking Fuhrman whether he was a racist who planted the bloody glove on Simpson's property. He denied planting evidence, but admitted to being nervous, explaining that "since June 13, it seems I've seen a lot of the evidence ignored and a lot of personal issues come to the forefront. I think that's too bad." Fuhrman also described an incident in 1985 in which he responded to a domestic disturbance call at Simpson's Brentwood mansion, only to find Nicole Brown Simpson crying on a car.   She told Fuhrman that her husband had smashed the windshield of her Mercedes with a baseball bat.

March 10, 1995

Prosecutors introduced a shovel, a towel and a large, heavy-duty plastic bag into evidence, which detective Mark Fuhrman testified that he found at Simpson's home shortly after the murders. Fuhrman also explained his actions in scaling a wall into the Simpson compound without a warrant, saying that officers had tried for 35 minutes to get someone to come to the door, then discovered what appeared to be blood on the door of Simpson's Bronco which was parked around the corner from the main gates of the residence.   Officers feared that someone inside might be injured or dead, and so took immediate action.   Fuhrman testified that detective Philip Vannatter made the final decision to enter Simpson's home without a warrant.

March 13, 1995

As questioning of Fuhrman continued, the detective acknowledged that the large plastic bag he found in the Bronco was standard equipment in such vehicles. Fuhrman then described finding a bloody glove as he went down a rear walkway toward the point where Brian "Kato" Kaelin told him that he had heard thumps hours earlier. Defense attorney F. Lee Bailey began a cross-examination of Fuhrman, asking the detective why Kathleen Bell or a real estate agent named Andrea Terry would lie about Fuhrman's allegedly racist remarks. Fuhrman said he didn't know. Then Bailey questioned Fuhrman at length in an effort to show that he had the time and the opportunity to plant evidence on June 13th.   Fuhrman admitted that he spent about 10 minutes alone on the path in Simpson's estate where he said he found a right-handed glove. Bailey got Fuhrman to admit that he had been upset at having the case taken over by other detectives, and suggested that Fuhrman planted evidence so that he could become an important witness.

March 15, 1995

Detective Fuhrman, under continuing cross-examination by F. Lee Bailey, again denied ever making racial slurs.   "You say under oath that you have not addressed any black person as a nigger or spoken about black people as niggers in the past ten years, Detective Fuhrman?" Bailey asked. "That's what I'm saying, sir," Fuhrman responded.

March 16, 1995

Detective Mark Fuhrman spent his fifth day on the witness stand, responding to questions from prosecutor Clark's re-direct examination. Clark tried to show that Fuhrman did not have enough knowledge about *the crime, including the time of the murders, whether Simpson had an alibi, whether there might be important witness to contradict the finding of the glove, etc., for him to so quickly decide to plant evidence at the Simpson estate. LAPD Lt. Frank Spangler, who followed Fuhrman, testified that he never saw Fuhrman alone near Ronald Goldman's body and the bloody glove, and that he never saw more than one glove at the crime scene. LAPD detective Philip Vannatter then testified that he was led to the bloody glove on the walkway at Simpson's estate by Fuhrman. Vannatter also said that he, and not Fuhrman, had made the decision to visit Simpson's estate after the murders. Crucial to the prosecution's case, Vannatter said he was concerned that someone on the premises might be hurt because he had just left an "extremely bloody murder scene," and had noticed what could have been blood on the white Ford Bronco parked on the street — thereby explaining the police decision to enter the Simpson compound without a warrant. Fuhrman was chosen to climb the wall into Simpson's estate because he was the youngest and fittest of the four detectives at the scene, Vannatter explained. A portion of his testimony follows. Note, as well, that Vannatter stated that O.J. Simpson was not a suspect in the killings at the time he decided to enter the Simpson estate.*

Q (By Christopher Darden) Okay. Now, you mentioned a moment ago that you and Detective Fuhrman had a discussion as to whether or not you should enter the property.

A (By Detective Vannatter) Well, it was more — it was more my discussion. I was telling him my concerns, that I felt that we needed to enter the property. He voiced the same concerns.

Q Well, who brought up the issue first if you recall?

A I did.

Q Are you sure?

A I'm positive.

Q Detective Fuhrman didn't attempt to convince you of the need to enter the property?

A Detective Fuhrman could not convince me of anything. No.
I was concerned. No. I was the one who was concerned.

Q And if you will, detective, outline for us the information that you had at that time up to that point that caused you to be concerned that someone on the property might be injured.

A Certainly. I had a location that appeared to be occupied that had lights on in it. I had vehicles parked in the driveway. I had information that there was supposedly a live-in maid at the location and I had what appeared to me to be blood on the outside. After leaving a very violent bloody murder scene, I believed something was wrong there. I made a determination that we needed to go over — to go into the property.

Q You say that you had information that there was supposed to be a live-in maid on the property?

A   That's correct.

Q   **Where did you get that information?**

A   Came from Westec Security.

Q   **Okay. And so to be clear, the information you had at that time that caused you to be concerned was the lack of any response from a live-in maid?**

A   The lack of any response from anybody.

Q   **Okay. The lights were on inside the house?**

A   That's correct.

Q   **The fact that there were cars in the driveway?**

A   Vehicles in the driveway.

Q   **You just left a bloody homicide scene?**

A   Extremely bloody homicide scene.

Q   **There seemed to be blood on the door of the Bronco?**

A   That's correct.

Q   **And you had some inclination that the bronco was owned by Mr. Simpson?**

A   Yes.

Q   **Okay. Well, had you ever met Mr. Simpson prior to that morning?**

A   No.

Q   **Or that day, rather?**

A   No.

Q   **Had you watched him play football over the years?**

A   Yes, I've seen him play football.

Q   **Do you dislike Mr. Simpson for any reason?**

A   No. I didn't know him. I thought he was a great football player.

Q   **Did you confer with Detective Lange on the issue of whether or not you should enter onto the property?**

A   Yes.

Q   **Did you discuss that issue with Detective Phillips as well?**

A   Detective Phillips was there, but I believe the discussion was between myself and my partner.

Q   **Okay. During that discussion, did any detective voice any opposition to scaling the wall?**

A   No.

Q   **At that point, did you consider Mr. Simpson a suspect in the murder of Nicole Brown and the other man?**

A   No.

March 17–20, 1995

Detective Philip Vannatter continued his testimony, telling how he found eight drops of blood on Simpson's driveway between the Bronco and the front door. Judge Ito dismissed another juror — a 52-year-old Amtrak manager, replacing him with a 60-year-old woman.   The juror was thought to be writing a book.

   Defense attorney Robert Shapiro cross-examined detective Vannatter about a cut on Simpson's hand.   At Shapiro's request, Simpson stood up and showed his left middle finger to the jury.   Although the prosecution claimed he cut it during the killings, the defense maintained that it was cut on a glass in his Chicago hotel room.   Vannatter had previously testified about noticing the cut on Simpson's hand the day after the murders, and said the injury contributed to Simpson's being a suspect in the murders.   To counter defense claims that police investigators had "rushed to judgment" in the case, failing to consider any suspects other than Simpson, Deputy District Attorney Christopher Darden concluded his questioning of Vannatter by asking him: "Did you rush to judgment in this case?"   A portion of the testimony follows.

Q   (By Mr. Darden): Now, detective, when you testified Friday, you told us that you asked officer Thompson to do something; is that right?

A   Yes.

Q   What did you ask him to do?

A   I asked him if — to detain Mr. Simpson at the front gate if he showed up at the location and not to let him enter the residence.

Q   Now, you had a search warrant at that time; is that right?

A   Yes.

Q   If you know, detective, does the fact that you have a search warrant for the premises, does that allow you to prevent persons or other persons or civilians from entering the property to be searched?

A   Yes. It was a secured crime scene.

Q   Did you ever tell Officer Thompson to handcuff Mr. Simpson?

A   No.

Q   Where were you when you first saw Mr. Simpson handcuffed?

A   Standing in the kitchen area of the residence.

Q   Okay. What did you do when you saw the handcuffs on Mr. Simpson?

A   I immediately responded to his location.

Q   I'm going to replay the video at a slower speed and I'm going to ask you to identify some of the persons you see in the video. Okay.

(At 9:34 a.m., People's exhibit 124, a videotape, was replayed.)

Q   (By Mr. Darden): Let me stop right there. There is an officer in the background there. Who is that officer, if you know?

A   I believe that is Officer Thompson.

Mr. Darden: Let it play some more.

(The videotape continues playing.)

Q (By Mr. Darden): Is Mr. Simpson handcuffed at this point?
A Yes.
Q Okay. Now, stop there. You are having a conversation with Mr. Simpson; is that right?
A Yes.
Q Okay. Now, at this point had you removed the handcuffs?
A No.
Q Okay. You did not immediately take — take the handcuffs off Mr. Simpson?
A No, I didn't immediately.
Q Okay. How much time elapsed between your first contact with Mr. Simpson and your removal of the handcuffs?
A Very short time. A couple of minutes maybe, two, three minutes.
Q Is there some reason that you delayed two to three minutes before taking the handcuffs off Mr. Simpson?
A I was explaining the — the situation to him, what was going on and was awaiting his attorney's arrival there.
Q You were expecting Mr. Weitzman to approach you and Mr. Simpson?
A Yes.

(The videotape continues playing.)

• • •

Q (By Mr. Darden): Now, someone else has joined you here; is that right?
A Yes.
Q Who is that person?
A It would appear that it is attorney Howard Weitzman.
Q Okay. Now, at this point is Mr. Simpson still handcuffed?
A No.
Q You removed the handcuffs?
A Yes.
Q Is Mr. Simpson under arrest at this point, that is, as you walked down the driveway?
A No.
Q Is he free to leave?
A Yeah, he could have.
Q Is that Officer Thompson there, the African-American officer?
A Yes.
Q Did you place Mr. Simpson inside your vehicle?

A   No.

Q   **You heard Mr. Cochran refer to a term, "rush to judgment," detective?**

A   Yes, I've heard that.

Q   **Did you rush to judgment in this case?**

A   No.

On re-direct examination, prosecutors questioned Vannatter about the handling of blood-stain evidence gathered at Simpson's estate, in an effort to show that that evidence could not have been planted. Vannatter explained how he personally took blood samples to a criminalist working at Simpson's estate. Vannatter also testified that he had timed the drive from Simpson's house to the crime scene, and that driving at the speed limit it took about five minutes. During cross-examination, defense attorney Shapiro tried to show that the police had bungled evidence gathering and that the work of investigators and criminalists had been sloppy.

March 21, 1995

Under continuing cross-examination, Detective Vannatter was asked why there was no cut in the glove found at the murder scene and why there was no blood around the glove found on Simpson's property (although the glove itself was bloody). Defense attorneys argued that if a bleeding Simpson dropped the glove on his property that then there should have been blood drops on the walkway.

Q   **(By Mr. Shapiro): Now, one of the things that you have told us about is a path of blood that led from the control gate at Rockingham to the front entrance of the house at Rockingham; is that correct?**

A   Well, I don't think it was a path. There was blood droplets that appeared to be a trail, yes.

Q   **How many blood droplets constitute a trail?**

A   Well, it could go from — from one, two, to 5000, if it proceeded that far.

Q   **And it was your opinion that the person who dropped the glove at Rockingham was involved in the murders of Nicole Brown Simpson and Ronald Goldman; is it not?**

A   Yes, it is.

Q   **I take it then that if there was blood coming from Rockingham to the entrance of the house, that same person would be bleeding at the time that the glove was placed in the condition — in the area outside of Kaelin's room; is that correct?**

Mr. Darden: Objection, calls for speculation.

The Court: Sustained.

Q **(By Mr. Shapiro): Is it — is it — did — is it your opinion that the person who did the killing was bleeding at the time he came or she came to Rockingham?**

A Yes.

Q **I take it then there was a thorough search for blood from the area of Rockingham — from Rockingham to the area where the glove was found?**

A Yes, that's correct.

Q **How much blood was found there?**

A None. None that I am aware of.

Q **I take it a thorough search was done of the adjacent property for blood; is that correct?**

A The area was searched, yes.

Q **For blood?**

A Well, searched for any type of evidence.

Q **Was it searched for blood?**

A Yes, sir, that would include any type of evidence.

Q **How much blood was found there?**

A None.

Q **I take it a thorough search of the fence was undertaken if somebody climbed the fence for blood?**

A Yes.

Q **How much blood was found there?**

A None.

Q **I take it a thorough search was done of the walls?**

A That's correct, yes.

Q **How much blood was found there?**

A None.

Under re-direct examination by District Attorney Christopher Darden, Detective Vannatter explained that he might not have seen blood drops around the area where the glove was found at the Simpson estate because it was so overgrown with vegetation that blood could not be spotted. A portion of Detective Vannatter's testimony during the re-direct examination conducted by Darden follows:

Q **Now, you've also described for us your finding of the glove, or rather, your viewing of the glove on the south side of the defendant's property, right?**

A Yes.

Q **Okay. Now, you didn't find any blood drops in the area of the glove found at Rockingham?**

A I did not.

Q   But you did find blood drops at Bundy?

A   Yes.

Q   Now, what is the surface composed of, that is, the surface at Bundy where you found blood drops?

A   It is a — it is a cement — cement walkway that runs on the north side of the — of the residence and runs east and west from the front walkway to the alley.

Q   Okay. And the surface where you found or rather where Detective Fuhrman found the glove at Rockingham, what is that surface composed of?

A   That is also a cement surface that is on the south side of the residence that was heavily covered with debris and leaves and —

Mr. Darden: If we can just pull up 116, your honor, the glove board.

The Court: Yes. Mr. Fairtlough.

Q   (By Mr. Darden): showing you people's 116, detective ... are the leaves on the walkway as depicted in those photographs, detective?

A   Yes, sir.

Q   They are all over the place, aren't they?

A   Yes, sir, they are.

Q   Did you pick up each and every leaf on the south side of that property and examine it?

A   I did not, no, sir.

Q   Did you turn each leaf over and examine it?

A   No. I did not.

Q   You told Mr. Shapiro that you found no blood on the fence or on the gate or on the wall?

A   That's correct.

• • •

Q   But you did find blood in the driveway?

A   At Rockingham, yes.

Q   Yes. Is it your opinion that the person who dropped the glove climbed over the fence at Rockingham?

Mr. Shapiro: Objection, calls for speculation.

The Court: It is leading, "is it your opinion that." Leading.

Q   (By Mr. Darden): Do you have an opinion as to how the person who dropped the glove at Rockingham entered the property?

Mr. Shapiro: Calls for speculation. Objection.

The Court: Overruled.

The Witness: Yes.

Q **(By Mr. Darden): How?**
A   I believe they — I believe he used a key to come through the
Rockingham gate after parking the vehicle in the street there, just
north of the gate, walked down to the south side of the house.
Q **Which gate are you referring to?**
A   The Rockingham gate.

• • •

Q **You told us that you did not find — or have not found the
murder weapon?**
A   That's correct.
Q **Is that uncommon in a situation like this, that is, not to find
the murder weapon?**
A   No. That is not uncommon at all.
Q **Are you surprised at all that you haven't found the murder
weapon?**
A   No.
Q **Why not?**
A   The knife is a very easy item to dispose of. It could be disposed of
any place. I have cases that I have never found the bodies on, so it
is not unusual not to find a murder weapon.

*Brian "Kato" Kaelin, perhaps the most entertaining witness to testify, and
a former houseguest of O.J. Simpson, took the stand to testify that
Simpson told him that he had given up attempts to reconcile with ex-wife
Nicole. When Clark suggested that Kaelin was a friend of Simpson's and
that he was indebted to him for helping with his acting career, Kaelin
joked, "I don't think we were going for the same parts."*

March 22

*Brian "Kato" Kaelin told the court about the time he spent with O.J.
Simpson the night of the murders, saying that after Simpson returned
home from his daughter's dance recital, the two had gone together in
Simpson's Bentley to a local McDonald's restaurant. Kaelin said Simpson
complained about the tight and revealing dress Nicole had been wearing,
and told him that his relationship with Nicole was "over." After they
returned home (about 9:40 p.m.), shortly before the murders took place,
Kaelin said, he didn't see Simpson for more than an hour. Kaelin also
told of hearing three loud bumps against the outside wall of his guest*

room while he was talking to a friend on the phone — thumps that prosecutors claim were made by Simpson running down the alleyway as he dropped one of the gloves. The thumps, said Kaelin, happened around 10:40 p.m. Here's how the questioning proceeded.

Q **(By Prosecutor Marcia Clark): All right. You indicated that you placed a phone call to Rachel Ferrara at about 10:10 p.m.**

A Yes.

Q **And that during that phone call you were seated on the bed with your back up against that headboard?**

A Yes.

Q **During that phone call, sir, did something unusual occur?**

A Yes.

Q **And what was that?**

A I heard a thumping noise.

Q **How many thumps did you hear?**

A Three.

Q **Can you demonstrate for us how loud it was?**

A Somewhat, yes.

Q **Go ahead.**

A Here?

Q **Go ahead.**

A Thump, thump, thump. *(Witness pounds on witness stand).*

Q **Where did that noise seem to be coming from?**

A From the back of the wall.

Q **From behind you where you were sitting?**

A Right, from behind the wall from where I was sitting.

Q **Did you notice anything occur in your room as a result of those thumps on the wall?**

A Yes.

Q **What?**

A There is a picture that moved.

• • •

Q **At that point that you heard the thumps on the wall, sir, approximately how long had you been on the phone with Rachel Ferrara?**

A About a half hour.

Q **And so approximately what time was it when you heard the thumps on the wall?**

A At about 10:40.

Q **Is that exact, 10:40?**

A Well, what I remember. I didn't look at the clock, but around 10:40.

• • •

Q   **So at approximately 10:40 to 10:45, when you heard the thumps and you saw the picture move, what did you do?**

A   Well, I was on the phone still and I was talking to Rachel and I thought — I said to Rachel — I asked her, "Did we just have an earthquake?"

Q   **Did those thumps alarm you, sir?**

A   After she said we didn't have one, yes.

Q   **And why were you alarmed?**

A   Well, if it wasn't that, then I thought there was, you know, someone back there.

Q   **Someone back there and where would "there" be?**

A   "There" is behind the wall on the path that we showed before.

Q   **And that path that we have shown before, that is the south pathway that runs along the outside of your exterior wall?**

A   Yes.

• • •

Q   **All right. When Rachel told you that it was not an earthquake, you became alarmed thinking someone was back there. What happened next?**

A   Well, I was on the phone with her and I told her that I was going to check on it.

Q   **And what — how long did you speak to her after you heard the thumps on the wall?**

A   You know, two to three minutes.

Q   **And when you say you were going to go and check on it, what did you intend to do?**

A   Well, that — see the dresser right there next to the bed? On the top drawer I have like a little light, flashlight. I was going to take that light and look behind there.

Q   **Look behind where?**

A   Behind the path.

Q   **The path that you have earlier identified?**

A   Yes.

Q   **How did you feel about going back there onto that little pathway?**

A   Scared.

Q   **Why?**

A   Because there could be someone back there and I just had a little flashlight.

Q   **Okay. And what was that pathway like?**

A   Well, it is dark and there is leaves. It is very narrow.

Q   **How well-lit — you said it was dark?**

A   Yes.

Q   **And you had — what was the size of that flashlight you had?**

A   This size, (indicating). It was a little, you know, thicker around, but it was about that same length.

Ms. Clark: Okay. For the record, the witness is holding up a pen.

The Court: Yes.

• • •

Q   **What did you do next?**

A   Okay. I hung up the phone and I got the flashlight and I walked the pathway, the front pathway out of my front door, to the driveway.

Q   **Okay. Now, when you went to the driveway, you said you took a pathway and that pathway led you through what?**

A   You go by the pool and when you go by the pool you go to the side of the house, the side that would face Ashford, and then you go and you hit the driveway.

• • •

Ms. Clark: For the record, the witness is tracing the pathway that goes through the lawn area along Ashford Street.

The Court: Yes, out to the driveway.

Ms. Clark: Thank you, your Honor.

Q   **Okay. You indicated that you heard the thumps at 9:40 to 9:45?**

A   Not at that time, no. It was 10.

Q   **I'm sorry, 10:40 to 10:45. Thank you, sir. And you remained on the phone with Rachel Ferrara for another two to three minutes?**

A   Yes.

Q   **So at approximately what time was it that you exited your room to go out to the pathway?**

A   So it was about two to three minutes after that time, 10:43, 10:44.

Q   **Okay. And when you went out to the pathway, did you — when you went out on the lawn area?**

A   Yeah, but I stayed on this path, (indicating).

Q   **All right. What did you see when you were on that path?**

A   On this path?

Q   **Yes.**

A   Nothing. I didn't see anything until I got to the driveway.

Q   **When you got to the driveway area where the path meets the driveway?**

A   Yes.

Q   **What did you see?**

A   I saw a limousine.

Q   **Where was that limousine?**

A   It was right behind the gate on Ashford, (indicating).

Q   **Was it facing into that Ashford gate?**

A   Yes.

Brian "Kato" Kaelin gestures during a difficult day of questioning.   Photo: Lee Celano, Pool/AP/Wide World Photos.

At that point, said Kaelin, Simpson came out of the house and he helped him load his luggage into the waiting limousine. Kaelin testified that there was one item, a black knapsack, that Simpson insisted on carrying personally. The prosecution suggested that the bag contained bloody clothing or a weapon which Simpson intended to dispose of. Kaelin said he did not see any injuries on Simpson's hands.

March 23, 1995

Direct examination of Brian "Kato" Kaelin by the prosecution concluded. Kaelin testified that he had planned to move into a room in Nicole Brown Simpson's condominium which she bought in January 1994, but that

Simpson convinced him that it "wasn't right" to live there while O.J. and Nicole were trying to reconcile.

March 27, 1995

The prosecution asked for and was granted permission to treat Brian "Kato" Kaelin as a hostile witness because of his apparent desire to protect Simpson during certain lines of questioning. The judge's decision gave Deputy District Attorney Marcia Clark the opportunity to ask more probing questions. Kaelin then changed his testimony to say that Simpson appeared "upset" after the dance recital over an incident with his daughter. Simpson was also upset by the way Nicole was dressed, and by the way she treated him — denying him the opportunity to spend time with his daughter, and not inviting him to dinner after the recital. Under cross-examination by defense attorney Robert Shapiro, Kaelin said only that Simpson was upset, but not angry or agitated. He also said that he didn't notice anything unusual about Simpson's behavior either at 9:35 p.m. or at 11 p.m. on the night of the killings.

March 28–29, 1995

Limousine driver Allan Park was called to the stand by prosecution attorneys, and testified that when he arrived at Simpson's residence Simpson did not answer the door. Similarly, Park said, he did not see Simpson's Bronco parked near the home. The prosecution, in an effort to show that Simpson was not at home at the time of the murders, questioned Park at length about his activities that evening. Marcia Clark conducted the direct examination of Allan Park, a portion of which is reproduced below:

Direct examination by Ms. Clark:

Q **Good morning, Mr. Park.**
A Good morning.
Q **Sir, as of June the 12th, can you tell us where you are employed?**
A Uh, I was employed for Town and Country Limousine.
Q **As what, sir?**
A As a limousine driver.
Q **And how long as of June the 12th had you been working there?**
A Uh, it was about two and a half, three months.

• • •

Q **On the date of June the 12th, 1994, did you have an order for a pickup on that date for the evening to go to the airport?**
A Uh, yes, I did.

Q **What was your order?**
A Uh, my order was to pick up Mr. Simpson at 360 Rockingham.
Q **At what time?**
A Uh, 10:45.
Q **10:45?**
A Yes.
Q **And did you — were you made aware of what flight you had to get him to?**
A Uh, not a flight number, but just to get him to LAX, uh, for an 11:45 flight out from American Airlines.
Q **And were you aware of where that flight was going to?**
A Uh, I believe Chicago.
Q **Had you ever driven Mr. Simpson to the airport before?**
A No, I haven't.
Q **Or have you ever driven — had you ever driven Mr. Simpson anywhere before?**
A No.
Q **Now, as of June the 12th, 1994, had you ever been to the Brentwood area?**
A Uh, no.
Q **Can you tell us, sir, at what time you left to pick up Mr. Simpson to take him to the airport on June the 12th?**
A What time I left my place?
Q **Yes.**
A Uh, it was about 9:45.
Q **And the area was — not your address at that time, but the general area you were leaving from?**
A Uh, Torrance.
Q **Okay. So you left at 9:45?**
A Yes.
Q **Were you anticipating it would take you an hour to get to Brentwood from there?**
A Uh, I had no idea how long it would take. I knew it would be somewhere around there.
Q **Okay. Now, were you scheduling yourself to arrive exactly at 10:45?**
A No, I wasn't.
Q **What time were you scheduled to actually arrive there?**
A Well, they like us to be there 10 minutes early.
Q **So what time were you trying to arrive at the defendant's house in Brentwood?**
A 10:35.
Q **Now, when you were — when you were driving to the defendant's house, what kind of car — what kind of limousine were you driving?**
A Uh, it was a stretch.

Q   A stretch limousine?

A   Yes.

● ● ●

Q   So while you were driving, what route did you take to Mr. Simpson's house?

A   I took the 405 freeway north to Sunset, made a left off of Sunset going west to Rockingham, I made a right and headed up Rockingham to the residence.

Q   During your drive to the residence, sir — is that car, that limo that you were driving that night, that stretch limo, is it equipped with a cell phone?

A   Yes, it is.

Q   And is it the kind of phone that is fixed in the car or can you remove it and take it around with you?

A   It's fixed in the car.

Q   Did you receive any phone calls during your trip to Rockingham?

A   Uh, from what I remember, I received one from Dale, just —

Q   I'm sorry. Dale St. John?

A   Yes.

Q   That was your boss?

A   Yes.

Q   He called you in the car while you were en route to Rockingham?

A   Yes.

Q   All right. Do you recall what time it was when you drove — when you indicated to us just now, you turned right up onto Rockingham and drove up Rockingham, do you recall what time it was when you got to the location on Rockingham where the defendant's house was?

A   Uh, it had to have been around 9:22, 9:23.

Q   9:22?

A   No. Excuse me. 10:22, 10:23. I'm sorry.

Q   Now, how was it that you — you knew what the address was; is that correct?

A   Yes.

Q   360 North Rockingham?

A   Yes.

Q   How were you able to locate which house on Rockingham was the defendant's as you drove up Rockingham?

A   There was addresses on — painted on the curb.

Mr. Fairtlough: 62-A.

Q (By Ms. Clark): all right. Do you see the photograph that's being shown to you as people's 62-A, sir?

A Yes, I do.

Q Can you indicate to us — well, strike that. Did you locate the address on the curb that belonged to the defendant, 360, as you drove up Rockingham in that stretch limo?

A Yes.

Q And do you see the location that you noticed the address in painted on the curb in this photograph?

A Yes, I do.

Q I'm going to ask you to direct the arrow to the address you saw on the curb on June the 12th. How about a different color? Red? Tell us — tell the arrow where to go, Mr. Park.

A Uh, go down behind the bronco, back up a little bit, uh, up, there you go, right there (indicating).

Q All right. Could you put a circle around that, John? All right. So you were able to see the address on the curb there?

A Yes.

Q So at the time that you were looking at that location, the address on the curb, did you see a car parked in that location?

A No, I didn't.

Q You see that white Bronco in this photograph, sir?

A Yes.

Q Was that white Bronco there at the time you drove by at about 10:22?

A I didn't see it.

Q And you were looking at that curb; were you not?

A Yes.

Q When you saw the address on the curb, what happened next? What did you do?

A Uh, I was driving a little bit quick. So by the time I saw it, uh, I noticed that was the house and I should turn around. As I got a little bit farther, uh, I noticed another side street, Ashford.

Q And how far was that side street past the location of the curb where you saw the address?

A It's about another 40, 50 yards.

• • •

Q And is that the street that you indicated was the side street that you saw?

A Yes.

Q And when you got to that side street, what did you do?

A I turned right and drove down the street a little ways and made a u-turn and came back and parked on the opposite side of Mr. Simpson's house almost parallel to the gate with my front window.

Q   **Almost parallel to the Ashford gate?**
A   Almost, yeah.

· · ·

Q   **All right. And what happened next after you parked? What did you do?**
A   Uh, I got outside. I walked towards the back of the car, uh, had a cigarette. I got back inside the car, listened to the radio for a few minutes and then just at about 10:39, I proceeded to drive up to the driveway.

Q   **Okay. So you smoked a cigarette, listened to the radio and then got back inside?**
A   Yes.

Q   **After you got back inside, did you look at the clock again?**
A   Yes, I did. I wanted to — I wanted to make sure that I was right on my 10 minutes early.

Q   **Okay.   And you got back into the car at what time?**
A   It was around 10:39.

Q   **10:39?**
A   Yes.

Q   **And how do you know that?**
A   From looking at the clocks.

Q   **What did you do next?**
A   Uh, I started the car and drove back onto Rockingham, made a left and drove up to the Rockingham gate.

· · ·

Q   **Okay. And as you pulled down Rockingham this time going southbound on Rockingham and looked into the Rockingham gate, did you see any car, white Bronco, parked to the left of the gate as you faced it?**
A   No, I didn't.

Q   **And was that location in your field of view at the time you looked into the Rockingham gate?**
A   Yes.

Q   **What were you trying to do when you looked through — what were you trying to determine when you looked through the Rockingham gate to your left?**
A   I was just looking at the driveway and seeing how easy it would have been to pull into the driveway and if I can exit out onto Ashford. Uh, just the way the cars were parked and where the garage was, it didn't look, you know, very easy to make that turn.

· · ·

Q   **Okay ... then what did you do?**
A   Pulled — I pulled up to the Ashford gate with my bumper just about touching the — just about touching the gate and, uh, turned off my lights. I only had my parking lights on.
Q   **Okay.**

• • •

Q   **And did you see any car — any white Bronco parked to your left at — north of the Rockingham gate?**
A   No, I didn't.
Q   **I'm sorry. you did not see any —**
A   No.
Q   **— Bronco parked to the north of the Rockingham gate?**
A   No, I didn't.

• • •

Q   **When you pulled up to the Ashford gate, sir, the location shown by the green arrow, can you tell us what time it was?**
A   That was at 10:40.
Q   **And how do you know that?**
A   Because I looked at the clocks again.
Q   **I'm sorry?**
A   I looked at my watch and the clock again.
Q   **And the clock?**
A   Yeah.
Q   **You looked at your clock and your watch a lot that night.**
A   A lot.
Q   **Why is that?**
A   Because when you're a limo driver, you're set pretty much on schedules. So you're looking to see if you're on time, how long you have to get to the airport, things like that.
Q   **Now, you indicated I think that you turned off your head lights and you left only your parking lights on?**
A   Yes.
Q   **All right. At 10:40?**
A   Yes.
Q   **What happened next?**
A   That is when I got out of the car. And there is an intercom at the gate, and I was using that intercom to buzz the house. And I buzzed it and there was no answer. I proceeded to buzz it a few more times. There was still no answer. So I, uh — that's when I decided to get back in the car and, uh, call my boss' voice mail.
Q   **Okay. When you — was it something you pressed, a button you pressed?**

A   I think it was a button, yes.

Q   And when you pressed that button, could you hear a sound?

A   Yeah. It — it made a ringing or a buzzing noise.

Q   Do you remember whether it was ringing or buzzing?

A   No.

Q   Okay. But it was a sound.

A   Yes.

Q   How many times did you press the button at 10:40?

A   It was a good two or three, four times.

Q   And did you get any answer?

A   No, I didn't.

Q   So after you pressed the buzzer two or three or four times and got no answer, what happened next?

A   That's when I stepped back into the car and, uh, used the cell phone to call my boss' voice mail.

• • •

Q   I'm going to show you phone records, sir.

Ms. Clark: Your Honor, I have here a photocopy of a phone bill I'll be marking —

The Court: People's next in order is 148.

Ms. Clark: People's 148. Thank you. I'll be marking a different copy of this same for actual admission at some point.

The Court: All right.

Ms. Clark: But for now, I'll just use this Xerox if that's all right.

(People's 148 for ID = Phone bill)

Q   (By Ms. Clark): Sir, I'm directing your attention to this document in front of you and I'm going to be asking you a few questions about it.   Do you see here an entry for June the 12th, '94, the time 2205:36?

A   Yes, I do.

Q   First of all, are you familiar with military versus regular time?

A   Yes.

Q   Okay. And 2205:36, would that be 10:05 and 36 seconds p.m.?

A   Yes, it would.

Q   All right. Does that show a phone call placed to and from a given number here?

A   Yes, it does.

Q   **Okay. The number stated here for this first call at 10:05 on this bill, do you recognize that number?**

A   Do I — well, I don't recognize it, no. I know what it is, but —

Q   **What is it?**

A   That's — it's the phone number to the limousine.

Q   **Okay. The car — the phone that you had in your car?**

A   Yes.

Q   **All right. And does that reflect a call that came into you at 10:05?**

A   Yes.

Q   **Who would that be from?**

A   That would be from Dale St. John.

Q   **Your boss?**

A   Yes.

Q   **Okay. Do you see then a call at 10:43 on June the 12th?**

A   Yes, I do.

Q   **And do you recognize the phone number to which the call was placed?**

A   Yes, I do.

Q   **Whose phone number is that?**

A   That is Dale St. John's business line.

Q   **Okay.   And when you say business line, you earlier indicated to us that you placed a phone call to his pager?**

A   Yes.

Q   **Is that the same as his business line?**

A   Yes, it is.

Q   **Okay.   Now, directing your attention — okay. All right. After you placed the call to Dale St. John's pager, what did you do next?**

A   Uh, I made the call and, uh, I left the number that, uh — to call me back, and after that, I got back out of the car and proceeded to ring the intercom a few more times.

Q   **Okay. Let me ask you something, Mr. Park. When you say you left a number for him to call you back, what number did you leave? The number to what?**

A   Actually, I think I left like 911, because I never knew the phone number to the — to the limousine. I never knew what the — never knew what the number to the limousine phone was. So I couldn't leave him a number I didn't know. So I just left him 911 figuring he'd figure that out, realize I was in some kind of trouble.

Q   **And what kind of trouble were you in that you left the 911?**

A   Uh, that nobody was answering, that I didn't think anyone was home. So I wanted to find out what his instructions were from there to, uh, figure out what to do.

Q   **All right. And that was at 10:43, was it, p.m.?**

A   Yes, it was.

        • • •

Q   **All right. Now, as you were seated in the limousine speaking to your boss did you — did you say something to your boss?**

A   Yeah. I told him that I thought nobody was home.

Q   **And then what happened? Did he respond to you?**

A   Yes. He —

Q   **Did he tell you to do something?**

A   Well, he asked me to —

Q   **Okay. What did your boss tell you?**

A   Well, first he told me, he said — he said, "O.J.'s usually running a little late so hang out until about 11:15. If he is not there by then, go ahead and come on home."

Q   **Okay.**

A   He also asked — because I told him there was no lights on downstairs — he asked me to look at the pantry area, what he called a pantry area where there was what resembled some sunroofs or skylighting toward the garage area and he asked me if there was any lights on in there.

Q   **Okay.**

A   He said he usually watches TV in there.

        • • •

Q   **And did you see any lights on in that area?**

A   No, I didn't.

        • • •

Q   **At some point during your phone conversation with Dale St. John did something attract your attention?**

A   Yes. A white male walked from behind the house area on a pathway and he had a flashlight in his hand and he stopped — he stopped before he got to the driveway.

Q   **Okay.**

A   So I — I told Dale that, you know, somebody is home.

        • • •

Q   **And that person that you are describing, have you since learned what his name is?**

A   Yes.

Q   **And what is his name?**

A   Kato.

        • • •

Q **What was he doing when you saw him?**
A He was just standing there, from what I observed.

* * *

Q **Now, at the same time that you saw Kato Kaelin in the side yard, did you see anything else?**
A Yes. I saw a figure come down — well, not come down, but I saw a figure come into the entranceway of the house just about where the — where the driveway starts.

* * *

Q **Okay. Can you describe the person that you saw — was that the first point at which you saw the person? ... Can you describe what he looked like, what that person looked like.**

* * *

A Six foot, 200 pounds.
Q **(By Ms. Clark): six foot, 200 pounds?**
A All dark clothing.
Q **And could you tell anything else about this person?**
A No.
Q **Could you tell whether the person was Caucasian or African American?**
A Black.
Q **Okay. And how — in relationship to when you saw Kato Kaelin, when did you first see this person?**
A It was just — it was almost simultaneously. It was seconds after I saw him.
Q **And this six-foot 200-pound African-American person in all dark clothing, was this person moving quickly or slowly?**
A Not quickly, not slowly, a good pace walk it seemed to be.
Q **And moving in what direction, sir?**
A Into the house or toward the house.
Q **Did you form an opinion as to whether this was a male or female?**
A No.
Q **And when you saw that person, did that person walk into the entrance?**
A Yes.
Q **After that person walked into the entrance, what did you do?**
A I then proceeded to — well, I was still talking to Dale at the same time. I said "somebody's here." He said, "fine, finish the job, take him to the airport and I will see you tomorrow" or whatever. I

hung up the phone and I still waited another — it was about
another thirty seconds or so before I got out of the car, but I was
still waiting for some somebody to come open the gate. I figured
somebody was going to come open the gate for me. They still
didn't.

• • •

Q **And so you would have hung up with him at 10:55 and 12
seconds?**
A Yes.
Q **And it was within the last ten to thirty seconds of that call at
10 — of ending that call at 10:55 that you saw this six-foot
200-pound person go into the entrance?**
A Yes.

• • •

Q **And did Kato Kaelin come over to let you in?**
A No, he didn't.
Q **And did the six-foot 200-pound person dressed in all dark
clothing come to let you in?**
A No.
Q **And after thirty seconds what did you do?**
A That is when I got back up and out of the car and rang the
intercom. This time there was an answer, which was Mr. Simpson.
He told me that he overslept and he just got out of the shower and
he would be down in a minute.
Q **Okay. How many times did you have to ring the buzzer this
time before it was answered?**

• • •

A Oh, it was just — he answered it pretty much immediately.
Q **As soon as you rang?**
A Yes.

• • •

Q **(By Ms. Clark): You have seen the defendant, Mr. Park?**
A Yes.
Q **Can you tell us if that appears to be the size of the person that
you saw enter the front entrance of the house at Rockingham?**

• • •

A Yes, around the size.

Park also testified that Simpson brought five bags with him for his trip to Chicago. Park said that a high-priced Louis Vitton garment bag and golf bag were placed in the trunk, but that Simpson carried two duffel-type bags into the back seat of the limousine. He said that he also saw Simpson pick up a knapsack but did not see what happened to it. Upon arrival at the airport, Park said, he unloaded the luggage, but didn't see the knapsack. Simpson, said Park, went over to a trash container and set his gold bag on top of it.

Park also told defense attorneys that he didn't see a cut on Simpson's left hand, but admitted on redirect examination that he shook Simpson's right hand, not the left.

March 31, 1995

Charles Cale, a neighbor of Simpson's, testified that he walked his dog around the Simpson estate about 9:45 p.m. on the night of the killings, but that he did not see Simpson's Ford Bronco parked outside of the home. It was there the next morning, he said.

April 3–5, 1995

LAPD criminalist Dennis Fung began his testimony by explaining to the jury the process whereby evidence is collected, tagged, and stored.

Fung also testified about the blood stains collected from O.J. Simpson's Bronco on June 14, two days after the murders. Fung described how he collected blood stain evidence from the steering wheel, carpet, instrument panel and console.

Under cross-examination by defense attorney Barry Scheck, Fung admitted that investigators made some mistakes in gathering evidence at the murder scene which might have possibly contaminated some physical evidence. A portion of Fung's testimony, which specifically focused on a blanket removed by investigators from Nicole Brown Simpson's condominium, is reproduced below. Near the end of the exchange even Judge Ito agreed that attorney Scheck has made his point about cross-contamination of evidence.

Q **(By Mr. Scheck): The glove, the hat, the clothing of the victims, all those were important in terms of trace evidence?**

A Yes.

Q **Now, when you arrived at the crime scene, you saw that there was a blanket over the body of Nicole Brown Simpson?**

A I don't know — I don't recall being there that soon. When I got there, the body of Miss Simpson was being processed.

Q **Where — when was the first time you saw the blanket?**

A I saw the blanket when it was on the ground.

Q **It was on the ground in the area where Miss Simpson's body was?**

A   Yes.

Q   **And you came to learn in your investigation that day that the blanket had been used to cover the body?**

A   Yes.

Q   **And you came to learn that that blanket had come from the home of Nicole Brown Simpson?**

A   I did not know that.

Q   **Have you found that out?**

A   Since then, yes.

Q   **And did you make any inquiry on that day about where that blanket had come from?**

A   No, I didn't.

Q   **And would you agree, sir, that a blanket of that kind is a source of — a possible source of secondary transfer?**

A   Possibly.

Q   **And that if Mr. Simpson had been in that home and been sitting, lying on that blanket, his hairs could be in that blanket?**

Mr. Goldberg: Calls for speculation, your honor.

The Court: sustained.

Q   **(By Mr. Scheck): Well, within your expertise, is that the kind of blanket that if somebody were sitting on it, lying on it, one would expect to find hairs that they had shed on the blanket?**

Mr. Goldberg: Objection. Calls for speculation.

The Court: Sustained.

Q   **(By Mr. Scheck): Well, in your expertise as a criminalist, do you have to make judgments about different kinds of items that can be sources of possible secondary transfer?**

A   Yes.

Q   **You have to worry about such objects being brought into crime scenes?**

A   Yes.

Q   **You have to be worried about such objects being brought into crime scenes because they can be a source of contamination?**

A   Yes.

• • •

Q   **(By Mr. Scheck): Mr. Fung, again, assuming that Mr. Simpson had been in the Bundy residence and sat or laid on that** blanket, shed hairs on that blanket and that blanket is taken and put in the middle of this crime scene, could that in your expert opinion be a source of secondary transfer of his hairs to the crime scene?

A   It's possible.

Q   **Possible?**

A   Yes.

Q   **All right. And that would be what is known as contamination of the crime scene?**

A   Yes.

Q   **And if Mr. Simpson or his — any of his children or Miss Nicole Brown Simpson had been in Mr. Simpson's Ford Bronco, picked up fibers from that Bronco and at some point in time sat or lay on that blanket, there could be fibers from the Bronco on that blanket?**

A   Yes.

. . .

Q   **(By Mr. Scheck): And again, as a basis for this hypothetical, can you assume that if a dog were lying on this blanket in question or moving on this blanket in question, that dog hairs can be transferred to the blanket?**

. . .

A   Yes.

. . .

Q   **(By Mr. Scheck): All right. And the dog itself may have hairs and fibers from other people with whom it has been in contact?**

A   Yes.

Q   **That happens, right, in your judgment?**

A   It's possible.

Q   **And assuming that to be the fact, that a dog could have shed fibers and hairs on the blanket and people who had been the children of Mr. Simpson and Mr. Simpson himself and Miss Nicole Brown Simpson had been in and out of the Bronco and been on that blanket, hairs and fibers from the dog and from the Bronco could be on that blanket?**

A   It's quite a lot for me to —

Q   **Quite a lot, huh?**

A   For me to —

Q   **Assess.**

A   Yeah. There's a lot of factors in there.

Q   Yeah. I'm just asking you to — let's just assume all that occurred and those fibers are on that blanket. All right? You with me?

A   Yes.

Q   If that blanket was transferred and put right in the middle of the crime scene, there is a chance of secondary transfer of those hairs and fibers across this crime scene?

A   Yes, there is a chance.

Q   As a general principal as a criminalist, you try at all costs to avoid taking an object that could have lots of hairs and fibers on it and putting it right into the middle of a crime scene, don't you?

A   That's correct.

Q   That's a terrible mistake from the point of view of a criminalist, isn't it?

A   Yes.

Q   And it's a terrible mistake particularly when bodies are being removed and they're being dragged into the same area where that blanket was?

A   It can be, yes.

Q   Because that creates a situation where you can have cross contamination of the fibers from the blanket and it could come into contact with the clothing of Nicole Brown Simpson?

• • •

The Court: I agree terrible mistake, mistake, preference not to have been done, I think you've established the point.

Attorney Scheck also questioned the wisdom of Fung's allowing rookie criminalist Andrea Mazzola to collect most of the blood evidence taken from the scene. A sixth juror, a 38-year-old black woman named Jeanette Harris was dismissed, for failing to disclose a past history of exposure to domestic violence.

April 10, 1995

Judge Ito subpoenaed removed juror Jeanette Harris, after Harris made allegations during taped interviews with the press that jurors were discussing the case among themselves and with others, and claimed that sheriff's deputies overseeing the sequestered jury were biased in favor of white jurors.

April 11–13, 1995

The testimony of LAPD criminalist Dennis Fung resumed as defense attorney Barry Scheck challenged Fung's handling of physical evidence.

Fung denied gross mishandling of the evidence, but did concede however that some of the evidence at the crime scene had been moved to permit coroner's officers to remove the bodies. While questioning Fung, Scheck played a videotape made at the crime scene showing a bare hand holding an envelope in which prescription glasses were found next to Goldman's body. Fung denied that it was his hand in the videotape, and said that his fingerprints were not on the envelop. Fung also testified that no blood was found on the carpet in Simpson's bedroom, although investigators found a pair of blood-stained socks there.

Scheck then switched tactics to suggest that Fung lied about blood stain evidence, and insinuated that Fung participated in a plan to frame Simpson for the murders. Fung testified that detective Vannatter delivered a vial of O.J. Simpson's blood to him on June 13, one day after the murders, which Simpson had willingly provided at police headquarters. Vannatter earlier testified that he drove the blood to Simpson's estate, where Fung and Mazzola were collecting evidence, and handed it to Fung. Scheck, however, suggested that the vial of Simpson's blood was taken to Simpson's home by Fung, giving police an opportunity to plant evidence and frame Simpson. Scheck seemed to be implying that Fung was manufacturing dates related to evidence collection in an effort to protect detective Mark Fuhrman who may have planted evidence out of racist leanings.

Finally, Scheck accused Dennis Fung of intentionally destroying evidence to cover up that he lied about when he received a vial of O.J. Simpson's blood. Fung had earlier said that Detective Philip Vannatter handed him a vial of Simpson's blood at Simpson's residence on June 13, 1994. However, in a videotape played by Scheck, Fung and his assistant could be seen putting evidence in their vehicle at the Simpson estate on that date, and locking it before Vannatter arrived. Scheck used the disparity to attack Fung as a liar:

Q And when you saw these series of tapes, Mr. Fung, you realized that you had been caught in a lie, didn't you?

A No.

Q Well, you had told this jury yesterday that you carried the blood vial — blood sample either in a brown paper bag in the posse box or in your hands, correct?

A That's what I stated.

Q But when you saw the videotape, these videotapes, you realized, sir, that that — Detective Vannatter's car wasn't there when you put the brown paper bags and the posse box was put in the rear of the crime scene vehicle, correct?

A The — I — that didn't come to my attention at that time, no.

Fung then explained that he now remembered that his assistant, Andrea Mazzola, had carried the vial to the truck in a black plastic bag. Scheck attacked Fung, accusing him of engaging in a cover up, and pointing out that one page of the crime scene checklist (consisting of a total of eight notebook pages) had been replaced by Fung, and was not the original. Scheck's implication was that the notebook pages listing evidence gathered at the crime scene might have been tampered with by Fung (whose initials were on the replaced page) in order to allow investigators to substitute tampered evidence for original evidence.

When attorney Scheck finished his cross-examination, prosecutor Hank Goldberg, began a re-direct examination of Fung by asking whether Fung had participated in a conspiracy to frame Simpson. Fung said he did not, and explained that his lost notes were later recovered:

Q **(By Mr. Goldberg): Were you involved in some kind of a conspiracy with Andrea Mazzola to cover up receiving some item with your bare hands?**

A No.

Q **Were you involved in any conspiracy with detective Vannatter to allow him to keep a vial overnight so that you could do with it what he pleased?**

A No.

Q **Or with Detective Lange to allow him into the evidence processing room so that he could somehow maybe take the defendant's shoes and in some way get any DNA that might be on them on the swatches and the controls?**

Mr. Scheck: Objection, your Honor.

The Court: Grounds?

Mr. Scheck: This is leading, compound, speculative.

The Court: Sustained on the leading ground.

Q **(By Mr. Goldberg): Were you involved in any conspiracy whatsoever with Mr. Lange to allow him into an evidence processing room?**

A No.

Mr. Scheck: Objection, leading.

The Court: Overruled.

Q **(By Mr. Goldberg): Or would anyone in this case, Mr. Fung?**

A Nobody.

Q Now, Mr. Fung, do you recall that on cross-examination an issue came up as to one of the pages from the crime scene identification checklist, the original of which was missing?

A Yes.

Q And do you happen to have a Xerox copy of that page now?

A No.

Q Not the original, but a Xerox?

. . .

A I don't have one, no.

Q (By Mr. Goldberg): And did you find the original of that document?

A Yes, I did.

Q How did you do that?

A I opened up my notebook and examined that page and it was there.

Q Now, there are two notebooks that are sort of similar that you have seen. One is the notebook that I am holding in my hand; is that correct?

A Yes.

Q And then you have a notebook in front of you?

A Yes.

Mr. Goldberg: For the record, your honor, these are blue notebooks about an inch thick or so.

The Court: Appear to be.

Q (By Mr. Goldberg): Is your notebook your own personal notes that you maintained?

A Yes.

Q Okay. So you found the original of that document that was missing in your notebook.

A Yes.

April 17–18, 1995

Prosecutor Hank Goldberg continued a redirect examination of criminalist Dennis Fung in an effort to discredit defense accusations that Fung lied about when he received a vial of Simpson's blood in support of a police cover-up.

April 19, 1995

Judge Ito spent the day individually interviewing jurors about allegations made by former juror Jeanette Harris that jurors were discussing the case and that Sheriff's deputies were racially biased in their handling of jurors.

April 20, 1995

LAPD criminalist Andrea Mazzola was called to the stand. Prosecutor Hank Goldberg questioned her about her qualifications, and she described herself as a trainee. Mazzola was then called upon to support Fung's testimony that he received a vial of blood at Simpson's house. Although she said she couldn't remember the exact sequence of events, she agreed that Fung's version of things must have been correct. During cross-examination, defense lawyer Peter Neufeld attacked Mazzola's credentials and had her admit that she was still a probationary employee when she gathered evidence at the crime scene.

Judge Ito ordered that three Sheriff's deputies be replaced, and that others be assigned to oversee the jury. Los Angeles County Sheriff Sherman Block complained to the press that the judge improperly released the deputies without interviewing them. Also, a 25-year-old black female juror asked the judge to excuse her from continued duty, saying, "I can't take it any more."

April 21–24

A jury protest erupted over Judge Ito's dismissal of three deputies with 13 of the 12 jurors and six alternates refusing to board a bus to take them to court. The jurors sent Ito a note asking him to come to their hotel for a conference. Ito refused to come, and the jurors came to courthouse dressed in black clothing as a sign of protest. Ito held a series of meetings with some of the jurors in his chambers.

April 25, 1995

Testimony resumed with criminalist Andrea Mazzola facing cross-examination by defense attorney Peter Neufeld. Mazzola said she had been responsible for collecting most of the blood from both crime scenes, and said that Fung supervised her only part of the time. Her version of events differed from Fung's, who said earlier that he had gathered most of the evidence — although she agreed that the two had worked as a team. Neufeld played a videotape showing Mazzola at the crime scene behaving in ways which seemed unprofessional — dropping cotton swabs, brushing her hand on her dirty knee, and wiping a pair of tweezers with a dirty hand. Neufeld also got Mazzola to admit that she used the same cotton swab on different blood stains in the Ford Bronco, even though her training required her to use separate swabs. Like other police officers who testified, Mazzola denied that investigators or anyone in the crime lab altered evidence in an effort to frame Simpson.

April 26, 1995

Without the jury present, Judge Ito admonished lawyers for both sides, telling them to move more quickly and to be less argumentative. He estimated that he had already sustained 1,000 objections for argumentative questions.

Criminalist Andrea Mazzola underwent a third day of cross-examination by defense attorney Peter Neufeld. Neufeld continued to describe Mazzola as an inexperienced investigator and hammered away at Mazzola's forgetfulness concerning a vial of blood supposedly taken from Simpson on the day following the murders. Although Dennis Fung had testified that Mazzola had carried the blood out of Simpson's home in a plastic bag, she denied knowing that she had had the blood in her possession. She said she may have looked away at the time she was handed evidence, she said, not realizing that it was a vial of blood. That comment prompted this exchange between attorney Neufeld and criminalist Mazzola:

Q Now, in your current memory of what transpired back at Mr. Simpson's house, after you left Mr. — Mr. Fung's side, where did you go?

A I went into the living room.

Q And was this after about, what, five or ten minutes standing in the foyer with Mr. Fung?

A I don't recall where I was standing with Mr. Fung and I don't recall how long.

Q Well, you said that you first came into the house and on the way in you picked up item 16, right?

A Correct.

Q And then a couple of minutes later, a few minutes later, Mr. Fung picked up item 15; isn't that right?

A Correct.

Q And then you were standing in the foyer with Mr. Fung and with other detectives; isn't that right?

A I do not believe that we were standing in the foyer. It could have been in the kitchen. I don't recall.

Q Standing there with other — other detectives?

A Correct.

Q And during those minutes that you were standing there, you asked if someone could get you a trash bag to put items in?

A I believe Mr. Fung and others went looking for a bag.

Q And then someone brought a bag back for you?

A Correct.

Q And you put the items 15 and 16 into that bag?

A Correct.

Q And did you also put the cards, those number — those photo i.d. cards back into the bag at that point?

A Yes.

Q You put them in?

A Yes.

Q **And you held that bag?**

A Yes.

Q **And then you walked into the living room to sit down?**

A At some point, yes.

Q **And didn't you take that bag with you when you went to sit down?**

A I don't believe I had the bag at my side when I went to sit down.

Q **Why did you give up the bag, ma'am?**

A There was no reason to carry it with me.

Q **What did you do? Did you put it on the floor?**

A I believe I had put it out where we had our kits previously in the foyer.

Q **Where were your kits?**

A In the foyer.

Q **And you simply left this bag with evidence in it with the kits in the foyer?**

A The kit was not there, but that is where we had the kit before and the area was secured.

Q **And you simply left it there and walked into the living room?**

A Yes.

Q **And after you went into the living room you then sat down on the couch?**

A I sat down, yes.

Q **And as you sit here today, ma'am, you have — do you have an independent recollection of your eyes being closed while you are sitting in that living room couch?**

A I believe they were closed for partial — bit of time.

Q **Miss Mazzola, did you invent this notion that your eyes were closed so that Mr. Fung could testify that he received the vial without you seeing it?**

Mr. Goldberg: Argumentative.

The Court: Sustained.

Mazzola also testified under cross-examination by attorney Neufeld that she didn't have an "independent recollection" of picking up two crucial items of evidence at the murder scene: a glove and ski cap. "Yet, you have an independent recollection that while you were sitting on a couch you closed your eyes? You had that recollection ten months later?" asked Neufeld. "Yes," Mazzola replied.

Prosecutor Hank Goldberg began a redirect examination, asking criminalist Mazzola if she was involved in a conspiracy to frame Simpson. Mazzola responded by saying that she was not part of such a conspiracy, and that she didn't even know who Simpson was when she and Fung start collecting evidence on the night of the murders. Part of the re-direct went like this:

Q   When you arrived at the Rockingham location had you ever heard of someone named Orenthal Simpson commonly known as O.J. Simpson?

A   At that morning it did not ring a bell in my mind.

Q   You didn't have any conception that there was a sports figure or a television personality or movie personality that went by that name when you arrived at the scene?

Mr. Neufeld: Objection, leading.

The Court: Sustained.

Q   (By Mr. Goldberg): Had you any conception of that when you arrived at the scene?

A   No.

Q   When did you first become aware that Orenthal Simpson was someone of public notoriety?

A   Mr. Fung, after he was done with the detectives, he came and kept saying, "O.J.'s house, it is Mr. Simpson's house." And I said, "O.J. Who?" And he said, "movies, sports," and it just did not ring a bell.

April 27, 1995

Deputy District Attorney Hank Goldberg continued the redirect examination of Andrea Mazzola, attempting to show that she was a competent criminalist who had no reason to want to frame Simpson.

In a recross-examination, defense attorney Peter Neufeld attempted to demonstrate that Mazzola may have been involved in covering-up mistakes made by criminalist Dennis Fung. Neufeld reminded Mazzola that during a pretrial hearing she has said that she had initialed all of the envelopes and containers used to preserve blood samples taken from the crime scene. He then asked Mazzola to look at all the evidence, whereupon she was unable to find her initials on any of it. Neufeld asked Mazzola when she discovered that her initials were not on the sealed evidence. She said she first noticed it when she walked through the serology laboratory and saw the evidence lying on a table. "Did you realize that if the prosecutors could not produce the original bindles, that that would be devastating," Neufeld asked. Immediately after the question was raised Judge Ito sustained an objection from the prosecution and Neufeld ceased questioning Mazzola.

May 1, 1995

Gregory Matheson, chief forensic chemist in the LAPD crime laboratory was called to testify by prosecutor Hank Goldberg. Matheson testified that, from a scientific point of view, it doesn't matter which criminalist gathers evidence at a crime scene as long as they follow established guidelines for evidence collection. Matheson responded to Goldberg's questions about the previously shown video of an apparently sloppy Mazzola gathering evidence by saying that while Mazzola may have done a few sloppy things, she didn't do anything which would have necessarily contaminated the evidence she collected, nor did she do anything which would have made the results of the analysis of the evidence she collected unreliable.

A black female flight attendant serving as a juror, who had asked Judge Ito to remove her from the jury was sent home. She was replaced by a 28-year-old female Hispanic real estate appraiser.

May 2–4, 1995

Gregory Matheson continued his testimony, telling the jury that a blood sample taken from a bloody trail near the murders was consistent with O.J. Simpson's blood type. The blood was found next to a trail of bloody shoeprints found leaving the murder scene. Simpson, said Matheson, has a rare blood type — consistent with only 0.5 percent of the population — or 1 person in every 200. Blood found on a glove at the crime scene matched that of Ronald Goldman, said Matheson, while Nicole Brown Simpson's blood type was found on the front gate to her home. Matheson said the type of blood analysis he performed was conventional, and did not involve DNA testing. It's purpose, he explained, was not to positively identify a killer, but to eliminate suspects. Matheson also testified that the blood found under Nicole Brown Simpson's fingernails was very likely hers.

During cross-examination of Matheson, defense attorney Robert Blaiser forced the admission that some important evidence may possibly have been mishandled. Matheson said that criminalist Andrea Mazzola did not follow guidelines when she wrongly used the same cotton swatch on several blood samples in Simpson's Bronco. She also made an error in rolling some of the carpet in the vehicle, because blood from one part of the carpet may have then spread to other parts. Even so, Matheson said, the mistakes made by Mazzola were merely technicalities and did not effect the crime lab's ability to work with the evidence, nor did they negatively impact the integrity of the evidence.

Blaiser also showed Matheson several scientific articles describing the process by which type BA blood may appear to degrade into type B. Matheson agreed that blood samples taken from beneath Nicole Brown Simpson's fingertips could have come from someone other than O.J. Simpson. Blaiser also tried to show that a small amount of sample blood taken from O.J. Simpson — 1.5 milliliters from a total sample of 6.5 milliliters — could not be accounted for, and could have been used as part of a conspiracy to plant evidence and frame Simpson. Matheson responded by saying that the sample taken from Simpson was used for comparison purposes, that some may have been consumed during the testing process that wasn't accounted for, and the crime laboratory didn't keep a strict accounting of how much was used or discarded. Finally, Blaiser attempted to get Matheson to admit that a preservative known as "EDTA" may have been present in some of the blood samples taken from the crime scene — suggesting that the blood had come from the Simpson sample, and adding weight to the suggestion that it had been planted. On redirect examination prosecutor Hank Goldberg allowed Matheson to describe the different ways in which type BA blood could degrade into type B — demonstrating, once again, that the blood under Nicole Brown Simpson's fingernails could have been hers.

Matheson responded to questions about the defense's claim of missing blood by saying that some of the blood may have adhered to pipettes, gloves, and other laboratory instruments. Tests he conducted after the issue arose, said Matheson, showed 0.5 milliliters of blood adhering to test instruments under stimulated laboratory conditions. Repeated tests, said Matheson, may have used more of the blood.

May 8, 1995

DNA expert Dr. Robin Cotton director of Cellmark Diagnostics's laboratory in Germantown, Maryland, was led by prosecutors to describe the process known as "DNA fingerprinting." DNA fingerprinting, explained Cotton, used genetic residue left at a crime, such as blood and semen, to determine who may have been there. Since the DNA of each person is different (except in the case of identical twins), there is very little chance for erroneous identification when tests are properly conducted. Cotton described a process known as "RFLP," or Restriction Fragment Link Polymorphism, which, she said, is the most accurate method available for the testing of DNA. Cotton also explained that the degradation of blood would not change its DNA characteristics.

May 9–12, 1995

Much of the day was spent in discussions between attorneys and the judge outside of the presence of the jury. Near the close of the day, however, the testimony of Dr. Cotton resumed and jurors saw x-ray pictures, called "autorads," of DNA fragments from O.J. Simpson and the two murder victims. Cotton, director of Cellmark Diagnostics' laboratory in Germantown, Maryland, showed how DNA test results directly linked O.J. Simpson to the murder scene. Cotton said that DNA testing showed a near-perfect genetic match between Simpson's blood and blood stains found near the bodies of the two murder victims. Cotton also testified that a small blood stain on a sock found by police in Simpson's bedroom must have come from Nicole Brown Simpson. Cotton said that DNA patterns found in a blood spot at the crime scene showed almost conclusively that *the blood had come from O.J. Simpson. Cotton estimated the odds that blood found at the scene of the crime could have come from anyone other than Simpson were about one in 170 million. Odds that the blood found on the sock at the base of Simpson's bed could have come from anyone other than Nicole Brown Simpson, said Cotton, were approximately one in 9.7 billion. Such statistics, Cotton testified, were calculated from previous DNA experimentation conducted by Cellmark Diagnostics.*

Defense attorney Peter Neufeld challenged Cellmark's statistical estimates, saying that it had used only a limited number of DNA samples taken from a few hundred people in Detroit. Neufeld got Cotton to admit that some of the evidence collection techniques employed by the police were not ones she would have chosen.

May 16–22, 1995

Gary Sims, senior criminalist with the California Department of Justice's DNA laboratory, testified that DNA testing showed that blood taken from the glove found on Simpson's estate matched Ron Goldman's blood. Sims also told jurors that blood found on the ankle area of socks in O.J. Simpson's bedroom showed genetic matches to the blood of Nicole Brown Simpson. The chance that it had come from someone other than Nicole Brown Simpson, said Sims, was around 1 in 21 billion. Other blood, found in the toe area of one of the socks, was consistent with O.J. Simpson's. Another analysis, said Sims, showed that blood matching Simpson's and the two victims was found inside the Bronco. The glove found on Simpson's property, said Sims, was soaked with the blood of Simpson and both victims.

During cross-examination, defense lawyer Barry Scheck pointed out that if the blood in question had been contaminated, Sims would have had no way of knowing it. "Do you know from your own personal knowledge how and when that blood got on the sock," Scheck asked. "No," said Sims.

May 24, 1995

Prosecution witness, Collin Yamauchi, testified about further DNA matches, adding that when he performed the first tests he had heard from the radio that Simpson had an "airtight alibi" — that "he's in Chicago."

May 25, 1995

Another juror, a 38-year-old white woman, was removed from the case.

May 30–31 1995

Defense attorney Barry Scheck cross-examined police criminalist Collin Yamauchi, trying to show that Yamauchi did not handle proper procedure during evidence collection — leading to the possibility that evidence may have been contaminated. Scheck was able to show that Yamauchi had not changed his gloves when handling different pieces of evidence, and got Yamauchi to admit that he did not see initially see blood spots on the dark socks found in O.J. Simpson's bedroom. Yamauchi also conceded that he had inadvertently gotten some of Simpson's blood on his plastic glove before handling the leather glove found on Simpson's property. Yamauchi testified that he wrote his initials on the glove being used as evidence, gripping the glove by wrist area — the only spot where Simpson's blood was found on the glove.

Under redirect examination by prosecutor Rockne Harmon, Yamauchi denied being part of a police conspiracy to frame Simpson.

June 5, 1995

Two more jurors were dismissed. One was a 28-year-old female real estate appraiser, and the other was a 54-year-old male postal operations manager.

June 6–13, 1995

Los Angeles County Coroner Lakshmanan Sathyavagiswaran, who had originally taken the stand on June 2, offered detailed testimony about the manner in which of Nicole Brown Simpson and Ronald Goldman had been killed. Grisly autopsy and crime scene photographs were shown to the jury. One photo of Nicole Brown Simpson showed a gaping neck wound — a slash so deep that it exposed her spinal chord. When asked by prosecutors, Dr. Sathyavagiswaran demonstrated the way in which Nicole Brown Simpson had been killed, grabbing prosecutor Brian Kelberg's hair, pulling his head back, and running a ruler across his throat. Sathyavagiswaran testified that a contusion on Nicole Brown Simpson's brain indicated that she had been beaten unconscious, and was probably face down on the ground when her throat was slit, causing her to rapidly bleed to death. A lack of significant amounts of blood in her air-pipe and lungs caused him to conclude that she was in the face-down position when she died.

As Nicole Brown Simpson lay unconscious on the ground, her attacker most likely turned on Ronald Goldman and killed him, Dr. Sathyavagiswaran testified. She was killed after Goldman died, theorized Sathyavagiswaran.

Sathyavagiswaran also said that he believed the killer taunted Goldman, holding him from behind as he lightly ran the knife across his throat before making the deep cut that severed Goldman's jugular vein and damaged his aorta.

Sathyavagiswaran described what appeared to be "defensive wounds" on Goldman's hands, saying that they were probably not caused by a fight with his assailant, but were more likely caused by Goldman's *open hands flailing about as he was held from behind, or as he attempted to flee from his attacker. His hands appear to have hit a tree, a gate or some other hard surface.*

Sathyavagiswaran concluded that Goldman died from any one of four wounds which would have been fatal: two slashes in the chest that punched through ribs and punctured Goldman's lung, and a separate stab injury which hit the aorta, and a sliced throat. It appeared, said Sathyavagiswaran that Goldman's attacker poked him in the face at least four, or five times with the knife to be sure he was dead.

June 14, 1995

Defense attorney Robert Shapiro sounding almost mocking during the cross-examination of Dr. Sathyavagiswaran, saying that the coroner had really established only four facts during eight days of testimony: Those facts, according to Shapiro, were: 1.) Nicole Brown Simpson and Ronald Goldman were murdered, 2.) the wounds were caused by a knife or other sharp instrument, 3.) the victims' throats were cut, and 4.) they both bled to death. Shapiro got Dr. Sathyavagiswaran to conceded that he could not say, with certainty, how many killers had been present, nor whether only one single-edged knife was used in the attacks.

June 15–16, 1995

During a dramatic moment in the trial, prosecutors asked O.J. Simpson to put on the gloves which they claimed he wore while committing the murders. Simpson, who had first put on latex gloves, stood before the jury and struggled to put the gloves on. His facial expressions gave a clear indication to the jury of the struggle he made. Prosecutors were quick to declare that Simpson was acting for the jury, and the extra-large gloves should have fit hands his size. Richard Rubin, a well-known glove designer for Isotoner, was then called to testify that wet leather gloves will shrink when dried. Also, in continuing efforts to overcome the apparent fiasco caused by the gloves not fitting Simpson, prosecutors questioned a saleswoman from New York's Bloomingdale's department store, who testified that Nicole Brown Simpson bought two pairs of extra-large Isotoners in January of 1990. During cross-examination by, Johnnie Cochran, however, Rubin admitted that the small amount of blood absorbed by the gloves (estimated to have been about 3 cubic centimeters) should not have caused noticeable shrinkage.

June 19, 1995

FBI expert William Bodziak testified that prints from expensive Italian shoes found at the crime scene showed that the person who killed Nicole Brown Simpson and Ronald Goldman wore shoes that would fit O.J. Simpson. The prints, said Bodziak, were left by size 12 Bruno Magli *shoes which sell for around $160. Such shoes are very rare in the United States, said Bodziak, who testified that he had to make a trip to Italy to properly identify the shoes in question. Only 12 pairs of Bruno Magli shoes in that size had been sold in the United States, said Bodziak.*

During cross-examination F. Lee Bailey pointed out that anyone wearing size 12 shoes might have left the questionable footprints. Bailey also suggested that a killer may have worn overly-large shoes to confuse investigators. Bodziak discounted the contention, however, saying that shoes which are too large would have caused the killer to stumble — something for which no footprint evidence was found.

June 21, 1995

Prosecutors once again asked O.J. Simpson to try on a pair of Aris Isotoner gloves. The new gloves were the same size as the gloves entered into evidence, and seemed to fit Simpson's hands perfectly.

Telephone company witnesses were called to discuss records showing that Simpson made cellular phone calls on the afternoon of the murders. The calls included: 1.) a 3 minute call to Nicole Brown Simpson at 2:18, 2.) two unanswered calls to girlfriend Paula Barbieri's Florida number at 2:22, 3.) a 2:23 unanswered call to Barbieri's Los Angeles number 4.) a 2:24 unanswered call to Barbieri's Florida number, and 5.) two calls at 10:03 p.m. to Barbieri's Florida number, and another to her Los Angeles number — both of which went unanswered.

June 26, 1995

During cross-examination by defense attorney Peter Neufeld genetic statistician Bruce Weir questioned whether the large probabilities of DNA matching alluded to earlier by personnel from by Cellmark Diagnostics and the California Department of Justice laboratory were accurate. Neufeld suggested that while investigators should have used a representative sample, they had instead used what he termed "convenient samples."

June 27–28, 1995

Winding up its case on physical evidence, the prosecution solicited testimony from Susan Brockbank, a police department expert in the trace analysis of hairs and fibers. Brockbank testified that she had collected hair and fiber evidence from the bloody glove found at the crime scene and from the victims' clothing and a blue knit cap found at the crime scene. Then, said Brockbank, she collected 93 hairs from Simpson for comparison purposes.

June 29–30, 1995

FBI evidence expert Doug Deedrick testified that hairs very similar to O.J. Simpson's were found on the knit cap found at the murder scene.

Deedrick also said that hair similar to that of Nicole Brown Simpson was found on both bloody gloves. Hairs similar to Goldman's were on the glove found on the walkway at Simpson's home, while hairs similar to Simpson's head hair were found on Goldman's shirt.

July 5, 1995

Defense attorney F. Lee Bailey attacked Deedrick's expertise, claiming that he was a poorly qualified witness because he is not a member of any relevant professional societies, and has written only a few articles about forensic science.

July 6, 1995

Cross-examination of Doug Deedrick concluded, with F. Lee Bailey getting the FBI expert to admit that no hair from the victims had been found in Simpson's Bronco, none of Nicole Brown Simpson's or Ron Goldman's hair had been found on the bloody socks discovered in Simpson's bedroom. Bailey also raised what some called the "dandruff defense," showing that while Simpson appeared to have dandruff when examined in jail, no dandruff had been found on any African-American-like hairs taken from the evidence. On re-direct examination by Marcia Clark, Deedrick said that Simpson's hair is very unusual, and that it had the same characteristics as hairs found on the knit cap at the crime scene and on Goldman's shirt.

As cross-examination concluded, the prosecution rested its case. In total, it had called 58 witnesses and presented 488 exhibits.

July 7, 1995

The defense made, and Judge Ito rejected, a routine motion to dismiss the case against Simpson for lack of evidence.

Chapter 4
Presentation of Evidence:
Witnesses for the Defense

North Carolina screenwriter, Laura Hart McKinny, testifying for the defense.   Photo: AP/Wide World Photos.

INTRODUCTION

In a criminal trial, after the prosecution rests it's case, the defense is given an opportunity to present evidence. Defense strategy dictates which witnesses will be called to testify, and what kinds of questions they will be asked. Strategies commonly used include defenses based upon alibi, insanity (whereby a defendant admits to committing the offense, but claims that he or she should not be held responsible by reason of insanity), self-defense, duress (where a person was forced to do something), and entrapment (wherein it is claimed that the police actually instigated the crime, not the person charged with it). Other strategies may also be employed, and a number of innovative defense claims — previously unheard of — have become common in recent years. Some of these include 1.) black rage (suggested in the case of Colin Ferguson, the man convicted of killing 6 and wounding 19 others in a December 1993 shooting on the Long Island Railroad), 2.) urban survival syndrome (a kind of predilection to engage in violence in order to prevent oneself from being victimized), and 3.) defense against abuse (in which the person being abused kills or otherwise injures their tormentor). In the murder trial of O.J. Simpson, multiple defense strategies were discernible. They included 1.) outright police fraud predicated upon racism, under which it was claimed that some police officers investigating the case were biased against blacks, and against Simpson in particular, and may have planted evidence to make it look as though Simpson was the killer, 2.) alibi, wherein it was claimed that the time of the murders could not be conclusively established, and that Simpson's whereabouts could be accounted for most of the time, 3.) the claim that Simpson was not in the physical condition needed to commit the murders, 4.) the claim that the killings were perpetrated by drug "enforcers" who had targeted Faye Resnick, a friend of Nicole Brown Simpson's, an admitted drug user — possibly killing Nicole Brown Simpson and Ronald Goldman by mistake, 5). claims of seriously compromised and contaminated evidence, and 6.) a two-killer theory.

In most cases where multiple defenses are offered jurors may become confused and therefore tend to discount all defense claims — especially when multiple explanations make it seem that defense attorneys are grasping at straws instead of adhering to one supportable position.

As the defense presents its witnesses, the prosecution has the opportunity to cross-examine each one. Defendants, however, under the Fifth Amendment, have a constitutional right not to testify, and are usually called to testify (if at all) only by their own lawyers. If a defendant chooses not to testify, prosecuting attorneys may not allude to that fact in their closing arguments to the jury, since doing so would tend to imply guilt. At the close of the Simpson trial, defense attorneys, after much apparent consternation, decided not to call O.J. Simpson to the stand — apparently fearing that cross-examination by prosecutors would harm their case.

THE DEFENSE CASE BEGINS

July 10, 1995

The defense began presenting its case. Three Simpson family members and two close friends took the stand, one after the other, to testify that

O.J. Simpson was acting normally prior to hearing of the killings, but became distraught and grief stricken after learning of the death of his former wife. Testifying were 1.) Simpson's 26-year-old daughter, Arnelle, 2.) his sister, Carmelita Simpson-Durio, 3.) Simpson's 73-year-old mother, Eunice, 4.) Carol Conner, a songwriter and long-time Simpson friend, and 5.) Mary Collins, Simpson's interior designer who had met with him on the day of the killings.

During cross-examination, prosecutor Marcia Clark made it clear that none of Simpson's family members could account for his whereabouts at the time of the murders.

July 11, 1995

Dan Mandel and Ellen Aaronson, who had been out on their first date on the night of the murders, and who had strolled past Nicole Brown Simpson's home at about 10:30 p.m. that evening, testified that they saw and heard nothing unusual. A third defense witness, and neighbor of Nicole Brown Simpson, Robert Heidstra, testified that as he was walking his dogs on the night of the murders he heard two men arguing around 10:40 p.m. near Nicole Brown Simpson's condominium. Portions of Heidstra's testimony follow:

Q (By Johnnie Cochran): When you left your residence, can you tell the court and jury on which — which direction did you go to walk these dogs that night, that is, June 12th of 1994?

A Oh, yes. At 10:15 I left and I went toward Westgate.

Q Okay.

A Toward Westgate about a couple of buildings from my place.

Q All right. ... What did do you when you got to Westgate?

A I turned north on Westgate, a block north on Westgate.

Q And then did you proceed down Westgate?

A No, no, I turned west on Gorham.

Q All right. You went north on Westgate to Gorham?

A Yeah.

Q And you —

A One block.

Q You turned west on Gorham?

A Yeah.

Q All right. As you proceeded down Gorham, in which direction on Gorham did you come?

A I went west — I went west on Gorham.

Q All right.

A A long block. A long block.

Q That is a long block?

A Very long, yeah.

Q Does Gorham ultimately run into Bundy?

A   Yeah.

Q   **Did you come down to Bundy?**

A   Yeah. Well, I went almost into Bundy. It is a big curve there that comes together with Gorham.

Q   **All right. And when you got — what happened before you got to that curve, if anything?**

A   Nothing. Very quiet. Very quiet at night.

Q   **It was very quiet at that point?**

A   Yeah, no problem.

Q   **Before I ask you to look at a diagram, did you ultimately go down Bundy or any street parallel to Bundy?**

A   No. I stopped at Bundy.

Q   **All right. And then which way did you go at that point?**

A   Then I stopped because I heard all of a sudden from nowhere Akita barking like crazy hell broke loose with the Akita.

· · ·

Q   **Can you tell us about what time it was, sir?**

A   Oh, it takes me about twenty minutes to get down there, so from 10:15, 10:30, 10:35.

· · ·

Q   **And now, when you got to that point did you see anything at that point when it is 10:35 and you are at Bundy and Gorham?**

A   Nothing.

Q   **All right. now, you are still walking your dogs?**

A   Right.

Q   **Do you have the dogs — are they on a leash of any kind?**

A   Yeah, one is on a leash, the older one. Another one is always next to me loose.

Q   **All right. He is loose at that point?**

A   Yeah.

Q   **Okay. When you got to that location — which is kind of a fork in the road at Bundy and Gorham?**

A   Uh-huh.

Q   **Tell us then what happens at that point? Which direction did you go at that point?**

A   I stopped here because the Akita all of a sudden started to bark like crazy.

· · ·

Q   **Now, you walked this route many nights, have you?**

A   Hundreds of times.

Q   **How many times?**

A   Hundreds of times in the years.

• • •

Q   **(By Mr. Cochran): Was there an Akita who lived somewhere in that neighborhood?**
A   I have seen him before there behind the gate.
Q   **At what residence did the Akita live?**
A   That is the Akita from Nicole's condo.
Q   **The Akita at Nicole's condo?**
A   Yeah, right.
Q   **Nicole Brown Simpson's condo?**
A   Yeah, right.
Q   **You heard this Akita start to bark?**
A   Oh, yeah, hysterically panicking.
Q   **And you heard that at about 10:35?**
A   10:35, right.
Q   **Prior to that had you heard that Akita dog barking that night?**
A   No, not at all.
Q   **And at that point you were at the intersection of Bundy and Gorham when you heard that sound?**
A   Yeah.
Q   **Is that right?**
A   Yeah.
Q   **All right. When you heard that sound what, if anything, did you do?**
A   Well, I was a little confused, what is going on there, and I was afraid more for my dogs because the Akita is a big dog and they are pretty protective, so I didn't want to go further with my dogs into Bundy.
Q   **All right.**
A   So I —
Q   **Let me ask you this: in your normal route would you ever walk down Bundy?**
A   Oh, yes, I would have gone around the block and come back to Dorothy.
Q   **All right. But after you heard this noise with the Akita, which direction did you go?**
A   I stopped immediately and turned around with my dogs. Like I said, I was afraid for my dogs.
Q   **All right. When you turned around with your dogs where did you go?**
A   Well, I decided I didn't want to go back the same way Gorham where I came from.
Q   **So where did you go?**

A   So I stopped parallel to Nicole's condo, there is houses on the other side and there is an alley.

Q   **All right. There is an alleyway?**

A   Alleyway, yeah.

. . .

Q   **Show us, if you can, on this photograph, the right side where you were and the approximate area where you were.**

A   It must have been down here, (indicating).

Q   **All right. So you are at an area off the aerial photograph; is that correct?**

A   Yeah, right.

Q   **To the right?**

A   Yeah, here, (indicating).

Q   **You told us because of the fear for your dog you then took another route and talked about an alleyway; is that correct?**

A   Exactly, yeah.

Q   **Now, can you point out on this exhibit for the jury the alleyway that you decided to take down?**

A   (indicating).

Q   **All right.**

A   It is here, here, (indicating).

Mr. Cochran: Your Honor, the witness is referring to an alleyway that apparently runs parallel to Bundy.

Q   **Is that correct?**

A   Exactly.

The Court: Yes, it is. The foreground of the photograph to the right on Defense 1239.

Mr. Cochran: Thank you, your Honor.

Q   **And that is the route that you started to take, that route?**

A   Exactly, yeah.

. . .

Q   **Now, so that we are clear, Nicole Brown Simpson's condo, if you can point to it again, and show us approximately where you believe it is?**

A   There, (indicating).

Mr. Cochran: All right. He is pointing to a residence on the west side of Bundy, your Honor, and he is pointing to it on Defendant's 1239.

The Court: Yes. It appears to be the residence that is just to the south of the parked car that is to the left of Bundy on the west side of that street.

Mr. Cochran: Thank you, your Honor.

· · ·

Q **I think the court reporter is having trouble. You said the sound didn't bother your dogs, thank God?**
A They didn't bark back when they heard the Akita.
Q **Your dogs didn't bark?**
A No, they were quiet.
Q **After your dogs didn't bark, what did you do then, sir?**
A I decided to turn around and not go any further there.
Q **In which direction did you go at that point?**

The Court: Counsel, I think we have already gone through this. He has already gotten to the point where he was going in the alley.

Mr. Cochran: I'm trying get back in the alley, yes.

Q **You are going down the alley; is that correct?**
A I went up in the alley there to high level ground.
Q **In the alley, you are now going at that point southbound in the alley; is that right?**
A Yeah, right.
Q **All right. And as you go southbound in the alley, do you go a distance and do you hear something else at some point?**
A Well, I — the Akita never stopped barking. It was hysterical barking all the time and never stopped until I reached the middle of the alley.
Q **All right.**
A In the middle.
Q **Okay. Show us about where you were, the middle of the alley. Point to that.**
A Yeah. Just opposite Nicole's. It is about the middle here, (indicating).
Q **All right.**
A Opposite Nicole's condo.
Q **Okay. When you say "Nicole" you are talking about Nicole Brown Simpson, right?**
A Yeah.

Mr. Cochran: So your Honor, what he has done is drawn a line basically I guess perpendicular to where he believes the condo is toward the alleyway.

The Court: Yes.

Q **(By Mr. Cochran): And when you get to that location in the alley — which you say is about halfway through the alley?**
A   Yeah, in the middle of the alley.
Q **Middle of the alley?**
A   Yeah.
Q **What happens at that point?**
A   Well, I stood there listening to the commotion of the dog, the Akita.
Q **All right.**
A   For a minute or so, more than a minute, and I heard also another dog started to bark, a little black dog that the lady has in the alley. The dog started to bark.
Q **A second dog starts barking?**
A   Oh, yeah. Crazy, too.
Q **All right. Now, where is the — if you can show us, the little black dog that starts to bark, where does that dog live?**
A   This one live in this house here, (indicating). This here, (indicating).

Mr. Cochran: Your Honor, again he is pointing to a house.

The Witness: This house, (indicating).

The Court: Appears to be the house that is across the street from Nicole Brown Simpson's condo?

The Witness: Yeah, exactly.

Q **(By Mr. Cochran): That is the house that is —**

The Court: On the east side of Bundy.

Mr. Cochran: East side of Bundy.

Q **It is right near the area where you stopped in the alley?**
A   Exactly.
Q **You see this little black dog at that point?**
A   I didn't see him, no, but I heard him bark.
Q **You knew this dog from before?**
A   I have seen him before.

Q You now hear two dogs barking, right, from that location?
A Like crazy.
Q **Your dogs weren't barking?**
A No, no, they were alert but not barking.
Q **They what?**
A Alert.
Q **What time is it by this time now when you now hear at least two dogs barking? Give us your time, the best time that you —**
A Around 10:40 or something.
Q **About 10:40 P.M.?**
A Yeah.
Q **All right. And at that point you are in the alley and it is 10:40 on June 12th, 1994. What happens next?**
A Well, like I said, I was listening to the dogs and all of a sudden I heard two voices.
Q **All right. You heard two voices?**
A Yeah.
Q **All right. What did you hear these two voices say?**
A Well, the first one I heard was a clear male young adult voice that said, "Hey, Hey, Hey!"
Q **All right. Had you ever heard that voice before?**
A No, no, no, just from nowhere.
Q **You heard this voice say, "Hey, Hey, Hey"?**
A Three times, yes.

• • •

Q **And at the time you hear this sound, "Hey, Hey, Hey," what happens after that, Mr. Heidstra?**
A I heard another voice fast talking back to him, to the person who said, "Hey, Hey, Hey."
Q **Did you hear what the other voice said?**
A Could never hear. The dogs were barking so loud I couldn't hear nothing.
Q **So you heard another voice after the first voice yell, "Hey, Hey, Hey," is that correct?**
A Yeah, right, right.
Q **But you couldn't make it out?**
A No, nothing.
Q **All right. How long did the second voice continue, if you know?**
A A few seconds, very short, very short.
Q **Very short?**
A Very short time.
Q **All right. Are you still at the same location?**
A Yeah.

Q   All right. What happened next?

A   Next time I heard just it was about fifteen seconds. That argument I guess. Sounded like an argument. Two men talking to each other.

Q   **All right. Let me back up.   The — you thought that you heard an argument at that point?**

A   Sounded like an argument, yes.

Q   **All right. The argument sounded like it was between two men?**

A   Yeah, two male voices.

Q   **Two male voices?**

A   Yes.

Q   **All right. And could you discern or could you make out any other words spoken during this argument at all, Mr. Heidstra?**

A   Not at all. Not at all. Not at all.

Q   **All right.   So you then, after you heard the "Hey, Hey, Hey," and then the response, the argument, what happened after that?**

A   Then I heard a gate slamming, "Bang!"

Q   **All right. How many times did you hear a gate slam? Once, twice, how many times?**

A   Once, just once.

Q   **All right. You heard a gate slam?**

A   Yeah.

Q   **All right. And could you see anything at this point?**

A   No, no, no, I couldn't see anything.

Q   **But you heard the gate slam?**

A   Yes.

Q   **And after you heard the gate slam what did you hear next?**

A   Nothing any more.

Q   **All right. Was the — you heard no more voices?**

A   Nothing, nothing.

Q   **And by the time the gate slammed, what time was it at that time, Mr. Heidstra?**

A   About around 10:40 I would say, something like that, 10:40, about that time.

Q   **About 10:40, thereabouts?**

A   I would say so, 10:40.

Q   **And the gate, did it sound like a metal gate?**

A   Oh, yes. I recognized the gate immediately. I recognized the gate from the Akita — where the Akita is behind all the time.

Q   **You heard what sounded like a metal gate?**

A   Yes.

Q   **All right. After you heard this metal gate and you heard the "Hey, Hey, Hey," and this other voice, what did you next hear, if anything?**

A   I heard, well, the dog still barking, of course. He never stopped barking.

Q   **All right. So the dog continued to bark, the dog you believe was the Akita?**

A   And that little dog, plus that little dog.

Q   **The little black dog?**

A   Both of them, yes.

Q   **All right. Did you then at that point continue southbound in the alleyway? Did you continue and move from your location at some point?**

A   Right, right, right, right, right.

Q   **You were — and where did you go as you moved southbound in the alley? Which direction did you go?**

A   Well, I moved out of the alley into Dorothy.

• • •

Q   **(By Mr. Cochran): you then proceeded out of this alleyway back to Dorothy; is that correct?**

A   Exactly.

Q   **And then was it your intent, when you did that, to go someplace?**

A   To go back home, the direction of my building where I live.

Q   **All right. Then ultimately did you go back home to your building?**

A   I went, yes ...I stood in front of my building listening to the two dogs still barking and I was puzzled. I say what's going on?

• • •

A   All of a sudden the two dogs started slower and slower barking and I said, ah, it is all over now. I don't know what is happening there ... so I went inside and turned my TV to the local news, every night I do at eleven o'clock ...

July 12, 1995

Under cross-examination Robert Heidstra testified that he saw a white vehicle much like the Bronco routinely driven by O.J. Simpson's leaving the area near the murders that night. He thought the car might have been a Blazer or a Jeep Cherokee, but observed that it was headed south — away from Simpson's home. Upon further questioning, he conceded that the vehicle may have been a Ford Bronco.

The defense also introduced testimony from airline employees who met with Simpson during his flight to Chicago on the night of the murders.

None of them thought he was acting abnormally, and none noticed any cuts on his hands.

July 14, 1995

Dr. Robert Huizenga, a physician who examined Simpson three days after the murders, testified that Simpson suffered from osteo and rheumatoid arthritis, and said that while he had "the body of Tarzan," he "walked like Tarzan's grandfather." Huizenga also said that, in his opinion, cuts on the fingers of Simpson's left hand probably were caused by glass, and not by a knife. The doctor also failed to find bruises or scratches on Simpson's body which have shown he had been involved in a struggle. During cross-examination Huizenga conceded that Simpson was still strong enough to kill two people with a knife. Prosecutors then played an exercise video taped a month earlier, showing Simpson performing a variety of exercises.

July 18, 1995

Jurors were shown a commercially-produced videotape made on May 26, 1994, picturing a jovial O.J. Simpson shadow boxing and joking. In the video Simpson said, "Get your space in if you're exercising with your wife, if you know what I mean ... You can always blame it on working out." Prosecutors also showed jurors a promotional video made by Simpson a few months earlier in which he extolled the virtues of a vitamin supplement named Juice Plus. He told viewers that Juice Plus had nearly cured him of his arthritis symptoms.

July 19, 1995

John Meraz, the towtruck driver who towed Simpson's white Bronco for the police a few days after the murders, said he did not see blood inside the vehicle. Meraz, who was fired by his employer, admitted to stealing paper receipts he found inside of the Bronco. During cross-examination prosecutors showed photographs of the Bronco taken before Meraz towed it. In those photos, bloodstains were clearly visible.

Richard Walsh, a fitness trainer with whom Simpson had filmed an exercise video a few weeks before the killings, testified that he was concerned about Simpson's physical condition and about his ability to complete the video. Under cross-examination, however, Walsh admitted that when he challenged Simpson to more exercise, Simpson was able to continue with vigorous exercise even after 12 hours of videotaping.

July 24, 1995

Defense witness Fredric Rieders, a forensic toxicologist, testified that the chemical preservative EDTA was present in drops of Nicole Brown Simpson's blood found on a sock in Simpson's bedroom and in a sample of Simpson's blood found on a back gate of Nicole Brown Simpson's condominium.

Rieders explained that EDTA is used by police criminalists to preserve blood samples, and that its presence at the crime scene may have indicated the blood was planted. Rieders was not, however, able to quantify the amount of EDTA in the blood, and upon cross-examination by prosecutors admitted that the chemical EDTA — in very small amounts — is naturally present in all human blood. Rieders also admitted that EDTA is found in laundry detergent, but said that tests did not find the chemical anywhere else on the bloody sock.

Prosecutor Marcia Clark attempted to discredit Rieders by questioning him about another murder case in which he had incorrectly identified the cause of death. Clark also questioned Rieders in an attempt to show that far more EDTA is naturally present in human blood than he admitted.

July 25, 1995

FBI expert Roger Martz testified that only very vague signs of what might have been the chemical EDTA could be detected in blood found on the sock at the foot of O.J. Simpson's bed. The same, he said, was true of the blood found on the gate near the crime scene. Although his testimony was not helpful to the defense case, defense attorneys had to put Martz on the stand since the previous day's witness, Fredric Rieders, had not conducted his own tests, but had instead relied upon interpretations of tests conducted by Martz. The testimony of Agent Martz, which is an excellent example of the kind of highly technical testimony sometimes given by expert witnesses, is partially reproduced below:

A   (By Mr. Martz): It—the one graph demonstrated or some of them did, in my blood, the gate and the sock, there's low levels of an ion that I look for with EDTA, very little levels compared to the EDTA preserved blood. I don't have the explanation as to what they're from. I believe they could be from other chemicals. It could be EDTA or it could be some artifact in the instrument due to some type of matrix effect with the blood.

Q   **(By Ms. Clark): And in that regard, the fact that it could be another compound, sir, in your opinion, in order to rule out any other compound as being the substance detected on the rear gate and the sock, would it be appropriate in your opinion to look at the Merck index for parent ions of a 292 weight?**

A   Well, what I would not do with the Merck index is just look at compounds with a molecular weight of 292. In my experiment that I conducted, I did daughters of 293. So people may assume that what I'm looking for is all compounds with a molecular weight of 292. But that's not the case.

Q   **No. I forgot to ask, what is the Merck index, sir?**

A   The Merck index is a reference book of about 10 thousand common chemicals that are used.

Q   **And does that index indicate for each of the compounds that it lists what the ions and what the ion count should be?**

A   Well, no, it doesn't. What it does list though is the molecular weight of the compound. So it's a way that you can determine how many compounds are of a various molecular weight.

Q   **And is it referenced only by the parent ion?**

A   Well, there's a lot of different references in the book. You can look up by molecular formula. Some of them you can look up by molecular weight. If you have the computer program, you can do a lot of searches.

Q   **Now, you indicated on direct examination that — some point this morning, you received additional compounds of the — of a similar molecular weight to the substance as you found in the evidence on the rear gate and the sock?**

A   Well, in the Merck index, I believe molecular weight 292 and 293, there were probably approximately about 50 compounds that would give those molecular weights. But what you have to consider is, there's probably multi-thousand compounds that have a higher molecular weight that you would also have to consider as giving the same results. Now, compound with a lower molecular weight, unless something adds to it, you can pretty much eliminate. But just looking at the Merck index and looking at compounds molecular weight 292 or 293, you can't eliminate all the compounds in the book with higher molecular weights that could give a similar response.

Q   **Well, how is that? If it has a higher molecular weight, how is it going to give a similar response to a 292 or 293?**

A   Well, with a mass spectrometer, I'm only allowing that one mass to go through. Now, there's nothing to preclude a compound of a larger mass breaking down to 293 and then breaking down to the 162 or the 160 ion. That's very possible, and that's why I make sure that I do a full daughter spectrum before I ever identify a chemical in mass spectrometry.

Q   **When you say a "Full daughter spectrum," what do you mean by that?**

A   Well, with EDTA, when you take the molecular weight or the molecular ion and you bombard it in the second quadrupole, it will fragment to ions. We talked earlier about some of those ions or Dr. Rieders did yesterday, the 160 ion. Well, you also have a 132 ion. And some of the molecular ion passes through the quadrupole, the 293 in this case, the quasi molecular ion. And you not only want those three ions, but you want them at a certain ratio. In this particular case, the 160 is what's called the base peak. That's the largest ion. And then the 293 would be the second largest and the 132. So we not only want all those ions before we identify. We want them in a particular ratio.

Q **Now, scientifically speaking, sir, is it very important to insist that the whole spectrum be shown and in the appropriate ratio before you're willing to identify a particular compound in a court of law or anywhere?**

A In the chemistry unit, we pretty much require that if we're dealing with mass spectrometry alone. Now, there are other ways to identify chemicals. But if we're doing mass spectrometry, we want a full daughter spectrum. Unfortunately, mistakes have been made in other laboratories where they do single ion monitoring or look for just certain ions. It's a very dangerous practice.

Q **And when you say "A very dangerous practice," by that, sir, do you mean that you may identify a compound, for example, in this case as EDTA when it really isn't?**

A That's correct.

Q **And in order to guard against that kind of error, is it important then to make sure that the full daughter spectrum is shown?**

A In my opinion, that is correct, yes.

Q **Was the full daughter spectrum shown in the evidence of the rear gate, the sock or your blood?**

A No, it was not.

Q **Conversely, sir, was the full daughter spectrum shown in the reference samples from the Defendant and Nicole brown?**

A Yes, it was.

Q **And for that reason, sir, in your opinion, is it scientifically correct or appropriate to identify the substance in the rear gate and the sock as EDTA in the absence of the full daughter spectrum?**

A In this particular case, it is not appropriate to identify EDTA based on the data that I have provided for the sock and the gate.

• • •

Q **All right, sir. Now, you indicated that you did not identify the substance found on the rear gate and on the sock or in your blood as EDTA because it did not present the full daughter spectrum for EDTA, correct?**

A That's correct.

Q **Now, you have met with Mr. Blasier in Washington D.C., correct?**

A Yes, I have.

Q **And you have spoken to him on the phone?**

A Yes, I have.

Q **You have been accessible to him, correct?**

A Yes, I have.

Q **And did you explain to him why you did not identify the substance on the rear gate and on the sock as EDTA?**

A I believe that I did, yes.

Q **Because of the absence of the full daughter spectrum?**

A That's correct.

Q **Did you refuse to answer any questions that he posed to you concerning this case?**

A No, I did not.

Q **Did he make any request of you that you conduct any of the experiments he outlined here in court today when you spoke to him on previous occasions?**

A No, I don't believe he did, no.

• • •

Q **All right. Now, you indicated that you continued testing on February 22nd even though you had determined there was no EDTA from a preserved test tube and you went into another mode to do that testing?**

A Yes. I conducted a positive ion mode looking for the 160 daughter from the 293 quasi molecular ion or the m-plus-1 parent ion.

Q **Now, did you—was there something different about the method of testing you used on the 22nd from the method you had used on the 19th?**

A It was the same method of extraction. The instrumentation perimeters varied.

Q **And what do you mean by that?**

A Well, with the instruments, you can look at the positive ions or the negative ions that are produced in the ionization. And the first day when I set up the experiment, I was looking for the negative ion, the EDTA form with the ion complex. On the second day or on the 22nd, I was looking for a protonated EDTA.

Q **And why did you do that? What would that give you more than you already got from your previous testing?**

A Well, I determined that it was a little bit more sensitive. So I would be able to detect lower amounts of EDTA that may be present naturally in human blood.

Q **Now, when you talk about doing these tests, sir, you indicated that you tested your own blood. Do you recall that?**

A Yes.

Q **Did anyone ask you to do that?**

A Not that I remember, no.

Q **It was just your idea?**

A Yes. That's correct.

Q **Nevertheless, did you generate graphs showing the results of the testing on your own blood?**
A Yes, I did.
Q **And did you generate graphs showing that your — showing your blood tested with EDTA and without?**
A Yes.
Q **Now, when I say with and without, I'm talking about adding EDTA preservative to it.**
A Yes.
Q **And those graphs were turned over to the Defense?**
A Uh, those were turned over when we met. I guess it was about weeks ago now.
Q **All right. Back to the testing on February 22nd.**
A Your Honor, I have here a series of four charts that I would like to be marked People's next in order, A, B, C and D.

• • •

Q **Now, this is the evidence from the sock itself, correct?**
A That's correct.
Q **Did you attempt then to determine whether or not you could get the full daughter spectrum, that is the 132 as well on the evidence of the sock?**
A Yes, I did.
Q **And showing you 543-B, does this graph depict your attempt to see whether or not you could detect the full daughter spectrum in the evidence of the blood from the sock?**
A Yes, it does.
Q **Now, you recall, doctor, you were present in court when Dr. Rieders testified?**
A Yes, I was.
Q **And you saw his—you heard his testimony concerning this graph that's now before the jury?**
A That's correct.
Q **Do you agree with the opinion that he gave on this graph?**
A No, I do not.
Q **Please explain why.**
A This particular graph depicts a lot of noise is all it depicts. As I mentioned before with the electro spray, everyone is running a 50-yard dash. Everyone is coming to the finish line about the same time. There are many, many, many chemicals in blood that are going to come across the finish line at the same retention time as EDTA. So we're going to get a lot of noise signal at that area. The noise in this case is no larger really than—than—it—it just doesn't increase anywhere, and where it increases may be slightly where Dr. Rieders was pointing out in the one area. That's only because

everything was coming out of the instrument at one time and it caused electrical noise. This is not real peaks. This is electrical noise. This is very common in mass spectrometry. It's electrical noise. It is not signal. Any time you would identify something as signal, you would want something larger than the noise. There's nothing here that's larger than the noise. It's random noise that's very common in mass spectrometry, especially in electro spray where you're using different I should say electrical settings than you're using with conventional mass spectrometry. This is standard noise in electro spray mass spectrometry. This should never be considered signal or should never be interpreted as anything other than noise.

What you would want to do and what I did, and unfortunately I didn't print it out, but there was a mass spectrum taken of that particular peak, and it showed that it was just noise. Since there was nothing there, I didn't print it out. But for someone to try to make this into something other than noise is totally wrong.

Q **In your opinion then, is his—scientifically speaking, was it scientifically and forensically inappropriate for Dr. Rieders to have interpreted this graph in the manner that he did?**

A In my opinion, it was, yes.

· · ·

Q **And do you think that—strike that. To your knowledge, has Dr. Rieders ever operated the electro-spray?**

A To my knowledge, he has not. He admitted that yesterday.

Q **And what impact, if any, would that have on the knowledge that retention time is not a discriminating factor in your machine?**

A Well, it could have some.

· · ·

Q **Now, given that you would not—you said signal to noise. The random peaks that you see on the chart before you on 543-A, how would you characterize those?**

A Well, the first indication that you don't want to give much credence to this is the fact that we've got 10 to the minus fourth for noise. I mean, this is a large count. So someone that didn't know a lot about mass chromatography would want to know why do you have noise that's that large. I mean, that's a thousand ions or something. Why do you have electrical noise that's a thousand ions. I mean, that's the first thing if I didn't know anything about electro spray or how this was done, I would want to know that before I made any interpretation. Generally, with most instruments, your noise level is going to be very, very small. Now, electro spray, the manufacturer suggests that you use the higher settings because they determine that it works better that way. And this is not normal noise level that you would expect in a mass spectrometer, plus your noises increase by the fact that you're doing tandem mass spectrometry. So you've got two different techniques here that require you to have this very large noise. And any time you have noise that's a thousand counts high, you'd better be very, very careful before you try to interpret and make a peak out of that noise.

Q Because?
A Because it's just noise. It's not a peak.
Q It's not — it's not a readable?
A It's random noise. I mean, I certainly would want something at least three times the noise before I would even consider it to be a signal ... I consider all that to be electrical noise.

July 26, 1995

Judge Ito granted defense attorney Robert Blasier's request to treat FBI Special Agent Roger Martz as a hostile witness. Such a declaration allowed Blasier to ask Martz "leading questions." Blasier asked Martz if he was biased in favor of the prosecution, but Martz denied the claim.

July 27, 1995

Herbert MacDonnell, a blood splatter expert and member of the International Association of Blood Stain Pattern Analysts, testified that stains on socks in Simpson's bedroom seemed to have been applied to the socks. Some of the blood on the sock, said MacDonell, had soaked through — something which, he said, would be unlikely to happen if the sock had been worn at the time it came in contact with blood. The stains on the socks, MacDonnell said, appeared to be smears rather than "splatter stains."

During cross-examination Prosecutor Marcia Clark asked MacDonnell whether it was possible that the socks had been so wet with perspiration and blood before they were taken off that, had they been laid flat blood would have seeped through. MacDonell agreed that such a scenario was possible.

August 2–7, 1995

Dr. John Gerdes, clinical director of Immunological Associates in Denver, Colorado, testified as an expert witness for the defense, saying that — in his opinion — the LAPD crime lab has the worst contamination problems he has ever seen. The laboratory is so rife with contamination and poor procedure that it should be shut down, Gerdes said. Even tests which in this case were conducted by outside laboratories were open to suspicion, Gerdes said, because all of the biological evidence had been gathered by LAPD specialists.

Under cross-examination, Gerdes admitted that he is not a member of any professional forensic associations and has never conducted a forensic experiment on his own. He also admitted that he could not categorically deny that blood in question came from O.J. Simpson or the victims.

August 10–11, 1995

Defense expert witness Dr. Michael Baden, the forensic pathologist who led a commission which reopened the investigation into the assassination of President John F. Kennedy, questioned the prosecution's version of how the murders took place. Baden suggested that Nicole Brown Simpson may have engaged in a lengthy struggle with her attacker, and may not have been lying on the ground when her throat was cut.

Baden also told jurors about a number of mistakes investigators made which may have led to contamination of evidence or lost evidence. Baden said that the hands of Nicole Brown Simpson should have been wrapped when her body was moved in order to protect evidence under the fingernails, and that the investigators had failed to properly examine blood drops found on her back.

During cross-examination prosecutor Brian Kelberg showed that Baden had never published a scientific article in his area of expertise, and had him admit that his real area of expertise is death by drug abuse. Baden also said that he will receive about $165,000 for his services on behalf of the defense. Kelberg also won an admission from Baden that the autopsies performed on Nicole Brown Simpson and Ronald Goldman were very well done, and even "better than the autopsy of President Kennedy."

August 17, 1995

A witness for the defense, Gilbert Aguilar, a fingerprint specialist with the Los Angeles Police Department, testified that none of the 17 crime scene fingerprints examined by him were O.J. Simpson's. Defense attorneys suggested that unidentifiable prints at the scene could have belonged to an unknown killer. Prosecutor Christopher Darden cross-examined Aguilar in an effort to show that the questionable prints could have belonged to almost anyone. Aguilar also testified that fingerprints would not have been left by someone wearing gloves.

August 18, 1995

Larry Ragle, the former director of the Orange County Sheriff Department's crime laboratory testified that, from a forensics viewpoint, the investigation in the Simpson case had fallen below a "minimum *standard* of acceptability. Ragle point out that critical evidence may have been lost because ten hours had passed before representatives of the coroner's office arrived at the crime scene. Ragle also criticized police for using a blanket from inside Nicole Brown Simpson's condominium to cover her body instead of examining it separately for fiber and other evidence.*

During cross-examination prosecutor Hank Goldberg pointed out that Ragle has never read many leading forensic criminology textbooks, and that he is not a detective. Goldberg also had Ragle admit that he himself had failed to wear gloves when examining the inside of Simpson's Bronco.

August 22–25, 1995

Crime scene reconstruction expert Dr. Henry Lee testified that he found what appeared to be shoe prints on a piece of paper and an envelope at the murder scene. The prints, said Lee, did not come from the Italian shoes identified as having been worn by an unknown person at the crime scene. Lee, who is a forensic laboratory manager in Connecticut, said that he found the paper and envelope at the murder scene 13 days after the crime — indicating that LAPD investigators had not conducted a thorough investigation of the scene.

Lee also testified that he saw patterns that appeared to be footprints on Goldman's blood-soaked jeans. Lee also said that something was "wrong" with the way in which LAPD investigators handled blood evidence collected at the crime scene — suggesting that the evidence was tampered with. Stains inside the packaging material surrounding the evidence suggested that the evidence had been either improperly handled, or handled more than one time.

Under cross-examination by prosecutors Lee admitted that he was not sure if the imprint patterns he observed were in fact footprints. If they were prints, Lee admitted, they might have been left by investigating officers.

August 29, 1995

Laura Hart McKinny, called as a witness by the defense, traveled from North Carolina to testify about conversations she had had with detective Mark Fuhrman. With the jury out of the courtroom, McKinny told court officials that Fuhrman approached her in a Los Angeles coffee shop in 1985. Fuhrman said he wanted to talk about her laptop computer, but quickly told McKinny about being a member of a group called Men Against Women, which was dedicated to keeping women off the LAPD force. Defense attorneys then played tape recordings McKinney had made of conversations with Fuhrman. The tapes consisted of interviews with Fuhrman recorded between 1985 and 1994 which McKinny intended to use as material for a screenplay about women in police work. On the tapes Fuhrman could be heard using the word "nigger" 41 times, and boasting about instances of police brutality and about concocting probable cause to arrest anyone he wanted.

Defense attorneys spent much of the day arguing for the admissibility of the tapes, telling the judge they wanted to play them for the jury because of their tendency to prove that Fuhrman was a liar, and that he had earlier lied under oath when he denied using what they called "the N-word."

Prosecutors responded by saying that since defense attorneys had not produced any conclusive material which might show that Fuhrman planted evidence in the Simpson case his racially-charged comments were irrelevant and would only serve to inflame and bias the jury. Moreover, prosecutors argued, many of Fuhrman's comments were eight or nine years old, making them less relevant to the present case. "Because of the inflammatory nature of the remarks at issue, especially in front of this predominantly African-American jury," said prosecutors, "it does have a substantially undue impact ... With all due respect to people of color everywhere, I submit that whether or not he used the N-word at some point in the remote past is not a material part of his testimony." Marcia Clark told Judge Ito that to admit the "Fuhrman tapes" into evidence would be like "telling the jury: 'Disregard the case. Look somewhere else.'" Before the hearing was over, prosecutor Christopher Darden cross-examined McKinny, getting her to admit that she was in the process of creating a work of fiction, and suggested that what Fuhrman said may have been fictional.

August 30, 1995

Court was in recess while Judge Ito considered how to rule on the admissibility of the Fuhrman tapes.

August 31, 1995

Judge Ito ruled that jurors would be allowed to hear only 2 of the 41 instances on the Fuhrman tapes in which Fuhrman referred to black people as "niggers." The judge also ruled that defense attorneys could not use Fuhrman's statements about police misconduct. The two phrases which the jury was allowed to hear were Fuhrman saying: "We have no niggers where I grew up;" and Fuhrman responding to McKinny's question about residential areas by saying, "That's where niggers live."

The judge did rule that defense attorneys could ask McKinny to testify that Fuhrman used the word "nigger" 41 times during interviews she conducted with him.

September 5, 1995

A number of witnesses told stories to the jury about Detective Fuhrman's penchant for racist talk. The first, Kathleen Bell, testified under direct examination by F. Lee Bailey that she met Fuhrman in 1985 or 1986 at a Marine recruiting center. A portion of her testimony follows:

Direct examination by Mr. Bailey:

Q   **Miss Bell, without giving a street address, can you tell us where you live?**
A   (by Ms. Bell) In Long Beach.
Q   **And how long have you lived in that area?**
A   Since, let's see, about a year and a half.
Q   **All right. In 1985 and '86 where were you living?**
A   In Palos Verdes.
Q   **And did you have an occupation or profession at that time?**
A   Yes, real estate agent.
Q   **And who did you work for as a real estate agent?**
A   Century 21, Bob Maher realty in Redondo Beach.

• • •

Q   **When did you begin working for Bob Maher at century 21?**
A   I received my real estate license in September of 1985 and I started working for Bob Maher I believe in October.
Q   **Can you tell me whether or not in the immediate vicinity of your real estate office there was located a Marine recruiting station?**
A   Yes.
Q   **Did you know any of the personnel who worked in that station?**
A   Yes.
Q   **Can you name any of them?**
A   Joe Foss and Ron Rohr.

• • •

Q   **Was your office immediately above theirs?**
A   Umm, it was above the Marine recruiting center.

• • •

Q   **All right. Do you know a person named Mark Fuhrman?**
A   Yes, I do.
Q   **When did you first see Mr. Fuhrman, according to your best recollection?**

A   Umm, between the time that I was working for Bob Maher realty Century 21, it was between 1985 and '86.

Q   **And what were the circumstances the first time you saw him, as opposed to encountered him?**

A   The first time I saw him I walked down to the Marine recruiting center just to say hello to the Marines and they had a man sitting there and I thought that they were in a meeting, so I just kind of tapped on the window and waved and went back upstairs.

Q   **Were you introduced to Mr. Fuhrman at that time?**

A   No.

Q   **Did you have any conversation with him or anyone else inside the station?**

A   No, I did not.

Q   **Could you see what they were doing as you walked by?**

A   They were just speaking to each other.

Q   **Did you notice anything unusual about Mr. Fuhrman at that time?**

A   Umm, I thought that he was handsome.

Q   **All right.**

A   And I did notice that.

Q   **Did you notice anything about his height?**

A   He was sitting in a chair but I could tell that he was tall, yes.

• • •

Q   **When you next saw Mr. Fuhrman in their office, what did you do?**

A   I went inside the Marine recruiting center and I introduced myself and I just began speaking to all of the men.

Q   **Who was present at the time?**

A   Joe Foss, Ron Rohr and Mark Fuhrman.

Q   **All right. Had you at that time any special reason for wanting to meet Mr. Fuhrman?**

A   I thought that he would be interested in meeting my girlfriend Andrea Terry.

Q   **What is there about Andrea Terry that you thought might match up well with Mr. Fuhrman?**

A   She is six feet tall and really beautiful and I thought that—she liked tall men and so I thought that she might want to meet him as well.

Q   **All right. How did you introduce yourself to Mr. Fuhrman?**

A   Umm, I just said "hello," and the Marines actually introduced me, and I don't remember the first kind of shooting the breeze part of the conversation. It was just very mild and I was talking about Andrea. I began talking about Andrea.

. . .

Q   Did you tell Mr. Fuhrman something about a girl named Andrea Terry, without saying precisely what it was?
A   Yes, I did.
Q   All right. In the course of giving him that information did you mention the name of anyone who is a public figure?
A   Yes.
Q   What was that name?

Mr. Darden: Hearsay, your Honor.

The Court: Overruled.

A   Marcus Allen.
Q   What happened when you mentioned the name Marcus Allen to Mark Fuhrman?
A   His demeanor changed and his attitude toward me changed.
Q   And what, if anything, did he say?
A   He said that if — when he sees a black man with a white woman driving in a car he pulls them over.
Q   And what did you say?
A   I was taken back a little bit and so I kind of paused and I looked at the Marines and I just said, "Well, what if they didn't do anything wrong?"
Q   What did he say?
A   He said he would find something.
Q   All right. And did you talk any further about that hypothetical of a black man riding with a white woman being pulled over?
A   Yes.
Q   What else was said?
A   I asked, "What if they are in love?"
Q   And what did he say to that?
A   He said, "That is disgusting."
Q   The fact that a black man might be in love with a white woman was disgusting?

Mr. Darden: Objection. That is leading, your Honor.

The Court: Rephrase the question.

Q   Okay. What was he referring to in your understanding when he used the word "Disgusting"?
A   That I said—I asked him what if they were in love and I think the idea of them being in love was disgusting to him.

Mr. Darden: Objection, objection to strike, calls for speculation.

The Court: Overruled.

Q   After the word "disgusting" was uttered, what was next said by either of you?

A   Well, again I looked at the Marines because I had spoken to them before and they didn't seem to be mean people, and so I was waiting for some kind of reaction from them, and then, umm, I just was kind of—I just kind of paused and then he said, "If I had my way I would gather ... All the niggers would be gathered together and burned."

Q   All right. And what was your reaction when he told you that he would gather the niggers all together and burn them?

A   Umm, I'm sorry, I didn't—I thought that that was—nobody ever said that to me before. I heard the "N" word before, but nobody ever said something like that to me before.

Another witness, Natalie Singer, testified that her roommate dated Fuhrman's partner in 1987. Both Fuhrman and his partner frequented her apartment, she said.

Q   (By Mr. Bailey): Tell me the circumstances within your apartment surrounding your first encounter with Mark Fuhrman and his partner Tom?

A   (By Ms. Singer): Okay, okay. You walk in the front door and there is — there is two couches in the living room. There is a living room area. There is one couch facing that wall and there is one couch facing that wall. Karel was excited. This was going to be the first time, you know, they are coming over, and I want you to meet them, and you know, all that stuff, and they stopped by while they were on duty, because there is no other reason for a man to pick up a date with another guy, you know. They would just drop by.

Q   But did they say they were on duty or this is a conclusion?

A   No, they were on duty. Well, I mean, I—being that they had all that paraphernalia dangling off of them.

. . .

Q   At some point during that evening were you sitting in proximity to Karel Hannak, Tom Veterano or Vettraino and Mark Fuhrman?

A   Yes, yes, yes.

Q   How close was the group?

A Okay. Tom and Karel were sitting on this couch, *(indicating)*. Mark Fuhrman sat here, *(indicating)*. I sat here, *(indicating)*. I—okay, that is it. That is all I want to say. Okay.

Q **At some point was inquiry made by someone as to what these two officers did?**

A Yes.

Q **Their work? And what was the response to the type of work that they did?**

A Fuhrman said "We work with gangs."

Q **All right.**

A Gang unit.

Q **Being very careful with your answer. Did he, in describing the gangs that he worked with, describe any particular race?**

A Yes.

Q **Did he use an epithet well-known to the world that denotes black people and begins with "N"?**

A Yes.

Q **What was your reaction to his use of that word on your first encounter?**

A *(No audible response.)*

Q **How did you feel?**

A Well, in the context that it was in, that that word was used in, I was shocked, stunned. I never met anyone that talks that way.

Q **All right.**

• • •

Q **Is it fair to say that the description of the way the "N" people were treated, according to Fuhrman, was abusive?**

A Absolutely.

• • •

Q **You can stop there. Later in the conversation did he make another reference to "N" people?**

A Yes, he did.

Q **Can you tell us what he said?**

A *(No audible response.)*

Q **You may use the "N" word, if you wish.**

(Discussion held off the record between defense counsel.)

The Court: Do you remember the question?

Q **(By Mr. Bailey): Let me rephrase it if I may, your Honor. Did he make a reference to the African American race using a word we have discussed that begins with "N"?**

A   (By Ms. Singer): And you are not referring to the first reference?

Q   **No, no.**

A   You are referring to that second kind of saying.

Q   **Later in the conversation?**

A   Yes.

Q   **What did he say?**

A   It is okay to say that?

Q   **Yes.**

A   He said, "The only good Nigger is a dead Nigger."

Another witness, Roderic Hodge, a black man who had been arrested by Fuhrman in 1987 said Fuhrman had said to him, "I told you we'd get you, nigger."

Defense attorneys also played brief portions of screenwriter Laura McKinny's tape recorded conversations with Fuhrman. Commenting on women police officers, Fuhrman could be heard saying, "They don't do anything. They don't go out and initiate contact with some 6'5" nigger that's been in prison for seven years pumping weights."

McKinny took the stand to describe how she had met Fuhrman, and told the jury that the detective had used the "N-word" 41 times in ten years of tape recorded interviews while describing his life as a Los Angeles police officer. A portion of her testimony follows.

The Court: All right. Thank you, ladies and gentlemen. Be seated. Mr. Cochran, you may conclude for the day.

• • •

Q   **(By Mr. Cochran): Miss McKinny, the — Mr. Fuhrman said, "We have no niggers where I grew up." I think you have indicated that was in the early part of 1985?**

A   Yes.

Q   **All right. And the statement about prison and six-foot-five-inch people, when was that?**

A   That was approximately the same time, later in that month of April or possibly in the beginning of May.

Q   **Of 1985?**

A   Of 1985, yes.

Mr. Cochran: All right. Mr. Harris, are we ready?

• • •

(A videotape and audiotape were played.)

Q (By Mr. Cochran): Do you recognize the voice of the person who was saying, "They don't do anything. They don't go out there and initiate a contact with some six-foot-five-inch nigger that has been in prison for seven years pumping weights"? Who said that?

A Officer Mark Fuhrman.

Q **When did he say that?**

A In April or early May of 1985.

Q **And that was his voice; is that right?**

A Yes.

Q **No doubt about it?**

A No doubt about it.

· · ·

September 6, 1995

During cross-examination of playwright Laura McKinny, prosecutor Christopher Darden asked why she had used the "N-word" word in a screenplay if she found it offensive. Portions of the cross-examination are reproduced below:

Q **Was it your testimony yesterday that you were offended when you heard Mark Fuhrman use that epithet?**

A Yes.

Q **Now, when you met with Miss Clark and Miss Lewis and Mr. Hodgman and myself on August 17, do you recall me asking you what you thought or what came to mind when you first heard Fuhrman use that epithet?**

A Yes, I do.

Q **And you told me that nothing came to mind; is that correct?**

A That's correct, that I couldn't remember anything coming to mind the first time. Your question was what came to mind the first time you heard that word, I believe.

Q **But you don't remember what came to mind at the time?**

A No. That would have been about ten years ago. I could not remember the first time I heard that word used what came to my mind.

Q **You don't remember a white police officer using this epithet in your presence and your not being offended by it?**

Mr. Cochran: Object to the form of that question and the tone of the voice.

The Court: Sustained. It is argumentative.

Q **(By Mr. Darden): You understand that that word is the most vile word in the English language?**

A   I think it is one of the most vile words in the English language, yes.

Q **You think there are worse?**

A   Yes, I certainly do. Why are we having this adversarial relationship? I don't understand that. It is a vile word. Why do I have to define it more so than it is?

Q **You wrote a screenplay, right?**

A   That is accurate.

Q **Did you use that word in the screenplay?**

A   Yes.

Q **Did you attempt to go out and sell that screenplay?**

A   Certainly.

Q **You are using that word in your screenplay to help make money, right?**

Mr. Cochran: Object to the form of that question, your Honor. That is argumentative.

The Court: Sustained. Sustained.

Q   (By Mr. Darden): Are you trying to make money off of the use of that word?

Mr. Cochran: Object to the form of this question, your Honor. Object.

The Court: Overruled. Overruled. It is an appropriate question.

Q **(By Mr. Darden): When you met Detective Fuhrman you told him that you were a screenwriter?**

A   That is accurate.

Q **And you told him that you had written other screenplays?**

A   Yes.

• • •

Q **Are you a member of the writer's guild?**

A   No, I am not.

Q **You have had one screenplay published or made into a film?**

A   Have I had one screenplay made into a film?

Q **Yes.**

A   No.

• • •

Q   **(By Mr. Darden): When Mark Fuhrman used these words in your presence why didn't you just tell him to stop?**

Mr. Cochran: Your Honor, I object to the form of that question. I object to the form of that question.

The Court: Overruled.

Mr. Cochran: Argumentative.

The Court: Overruled.

A   For the same reason I didn't tell him to stop when he told me of police procedures, cover-ups, other information that I felt were important for me to have a clear understanding in context of this material that I was writing. He told me many things that I thought were important for me to understand, many things I hadn't been aware of, as did other officers of the Los Angeles Police Department, as did many of the other interviews that I did and ride-alongs I went on.

    I was in a journalistic mode. I was not judgmental. And I needed that information to help me write a more realistic journalistic piece and I did not ask him to stop using the type of normal ordinary language he would use or other officers would use. I needed to know how he would speak.

Q   **(By Mr. Darden): You told us yesterday that there was no racial subplot to the screenplay you were planning to write, correct?**
A   That is accurate.
Q   **And yet you use this epithet in your screenplay anyway; is that also correct?**
A   That is true.

· · ·

Q   **Okay. Now, you asked a moment ago why we are involved in some adversarial relationship. Do you recall asking that?**
A   I felt that you were. I don't feel adversarial toward you, but I felt that there was something negative coming from some of your questions, yes.
Q   **Okay. You didn't stop him the first time he used the epithet, correct?**

Mr. Cochran: Your Honor, that has been asked and answered.

The Court: It has.

Q　By Mr. Darden: Well, you didn't stop him the twentieth time he used the epithet?

Mr. Cochran: Asked and answered.

The Court: That has not. Overruled.

Q　(By Mr. Darden): Correct?
A　That's correct.
Q　You didn't stop him the fortieth or forty-second time that he used the epithet, correct?
A　I didn't abridge his dialogue or conversation during an interview, no.
Q　Given the fact that you have included this epithet in your screenplay, do you feel that it is appropriate under some circumstances to utter or use this word?

Mr. Cochran: Your Honor, I object to the form of this. Object to the form of that question.

The Court: Overruled. Overruled.

The Witness: Do I personally feel it is appropriate?

Q　(By Mr. Darden): Yes.
A　No, I don't.
Q　Why then include it in a screenplay, a screenplay that you intend to make into a movie?
A　Because it is reflective of particular officers or officer's dialogue, feelings at a particular time. It is representative of what would be said.

Mr. Darden: That is all I have.

The Court: Thank you, Mr. Darden.

At the request of defense attorneys, former detective Mark Fuhrman returned to the courtroom.. Outside of the presence of the jurors, and with his lawyer by his side, Fuhrman invoked his Fifth Amendment privilege against self incrimination when attorneys asked if he had previously lied under oath, or if he had planted evidence or filed false reports in the Simpson case. (Fuhrman had retired from the LAPD at this point, although he was still referred to by the judge as "Detective" Fuhrman.) Here is how the hearing went:

The Court: All right. Mr. Uelmen, I take it at this point then, you wish to recall Detective Fuhrman.

Mr. Uelmen: Yes, your Honor.

The Court: All right. And so that the record is clear, my recollection is that Detective Fuhrman, who is now present in court with counsel, Mr. Mounger, my recollection is that Detective Fuhrman was excused, but not released and was subject to recall. Is that your recollection?

Mr. Uelmen: That is correct. Your Honor.

The Court: All right.

Mr. Uelmen: He was not excused.

The Court: Well, let me rephrase that. Subject to recall. Excused for the day, subject to recall, not terminated as a witness before the court.

Mr. Uelmen: That's correct.

The Court: All right. And, Mr. Mounger, if you wish to stand next to your client, you may.

Mr. Mounger: Thank you.

The Court: All right. Detective Fuhrman, would you resume the witness stand, please.

Mark Fuhrman, recalled as a witness by the defendant, pursuant to Evidence Code Section 402, having been previously sworn, testified further as follows:

The Court: All right. Good afternoon, detective.

The Witness: Good afternoon, your Honor.

The Court: You are reminded, sir, that you are still under oath. Mr. Uelmen, you may proceed.

Direct examination by Mr. Uelmen:

Q   Detective Fuhrman, was the testimony that you gave at the preliminary hearing in this case completely truthful?
A   I wish to assert my 5th Amendment privilege.
Q   Have you ever falsified a police report?

A   I wish to assert my 5th Amendment privilege.

Q   Is it your intention to assert your 5th Amendment privilege with respect to all questions that I ask you?

A   Yes.

Mr. Uelmen: Can I have a moment?

The Court: Certainly.

(Discussion held off the record between defense counsel.)

Mr. Mounger: Your Honor, further questions don't serve any purpose since my client has already answered that he will not answer any question and will assert his 5th Amendment privilege. Anything further can only be a show.

Mr. Uelmen: I only have one other question, your honor.

The Court: What was that, Mr. Uelmen?

Q   (By Mr. Uelmen): Detective Fuhrman, did you plant or manufacture any evidence in this case?

A   I assert my 5th Amendment privilege.

The Court: All right. Based upon the witness' answers, the representation by his counsel, Mr. Mounger —

Ms. Clark: Your Honor, the People make an objection to the last question and ask the court to strike it as being improper and does nothing but headline.

The Court: Overruled. The answer will stand. All right. Miss Clark, do you have any questions of this witness?

Ms. Clark: No questions.

The Court: All right. Then, given the assertion of the 5th Amendment privilege, we will not conduct any further inquiry as to Detective Fuhrman. And — but, however, detective, I am going to release you from further attendance this afternoon. However, you are still subject to recall. All right. Thank you, sir.

The Witness: Thank you, your Honor.

On the basis of the claim that Fuhrman couldn't be trusted to testify truthfully given the fact that he had lied about his use of the "N-word," and suggesting that Fuhrman might have planted evidence, defense attorneys asked Judge Ito to suppress all evidence taken from Simpson's estate after Fuhrman said that he had found blood on Simpson's car hours after the murders. The search of Simpson's residence, said Simpson's attorneys, must have been illegal since it was conducted without a warrant and Fuhrman's earlier avowed concern that injured parties might be inside the residence now seemed questionable. Judge Ito took the defense request under consideration.

September 7, 1995

Judge Ito ruled that Fuhrman could not be forced to testify further before the jury. California law, said Ito, makes it inappropriate to present to the jury a witness whom the court already knows will invoke the Fifth Amendment right against self-incrimination.

Ito also ruled that the material on the Fuhrman tapes did not support exclusion of evidence gathered at the Simpson estate on the morning following the killings. Fuhrman's testimony, wrote the judge "is corroborated by the testimony of other witnesses."

In a separate matter, defense attorney F. Lee Bailey said that Simpson would not take the stand to testify in his own defense.

Chapter 5
Rebuttal, Rejoinder, and Closing Jury Instructions

Judge Lance Ito reviews California jury instructions at the close of rebuttal. AP/Wide World Photos.

INTRODUCTION

At the conclusion of the defense's case, in what is known as the **rebuttal** stage of the trial, the prosecution is allowed to present additional evidence which may rebut the evidence the defense has presented. Prosecutors may also present evidence which challenges the credibility of defense witnesses. It is improper during the rebuttal, however, for prosecutors to offer new and significant evidence which is part of their "case in chief," and which should have been offered when they had the opportunity to present their case — unless the new evidence was not available at that time, and prosecutors can convince the judge that it should be allowed during the rebuttal. Following the rebuttal, the defense has a final opportunity to challenge any new assertions made by the prosecution in what is called a defense **rejoinder**.

On September 11, 1995, the prosecution began offering its rebuttal, even though the defense had not yet rested it's case. Key aspects of both the rebuttal and rejoinder are summarized below.

PROSECUTION REBUTTAL BEGINS

September 11, 1995

Prosecutors called professional photographer Michael Romano to the stand to testify that he was the photographer who took a picture of O.J. Simpson during a Chicago Bears football game in 1990 which showed Simpson wearing a pair of gloves which appear to be the same ones found at the murder scene and at Simpson's home after the killings. The photo showed Simpson wearing a pair of dark gloves and holding a microphone.

September 12, 1995

Former Isotoner executive Richard Rubin testified that the gloves worn by O.J. Simpson in 1990 photographs and videotapes were the same gloves as those found at the crime scene and at Simpson's home. Rubin said that only 300 pairs of the gloves had been manufactured. During cross-examination, Rubin said that he could not say with certainty that the gloves shown on the videotapes were the same as the ones found by police.

In a separate issue, defense attorneys asked Judge Ito to end the jury's sequestration. Ito did not rule on the request.

September 13, 1995

Gary Sims, a criminalist for the California Department of Justice, testified that new DNA test results confirmed the finding that blood from both O.J. Simpson and Ronald Goldman were found in Simpson's Bronco. Defense attorney Barry Scheck cross-examined Sims, suggesting once again that the blood in the Bronco had been planted. The prosecution also played a videotape showing Thano Peratis, a police department nurse, who had recently been hospitalized, saying that he had overestimated the amount of blood drawn from Simpson after the killings. Peratis's taped statement discounted the likelihood of missing blood, implying that none was available for the police to use in planting evidence.

Judge Ito also ruled on the request by the defense to un-sequester the jury, ruling that the jury would remain sequestered.

DEFENSE REJOINDER

September 14, 1995

FBI Special Agents Douglas Deedrick and William Bodziak, who had testified earlier during the trial, were again called to the witness stand. They refuted claims by expert witness for the defense, Dr. Henry Lee, who had earlier maintained that imprints on Ronald Goldman's jeans and on an envelope and piece of paper found at the crime scene indicated a second set of shoe prints. Deedrick, a forensic expert, testified that he believed that the marks may have been imprinted on the items in question by Goldman's bloody clothing during the struggle. Special Agent Bodziak, who specializes in footprint analysis for the FBI, testified that the marks in question could not have come from a shoe. Cross-examination by defense attorney Barry Scheck found Deedrick admitting that he is not a blood pattern expert.

September 15, 1995

FBI Special Agent William Bodziak continued to testify, saying that defense expert Dr. Henry Lee's claim of a second set of footprints at the crime scene was erroneous. Marks identified by Lee as footprints, said Bodziak, resulted from impressions left in the concrete walkway by the workmen who poured it.

September 18, 1995

FBI Special Agent Bodziak testified that there could not have been a second killer. "It's impossible," he said, "unless the person that committed the crime can fly." Defense attorney Scheck suggested that a second killer could have gone from the scene without leaving footprints if Ronald Goldman died before Nicole Brown Simpson's throat was cut. "Are you asking me to assume there were two independent murders at the same place 10 minutes apart?" an incredulous Bodziak responded.

September 19, 1995

Defense attorneys called two former organized crime figures — brothers Larry and Craig ("Tony the Animal") Fiato — who had become government informants in police investigations of mob activity and are now in the federal witness protection program. The Fiato brothers testified that lead detective Philip Vannatter had remarked to them that O.J. Simpson was a suspect in the murders immediately after they happened. Craig Fiato said, however, that Vannatter only remarked that when a woman is killed, "the husband is always the suspect." The Fiato brothers testified without television coverage because of fears that they might be endangered having their images broadcast.

September 22, 1995

Judge Ito asked Simpson to make a routine wavier of his right to testify. Following Simpson's statement defense attorney Johnnie Cochran made a routine motion to dismiss the case, which Ito denied. The judge then asked the Bailiff to recall the jurors and proceeded to give them closing instructions. Although closing instructions to the jury are routinely given after both the defense and the prosecution have concluded their closing arguments, Judge Ito decided that earlier instructions were appropriate.

SIMPSON WAIVES HIS RIGHT TO TESTIFY

Ms. Clark: Mr. Kelberg points out absolutely correctly that all the Court need do at this time is advise Mr. Simpson of his right to testify, that it is his personal right to use and to invoke, that he may testify over the objections of his lawyers if he so chooses, and that if he declines to do so, then he has waived that right. And that is all the Court need do.

Mr. Cochran: May I respond, Your Honor?

The Court: Briefly.

Mr. Cochran: There seems to be this great fear of the truth in this case. This is still America. And we can talk. We can speak. Nobody can stop us.

And the Court asked me about Mr. Simpson, and I respectfully indicated to him that he just wanted to briefly address the Court. And it's interesting that at this time — and I won't sink to this at this time. We won't start the arguments until Tuesday.

But the Court asked about the waivers of right to speak with regard to the waiver, and they can't stop him from speaking. And that's what it boils down to.

The Court: It also boils down to the Court can control the orderly process. And all I'm interested in at this point now is that I've been told that the defense intends on resting and not presenting any further witnesses or any further evidence other than their proffer that Mr. Simpson understands his right to testify as a witness, and that after discussing that with his lawyers, he's making an intelligent decision not to testify.

Mr. Cochran: The Court asked me about that, and I would indicate to the Court that Mr. Simpson would like to respond to the Court personally.

The Court: Mr. Simpson, good morning, sir.

The Defendant: Good morning, Your Honor. As much as I would like to address some of the misrepresentations made about myself and Nicole concerning our life together, I'm mindful of the mood and the stamina of this jury.

I have confidence, a lot more it seems than Ms. Clark has, of their integrity, and that they'll find — as the record stands now — that I did not, would not, and could not have committed this crime. I have four kids — two kids I haven't seen in a year. They asked me every week, "Dad, how much longer?"

The Court: All right.

The Defendant: I want this trial over.

The Court: All right. Thank you. Mr. Simpson, you do understand your right to testify as a witness?

The Defendant: Yes, I do.

The Court: And you choose to waive your right to testify?

The Defendant: I do.

The Court: All right.

THE DEFENSE RESTS

The Court: All right. Anything else before I we invite the jurors to join us? I'm sorry. Mr. Cochran, you wanted to make an 1181 motion?

Mr. Cochran: Yes, Your Honor. I would just I would just briefly move for a judgment of acquittal pursuant to 1181 of the Penal Code and submit it.

The Court: Ms. Clark?

Ms. Clark: Submitted.

The Court: All right. Motion will be denied. All right. Deputy Smith, let's have the jurors, please.

• • •

The Court: Ladies and gentlemen, please be seated. And let the record reflect that we have now been rejoined by all the members of our jury panel. Good morning, ladies and gentlemen.

The Jurors: Good morning.

The Court: All right. Mr. Cochran, on behalf of the defense, do you have any further testimony or evidence to present?

Mr. Cochran: Good morning, Your Honor. Good morning, ladies and gentlemen.

The Jurors: Good morning.

Mr. Cochran: Your Honor, I'm very pleased to say we have no further testimony to present at this time. And, as difficult as it is, the defense does rest at this point.

JUDGE ITO'S CLOSING INSTRUCTIONS TO THE JURY

After the defense rested its case, Judge Lance Ito read instructions to the jury for about 36 minutes. In most jurisdictions, after closing arguments have concluded, the judge will charge the jury to "retire and select one of your number as a foreman...and deliberate upon the evidence which has been presented until you have reached a verdict." The words of the charge will vary somewhat between jurisdictions and among judges, but all judges will remind members of the jury of their duty to follow the law, and to consider objectively only the evidence which has been presented. They will also remind jurors of the need for impartiality. The judge's charge includes a review of the statutory elements of the alleged offense, of the burden of proof which rests upon the prosecution, and of the need for the prosecution to have proven guilt beyond a reasonable doubt before a guilty verdict can be returned.

In their charge many judges will also provide a summary of the evidence presented, usually from notes they have taken during the trial, as a means of refreshing the juror's memories of events. About half of all the states allow judges the freedom to express their own views as to the credibility of witnesses and the significance of evidence. Other states only permit judges to summarize the evidence in an objective and impartial manner.

Following the charge, typical procedure is to order the jury removed from the courtroom to begin deliberations. In the absence of the jury, defense attorneys may choose to challenge portions of the judge's charge. If they feel that some oversight has occurred in the original charge, they may also request that the judge provide the jury with additional instructions or information. Such objections, if denied by the judge, often become the basis for appeals when a conviction is returned. In the Simpson case, Judge Ito decided to change the usual order of events, charging the jury prior to the presentation of closing arguments. Judge Ito's final instructions to the jury are presented below in summarized form.

The Court: All right. Upon receipt of the exhibit from both sides, both sides having now rested, ladies and gentlemen, as you heard, the counsel for both the prosecution and the defense have rested their case. There will be no further testimony or evidence presented to you.

And it is now going to be my duty to instruct you on the law that applies to this case. After I finish instructing you on the law, then we'll hear the arguments of the attorneys, and that will commence on Tuesday, September the 25th.

On Monday, September the 25th, I will be here with the attorneys who are available. We'll organize all the exhibits so that when the argument commences, it will go forward in an orderly and efficient and quick manner, I hope.

Having said that, there is a proposal that has been made that I am contemplating with regard to the arguments by the attorneys, and that is to extend the Court hours for next week.

The proposal is to start with the normal morning session at nine o'clock, go until noon, start the afternoon session and go till approximately five or six in the evening, take a break for an evening meal, and then have a session in the evening to approximately 8 or 9:00 in the evening. And it's my feeling that by doing that that we can finish the arguments perhaps next week or as soon as possible thereafter.

I know, however, that that would disrupt your schedule. It would place an extra burden on the court staff, and this is something that I have not decided yet to do. But I would like your input to see whether or not you would be willing to stay for an additional evening session each day until we have concluded the arguments, and I'm actually — I've seen 8 nods affirmative. I see smiles. Everybody?

Well, we have one unanimous decision already. All right. All right. Then this is also subject — I also, as you know, I have to make arrangements to get you all fed, the bailiffs have to change their schedules. I may have to bring in a third court reporter. It will be — I have some logistical things to do before we make that in stone, but I wanted to know first whether or not you would do that and having got an affirmative answers, I will pursue that this afternoon.

All right. Ladies and gentlemen of the jury. You have heard all the — excuse me. I'm sorry. Deputy Bakshmanan, now that I'm starting the instructions, nobody is to enter or leave the courtroom during the Court's instructions.

All right, ladies and gentlemen of the jury, you have heard all the evidence, and it is now my duty to instruct you on the law that applies to this case. After I conclude reading these instructions to you, we will commence with the argument of counsel. The law requires that I read these instructions to you here in open court. Please listen carefully. It is also my personal policy that you will have these instructions in their written form in the jury room to refer to during the course of your deliberations.

You must base your decision on the facts and the law. You have two duties to perform first, you must determine the facts from the evidence received in the trial and not from any other source. A fact is something that is proved directly or circumstantially by the evidence, or by stipulation. A stipulation is an agreement between the attorneys regarding the facts. Second you must apply the law that I state to you to the facts, as you determine them, and in this way, arrive at your verdict, and any finding you were instructed to include with your verdict.

You must accept and follow the law as I state it to you, whether or not you agree with the law. If anything concerning the law said by the attorneys in their arguments or at any other time during the trial conflicts with my instructions on the law, you must follow my instructions. You must not be influenced by pity for a defendant or by prejudice against him. You must not be biased against the defendant because he has been arrested for this offense, charged with a crime, or brought to trial. None of these circumstances is evidence of guilt, and you must not infer or assume from any or all of them that he is more likely to be guilty than innocent. You must not be influenced by mere sentiment, conjecture, sympathy, passion, prejudice, public opinion, or public feeling. Both the prosecution and the defendant have a right to expect that you will conscientiously consider and weigh the evidence, apply the law and reach a just verdict, regardless of the consequences.

If any rule, direction or idea is repeated or stated in different ways than these instructions, no emphasis is intended, and you must not draw any inference because of its repetition. Do not single out any particular sentence or any individual point or instruction, and ignore the others. Consider the instructions as a whole and each in light of all the others. The order in which the instructions are given has no significance as to their relative importance.

Statements made by attorneys during the trial are not evidence, although if the attorney has stipulated to or agreed to a fact, you must regard that fact as conclusively proven. If an objection was sustained to a question, do not guess what the answer might have been, do not speculate as to the reason for the objection. Do not assume to be true any insinuation suggested by a question asked of a witness. A question is not evidence, and may be considered only as it enables you to understand the answer. Do not consider for any purpose any offer of evidence that was rejected by the court, or any evidence that was stricken by the court. You must treat it as though you had never heard it.

You must decide all questions of fact in this case from the evidence received here in court in this trial and not from any other source. You must not make any independent investigation of the facts or the law, or consider or discuss facts as to which there has been no evidence. This means, for example, that you must not on your own visit the scene, conduct experiments or consult reference works or persons for additional information. You must not discuss this case with any other person except a fellow juror, and you must not discuss the case with a fellow juror until the case is submitted to you for your decision, and then only when all 12 jurors are present in the jury room.

Evidence consists of the testimony of witnesses, writings, material objects, or anything presented to the senses and offered to prove the existence or non-existence of a fact. Evidence is either direct or circumstantial. Direct evidence is evidence that directly proves a fact without the necessity of an inference. It is evidence which, by itself, if found to be true, establishes that fact. Circumstantial evidence, is evidence that if found to be true proves a fact from which an inference of the existence of another fact may be drawn. An inference is a deduction of fact that may logically and reasonably be drawn from another fact or group of facts established by the evidence. It is not necessary that facts be proved by direct evidence. They may be proof also by circumstantial evidence, or by a combination of direct evidence and circumstantial evidence. Both direct evidence and circumstantial evidence are acceptable as a means of proof. Neither is entitled to any greater weight than the other. However, a finding of guilt as to any crime, may not be based on circumstantial evidence unless the proof circumstances are not only: one, consistent with the theory that the defendant is guilty of the crime; but: two, cannot be reconciled with any other rational conclusion. Further, each fact which is essential to complete a set of circumstances necessary to establish the defendant's guilt, must be proved beyond a reasonable doubt. In other words, before an inference essential to establish guilt may be found to have been proved beyond a reasonable doubt, each fact or circumstance upon which such inference necessarily rests, must be proved beyond a reasonable doubt.

Also, if the circumstantial evidence as to any particular count is susceptible of two reasonable interpretations, one of which points to the defendant's guilt, and the other to his innocence, you must adopt that interpretation which points to the defendant's innocence and reject that interpretation which points to his guilt. If, on the other hand, one interpretation of such evidence appears to you to be reasonable, and the other interpretation to be unreasonable, you must accept the reasonable interpretation and reject the unreasonable.

If you find that before this trial, the defendant made a willfully false or deliberately misleading statement concerning the crimes for which he is now being tried, you may consider such statement as a circumstance tending to prove consciousness of guilt. However, such conduct is not sufficient by itself to prove guilt and its weight and significance, if any, are matters for your determination.

Certain evidence was limited — excuse me — certain evidence was admitted for a limited purpose. At the time this evidence was admitted, you were admonished that it could not be considered by you for any other purpose other than the limited purpose for which it was admitted. Do not consider such limited evidence for any purpose, except a limited purpose for which it was admitted. Neither side is required to call as witnesses, all persons who may have been present at any of the events disclosed by the evidence, or who may appear to have some knowledge of these events, or to produce all objects or documents mentioned or suggested by the evidence.

Testimony given by a witness at a prior proceeding, who was unavailable at this trial, has been read to you from the reporters transcript of that proceeding. You must consider such testimony as if it had been given before you in this trial. With the exception of Nurse Thano Peratis, evidence that on some former occasion, a witness made a statement or statements that were inconsistent or consistent with his or her testimony in this trial, may be considered by you, not only for the purpose of testing the credibility of the witness, but also as evidence of the truth of the facts, as stated by the witness on such former occasion. Evidence of the Thano Peratis videotaped statement, which is People's exhibit 615, which may include statements that were consistent or inconsistent with his former testimony, presented by reading the transcript of his former testimony, given before both —

excuse me — given at the preliminary hearing, may be considered by you solely for the purpose of testing the credibility of Mr. Peratis's former testimony. If you disbelieve a witness testimony that he or she no longer remember a certain event, such testimony is inconsistent with a prior statement or statements by him or her, describing that event.

Every person who testifies under oath is a witness. You are the sole judges of the believability of a witness and the weight to be given the testimony of each witness. In determining the believability of a witness, you may consider anything that has a tendency and reason to prove or disprove the truthfulness of the testimony of the witness including, but not limited to any of the following: the extent of the opportunity or the ability of the witness to see or hear or otherwise become aware of any matter about which the witness has testified, the effects, if any, from the use of consumption of alcohol, drugs or other intoxicants by the witness at the time of the events about which the witness has testified, or at the time of his or her testimony, the ability of the witness to remember or to communicate any matter about which the witness has testified, the character and quality of that testimony, the demeanor and manner of the witness while testifying, the existence or nonexistence of a biased interest or other motive, evidence of the existence or non-existence of any fact testified to by the witness, the attitude of the witness toward this action or toward the giving of testimony, a statement previously made by the witness that is consistent or inconsistent with the testimony of the witness, the character of the witness for honesty or truthfulness or their opposites, an admission by the witness of untruthfulness.

Discrepancies in a witness's testimony, or between his or her testimony and that of others, if there were any, do not necessarily mean that the witness should be discredited. Failure recollection is a common experience, and innocent misrecollection is not uncommon. It is also a fact that two persons witnessing an incident or transaction often will see or hear it differently. Whether a discrepancy pertains to a fact of importance, or only to a trivial detail, should be considered in weighing it's significance.

A witness who is willfully false in one material part of his or her testimony, is to be distrusted in others. You may reject the whole testimony of a witness who has willfully testified falsely as to a material point unless, from all the evidence, you believe the probability of truth favors his or her testimony and other particulars.

You are not bound to decide an issue of fact in accordance with testimony of a number of witnesses which does not convince you, as against the testimony of a lesser number or other evidence which appeals to your mind with more convincing force. You may not disregard the testimony of the greater number of witnesses merely from caprice, whim, prejudice or from a desire to favor one side as against the other. You must not decide an issue by the simple process of counting the number of witnesses who have testified on the opposing sides. The final test is not in the relative number of witnesses, but in the convincing force of the evidence.

You should give the testimony of a single witness whatever weight you think it deserves. However, testimony by one witness which you believe concerning any fact is sufficient for the proof of that fact. You should carefully review all evidence upon which the proof of such fact depends. A person is qualified to testify as an expert if he or she has special knowledge, skill, experience, training or education sufficient to qualify him or her, as an expert on the subject to which his or her testimony pertains. A duly qualified expert may give an opinion on questions and controversy at a trial. To assist you in deciding such questions, you may consider the opinion with the reasons given for it, if any, by the expert who gives the opinion. You may also consider the qualifications and the credibility of the expert. You are not bound to accept an expert opinion as conclusive but should give to it the weight to which you find it to be entitled. You may disregard any such opinion if you find it to be unreasonable.

In examining an expert witness, counsel may propound to him or her a type of question known in the law as a hypothetical question. By such a question, the witness is asked to assume to be true a set of facts and to give an opinion based upon that assumption. In permitting such a question, the Court does not rule and does not necessarily find that all the assumed facts have been proved. The Court only determines that those assumed facts are within the probable or possible range of the evidence. It is for you, the jury, to find from all the evidence whether or not the facts assumed in a hypothetical question have been proved. If you should find that any assumption in such question has not been proved, you are to determine the effect of that failure on the proof. Excuse me. You are to determine the effect of that failure of proof on the value and weight of the expert opinion based on the assumed facts.

In resolving any conflict that may exist in the testimony of expert witnesses, you should weigh the opinion of one expert against that of another. In doing this, you should consider the relative qualifications and credibility of the expert witnesses as well as the reasons for each opinion and the facts and other matters upon which it was based. In determining the weight to be given the opinion expressed by any witness who did not testify as an expert witness, you should consider his or her credibility, the extent of his or her opportunity to perceive the matters upon which his or her opinion is based and the reasons, if any, given for it. You are not required to accept such opinion but should give to it the weight, if any, to which you find it to be entitled.

The Court has admitted physical evidence, such as blood, hair and fiber evidence, and experts' opinions concerning the analysis of such physical evidence. You are the sole judges of whether any such evidence has a tendency and reason to prove any fact at issue in this case. You should carefully review and consider all the circumstances surrounding each item of evidence, including, but not limited to, its discovery, collection, storage and analysis. If you find any item of evidence does not have a tendency and reason to prove any element of the crime's charge or the identity of perpetrator of such of the crime's charge, you must disregard such evidence.

You have heard testimony about frequency estimates calculated for matches between known reference blood samples and some of the bloodstain evidence items in this case. The random match probability statistic used by DNA experts is not the equivalent of a statistic that tells you the likelihood of whether a defendant committed a crime. The random match probability statistic is the likelihood that a random person in the population would match the characteristics that were found in the crime scene evidence and in the reference sample. These frequency estimates are being presented for the limited purpose of assisting you in determining what significance to attach to those bloodstain testing results. Frequency estimates and laboratory errors are different phenomena. Both should be considered in determining what significance to attach to bloodstain testing results.

Evidence has been introduced for the purpose of showing that the defendant committed crimes other than that for which he is on trial. Such evidence, if believed, was not received and may not be considered by you to prove that the defendant is a person of bad character or that he has a disposition to commit crimes. Such evidence was received and may considered by you only for the limited purpose of determining if it tends to show a characteristic method, plan or scheme in the commission of criminal acts similar to the method, plan or scheme used in the commission of the offense in this case, which would further tend to show the existence of the intent, which is a necessary element of the crime charge. The identity of the person who committed the crime, if any, of which the defendant is accused, or a clear connection between the other offense and the one of which the defendant is accused, so that it may be inferred that, if the defendant committed the other offenses, the defendant also committed the crimes charged in this case. The existence of the intent, which is a necessary element of the crime charged, the identity of the person who committed the crime, if any, of which the defendant is accused, a motive for the commission of the crime charged.

For the limited purpose for which you may consider such evidence, you must weigh it in the same manner as you do all the evidence all the other evidence in this case. You are not permitted to consider such evidence for any other purpose. Within the meaning of the preceding instructions, such other crime or crimes purportedly committed by a defendant must be proved by a preponderance of the evidence. You must not consider such evidence for any purpose unless you are satisfied that the defendant committed such other crimes or crimes. The prosecution has the burden of proving these facts by a preponderance of the evidence. Within this limited context, preponderance of the evidence means evidence that has more convincing force and the greater probability of truth than that opposed to it. If the evidence is so evenly balanced that you are unable to find that the evidence on either side of an issue preponderates, your finding on that issue must be against the party who has the burden of proving it. You should consider all the evidence bear upon bearing upon every issue, regardless of who produced it.

Motive is not an element of the crime charged and need not be shown. However, you may consider motive or lack of motive as a circumstance in this case. Presence of motive may tend to establish guilt. Absence of motive may tend to establish innocence. You will therefore give its presence or absence, as the case may be, the weight to which you find it to be entitled.

A defendant in a criminal trial has a constitutional right not be compelled to testify. You must not draw any inference from the fact that a defendant does not testify. Further, you must neither discuss this matter, nor permit it to enter into your deliberations in any way. In deciding whether or not testify, the defendant may choose to rely upon the state of the evidence and upon the failure, if any, of the prosecution to prove beyond a reasonable doubt every essential element of the crime charged against him. No lack of testimony on the defendant's part will make up for a failure of proof by the prosecution, so as to support a finding against him on any such essential element.

An admission is a statement made by the defendant, other than at his trial, which does not by itself acknowledge his guilt of the crimes for which such defendant is on trial, but which statement tends to prove his guilt when considered with the rest of the evidence. You are the exclusive judges as to whether the defendant made an admission, and if so, whether such statement is true in whole or in part. If you should find that the defendant did not make the statement, you must reject it. If you find that it is true in whole and in part, you may consider the part which you find to be true. Evidence of an oral admission of the defendant should be viewed with caution.

No person may be convicted of a criminal offense unless there is some proof of each element of the crime independent of any admission made by him outside of this trial. The identity of the person who is alleged to have committed a crime is not an element of the crime, nor is the degree of the crime. Such identity or degree of the crime may be established by an admission.

Witness Ron Shipp testified to a statement alleged to have been made by the defendant concerning dreams. You must first determine whether such statement was made by the defendant. If you find the statement was not made by the defendant, you shall disregard the statement. If you find that the statement referred to subconscious thoughts while asleep, you are to disregard the statement. If you find that the statement referred to an expression of a desire or expectation, you may give to such statement the weight to which you feel it is entitled. Evidence of oral statements by a defendant should be viewed with caution.

A defendant in a criminal action is presumed to be innocent until the contrary is proved, and in case of a reasonable doubt whether his guilt is satisfactorily shown, he is entitled to a verdict of not guilty. This presumption places upon the prosecution the burden of proving him guilty beyond a reasonable doubt.

Reasonable doubt is defined as follows. It is not a mere possible doubt, because everything relating to human affairs is open to some possible or imaginary doubt. It is that state of the case which, after the entire comparison and consideration of all the evidence, leaves the minds of the jurors in that condition that they cannot say they feel an abiding conviction of the truth of the charge.

The prosecution has the burden of proving beyond a reasonable doubt each element of the crimes charged in the information and that the defendant was the perpetrator of any such charged crimes. The defendant is not required to prove himself innocent or to prove that any other person committed the crimes charged.

In the crimes charged in counts one and two, there must exist a union or joint operation of act or conduct and a certain specific intent or mental state in the mind of the perpetrator. Unless such specific intent and/or mental state exists, the crime to which they relate is not committed. The crime of murder in the second degree requires to specific intent to kill, known as express malice. The crime of murder in the first degree requires the specific intent to kill, known as express malice, and the mental state of premeditation and deliberation. These terms are more fully defined later in these instructions.

The specific intent or mental state with which an act is done, may be shown by the circumstances surrounding the commission of the act. However, you may not find the defendant guilty of the crimes charged in courts one and two or the crime of second degree murder, which is a lesser crime, unless the proved circumstances are not only, one, consistent with the theory that the defendant had the required specific intent or mental state, but, two, cannot be reconciled with any other rational conclusion. Also, if the evidence as to any such specific intent or mental state is susceptible of two reasonable interpretations, one of which points to the existence of the specific intent or mental state, and the other to the absence of the specific intent or mental state, you must adopt that interpretation which points to the absence of the specific intent or mental state. If, on the other hand, one interpretation of the evidence as to such significant intent or mental state appears to you to be reasonable, and the other interpretation to be unreasonable, you must accept the reasonable interpretation and reject the unreasonable.

Evidence has been received for the purpose of showing that the defendant was not present at the time and place of the commission of the alleged crime for which he is here on trial. If, after a consideration of all the evidence, you have a reasonable doubt that the defendant was present at the time the crime was committed, you must find him not guilty.

The defendant is accused in counts one and two of having committed the crime of murder, a violation of Penal Code Section 187. Every person who unlawfully kills a human being with malice aforethought is guilty of the crime of murder, in violation of Section 187 of the California Penal Code. In order to prove such crime, each of the following elements must be proved: one, a human being was killed, two, the killing was unlawful, and, three, the killing was done with malice aforethought.

Express malice is defined as when there is manifested an intention unlawfully to kill a human being. The mental state — excuse — me when it is shown that a killing resulted from the intentional doing of an act with express malice, no other mental state need be shown to establish the mental state of malice aforethought. The mental state constituting malice aforethought does not necessarily require any ill will or hatred of the person killed. The word, "aforethought" does not imply deliberation of the lapse of considerable time. It only means that the required mental state must precede rather than follow the act.

All killing which is perpetrated by any kind of willful, deliberate and premeditated killing, with express malice aforethought is murder of the first degree. The word "willful," as used in this instruction, means intentional. The world, "deliberate" means formed, or arrived at, or determined upon as a result of careful thought and weighing of the considerations for and against the proposed course of action. The word, "premeditated" means considered beforehand. If you find that the killing was preceded and accompanied by a clear, deliberate intent on the part of the defendant to kill, which was the result of deliberation and premeditation, so that it must have been formed upon pre-existing reflection and not under a sudden heat of passion or other condition precluding the idea of deliberation, it is murder of the first degree.

The law does not undertake to measure in units of time the length of the period during which the thought must be pondered before it can ripen into an intent to kill which is truly deliberate and premeditated.

The time will vary with different individuals and under varying circumstances. The true test is not the duration of time, but rather the extent of the reflection. A cold, calculated judgment and decision may be arrived at in a short period of time. But a mere unconsidered and rash impulse, even though it includes an intent to kill, is not such deliberation and premeditation as will fix an unlawful killing as murder of the first degree. To constitute a deliberate and premeditated killing, the slayer must weigh and consider the question of killing and the reasons for and against such a choice and, having in mind the consequences, he decides to and does kill.

Murder of the second degree is the unlawful killing of a human being with malice aforethought, where there is manifested an intention unlawfully to kill a human being, but the evidence is insufficient to establish deliberation and premeditation. Murder is classified into two degrees and if you should find the defendant guilty of murder, you must determine and state in your verdict, whether you find the murder to be of the first or second degree.

If you are convinced beyond a reasonable doubt that the crime of murder has been committed by the defendant, but you have a reasonable doubt whether such a murder was murder of the first or of the second degree, you must give the defendant the benefit of the doubt and return a verdict fixing the murder as the second degree. Before you may return a verdict in this case, you must also agree unanimously, not only as to whether the defendant is guilty or not guilty, but also, if you should find him guilty of an unlawful killing, you must agree unanimously as to whether he is guilty of murder of the first degree or murder of the second degree.

If you find the defendant in this case guilty of murder in the first degree, you must then determine the following special circumstance whether the following special circumstance is true or not true. The defendant has, in this case, been convicted of at least one crime of murder in the first degree and one or more crimes of murder in the first or second degree. The prosecution has the burden of proving the truth of a special circumstance. If you have a reasonable doubt as to whether a special circumstance is true, you must find it to be not true. In order to find a special circumstance alleged in this case to be true or untrue, you must agree unanimously. You will state in your finding — excuse me — you will state your special finding as to whether this special circumstance is or is not true on the form that will be supplied to you.

To find the special circumstance referred to in these instructions as multiple murders convictions is true, it must be proved that the defendant has, in this case, been convicted of at least one crime of murder in the first degree and one or more crimes of murder in the first or second degree. You are not permitted to find a special circumstance alleged in this case to be true, based upon circumstantial evidence unless the proved circumstance is not only, one, consistent with the theory that a special circumstance is true, but, two, cannot be reconciled with any other rational conclusion. Further, each fact which is essential to complete a set of circumstances necessary to establish the truth of a special circumstance must be proved beyond a reasonable doubt.

In other words, before an inference essential to establish a special circumstance may be found to have been proved beyond a reasonable doubt, each fact or circumstance upon which such inference necessarily rests must be proved beyond a reasonable doubt. Also, if the circumstantial evidence is susceptible of two reasonable interpretations, one of which points to the truth of a special circumstance and the other to its untruth, you must adopt that interpretation which points to its untruth and reject the interpretation which points to its truth. If, on the other hand, one interpretation of such evidence appears to you to be reasonable and the other interpretation to be unreasonable, you must accept the reasonable interpretation and reject the unreasonable.

Each count charges a distinct crime. You must decide each count separately. The defendant may be found guilty or not guilty of either or both of the crimes charged. Your finding as to each count must be stated in a separate verdict form. If you are not satisfied beyond a reasonable doubt that the defendant is guilty of the crime charged, you may nevertheless convict him of any lesser crime if you are convinced beyond a reasonable doubt that the defendant is guilty of such lesser crime.

The crime of Second Degree Murder is a lesser to that of First Degree Murder. Thus, you are to determine whether the defendant is guilty or not guilty of First Degree Murder, as charged in Counts One and Two, or of any lesser crime. In doing so, you have discretion to choose the order in which you evaluate each crime and consider the evidence pertaining to it. You may find it productive to consider and reach tentative conclusion on all charges and lesser crimes, before reaching any final verdicts. However, the Court cannot accept a guilty verdict on a lesser crime unless you have unanimously found the defendant not guilty of the greater crime.

It is alleged in counts one and two that in the commission of the crime charged, the defendant personally used a deadly or dangerous weapon. If you find such defendant of the crime thus charged or a lesser included crime, you must determine whether or not such defendant personally used a deadly or dangerous weapon in the commission of such crime. A deadly or dangerous weapon means any weapon, instrument or object that is capable of being used to inflict great bodily injury or death. The term, "used a deadly or dangerous weapon," as used in this instruction, means to display such weapon in an intentionally menacing manner or intentionally to strike or hit a human being with it.

The prosecution has the burden of proving the truth of this allegation. If you have a reasonable doubt whether it is true, you must find it to be not true. You will include a special finding of that question in your verdict using a form that will be supplied to you for that purpose.

The purpose of the Court's instructions is to provide you with the applicable law so that you may arrive at a just and lawful verdict. Whether some instructions apply will depend upon what you find to be the facts. Disregard any instruction which applies to facts determined by you not to exist. Do not conclude that because an instruction has been given that the Court is expressing any opinion as to the facts of this case.

All right, ladies and gentlemen, this concludes the instructions that I am going to give to you prior to the arguments of the attorneys. As I indicated to you, we will stand in recess until Tuesday morning, September the 26th, to begin at nine o'clock with the arguments of the attorneys. It's an interesting date, because if you'll recollect, those of you who came to us in the first batch of jury selection, we actually started jury selection on September 26, 1994, and I see some people recollect that date.

Chapter 6
The Closing Argument
of the Prosecution

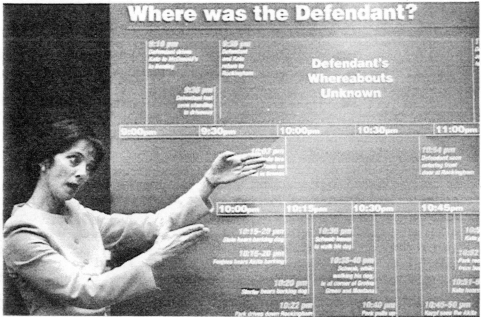

Prosecutor Marcia Clark used a time-line chart in closing arguments.
Pool photo by David Sprague.

THE PURPOSE OF CLOSING ARGUMENTS

At the conclusion of a criminal trial both sides have the opportunity for a final narrative presentation to the jury in the form of **closing arguments**, also called **summations**. These summations provide a review and analysis of the evidence. Their purpose is to persuade the jury to draw a conclusion favorable to the presenter. Testimony can be quoted, exhibits referred to, and attention drawn to inconsistencies in the evidence which has been presented by the other side.

States vary as to the order of closing arguments. Most, however, as is the case in California, require the prosecution to present its summation first, followed by the defense. An opportunity is then allowed for a final rebuttal by the prosecutor.

The Prosecution's Summation

September 26, 1995

Closing arguments began on September 26, 1995. Summarized below are the arguments made to the jury by Deputy District Attorneys Marcia Clark and Christopher Darden. The prosecution took six hours to present its closing argument.

The Court: All right. Deputy Terrara, let's have the jurors, please.

The Court: Let the record reflect that we've been rejoined by all the members of our jury panel. Good morning, ladies and gentlemen.

The Jury: Good morning.

The Court: My apologies to you for the late start. But we had some matters we had to get out of the way before we actually started with the arguments of the attorneys. However, we are now ready to commence. We are at that stage where the attorneys will have the opportunity to argue to you.

And I should let you know that previously I had contemplated placing a time limit on the lawyers in their argument. Some of the factors that I considered in whether or not I should place a time limit on them was the quantity of the evidence that was produced, the conflicts in the testimony, and the complexity of the issues that you'll have to resolve. And after considering the length of the case and the nature of the evidence, I have decided not to place a time limit on the argument of the attorneys. However, I have placed upon each side a limit of no more than two attorneys may argue to you for this part of the trial.

Now, the purpose of the argument by the attorneys is to discuss with you the facts and the evidence that have been presented to you, to discuss the law that I instructed you on earlier. And the attorneys may advance theories based upon the evidence, and they may urge conclusions that are fairly drawn from that evidence; however, during the course of their arguments, please remember my previous admonition to you that the comments and argument made to you by the attorneys are not evidence.

All right. Having said that, Ms. Clark, on behalf of the People, are the prosecution prepared to proceed their opening argument?

Ms. Clark: Yes, Your Honor, we are.

The Court: All right. You may proceed.

Ms. Clark: Thank you very much. Good morning, ladies and gentlemen.

The Jury: Good morning.

Ms. Clark: Finally, I feel like it's been forever since I talked to you; it kind of has. It's very weird to be in this courtroom next to you seeing you every day not getting a chance to talk to you. It's just very unnatural. And I have to tell you that as long as I've been doing this, as many years as I've been doing this, at this moment in a trial, I always feel the same. I feel like I want to sit down with you and say what do you want to talk about? Tell me what you're thinking.

• • •

I want to sit down, and I want to talk to you. I want you to tell me what do you want to know? You know, what do you want to talk about? Because that way I don't have to talk about stuff that you don't need to hear, stuff that you don't want explained, stuff that you're not interested in. And I can't. And I always have this sense of frustration. So I'm sorry if I say things that you don't need to hear or I explain things that are already very clear to you. Please bear with me because I'm not a mind reader, and I don't know.

Let me first—I want to take this opportunity to thank you, and I want to thank you from the bottom of my heart. You have been through so much. You have made a tremendous sacrifice. You haven't seen your children enough. You haven't seen your family enough. You haven't seen your loved ones enough. And all of this in the name of justice, in the service of justice.

Your dedication and your selflessness are truly beyond the pale. No one can say that any jury has sacrificed more for the cause of justice than you have. And I want you to know sincerely in my heart I appreciate it. I speak on behalf, I know, of the People of the state of California—this was a tremendous sacrifice. Your selflessness and your devotion will long be remembered by many, and I thank you. I think no one can understand how great their sacrifice has been, how terrible the pressure has been, how awful it must be for you to have your lives kind of out of control this way at the mercy of us taking longer than we should have, and you having to put your lives aside longer than you should have had to do. I'm sorry for that. I apologize for that.

. . .

Now, in the course of presenting all of this evidence, in this trial, just like every trial, some evidence has been presented to you that really is not relevant to answer the core question of who murdered Ron Goldman and Nicole Brown. And it's up to you, the jury, to weed out the distractions, weed out the side shows, and determine what evidence is it that really helps me answer this question.

. . .

Now, you, as jurors, sit as judges of the evidence. You are called the trier of fact, and as such, your job it is to be neutral and impartial as you examine the testimony presented, and in this regard you are guided, just like any judge, by the law.

And the jury instructions that were read to you on Friday is the law that you will apply to the evidence to determine the answers to the question that is posed here, who murdered Ronald Goldman and Nicole Brown.

The instructions discuss a wide range of topics. They talk about guidelines for the determination of credibility of witnesses, both expert and lay witnesses, and they talk about what the people are required to prove to establish the defendant's guilt.

But they go beyond that and they also tell you the frame of mind that you just adopt when you look at all of the evidence. And one of the first instructions that was read to you by the judge on Friday, if you will recall, concerned your duties as a jury and it stated in part, "You must not be influenced by pity for a defendant or by prejudice against him. You must not be biased against the defendant because he has been arrested for this offense, charged with a crime or brought to trial."

Now, of course, that makes sense, it's logical, and that means that we have to present proof to you, we just can't come in and say it's so, so I don't just get to get up here and say it's so, I have to prove it to you with evidence beyond a reasonable doubt. So that makes sense.

Now, the instruction goes on to read, "You must not be influenced by mere sentiment, conjecture, sympathy, bias, prejudice, public opinion or public feeling. Both the people and the defendant have a right to expect that you will conscientiously consider and weigh the evidence, apply the law and reach a just verdict regardless of the consequences.

In the course of this trial, you have heard some testimony of a very emotional nature. I expect that in the course of argument you are going to hear impassioned speeches, fiery speeches, speeches that may stir up feelings of anger, sorrow, pity.

Although your feelings may be aroused, as would be natural and understandable for all of us, as the instruction tells you, as the trier of fact, you, as the judges, are to remain neutral and impartial and not be influenced by some passion or sentiment, no matter how sorely tempted you may be to do so, and this applies to both sides, both sides.

Although the brutal and callous way in which Ron and Nicole were murdered may understandably make you feel sorrow, pity, even anger, it would be wrong to find the defendant guilty just because you felt sorry for them.

On the other hand, although it would be completely understandable if you were to feel angry and disgusted with Mark Fuhrman, as we all are, still, it would be wrong to find the defendant not guilty just because of that anger and disgust.

So as you listen to the arguments of counsel, please remember, when you weigh the evidence and you consider all of the evidence, remember that an appeal to passion and emotion is an invitation to ignore your responsibility as a juror. To be fair, we must examine all of the evidence in a calm and a rational and a logical way.

And let me come back to Mark Fuhrman for a minute, just so it's clear. Did he lie when he testified here in this courtroom saying that he did not use racial epithets in the last ten years? Yes. Is he a racist? Yes. Is he the worst LAPD has to offer? Yes. Do we wish that this person was never hired by LAPD? Yes. Should LAPD have ever hired him? No. Should such a person be a police officer? No. In fact, do we wish there were no such person on the planet? Yes.

But the fact that Mark Fuhrman is a racist and lied about it on the witness stand does not mean that we haven't proven the defendant guilty beyond a reasonable doubt, and it would be a tragedy if, with such overwhelming evidence, ladies and gentlemen, as we have presented to you, you found the defendant not guilty in spite of all that because of the racist attitudes of one police officer.

It is your duty, and it would be your challenge, to stay focused on the question you were brought here to answer, and the only question that you were brought here to answer, did the defendant commit these murders?

In seeking the answer to this question you look to all of the evidence presented to you, by both sides now, by both the people and the defense.

And you determine what evidence really answers that question. Because the defendant has thrown out many other questions, they throw out questions about whether LAPD has some bad police officers, does the scientific division have some sloppy criminalists, does the coroner's office have some sloppy coroners, and the answer to all these questions is, sure, yes, they do. That's not news to you. I am sure it wasn't a big surprise to you.

• • •

The question is what the evidence that was presented to you that relates to who killed Ron and Nicole, what does that tell you? Does that convince you beyond a reasonable doubt? No matter how much more qualified or how much better they could have done their job, still and all, did they present enough evidence to you? Did the evidence come to you in sufficient quantity and convincing force to convince you that the defendant committed these murders beyond a reasonable doubt? Ladies and gentlemen, I submit to you, that we have more than met our burden in this case.

Now, the defense has thrown out a lot of possibilities to you, the merest of possibilities, and a lot of them were just there to scare you. You heard Dr. Gerdes talk about it could be this, it could have been that, I see the validation studies, you know, kind of like — reminds me of a doctor when you have to go in for an operation, they give you all this list of things that could possibly happen to you.

Nevertheless — and they have to give you that warning, right? They have got to tell you that because otherwise you cannot give an informed consent and say, yes, knowing the risk, I am going to go and do this.

Now, if you really believed that all these horrible things were going to happen, no one would have an operation, you wouldn't take the risk, but you know, they have got to tell me everything, no matter how remote the possibility, and indeed, you go and you have the operation and you are fine and none of that stuff happens.

Well, in this case, it's actually they have raised all the possibilities of things that could happen in an effort to scare you away from the evidence. But we have done better than you could ever do in an operation because we have proven to you that nothing in this case did happen.

We have proven to you that it was not contaminated. We have even proven to you that it was not planted, for lack of a better term, and I am going to go through the evidence and demonstrate how we have proven is that to you.

So why were these issues raised? Why were these questions raised? Well, they are all questions and issues that were raised as a direction. There were roads raised — roads created by the defense to lead you away from the core truth and the issue that we are searching for the question — for the answer to, which is who murdered Ron and Nicole.

But these roads, ladies and gentlemen, these are false roads. They are false roads because they lead to a dead end. The false roads were paved with inflammatory distraction, but even after all their fearless efforts, the evidence stands strong and powerful to prove to you the defendant's guilt.

You know, I would like to show you a jury instruction that is very important, I think that both the prosecution and the defense will agree.

• • •

Reasonable doubt. Okay. This is an instruction that we'll talk to you about. They're going to talk to you about. This is a real important instruction. It's at the real heart of a case, every case, every criminal case, because it's the burden of proof that the People have. We don't guess anybody guilty, we prove it beyond a reasonable doubt, which is what we've done in this case.

Now, this tells you about reasonable doubt. It's kind of a funny definition, because it talks to you about reasonable doubt in very negative terms. It says that state of the evidence, which after the entire comparison you cannot say that you have an abiding conviction, it's very weirdly worded.

It's going to take you a while to go through this, so I'm going to take you through pieces at a time to try to give you a little hand here.

First of all, let me point out the first paragraph talks about the fact that it's our burden of proof. I think that one's fine, that's pretty easy. Now it talks about how reasonable doubt is defined. This is real important. It is not a mere possible doubt, okay, because everything relating to human affairs is open to some possible or imaginary doubt. That's very important.

If the doubt founded in reason—I'm going to amplify more on that with examples when we talk about the actual evidence in case. But bear in mind a possible doubt. I have a possible doubt that the sun will come up tomorrow. Do I have a reasonable doubt about it? No. I have doubt founded in reason that's going to happen. Just for a very basic example. So think about that, too. We're not talking about what possible doubt is. It's reasonable doubt.

Now, the other part of it, it is that state of the case which after entire comparison, the entire comparison and consideration of all the evidence. Now what that means, ladies and gentlemen, you can consider the defense case and you consider the prosecution case, you consider all of it. You'll probably hear from the defense multiple times "we don't have to prove anything," that's right, they don't.

In every criminal case, when the People complete their presentation, the defense can say, "no witnesses." We rest because they can sit and make the state prove their case without ever calling a witness, that's right, that's correct.

But when they do, when they do, then you must consider the quality and the nature of the evidence that they have presented. That goes into the mix. That's part of your consideration.

What kind of evidence did they present to demonstrate something to you, to prove something to you? If they try to prove something to

• • •

What have we shown you? We have the burden of proof. But you look at what they've shown you when you want to consider what was proven to you. I've got pieces of boards and exhibits everywhere in this courtroom.

All right. Now, all I'm telling you, ladies and gentlemen, is it's reasonable doubt and it's not possible doubt and we'll come back to it again.

But at the conclusion of all of our arguments, when you open up the windows and let the cool air blow out, the smoke screen that's been created by the defense with a cool wind of reason, you will see that the defendant has been proven guilty, easily, beyond a reasonable doubt.

Or to put it another way, the evidence has conclusively proven that when Detective Mark Fuhrman said he did not use racial epithets in the last 10 years, he lied. But it is also conclusively proven that the defendant is guilty beyond a reasonable doubt.

• • •

In the case, as in every case, there is certain evidence that is introduced that is directly proving a fact. For example, in this case Ronald Goldman left Mezzaluna at approximately 9:50, that's an approximate time, could have been a few minutes later. So we know that some time before 10:00 he left. We know he changed clothes, okay, but the direct thing we know is sometime shortly before 10:00 he left. We know he changed clothes because he was wearing something different when he was found.

We know how long it takes for him to get home because we have a witness telling us that. But what we don't know is exactly what time he left his house.

We know he left his house in time to be murdered and we'll talk about that shortly and in time for him to be there with the dogs barking, we have to make inferences, okay, we have to make an inference from the evidence that we know about as to when he got to Bundy.

Now, you can draw an inference that is reasonable or you can draw an inference that is unreasonable. What we are required to do here and what I must do is draw — inferences excuse me, that are reasonable.

Based on what we know, when he left the Mezzaluna, changing clothes, freshening up, and I think Stewart Tanner testified that he was — they had plans to meet at the Baja Cantina, he was going to get cleaned up to go somewhere.

Clark then spent a considerable amount of time reviewing the testimony of witnesses — trying to definitively establish the time line associated with the killings, while showing that Simpson had time to commit them, and that he didn't have a reasonable alibi. In this regard, Kato Kaelin is an especially important witness.

Now back to the timing. Kato told us that he was on the phone with a friend when the defendant came out to the pool area near his door. And he was able to pinpoint that — that time with the phone call bill that he had. Because the phone call was a long distance call. Now, the call was placed at 9:03 and it lasted for 7 minutes.

When he saw the defendant come out to talk to him, he hung up the phone. So it was about 10 after 9:00. I think — we do. At 10 after 9:00, approximately, just so we have 9:10 here, maybe it was 9:09, the defendant came out to talk to Kato. This is a very, very significant conversation that they have.

I'm going to come back to this a couple of times. So here's the first time. The defendant told Kato that he had only hundred dollar bills on him and he asked Kato if he had any fives for the skycap. You may recall that—asked him if he had fives. He realized he only had twenty dollars, so he gave the defendant a twenty which the defendant took.

• • •

Kato had several occasions to notice the defendant's hands during the drive to McDonald's and during the time that they paid and during the time they got changed. And he noticed that there were no cuts on the defendant's hands.

Or he didn't notice any cuts on the defendant's hands, to be more accurate. And that's actually an important distinction. You'll notice, too, when you look at the photograph of the defendant in the recital, you can see his left hand, and you can see that as of the time of the recital, when he's posing with Sydney, there's no cut on the back of the middle finger of the left hand. And that's important.

Now, what's probably even more significant than Kato's lack of observation of any cuts on the defendant's hand when they're in the — at the drive-through lane, is this: Kato wound up paying for the food with his own money, paid for both of them.

• • •

When they get back to Rockingham, Kato got out and he walked towards the house, expecting the defendant to follow him. But when he got to the front door, he turned and he realized, he's not here, and he saw the defendant still standing by the Bentley watching him, and he had not moved.

So as Kato told you, he took the hint, turned and went to his room. Now why didn't the defendant just walk in the house? Or if he intended to go somewhere, why didn't he just get back in the car and go? Either in the Bentley or in the Bronco. Why wait for Kato to be out of sight?

I'll come back to it. I just wanted us to think about it for a minute. Now, as soon as Kato got back to his room, he called a friend and fortunately the friend lived far enough away that it was a long distance call, so we have his phone bill that indicates what time it was.

And he indicated that he made that call as soon as he got back to his room. So he—the call was made at 9:37. So he left the defendant's presence at 9:36. And you can see here at 9:36 the defendant was last seen standing in the driveway. From 9:36 until 10:54, the defendant's whereabouts were unaccounted for. So we have the beginning of our window of opportunity at 9:36.

• • •

Now, in terms of timeline that night, what this tells you is that the defendant was outside — was out in his car at 10:03. Now, at that time he made phone calls to Paula Barbieri. You may recall we heard the testimony of the — I think it was LuEllen Robertson of Air Touch, and she told you — she interpreted the record for you and what it meant. And she told you that the calls were not completed. But we didn't need her to tell you that. The calls to Paula Barbieri were not answered because Paula Barbieri was in Las Vegas. She was not at home either in Florida or Los Angeles. She was in Las Vegas at the Mirage. You recall we had a witness testify to that. She checked into the Mirage at 2:00 p.m. on June the 12th. So she was not available to take those calls.

Now, I think we have further corroboration for the fact that the cell phone was in the Bronco in the fact that Allan Park, the limousine driver, testified that he saw — as they were loading up the limo, oh, he saw the defendant go out towards Rockingham, out to where we know the Bronco was parked and once or maybe even twice. So there is further corroboration for the fact that he went and got the cell phone out of the Bronco just before they left. Now, that — those phone calls are very significant in terms of their timing because at — you realize that at 10:03 when he's out in the Bronco and he's made those calls that the murders occurred about 10 to 15 minutes after that. We'll talk more about the state of mind that he was in at that time. We'll do it a little later.

• • •

Now, let's talk about Allan Park for a minute. You remember he was the young man who had never been to Brentwood before so he decided to make sure that he wouldn't be late. And although he was not supposed to be there until 10:45 for this pickup to LAX, he left at 9:45 to be on the safe side. And you may remember that this was a witness who was absolutely neutral, absolutely neutral. He was not going to strain to avoid answers. He was not going to make any effort to embellish anything. This was a witness who was just going to tell it straight and tell it honest all the way through no matter who was asking the questions, myself or the defense.

And he stood up there, and he took the grilling for a very long time. And I went back and I counted, the cross-examination and recross-examination by Mr. Cochran took up 175 pages of transcript in these proceedings. And he told you on that night he was driving down Sunset, he made a right at Rockingham and drove up Rockingham at 10:22.

Now, he looked at his clock and his watch many times that night. And the reason he did is very obvious. He's a driver. It's important that he be on time. It's important to him. It's important to his job. And this was an important job. I mean he's going to drive for Mr. Simpson. You know, it's not just me, something like that, or something the — ordinary average folk. It's important. He wants to do well. And he certainly doesn't want to be late, make Mr. Simpson miss his flight, so he was checking that clock. And at 10:22 he drives up at Rockingham, and he's looking at the curbs to see the address because he's never been there before, and he wants to see 360 Rockingham. This is also logical. I mean what do you do when you're looking for an address? You look at the curbs and you try to see where it is. And that's what he did. But when he did that, when he did that, he saw no Bronco parked on Rockingham, and he was looking right there at the curb.

• • •

So we know that at 10:22 the Bronco was not on Rockingham. But we know more because we know at this point when Allan Park had turned the corner onto Ashford, he told you he did not see any Bronco on Ashford either. So as of 10:22, that Bronco's gone, and the defendant is gone. That's further corroboration for what we told you with the phone calls in the Bronco. He was out in that Bronco on that night.

• • •

Now, at 10:39 he decided to check out the other gate, the Rockingham gate, and see if that would be easier to pull into than the Ashford gate. Because remember, he told you he had that stretch limo, kind of hard to maneuver. So what gate he went in and where he was, this was an important consideration for him. The logistics were not that easy with that car. When he drove down to the Rockingham gate, he told you that he pulled the driver's side window parallel with the driveway so that he could look into the driveway and see whether it would be easier for him to get the stretch limo up that side of the driveway because of the way it curved. And I'm sure you guys remember. You were there. You saw it's a curving driveway.

When he did that, the area where the Bronco was found on the curb just north of the Rockingham gate was well within his field of vision, but he didn't see it. Again, further corroboration. The Bronco was not there.

• • •

He wanted to let the defendant know that he was there. He pushed the buzzer, he told you, a good two or three times and he heard the buzzing and the ringing noise as he did that but he got no answer. He was concerned because the pick-up was supposed to be, he told you, for 10:45, starting to get up there now, so he called his boss and he wanted to ask him what he should do.

And I have a board that shows Allan Park's cell phone record, and that he was a very important cell phone record because that helps us to fix a lot of events that were testified to that otherwise would have been very approximate. With the help of his cell phone record, we have much more definite times, much more precise.

• • •

After he placed that call, he told you that he got out to ring the intercom a few more times, so now he rang the intercom at 10:40, no answer, 10:43, no answer, and he said he rang it a few times on each occasion, no answer. He noticed that there were no lights on downstairs, and that there was one light on upstairs. He got back in the car and he called his mother and he got his boss's home phone number and called him again at 10:49.

And you see that call — we have a lot more calls in here, but at 10:49 he called his boss again and he left a message because he got no answer. Now, when he left that message at 10:49 for his boss, after he hung up he got out and tried the buzzer again. Now, this is the third time he has tried to get someone to answer that buzzer at the gate, the third time that he rang two or three times, and this third time again he got no answer.

• • •

Back to Park. Now, after he tried the buzzer at 10:40 — after calling his boss at 10:49, he got out — it was when he was actually buzzing at that point — let me back up a for a second. He called his boss at 10:49 at home, he got no answer, he went out to the gate and he rang the buzzer again two or three times and got no answer.

While he was at the gate that third time he heard his car phone ringing and he went back into the car. It was his boss calling him. That call came in — that last call came in at 10:52, and he indicated — now, he told you about the fact that his boss called him, and he told his boss that no one had been home and he had been ringing for a while and he was very concerned because he was running late.

Now, at that time I asked him, were you seated in your car when you were speaking to your boss? He said yes. Where were you looking? I was looking through the gate right into the driveway. Well, what is the driveway lighting like, what is it like in there? Well, it's not really very well lit. The play area down in front — I am going to pull out a diagram of Rockingham and show you what I mean in a minute.

It was dark now, very little light. There was a light over the garage, but it gave very little illumination and it did not light up the south pathway area at all. So he sat in his car talking to his boss looking straight through the gate and at the driveway.

• • •

Well, Park checked the area, looked, and he couldn't see any lighting coming from that area and he told that to his boss. During that conversation Allan told you that he saw Kato come out on the side yard where the arrow is pointing, roughly in that area, I think it was a little bit farther back towards the tree, the other tree, that one, and he was holding a flashlight. Do you recall he told you that?

And at the same time, he said almost simultaneously, he saw a person approximately six feet tall, 200 pounds, African American, wearing all dark clothing walking at a good pace up the driveway...

• • •

I believe the testimony indicated that he saw this person at approximately where the arrow is, and he saw him walk up the driveway and into the entrance. Now, he hung up within 30 seconds of seeing that. Which means that according to the cell phone bill, according to the cell phone bill, the call ended at 10:55 and 12 seconds, approximately 30 seconds before that is when he saw the man walk into the house.

And immediately as soon as the man walked into the house, the lights started to go on and they went on downstairs. Now, Allan waited in his car thinking that someone would let him in, but no one did.

Now, if you recall, Kato said that he went out — he had gone out to that side yard to investigate the thumping noises. And when he saw the limo driver, he was thinking the limo driver was already taken care of and that the defendant would buzz him in.

He didn't worry about it. He went on to his business, that south pathway to start looking for what was going on back there. So Allan got out of his car and buzzed again. And this was now within a minute of seeing the man walk into the house, the lights go on, within a minute of that, Allan buzzed again, this is the fourth time.

This time he got an answer immediately. And the answer given to him was by the defendant. The defendant answered and told him he'd overslept and he'd just gotten out of the shower and he would be down in a minute.

Now, Allan told you that the man who he saw go into the house appeared to be the same size as the defendant and about the same height and weight. He would not stretch even one iota to draw the obvious conclusion that the man he saw walking up the driveway was the defendant. Of course it was. There was no one else there that night. It was the defendant. Who else could walk in the door, immediately turn on the lights and then answer the intercom? I mean, this is an easy reasonable inference to draw, easy.

But what's significant here is that he lied. Why did the defendant lie? Why, when he was just out in the driveway walking into the house, dressed in all dark clothing, why when he answered the intercom for Allan Park, did he lie and say I've overslept, I'm just getting out of the shower?

We know it's not true. We know it's not true. Why was it important for him to make Allan Park believe that he'd been at home? And I think we all know the answer to that question. Because he hadn't been at home. Because he'd just come back from Bundy.

● ● ●

And it was just as simple as that. Simple common sense tells you that the thumping, the gloves and the defendant's appearance on the driveway almost immediately thereafter are all part of one set of events, all connected in time and space. You don't need science to tell you that. You just need reason and logic.

After a luncheon recess, closing arguments by the prosecution continued.

When we left off, I was talking about the occurrence of the thumping, the gloves — the gloves dropping on the south pathway, and the defendant's appearance on the driveway within a couple of minutes of each other.

Now, while Allan Park was speaking to the defendant on the intercom, at that time Kato, who realized that — who wasn't worried about Allan being left outside, went over to the south pathway and looked down the gate.

. . .

Now, let me ask you this, why didn't the defendant let Allan Park drive into the driveway? Why leave him sitting out there at the gate? Why make him wait outside? Because the defendant was frazzled, ladies and gentlemen. He was hurried. And he needed to buy some time — time to wash himself up, wash off the blood, change the clothes, and to compose himself to appear normal, to appear calm, business as usual. So he bought himself that time and he did not let Allan in.

And when he came down — when the defendant came downstairs, he had changed clothes, no longer the dark clothing that Kato had described him in earlier that evening. He was wearing stonewashed denim jeans, denim shirt, and carrying a garment bag. You remember that Louis Vuitton garment bag? That's here in evidence. Allan estimated that the defendant came downstairs dressed like that carrying the garment bag about five to six minutes after he spoke to him on the intercom. I think Allan Park's words were a good five minutes, could have been longer. This was an estimate by him. But before the defendant actually came down, Kato went to let Allan Park in the gate. He let him in, and he immediately told Allan about the thumping noises he had heard. He asked him, "Did you feel an earthquake?" The same thing he asked Rachel Ferrara. If you recall, she told him she hadn't. Allan told him the same thing, "I didn't feel an earthquake."

. . .

Now, having heard about the thumping noises from Kato, hearing Kato's concern about it, how Kato was trying to figure out why that happened or what was the source of it and being very worried about it, knowing that he was going out of town, his daughter, Arnelle, staying on the property, and would be there alone with Kato, he did nothing to check on the source of the thumping.

He did none of the things you would expect someone to do under those circumstances, that is someone who didn't already know what caused the thumping, but, you see, he did, he knew, so, of course, he was unconcerned. He knew it was no prowler, certainly he knew it's no earthquake, because he knew the thumps were caused by him bumping into the wall.

And so he didn't have to be worried that Arnelle was going to be in danger, or even Kato in danger, or his home in danger, because it was not a question for him, it was something he knew about, and he acted like someone who already knew what the source of those sounds were, unconcerned.

Now, back to loading up the car. Allan and Kato described how they loaded up all the bags, all except one. You may recall that there was testimony about a small, dark bag that was on the edge of the driveway by the Bentley.

And Kato, as they were loading up the bags, offered to go and get that bag for him, I will go get that for you, defendant said, "no, no, no, no, no, I will go get it."

And the testimony was that all of the bags were loaded by either Kato or Allan Park, except for that one. And after the defendant walked towards it, after saying, no, I will get it, after he walked towards it, no one ever saw that little black — dark bag again, nor have we ever found the knife the defendant used, nor have we ever found the clothes that he wore during the murder, nor have we ever found the shoes that he wore during the murder.

And it's so typical. It's so common. They get rid of the murder weapon, they think that's it, can't get me, home free. But you see, as you have seen, it's not that easy. Evidence was left behind. So we don't need the murder weapon, because we have much, much more proof than that.

· · ·

Let me show you something. You recall the testimony that blood was collected from the bathroom upstairs that's just off the defendant's bedroom, and the blood is found very — it's found basically in between the sink and the shower in the defendant's bathroom. The defendant was bleeding in his bathroom when he was cleaning and changing his clothes, obviously.

That was before he went down to the limo, ladies and gentlemen, before he ever went to the Bronco. He already had that cut by the time he got downstairs. He got it long before he went out to that Bronco to get that cell phone.

So since we know he was bleeding upstairs in his own bathroom and before he went down to the limo, how come there wasn't any blood stains on the staircase? Obviously, he didn't fly, and just as obviously, he also bled downstairs. I show you that foyer picture, you have seen that quite a number of times with the blood spots on the floor, so he left blood downstairs, as well.

There are two possible reasons we didn't see photographs of blood stains on the staircase, number 1, they were there and they were missed, it seems unlikely, because it's a light carpet, but somehow, it's possible; or two, the cut temporarily stopped bleeding.

As you may remember, Dr. Huizenga testified that a cut will bleed, clot up, rebleed, and I am sure that isn't news to you, I mean, that's life experience, that's common to all of us, cut for a while, bleed for a while, and then maybe your hand will be still and then you will rebleed if you exercise it or you rub it against something, you irritate it somehow.

But in any case, by the time the defendant got downstairs with the garment bag and started loading up the limo, the cut was temporarily sealed. Now, here is the interesting thing about the blood trail on his driveway and the blood in the foyer. When you take into account the blood in the bathroom, doesn't it make sense that he actually reopened the cut while he was moving around getting ready to go?

You know you have the blood in the bathroom before he gets down to the limo, so he was already bleeding. You know that you don't have blood spots in between the bathroom and the foyer, so at some point the bleeding stopped before he left his bedroom. But you do know that you have more blood downstairs, you have blood leading out to the Bronco.

• • •

So by the time he opened the door, before he reached in and got the cell phone, that cut was bleeding again. You have him bleeding before he comes down to the limo in his bathroom, you have him going down to the Bronco and opening the door, but either way you look at it, he's already bleeding before he gets the cell phone. And that's shown to you by photographs.

Now, consider this possibility: He opened the car door, grazing his knuckle on that door, reopening the cut, and after getting the cell phone out, walks back up the driveway, dripping blood, walks into the foyer, talks to Kato about getting a flashlight that's better or stronger than the one he's got, talks to him about setting the alarm and while he's talking to him, he's standing in the foyer.

All right. He's standing in that foyer — can we get that close-up? All right. Now, you see those two drops down to the left of the number 12, it's kind of faint on this picture, you're going to have the pictures back in the jury room and I think they'll be better and clearer for you than this is. Those are big drops. Those are big blood drops, for example, not the kind you see from that little slice that Dr. Baden showed you on the defendant's finger, now we've all been living in this world for a while and you know when you get big drops of blood that's from a big cut.

You're not going to cut yourself, get a little slice like looking like a small slice on the inside of that finger and drip blood like that. It just makes — this is common sense stuff, it's just very logical. Those drops came from a big cut and we're talking about this cut on the middle finger.

• • •

So now we've talked about conduct. We've talked about opportunity and timing. Let's talk about the physical evidence. I'm not going to do it in the detail you've already heard it, heaven forbid. But although you already seen with the opportunity evidence, with the conduct evidence, we already have evidence to show you that the defendant did commit these murders without even really getting into the physical evidence. And once you see the vast array of physical evidence, you can see that there's virtually an ocean of evidence to prove that this defendant committed these murders.

What all of it does, all of this evidence, is it links the defendant to the victims and the crime scene at Bundy. Now, the defense has gone to great lengths to try and to show that they could discredit this evidence and the fact that they have included what have been some of the most bizarre and farfetched notions I think I have ever heard. They hinted that blood was planned. They've tried to create the impression that multiple other bloodstains were contaminated, and that somehow all the contamination only occurred where it would consistently prove the defendant was guilty. So now the little amplicons, the little DNAs, they're coconspirators, too, because they know they've got to rush to only the places where you can attribute the blood to the murderer. When you think about that, just think about that one point logically, obviously it's common sense if contamination is going on, you're going to see it going on all over the place.

• • •

Now, first of all, I want to hear Mr. Cochran actually stand up in front of you and tell you he believes the blood was planted, I want to hear that because that is incredible. That is absolutely incredible. When you think about that, think what evidence have you been given to show you how that blood was planted, to show you when that blood was planted, to show who planted that blood.

Now, the reason that they have to come up with this story about contamination and planting, and I want to hear if they really, really do that, say that to you, is because they can't get around the result.

• • •

If you are going to say that the blood was planted, then you are going to say that the blood was planted at or near the time it was collected, in which case the EDTA would not break down, in which case the EDTA would be intact, in which case you should see the kind of high, smooth arc that the graphs showed you from the reference tubes instead of the jagged noise that you actually saw.

And they brought in Dr. Rieders to try and tell you that that jagged noise looks just like that high arc, which is ridiculous, which is insulting to your intelligence, but the reason that they have to say this, defying logic, defying common sense, is because, ladies and gentlemen, his blood on the rear gate, with that match that makes him 1 in 57 billion people that could have left that blood. I mean, there is what, there is 5 billion people on the planet? That means you would have to go through 37 billion people to find the DNA profile that matches Mr. Simpson's. There is only 5 billion people on the planet.

Ladies and gentlemen, that's an identification. Okay? That proves it's his blood, nobody else's on the planet. No one. Now, they know that. Now, the blood on the socks, Nicole's blood on the socks, again, RFLP match, very powerful, showed from Cellmark, that was a 5-probe match, I believe, found to be 1 in 6.8 billion people, again, more than there are people on the planet, identification. An 11-probe match by DOJ showed that it was one in 7.7 billion people, again, her blood and only hers on this planet could be on that sock.

Now, how do you get around that? It wasn't wrong and they couldn't find an expert who would say it was contaminated because there is too much DNA. That is the blood, that type is the type, it is her blood. How do you get around that?

And if you know that that's true, if you know it's her blood on his socks that they find on the morning of June the 13th, that alone with the rear gate stain convicts him. You can't believe otherwise. You have so much proof now, how do they get around that?

They have to find a theory to get around that. And what do they do? This is what they come up with. So if it's low in volume DNA, it's contaminated; if it's high-volume DNA, it's planted and it's also very convenient, and ridiculous.

• • •

Yes, possibly we are all sitting on Mars right now, you know, and I am from Venus, anything is possible, let's talk about what did happen, let's talk about what we have got. They could have shown you proof that the Bundy blood drops were contaminated, not the mere possibility, no, I am talking about evidence that gives you a reason to conclude that that happened, and that they never could do.

And they could have done it if it were true, but they didn't. And not one expert they brought in on the DNA did even one test on the blood evidence, the evidence that we have that proves to you that the defendant committed these murders, not one, with all those experts you saw.

And the reason for that, ladies and gentlemen, is that it isn't true. The blood on the Bundy trail comes back to the defendant because it's his blood. The blood on the rear gate comes back to the defendant because it's blood he left there on the night of the murders.

So they took you through all this tortured and twisted road, one moment saying that the police are all a bunch of bumbling idiots, the next moment clever conspirators, and ask yourself did they ever prove who planted, when, how, and it's a fact that the defense doesn't have to prove anything, that's a fact.

But once they do decide to put on a case, once they decide to try and prove something, their witnesses are subject to the same scrutiny as the People's witnesses.

• • •

Saying it's so doesn't make it so. Having a lawyer stand up in front of you and say something, no matter how much it's said, doesn't mean it's true. I include myself in this, you know, I only argue what the facts show, what I believe the facts have shown, and any reasonable inferences that you can draw from them. That is all.

I cannot stand before you and tell you something that is false, that is untrue. You need to go with what is true, with the evidence, with what we have and the reasonable common sense deductions that you make from that evidence.

I don't ask you to take my word for anything. That's why we presented evidence. That's why we call witnesses. If it isn't in the record or it doesn't make sense to you as a logical inference from what you've heard, reject it. I don't care who says it, reject it. But do the same for the defense.

Hold me to that standard, hold them to that standard. When you hear them try to tell you that all of this evidence was either contaminated or planted, ask yourself, does this really make sense? Was it — what evidence was I given to prove that? Is there any evidence that really shows that? Or is it smoke and mirrors? Is it all the smoke to cloud everything, cloud all the issues, distract you, take a little piece here, take a little piece there.

Kind of reminds me of that story about all these guys that are blindfolded and each one goes to a different end of an elephant. One grabs the tail and he says, "Feels like a rope." And the other guy grabs the trunk and says, "Feels like a fire hose." And another guy grabbed the leg and says, "Feels like a tree."

Okay. Not one of them got it right, did they? Take off the blindfold, it's an elephant. You put all the pieces together, you put the whole picture together and you can see the truth.

But what they have done systematically is fragmented the case. This is not new. They did a very good job of it, they're fine lawyers.

And they challenged the People's case, as they should, that's good. You put the state to their proof. That's what we have to do, we have to deliver, we have to do our job. And we have.

But be aware what is happening here, they've fragmented little pieces out of context and focus on a little piece and a little piece of the picture, for example, on this little piece of the picture and forget about all the rest that puts it in context.

• • •

Now, back to DNA, I'm sorry, I digressed. Even when it's analyzed, using the PCR method, it's not quite so easily contaminated as the defense would have you believe. As you've learned, it's used every day to save lives.

And as you've also heard, it's used in very nonsterile conditions. It's used to identify war dead. What does that mean? War dead soldiers who die? Jungles and deserts, those are not sterile environments, ladies and gentlemen, those are very dirty environments, but they use PCR testing to identify those soldiers.

And why do they do that? So they can notify next of kin. That's a very serious responsibility. You better be right. You better be right. Now, if it's good enough to go and notify next of kin that their son, their daughter, their husband, their father has been murdered — or killed, excuse me — on a battlefield, then it better be good and reliable stuff.

So if it's good enough for that on body parts being recovered from jungles and deserts, it's pretty hearty, pretty durable.

Let me first say something to you about direct and circumstantial evidence. This instruction explains them both. I don't know how well, you know, I'm not a big fan of the way they're written, I think they could be a lot clearer, frankly, but they talk about direct and circumstantial evidence.

This one is just circumstantial evidence. You have another instruction that distinguishes between the two. You're told in these instructions that direct and circumstantial evidence are of equal weight, neither one is better than the other.

Now, an example of direct evidence would be an eyewitness, someone who would say, "I saw him, I saw that." We have an eyewitness in Allan Park, okay. His testimony seeing the man we know to be the defendant walking into the house at Rockingham.

Allan Park testified to his observations. That's direct evidence. Okay. Circumstantial evidence is evidence that leads you to infer, okay.

For example, in this case, the blood. The blood at Bundy dripped by the killer next to the bloody shoeprints. It's not direct, somebody didn't see the murder being committed, didn't see the murderer leaving the scene of the crime, but you have the blood of the murderer left behind.

It's kind of like — well, then you have the blood on the rear gate that actually identifies Mr. Simpson. That's kind of like the fingerprint, okay, that's circumstantial evidence as opposed to seeing it.

Now, in terms of quality, there's no difference, the law has no favorites. But when you think about it, you think about it logically, circumstantial evidence has a lot of benefits that direct evidence doesn't.

What is that? It gives you a lot of quality assurance. It gives you independent corroborating bases on which to believe that the defendant is guilty.

Instead of relying on one person's observation, one person who might be mistaken, who might be tired, who might not have observed very well, you know it happens because you saw it happen in this case.

What happens with an eyewitness, they started out saying, for example, you know, a robbery, okay.

I was standing on the street corner, I saw the defendant go over to the woman and grab her purse, okay, purse snatched. Okay, cross-examination, how far away were from you that woman? Where were you standing? Were they standing in shadow? Do you wear glasses? How much of the defendant's face did you see? Half? Three quarters? Only a quarter? What kind of hair did he have? What kind of shirt did he wear? What kind of pants did he wear? What color eyes did he have? Did he have a mustache? Did he have a beard? And so on and so forth. And the witness starts to get torn down. And if that's all you've got, that's all you've got is that person's observation. It can make you a little unsteady whether or not you have enough proof to give you that certainty you need.

Now, contrast that with the following: You have defendant committing a purse snatch. And what you have is someone who hears the woman scream, sees the back of a man running, and then a few minutes later the defendant is caught three blocks away holding her purse. Assume for a moment that she can't really identify her attacker. You've got him with her purse just a few minutes later. A lot of things can be said about how it got to him, but that's circumstantial evidence. But even that circumstantial evidence is not nearly as good. It doesn't come close to what we have in this case.

In this case you have circumstantial evidence of the blood, you have hair and fiber, and you have some of the conduct evidence and the opportunity evidence. You have a wealth of evidence in this case all pointing to one person, the defendant.

Now, this instruction, usually when I see lawyers argue this, they — they take out one paragraph, and they talk about that one. I'm going to talk about the whole instruction here. Okay. Begins in the very first paragraph with the fact "a finding of guilt as to any crime may not be based on circumstantial evidence unless the proved circumstances are not only, one, consistent with the theory that the defendant is guilty of the crime but, two, cannot be reconciled with any other rational conclusion."

You'll see the word reasonable, rational throughout these jury instructions because that's what it's all about — reason, common sense, logical, rational.

All right. Now here's — I'm going to jump around between us, and I'm going to come back and forth to this instruction because there's a lot here.

But in the third paragraph, this is what I told you about a little bit earlier, "If you have two reasonable interpretations," remember I talked to you, but I gave you the example of the Bronco that could have been on Ashford or could have been gone completely at the time that Charles Cale was walking his dog. You had two reasonable interpretations from that evidence. When he said he couldn't see the Bronco on Rockingham, at the point in time that he testified, based on his testimony, you had two reasonable conclusions to draw, either that it was not there at all or that it was on Ashford and he didn't see it. "When you have two reasonable interpretations, one of which points to guilt and the other to innocence, you adopt the interpretation that points to the innocence and reject that interpretation which points to his guilt." That is when they are equally susceptible of two reasonable interpretations. "If, on the other hand, one interpretation of the evidence appears to you to be reasonable and the other to be unreasonable, you must accept the reasonable interpretation and reject the unreasonable." Reasonable, rational.

The defendants will argue to you many things, inferences that could be drawn, just like the possibilities that I talked to you about. Ask yourself are they reasonable? Because if they are not, "if those inferences are not reasonable, then you are to reject them and accept the reasonable." And that's why I keep referring to common sense, rational, logical.

• • •

This is another important piece of evidence that proves the defendant's guilt. The shoeprints are all size 12. The shoeprints were all — and by the way, size 12, less than 10 percent of the male population wears that size. And the men who wear that size tend to fall within the height range of 5'11" to 6'4". The defendant is 6'2".

And these are not just any size 12s, they are expensive shoes, casual shoes that cost 160 bucks, not dress shoes; shoes that would be worn by a rich man, the kind of man who would wear cashmere-lined gloves.

And what's even more important is that those shoes were only sold in 40 stores in this country. Out of how many thousands, maybe even millions of stores in this country, these shoes are only sold in 40 of them, and one of those 40 stores was Bloomingdale's, the store the defendant shopped in regularly where he would buy shoes, both dress and casual, as you heard the testimony.

They stopped selling those shoes back in 1992, but during the time that they sold them, the defendant was shopping at Bloomingdale's.

Now, as we move down the walkway we see that there is only one set of bloody shoeprints. Mr. Bodziak made that very clear, especially on his last visit, only one set of the imprints were bloody shoeprints. And all of them were consistently Bruno Magli size 12.

• • •

Now on the rear gate, I think I've already talked to you about that. The blood that matches the defendant *was* typed 1 in 57 billion. In other words, that's identity. That is his blood.

And then when you go out to the driveway and you recall blood drop number 52 and that drop was also done with RFLP and in that blood drop out on the driveway, you have the typing, I think, determined with RFLP that was 1 in 170 million, the reason for the lower number is because they had fewer probes. It was a weaker sample.

• • •

So the blood that you see in the Bronco is actually, logically speaking, where you'd expect to see it from a cut hand or from a bloody glove that's dropped down next to the console. It's the amount you'd expect to see. It's where you'd expect to see it, given the circumstances of this case.

Now let's talk about the cut finger. Look at where we found blood on the door. You found blood inside the well of the driver's door handle, and you found some closer to the driver's window.

This blood in here, in the well of the driver's door handle inside the car, how do you get that blood there? Think about where you'd have to put your hand. Think about where you'd have to be sitting when you put your hand there.

• • •

There's also the blood of Ron and Nicole in that Bronco. And there are other people who saw that there was blood in that car at Rockingham in the early morning hours of June 13.

Recall another witness called by the defense, Officer Don Thompson, who was guarding the car and kind of taking care of business at Rockingham, he saw the blood in the Bronco, as well.

Now you may remember that the blood on the console was initially connected by console, I mean, the area here marked by number 31, this number tag. It's in-between the seats.

The testimony was that Dennis Fung collected blood from that console on June 14 at the print shed. That was before it went to Viertel's, that tow yard where it seems everybody and his brother went to look at that car. Before it went there, Dennis Fung collected that blood.

Now, the results of the blood collected by Dennis Fung in the morning of June 14 indicated with PCR testing the presence of blood from the defendant and from Ronald Goldman.

• • •

And those bloody shoeprints that lead away from the bodies of Ron and Nicole reach right into the defendant's Bronco.

All right. We have — you can — you already see we have such a wealth of evidence that we could probably stop right here but — frankly I'd like to, but I have to finish going through all of the evidence. And the Bronco went back to Rockingham. So let's go back to Rockingham as we trace the steps, and I'll quickly review the evidence for you at Rockingham.

All right. So he gets in the Bronco and he drives back to Rockingham parking it on Rockingham just north of the Rockingham gate where we see it in all of the photographs.

Now, as I've described earlier, the defendant runs down the south pathway, and you're saying to yourself why, why would he do that? And I talked to you about disposing of the knife. Really common, murderers want to get rid of the murder weapon. They think that's the one thing that can nail them. He's running back to the rear lot. He never gets there because he crashes into the air conditioner dropping the glove. Why would he need to put the knife on his own property? You're thinking why not drop it in a dumpster on the way home? Doesn't that make sense? Why not — why would you want to do that, leave it on your property or bury it on your own property? He can't. He can't because he's famous. If someone sees him hanging around near a dumpster on that night of all nights at that time of all times dropping something into a dumpster, they're going to recognize him, and he's going to have a witness, a witness who is going to put him very close to the scene of the crime at the very wrongest time he could be there, right after the murders. He can't dispose of evidence in public. Every move he makes is noticed. So he's got to find a private place. And that's the one that makes the most sense. And he doesn't have a whole lot of time to get real creative here. So what do we find on the Rockingham glove, the one he dropped? We find everything, everything.

We find fibers consistent with Ron Goldman's shirt, we find the hair of Ron, we find the hair of Nicole, we find the blood of Ron Goldman, we find the blood of Nicole Brown, and we find the blood of the defendant.

And we find Bronco fiber from the defendant's Bronco. We find blue-black cotton fibers just like those found on the shirt of Ron Goldman and on the socks of the defendant in his bedroom.

And on this glove he is tied to every aspect of the murder, to Ron Goldman, to Nicole Brown, to the car. And, of course, that's why the defense has to say that the glove is planted, because if they don't, everything about this glove convicts the defendant, where it's found, what's found on it, what's found in it, even a black limb hair found inside the glove, everything about it, convicts him.

Even though the planting theory is ridiculous, when you think about it, you give it a little rational thought and you realize, it's absurd, whatever you think of Mark Fuhrman, nobody thinks much of him, he couldn't have done this. Why couldn't he have done this?

It's not just the fact that all the other officers who were there before him saw only one glove, think about what he knew at the time he went out to the south pathway. He didn't know whether or not there were eyewitnesses to the crime that would say somebody else did it.

He didn't know if there was going to be someone who said I heard voices, they weren't his, they weren't Mr. Simpson's. He didn't know if the defendant had an airtight alibi and had maybe left on the 9 o'clock flight to Chicago. He didn't know any of that.

He could have — what he could have done by planting evidence is been wrong and completely fouled up the solution of the case because he is doing something like that without knowing anything about the case, subjecting himself, himself, think about his own self-preservation, to incredible — an incredible felony. He is in big trouble, in big trouble.

And all that has to happen is that an alibi is proven or an eyewitness comes forward, neither one of which he knows anything about. They could be out there. For all he knows, he probably thinks they are. So think about that when you consider this theory of the defense.

You know, I mean, it's like dismissing logic and reality and reason all at once, throw them out the window because nothing makes sense about that theory, nothing from even Mark Fuhrman's point of view.

But I think if you look clearly at the evidence, if you look straight on and you use your common sense, you are going to see this, you are going to know this. You will. But the bottom line is, and I think that you will reach the same conclusion, no one planted that glove. You know why? Because they are his gloves. They are his gloves. Think about all the evidence you heard now. Remember that he is a size extra large, the gloves are a size extra large, the glove at Rockingham is a mate to the glove at Bundy, they are a pair, a pair that are the same exact type purchased by Nicole on December 18th, 1990, one of only 200 pairs sold that year, gloves that are cashmere lined, gloves that cost $55, rich man's gloves, gloves that were exclusive to Bloomingdale's, gloves that were not sold west of Chicago, gloves that the defendant was wearing at football games from January of 1991 just a few weeks after he — she bought them until the last football season before the murders.

Now, you will recall that there was a photograph that was shown to you, first of all, the receipt, there was a receipt that was shown to you that showed that when she bought the gloves, she bought two pair of gloves and the muffler on December 18th of 1990, and there was a photograph shown to you during one of the football games that I am trying to remember the date of, I think it was '92, in which he is wearing a brown jacket, a brown muffler and the brown gloves.

Doesn't it make sense that when she brought the muffler, she bought it to match at least one of the pair of the gloves, and there he is wearing it. And you see him wearing those gloves in the photographs that we showed you right up until the last football season before the murders. And the gloves you saw him wearing in all of those pictures that we showed you at all those football games are the gloves that you have right here in evidence in this courtroom.

• • •

Okay? Now, I know that you recall the glove demonstration when the defendant put the gloves on, the crime scene gloves on. Now he mugged for you and he tried to act like it was real difficult, it was real hard for him and almost impossible to get it on. Well, I am sure it wasn't as easy as usual, he didn't have to ever wear them before over latex gloves. As Mr. Rubin told you, that makes it a great deal more difficult to put gloves on, and being old gloves, the blood that soaked into them soaked in and made them that much less stretchable because really the issue is stretchability, not so much size.

If he had had the chance to put them on, wear them for a while, they would have stretched back out, they would have been a better fit than they were, so it might have taken a little effort and a little time, but you ultimately would have seen that, of course, they do fit.

And it's no different than the experience that we all have in our lives, you have leather gloves, they get damp a little bit, you leave them to dry, you don't wear them for a while, you go back and you put them on, they are tight, they are tight, you got to drag them on, pull them on, you wear them for a little bit, they stretch back out.

And again, that's common sense, that's something that we have all had in our life experience, but if you are really trying, of course, you can do it. But have you ever tried to put shoes on a child that doesn't want shoes put on him or a jacket on a child that doesn't want the jacket to be put on? You know, you can't do it. They are going to kick, they are going to stream, they are going to avoid you, they are going to struggle, they are going to squiggle, and it's not going to happen.

And that's the same thing we have here. He doesn't want to put on those gloves — he doesn't want to show they fit. But did you see how quickly he snapped them off? If they were so hard to get on, how come they came off like that? And they did.

And I will tell you something else that really struck me, if I were asked to put on the gloves, the bloody gloves that were used to murder the father of my children, I would not be laughing, I would not be mugging, I would not be playing games.

I wouldn't think it was funny at all. Is that the attitude you expect? The laughing and the mugging, putting on the bloody gloves that were used to murder the mother of your children?

• • •

What do you do with gloves that don't fit? You throw them away. All right. That's why he was able to wear them. He would have brought gloves that did fit, that's what he would have done.

Now the testimony has told us that the gloves in evidence are smaller now than when they were new. So the issue with all that has been done to them, blood soaked, frozen, unfrozen, who knows what, the issue is how they fit at 10:00 p.m. just before the murders on the night of June 12.

• • •

Now, I've already talked to you about the significance of the blue-black cotton fiber, fibers from the clothes he wore, clothes that we never found. What are the fibers that share the same microscopic characteristics as those found on the shirt of Ronald Goldman doing on his socks and on the Rockingham glove? Those are fibers picked up from the clothes he wore that night. And we never found them. He got rid of them.

Now, the defendant's blood on that sock gave an RFLP match, once again, putting him within 1 in 57 billion people. You'd have to go through 57 billion people to find blood type like the defendant's as we found on that sock.

So that's his blood on the sock. That's an identification. But that's not all, we found Nicole's blood as well. Now, on this, on sock B, we have actually two stains for Nicole. Sock A, we have one stain.

Now, there's something interesting about the sock stains that perhaps was not made clear during the testimony. I want to bring it out now because it is very important to this notion of planting.

Gary Sims testified. And when he did, he told you about the fine spatter that he found above — on sock A that he found above the Nicole Brown stain on sock A, little dots. I think he said there were like ten of them above the Nicole Brown stain. And on sock B he found little tiny spatter between the stains, two Nicole Brown stains on sock B. Little fine spatter kind of like the little spatters you would get when you stepped in a puddle or a pool of blood.

Mr. MacDonell didn't want to talk to me about those little spatters. You know why? Because that little spatter proves to you that nothing was planted here. That blood got on his sock because he was wearing it at the crime scene when he was committing the murders, stepping in pools of blood. That's how that blood got there, and that's why you have that fine spatter.

· · ·

All right. So with all of this blood evidence, what we have done — and fiber and hair, look at all we've traced, look at all we've proven. We have linked the defendant to the crime scene. We have linked the defendant to the victims. We have linked the defendant and the victims to his car. And that link has reached from Bundy into his bedroom at Rockingham. They are all interwoven by time, by space, by occurrence, by science, all linked.

Now, let's turn to the murders themselves. And in this section I'd like to talk to you about the manner of killing. All right. In this section I'm going to talk to you — I'm not going to start this way, but ultimately I'm going to talk to you about the law of homicide, what the people are required to prove in terms of proving that a murder occurred, what's a first degree and what's a second degree murder.

Before I do that, I'm going to address some preliminary questions. These are not questions the law requires us to answer frankly. These are just kind of questions that you have, the things you might want to debate in the jury room. I'd like to give you some idea about these questions and ponder them with you for a little bit. But let me — Let me preface my remarks by saying this has nothing to do with the elements of the crime that we are required to prove in terms of our requirement of proof as to who did it and what they did. This has nothing to do with those, just so you know, because this is a matter of — as I told you, in the jigsaw puzzle, this is the piece of sky. But it's interesting, and it might be something that you're interested in. So in that light, I'm going to talk a little bit about it.

First of all, how could one person do this without the victims being able to scream or escape? How long did this take to accomplish? What about these murders leads us to believe that it was committed by only one person?

Okay. I'll start with the last question first. First of all, if someone else was involved, that certainly does not mean the defendant did it — didn't do it. It just means that he didn't get anybody — that he got somebody else to help him. It doesn't necessarily mean he didn't do it though. I'm not saying that he did. I'm not saying that there was a second person there. I'm just saying that that alone doesn't mean anything.

But secondly, first of all, if someone else was involved, on a purely basic level of observation, look at the nature of the wounds inflicted in each victim. I don't mean look physically because I'm not going to show them to you, but you can probably remember the nature of these wounds. You know, as I watch the testimony, I thought, only one person could have done this because they killed the same way. The stab wounds to the back of the head, the coup de grace slash to the neck, the — going — the targeting of the neck that way, the style of killing is the same. That's just a layperson's observation, but it's kind of a practical, common sense thing. The murders looked the same.

You also heard a great deal of testimony concerning the murder weapon, whether it was single or double-edged, remember that? And all of the wounds could have been inflicted by a single-edged knife. This is also information that goes to the determination as to whether or not you have one or two killers, although I must say two killers could have two single-edged knives because you can't tell any — I don't think you can — or there was no testimony indicating whether you could match a particular knife to a knife wound.

Dr. Lakshmanan testified in this regard that all of the major wounds were inflicted by a single-edged knife. He indicated to you also that there were certain other wounds, lesser wounds, in which he couldn't tell whether it was made by a single or a double-edge knife. But it would seem to make sense that if all the wounds are made with a single-edge knife, why would you come in there with a double-edged knife just to do little ones? So it kind of makes sense that just a single-edged knife was used. But beyond that, scientifically I think we had Doug Deedrick testify that he examined the damage in Ron Goldman's shirt, and he determined that — and a shirt, of course, is less elastic than — and less messy, if you will, than flesh. And he was able to see the damage in the shirt and see that it was the knife — that the cuts in the shirt were made with a single-edge, very sharp knife, which tends to support and corroborate what Dr. Lakshmanan said.

So the upshot of all that testimony is that to the extent that anything can be said based on what the wounds permit and in their description of the murder weapon, it would appear to be a single-edged knife.

Another indication that the murders were committed by one person comes from the blood evidence. And this was one of the areas there was no dispute as to the accuracy or the reliability of the result. And here's the result we haven't yet talked about. People's 100.

All right. You see that blood drop on the bottom of the boot, ladies and gentlemen? It was — That's a sole of Ron Goldman's boot. That's a photograph taken at the scene at Bundy after the coroner arrived because you can see he's lying on that sheet.

All right. Now, that blood drop was tested, and it was a high amount of DNA. It was a high amount of DNA because, as you can see, it was dripped on a part of the boot that doesn't look that dirty. And it obviously dried on that boot. So the DNA does not degrade as badly as it did on the concrete. Again, that's a nonabsorbent surface, it's plastic, so it was preserved better.

Now, what the result of that drop was a mixture of the blood of Ron and Nicole. Now, what does that blood drop mean? First of all, obviously that blood drop, and I think Henry Lee even testified to this, was dripped on the sole. And Ron Goldman was already down when it was dripped on the sole. How could it have dripped on the sole of the boot in that manner? Well, it had to have come from the murder weapon, from a knife those drops have dripped on, cast-off drops from the murder weapon, from the knife. And that means that Ron had already been cut badly enough to leave a quantity of blood on that knife, and it also means that Nicole had also been cut badly enough to leave a quantity of blood on that same knife. Because unless one knife has the mixture of blood of both victims on it, how can you get one blood drop from both victims? You see what I mean? The blood of Ron and Nicole mixed on the knife, it dripped onto the boot, and that's why you get a blood drop with a mixture of their blood. And that shows you one murder weapon.

Now, in addition to all of that, add the fact that you have virtually no evidence of the presence of a second killer. I mean there should be something left, but there was really virtually nothing.

• • •

So it's very clear. The crime scene really makes it very clear that there is evidence of only one killer and all of that evidence establishes that that is the defendant.

Next question, how long would it have taken? On this subject there really is some agreement. There is agreement that all of these wounds could have been inflicted very, very quickly. Even Dr. Baden didn't disagree with that.

Dr. Lakshmanan said it could have been just a few minutes. Now, when you realize — you look at this crime scene, look at what you have, look at where you have it. It is apparent from the evidence at the crime scene that Ronald Goldman was taken by surprise, and I will get to Nicole in a minute because there is evidence with respect to her, too, but first let's take Ronald Goldman because that's the one who struggled.

You see — do we have that picture? Thank you. Okay. This is 43E, Your Honor. All right. You see the envelope, and it's just — just inside the gate. Now, you remember because you were there how small that area is, that caged area in — at Bundy, it's very, very, very tight.

And that envelope is virtually with one step in the gate, it's dropped, and we have blood drippings on the envelope that indicate that it was dropped and then Ron bled, dripping onto that envelope. That indicates surprise.

I am going to show you in a moment where the keys were found, as well. He dropped his keys, also. Now, I know a lot of suggestions were made here about how you can use keys as a weapon. I don't see how that really makes a lot of sense, frankly. How do you use keys against a 6-inch sharp knife? And how do you see any evidence there that he even had them in his hands long enough to think about that?

Those keys were dropped and they were dropped right inside the gate, and I will show you the photograph of where they were found.

People's 56C. See the keys right by the gate? Now, those are a little bit — if this is the gate right here, if you step inside, it's a little bit down to my right as I am gesturing. But again, they are right inside the gate, they are right inside. Dropped. Ron is taken by surprise.

Now, Dr. Lee tried to say that the struggle with Ron was not a short struggle. What does that mean? What does that mean? More than a minute? More than five? The fact that Ron struggled is clear. But what is also obvious is someone who gets stabbed and is flailing about can get blood all over the place as he is struggling to back away from his attacker, and that happens very quickly.

You can imagine in your mind's eye somebody just flailing, flailing about trying to get away from their attacker, a big person with a knife in a very, very dark area, very confined space.

He hasn't very far to go, ladies and gentlemen, he has got only a few feet to move and he is backed into a corner like that. Where is he going to go? He flails backwards trying to avoid his attacker. A number of the contacts that you see, the bloody contacts on the fence are made at once, as he is flailing.

And that's what you see on that fence, you see a young man bleeding, backing and falling vainly trying to get away from the defendant who has him cornered in a cage and is coming at him with a very long knife.

Now, I am going to talk in a little more detail about how one person could do it, how. Dr. Lakshmanan spoke of the fact that Nicole suffered only two defensive wounds, one to the back of her left hand, I think it was one to the right of her palm. She struggled very little.

As Dr. Lakshmanan told you, there was — she was rapidly — I think — that's what he said, rapidly incapacitated, she was disabled very quickly.

There were stab wounds to the back of her head that indicated movement, perhaps as she tried to run, stabbing her in the back of the head. An abrasion to the right eyebrow indicates that she was pushed or fell to a hard surface such as the wall or the stairs.

She is stabbed in the left side of the neck four times. There was some movement shown on her part with respect to at least one of those stab wounds in the left side of her neck, which indicates there was still some effort at resistance.

And now most importantly Dr. Lakshmanan found evidence of a scalp and brain contusion caused by a blow to the head done by either a fist or the base of a knife, a contusion that was likely to cause unconsciousness which, in fact, we know it did because when the defendant cut Nicole's throat for the last time, there was no indication of any movement on her part. It was a clean cut. That final *coup de grace* had smooth margins that indicated no resistance on her part.

And there is a little bit more evidence of that that I will talk about later, but what's very important about these early wounds to the head and neck is that Dr. Lakshmanan told you there was evidence of bleeding in that brain contusion that showed that she lived after the infliction of those wounds for at least a minute and maybe more. Likely in an unconscious state, certainly disabled, at least a minute, maybe more.

Now look at the upper step, ladies and gentlemen, you can see she bled out on that step above her for a while before she came to the final spot at the foot of the stairs.

And Dr. Lakshmanan testified that Nicole was unconscious when the final throat cut was administered and she was put down at the base of those stairs.

If she lived for at least a minute, if not more, after she was hit on the head and struck unconscious, before her throat was slashed for the last time and she was up on that upper step where you see the first pool of blood, what was the defendant doing during that minute or more as she was laying unconscious or incapacitated on the upper step bleeding?

What was he doing before he came back to administer the final coup de grace. With Nicole disabled, the defendant had an opportunity to deal with an unsuspecting unarmed Ronald Goldman who had just come to do a favor for a friend.

And I remind you of the testimony — I remind you of the testimony of Dr. Lakshmanan in which he described the very narrow and confined space, the cage, in which the defendant cornered him. A cage that left Ron nowhere to run and nowhere to hide literally.

The defendant had all the advantage, no matter what Dr. Huizenga says. He talked about Tarzan's grandfather. He's built like Tarzan. He is built powerfully.

And even Dr. Huizenga said, admitted that whatever the defendant's disabilities may be, they did not prevent him from performing the actions necessary to commit these murders.

And the defendant had the advantage. He had the advantage of size. Ronald Goldman was only 5 foot 9, I think 175 pounds, Nicole Brown 5 foot 5, 125 pounds. The defendant 6 foot 2, 210 pounds.

He also had the advantage of the knife. He was the only one armed in this combat. He was the only one. And he had the advantage of surprise. He knew what he was going to do. But they didn't.

And don't forget, too, the adrenaline factor, that's real important, that's important. And Dr. Huizenga talked about that because adrenaline pumps you up. Even Dr. Huizenga talked about how football players get pumped up.

You know, they have to. They have to go running through these huge men. I've never seen men that size on the football field. You gotta be able to knock them down, run through them, you've got to get pumped. You gotta have a killer instinct to do that. And that's what the defendant did.

And that's what he did that night. And the defense can talk all they want about this new rare form of arthritis the defendant supposedly has that allows him to swing a golf club, lift a heavy set of golf clubs in that heavy golf bag.

You'll have it back there in the jury room. You'll see what I mean. Lifted it not once but a few times that night and carry heavy suitcases. That curious form of arthritis that somehow prevents him only from doing the movements required to stab and murder these people. But that's not what Dr. Huizenga, his witness, said. He could do it. He could do it.

Now let's talk about the attack of Ron. Ron was attacked with the defendant behind him, that much is clear. The wounds inflicted to the neck, those control wounds, I'll talk a little bit more about that, and some of the other stab wounds.

And Ron struggles, unlike Nicole, he's not so easily put down. He struggles and he grabs. The defendant, who's holding him from around the neck with his left hand and holding the knife in his right, Ron is struggling and he's grabbing at anything he can.

And he's grabbing at the hand that's holding him and that's how the glove comes off. And, by the way, that's why the right glove doesn't come off because the right glove, the right hand is holding the knife, holding the glove in place.

But from the point — from that point forward, after the defendant first attacked him, Ron's death was not a matter of if, it was just a matter of when. And Ron was totally on the defensive from the start, trying to ward off the knife and to back away.

And in the process, hitting the fence, the trees and everything around him in a desperate effort to survive. And all of this had to have happened very quickly, and I say this as a matter of common sense.

It didn't take Ronald Goldman and Nicole Brown more than a few minutes to be overcome and slashed to death, and that's not really surprising. Think about it. A boxing match, each round is, what, three minutes? And this is with men that are both prepared, ready to do battle in good condition who are not taken by surprise, who are prepared to do battle. And we know knockouts occur in the very first round, they certainly happen within a minute.

And that's with trained professionals. Same thing with martial arts matches, very quick. All right.

Next question: Why did he leave the cap and glove? This one's probably very easy. It was late. He had to catch a flight. This took longer than expected. Ronald Goldman was not expected at this scene. He was not supposed to be there.

But it is only because of him, because of the struggle that he put up that we have the cap, we have the glove and we have all this evidence, Ron's shirt, the blood. Because of the struggle with Ron, we have all of this evidence.

But it's not — I'm not saying that the defendant was not aware as he was leaving the scene that he knew he had lost evidence, because he was.

There was evidence given to you by Mr. Bodziak, who testified that he saw hesitation shoeprints down the Bundy walk, that he saw evidence that the defendant walked down the walkway, stepped back against the north wall and stepped out as though to look back at the crime scene.

And what that shows you is evidence that he — lost my cap, I've lost a glove, but he's thinking about going back, but doesn't dare, time is running out, he might be seen by someone. The longer he remains, the more likely to be detected. And probably the dog howling already. And so he has to leave.

Don't forget, too, that the glove and the cap are in complete darkness underneath that plant in that very dark, dark area in the front of Nicole's condominium.

Now, I know that I have not explained every move that was made by the defendant, which blow came first, which one came last, which one came in the middle. The law doesn't require us to do so.

And, of course, there's a simple reason. To do that, short of a videotape, we very rarely know exactly how any crime occurred. People who commit murder try not to do that in public and where everyone can see them. Their victims can't talk and they can't tell us what happened.

We have to look to the physical evidence and we have to use our common sense and our reason to make reasonable inferences to determine what happened, to the best of our ability. And even if we had a videotape, ladies and gentlemen, it wouldn't show you everything.

What happens before the tape starts? What happens after the tape ends? And what if — and, of course, a camera only picks up what's in its lens.

So if you saw, for example, a videotape of this that had Nicole, that was able to focus on Nicole, but not pick up Ron, and you saw the defendant killing Nicole and slashing her throat and then he stepped out of range to attack Ron, would you thereby conclude that he didn't kill Ron? No, of course not. Of course not.

So the law does not require that we prove how a murder was committed simply because in that case we'd have a — we'd have very, very few convictions for murder.

The law requires that we prove that a murder was committed, who committed it and what degree of murder it was. So the order of wounds makes very little difference. It doesn't answer any of those questions that we're required to answer and that's what we're here to determine is those questions that the law asks us to prove.

But there is one aspect of the nature of these murders that is a very telling point when you think about who did it. When you look at these pictures, ladies and gentlemen, you see rage, you see fury, you see overkill.

These — this is not the mark of a professional killer. These are not efficient murders. These are murders that are really slaughters, that are personal. And in that respect, they reveal a great deal about who did them. No stranger, no Columbian drug dealer. A man who was involved with his intended victim, one who wanted to control her and failed. And in failing, found the one way to keep her under control where she could never slip out of it again, and that man is this defendant.

Judge Ito orders a mid-afternoon recess, after which the prosecution's closing argument resumes.

Ms. Clark: We're really hanging out together today, aren't we? I hope you all had a real good dinner. ...And let me tell you briefly what I forgot to tell you in the very beginning. In all criminal cases because the People have the burden of proof, I argue to you first, and Mr. Darden will then argue to you, that's the prosecution. Then the defense will argue. Then because we have the burden of proof, we get to argue again. We get the last word, so to speak. But it's fair because it's our burden. Okay. So you're going to hear from me again.

• • •

All right. So let's talk about the degree of murder, is it first or is it second degree? Because you will be asked to determine this question also. And you will have the law of first and second degree murder back there. And if I can give you a hand stepping through the law as it applies to the facts, I would like to try to do that now and be of some help to you.

Defendant is charged with two counts of murder. And you're going to decide whether they are first degree or second degree. And in order to do that, what you do is you apply the law to the facts; that's what a judge does. And it's actually much simpler than it sounds.

And let me start with the basic law of murder. Legally speaking, what is murder?

You'll get some written forms back in the jury with you so if you have questions, you want to talk about them, you can go over them again.

All right. Every person who unlawfully kills a human being with malice aforethought is guilty of the crime in murder of violation of section 187 of the Penal Code. In order to prove such crime, each of the following elements much be proved.

Number one, a human being was killed. Ronald Goldman and Nicole Brown were obviously human beings. Element satisfied.

Two, the killing was unlawful. And what they mean by that is there was no legal excuse for the killing, that's not even an issue here.

Three, the killing was done with malice aforethought. Okay. That's the issue. Let's talk about that. Malice can be either expressed or implied. In this case, the only issue we have is express malice. What is express malice? Express malice aforethought means that a person had an intent to kill where there was no lawful reason to do so. And malice does not require any hatred or ill will of the victim. So, for example, regardless of whether the defendant liked or disliked Ron Goldman or even never knew him, malice is shown if the evidence shows that he intended to kill him.

Now, how do you determine if there was an intent to kill? We're not talking about premeditation. We're talking about an intent to kill. How do you prove that? Look at the pictures. This one is proven easily when you look at the nature of the injuries that were suffered by the victims in this case. The unlawful intent to kill is very obvious. These victims were virtually hacked to death, so you have malice shown in the nature of the injuries, the nature of the wounds that were inflicted upon them. So malice, express malice, is shown.

Just look at the pictures. Aforethought, malice aforethought, what does that mean? That just means that the intent to kill was formed before the actual killing occurred. It's not an afterthought. That doesn't mean premeditation or deliberation. And we'll talk about that in a minute.

And, again, with the nature and the number of wounds that were suffered by these victims, it's very obvious that the killer went to great lengths to disable and kill them with the throat slashing wounds alone. The preformed intent to kill is very clear. In fact, malice aforethought in this case, again, it's proven so clearly just with the coroner's photographs and the pictures that — of the victims at the crime scene where they were found. So you look at those photographs. You can see that there was a preformed — if it was just a second before — intent to kill these victims, and a great effort made to kill the victims with the nature of the wounds.

And there you go, we've applied the law to the facts just like you'll do back in the jury room to determine what was done. Let me give you an example aside from — let me give you an example.

This was a case I remember from a while back, a very simple example of second degree murder. In this example, a young man was standing on a street corner with his girlfriend. Another young man came and drove up to him — rode up to him on a bike, and he asked the young man on the corner, "Hey, where you from?"

The man — the young man on the corner responded, "I'm not from around here." Young man on the bike picked out — pulled out a gun, shot him to death, second degree murder. In that example, you have a preformed intent to kill, although no evidence that the young man planned to kill when he first rode up on the bike, but it was preformed in the second that the young man on the corner said, "I'm not from around here, (snaps fingers), second degree. Because when he pulled out the gun, he clearly meant to kill, even though it was — it was what you'd call a rash impulse; that's second degree murder. At a bare minimum in this case, at the very, very, very least in this case, we know we have second degree murder. That's the very least that we have.

But now we ask do we have more? Is there more? Do we have evidence that the murders were of the first degree? That is, premeditated and deliberate? In asking this question, what we're really asking is whether there is evidence that the defendant weighed and considered the question of killing and the reasons for and against the choice, because that's what we're talking about in terms of premeditation.

The answer to this question just like all the others comes from the evidence. We look to all the evidence in the case, and we ask is there evidence of planting? Is there evidence of premeditation in the manner of killing? Is there evidence of pre — or preparation for the act of killing? I'll address all these questions right now in the course of the argument, but I can tell you that the answer to these questions is yes. I'll briefly discuss the law with you, and then I'm going to show you how the evidence can be applied to the law to answer all of the questions that, yes, we do have premeditated and deliberate murder.

First of all, premeditated, let me see, I think we have a jury instruction for this. Premeditated is what it sounds like. It does mean considered beforehand. And it's important to remember here that there is no time requirement. The jury instruction states that the law does not undertake to measure in units of time how long the thoughts of killing were considered before they ripen into something that we call premeditation and deliberation. And the reason for that is very simple. And the law and the jury instruction will tell you so.

Circumstances vary in each case. Each case is unique, has a unique set of facts, and each defendant is unique and has unique thought processes, and so you cannot say, well, three minutes is not enough and five minutes is plenty. You can't do that, so it's not the consideration in terms of how much time because you can premeditate within just a few minutes, even seconds.

. . .

Here is what I was saying. You will have this in smaller form and it won't be highlighted, but you will have it back in the jury room.

This is the area I was directing your attention to. "The law does not undertake to measure in units of time the length of the period during which the thought must be pondered before it can ripen into an intent to kill which is truly deliberate and premeditated. The time will vary with different individuals and under varying circumstances."

And that's common sense. I mean, you would think that, wouldn't you? So the true test is not the duration of time but rather the extent of the reflection.

So even if you want to say, for example, that premeditation and deliberation happened in a mere few minutes or seconds, you are going to have to show that during that time there was deliberation.

Deliberation is really the issue. What do we mean by that under the law? Deliberation means that after giving careful thought and consideration, weighing the considerations for and against, the killer decides to and does kill, and that's really what the crux of the matter is in a premeditated and deliberate murder.

Can you show that kind of weighing and considering of the consequences? And this is to be contrasted with a second degree murder because in second degree murder you have what is known as just a rash impulse.

All right. Here is second degree murder. I just wanted to give you a chance to contrast it. Okay? Murder of the second degree, the unlawful killing of a human being with malice aforethought, we talked about that, that's intent to kill, when there is manifested an intention unlawfully to kill, there is an intent to kill but the evidence is insufficient to establish deliberation and premeditation.

Okay? So you have basic murder, murder of the second degree, and then if you have more, if you have premeditation and deliberation, you have murder of the first degree.

To give you an example of first degree murder, let's add to the example I gave you previously of the young man on the bike, he goes up and he shoots the young man standing on the corner.

To make this a first degree murder, this time assume the following: Assume that the shooter knows who his intended victim is. Assume further that the shooter is the member of a gang and that the intended victim is a member of a rival gang. Okay?

The young man standing on the corner, his gang recently killed somebody in the kid on the bike's gang. Kid on the bike knows this. He sees the victim on the corner, recognizes him as a rival gang member, a member of a gang that just killed a member of his gang, and he decides payback time, we are going to get this guy, we are going to show him, and it's my time to do it.

And now knowing who the victim is, knowing what his motivation is, knowing that he is going to pay him back, he rides up to the young man on the corner, goes up to him, pulls out his gun, shoots him at point blank range. There is first degree murder.

He has got a premeditated and deliberate idea of what he is going to do and why he is going to do it and then he goes and does do it. Now, in this example we see the evidence of planning and we see the cold, calculated decision to kill that is all accomplished very rapidly when he sees and recognizes the victim as a member of the rival gang.

Here is a non-criminal example of premeditation and deliberation. This is something that — to show you that we make decisions that are premeditated and deliberate every day. Let's say that you come downtown with some of your friends. You come downtown to have dinner one night, go into the restaurant, you have a good time, hour gets late and by the time you step out of the restaurant it's already — the streets are almost deserted, very, very little traffic on the streets.

You and your friends walk to the corner and when you walk to the corner you see that the "don't walk" sign is flashing. But it's late, you are tired, you don't want to wait. The "don't walk" sign is flashing. You step out, you look this way, you look that way, you don't see any traffic, you cross the street.

As you stepped off the curb, that was a premeditated and deliberate decision. Didn't take very long, but you weighed the consequences, pro and con. You said, well, I could get in trouble, there might be an officer around, I might get busted for jaywalking, but then again, doesn't look like anybody is there and it's probably okay and you cross the street. Premeditated and deliberate decision.

So you can see why it doesn't take long, it's not the length of time, it's the quality of the time spent.

Okay. So that's first degree and second degree murder. Second degree, a rash impulse, intent to kill with no premeditation and deliberation. First degree murder, premeditated and deliberate, a weighing of the consequences pro and con, and a clear and deliberate decision to act, and then the murder.

Now, the question is, do we have evidence of the premeditated and deliberate type in the murders of Ron Goldman and Nicole Brown. As I have told you, the answer to this question is yes.

Now, I would like to break down this evidence into three categories. For me this is the easiest way to analyze a case to see if there is premeditation and deliberation, and I hope it works for you, too.

Here is the first category, is motive. Do we have motive? Now, under this category would fall the subject matter that Mr. Darden is going to address so I am not going to discuss it with you other than to mention that the past episodes of domestic violence between the defendant and Nicole. That evidence is evidence of motive. I am not going to say any more about that because Mr. Darden will address it.

The next category is planning activity. What did the defendant do that shows us that he was planning to commit murder? Okay. Now I am going to come back to those questions I asked you to bear in mind early in the argument.

Remember when I asked you, what about this, why did he go out — why did the defendant go out and ask Kato for fives for the skycap to break the hundreds that he had if he was already going to go out and eat? Remember, I asked you that in the beginning of my argument.

The significance of that, of asking Kato for the fives, asking him for change, when he already knew he was going to go out and get something to eat and could obviously get the change at that point, he obviously didn't need Kato to give him those fives, so what was the point?

And even when he went out with Kato and he got the change back, he didn't keep it, so getting change from Kato was not the point. And none of his conduct is consistent with what he is telling Kato. None of it makes sense unless you look behind the words, what was he doing.

What he was doing was he was setting up an alibi with Kato. He is going out to see Kato so that Kato can say that he saw him. He can — then Kato can later say, I saw the defendant, I saw him at 9:00, ten after 9:00, he told me where he was going, he said he was going to get something to eat.

So if it is discovered that his whereabouts are unknown during the time of the murder, he at least has someone to say, well, wait a minute, he told me, he has a non-criminal explanation for where he was.

So he comes up with the pretext of needing change for the skycap. And it's a good way to remind Kato that he is going to be out of town, too. He will have Kato remember that alibi, too, I need change for the skycap.

Unfortunately, Kato stepped in his way. Kato invited himself along and the defendant would have been hard pressed to refuse because think about that. If Kato is going to be his alibi to tell anyone who later asks that I saw the defendant at thus and such a time and then he said he was just going to go out and get something to eat and then he says, you know, but I tried to invite myself along but he wouldn't let me go with him, then you have further evidence of consciousness of guilty. Then it's going to look suspension.

Why didn't he let him go with him? What's the big deal? He lets him live there. So the defendant agrees, takes Kato with him. This unexpected development, however, eats up time for him, time that he could have had out thinking about what to do, something that he was getting ready to do, getting ready to commit the murders.

So instead of going to a real restaurant, which he had the time to do, at ten after 9:00, the limo isn't going to get there until 10:45, even if you assume there is some packing to be done for a one-day trip, how long does that take?

They could have gone to a restaurant. But, no, they didn't. They went to McDonald's and they went to a drive-through, the quickest way you can possibly think of to get some food. And he went there in the Bentley.

Now think about that? Why take the Bentley? Why not take the Bronco if all you're going to do is go to McDonald's, unless there's something in the Bronco you don't want Kato to see, the knit cap, the knife, the gloves?

If Kato sees those on the night that he intends to commit those murders before he has committed them and the police get to him and say, "What did you see? Where were you? What did happen? What happened in this case?"

He's going to say, "That knit cap, I know where I saw that." These things have to pass through his mind. Now, he's got these things in the Bronco, he doesn't want Kato sitting in that Bronco with him. So they took the Bentley.

Now, once they got their food at McDonald's, the defendant eats his in the car, all the way home. Why do that? You got plenty of time to take it home, eat it in your house, relax, live a little. He doesn't have to be rushed like that. He eats it quickly. Why?

Because now his time has been eaten up by Kato coming along, time he doesn't have. Kato saves his. And it was interesting because he complained about being tired. It was about, what was it, 20 after 9:00, 25 after 9:00 they were in the car on the way back, I think it was, and he complained about being tired.

And he says, "Why don't you take a nap?" And he says, "I've got no time." And I heard, that's correct, got no time? The time is 9:25. The limo doesn't come until 10:45. You've got time to lay down, unless you're planning on doing something else.

But what was really telling was after they got back, when they both got out of the car and Kato walked straight for the house and the defendant stood there by the Bentley not moving, watching Kato.

Why do that? Why do you stand there and wait? Why not go in the house? Why not get back in your Bentley or get in the Bronco? Why do you wait for Kato to get out of sight unless you don't want him to see where you're going, unless you have it in mind that you're not going to go back in the house.

You don't want to take the time to do that. And you don't want him to see you going to the Bronco. Now, there's much more evidence of planning, planning that you see at the crime scene, itself.

And in that, I mean the defendant wore dark clothing, the dark blue-black cotton sweat suit that Kato described, perfect in the nighttime if you don't want to be seen, the dark blue-black cotton fibers that were found on Ronald Goldman, the socks, the Rockingham glove, the fibers of the clothing he wore.

The watch cap and the gloves, it was June 12, the summer night, why do you need these cashmere-lined gloves and a watch cap on a summer night? Unless you're going to commit a crime, unless you're planning, unless you're preparing to commit a crime.

Gloves are easy, why wear the gloves? Fingerprints, you don't want to leave fingerprints. And he didn't. You heard from the print people he didn't.

Watch cap. A partial disguise, if he has to walk around the house, if he's going to be standing at the front gate, he doesn't want someone glancing to make the immediate connection.

He doesn't want someone to see exactly who it is. Now, he doesn't intend to be there but a minute, but a watch cap over that head is going to make — that doesn't look like something that he would wear. And it throws someone off.

Now, those items alone show clear evidence of planning, planning activity, planning for a murder, preparation. But there's more. There's also timing. And by that, I mean we know that the children were asleep at the time these murders were committed, we know that from the evidence.

But who else would know when the children were going to be in bed? Who else would know when they would be safely out of the way? Who else would know when Nicole would be home alone with the children? Who else would know the perfect time to attack and get Nicole without the children being in the way? The defendant.

And that not only shows premeditation, it also shows identity, who did it. Now, there's one more thing that shows evidence of premeditation and deliberation, and that's the knife.

In the inventory tape that you have in evidence, the defendant's closet is shown, and it's shown that he had in that closet a gun. He had a gun. But he chose a knife. And this choice is evidence of planning. A gun makes noise. A knife doesn't, particularly if your intended victim is half your size.

A gun is registered, it can be traced. And bullets can be matched to guns. And even if you get rid of the gun, the type of bullet can be determined. It can be determined to have come from the type of gun you used to have.

So if you get rid of the gun, it's looking even worse, almost, than if they catch you in possession of it. Suddenly you don't have the gun after your wife was shot to death and a bullet that could have come from that gun. But not a knife.

A knife can't be identified to the exclusion of all other knives in making this wound or that wound, you can't match a knife to a murder. A knife isn't registered.

All of these things make a knife a better weapon of choice than a gun. But maybe more than all of that, a knife is up close and personal. And that's the kind of murders these are, ladies and gentlemen. These murders are up close and personal.

If your desire is to vent your rage on someone, a gun is far too sterile. It's far too removed. But a knife, it's lethal, but it affords the opportunity for the expression of violence, power and control at very close range. The choice of a knife is evidence of planning, and it, too, is also evidence that the defendant is the murderer.

· · ·

Now, that final gaping wound in [Nicole Brown Simpson's] neck was inflicted upon an unconscious victim, or at the very least, incapacitated. It's clear evidence of a cold and calculated decision to kill. When a victim is already incapacitated and the defendant goes back to her, pulling back her head, she's lying there basically unconscious, he pulls back her head, and he slashes the throat to such a degree that she's nearly decapitated, that was a cold and calculated decision to kill, to make sure she was dead. And it allows for no other reasonable inference.

Now Ronald Goldman. Now, once again a very significant point with respect to Ronald Goldman, as with Nicole, the neck is the target once again. And we know that from the neck wounds described on by Dr. Lakshmanan, why the neck, why is the neck the target, because it's a sure kill. It's something we've all heard about, go for the jugular. You go for the jugular because you cut it, you slice that neck, that person's dead. That's a sure bet. That's a sure thing. And the fact that the neck is the target for both victims indicates to you also a cold and calculated decision to kill. That is the epitome of a premeditated murder.

• • •

But beyond that, there is evidence in the wounding that the murder of Ron Goldman is of the first degree. The wound to his left abdomen, if you recall that one, the one that severed the aorta, a wound that ordinarily would have bled profusely into the abdominal cavity. And you expect to find all of that bleeding in the abdominal cavity if the blood pressure is normal. If the person is breathing, that blood pressure will force the blood into the cavity as a result of the wound to the abdomen. But there was very little blood to the abdominal cavity.

And like Nicole's final wound, there was no evidence of movement on Ron's part. The margins of the wound were clean, which indicated that there was no resistance offered by Ron. And this wound was inflicted when Ron was very near death already. It was an unnecessary wound. It was a wound inflicted to make sure that Ron was dead. And it shows that the defendant took great pains to go back and deliver the final *coup de grace* of Ronald Goldman.

But no matter when each wound was inflicted in what order, the bottom line is very clear, the defendant could not leave a witness alive, alive to tell what he saw. He had to deliver the fatal blows and make sure that they were fatal. The defendant surely didn't anticipate that Ron would be there that night. He came to murder Nicole. But once Ron showed up, he could not allow him to walk away with the knowledge of what he had seen.

Ron was a witness who had seen what no one was supposed to see. Ron was the ultimate threat, so Ron had to die. And the intent to eliminate a witness, ladies and gentlemen, is a premeditated and deliberate decision. It is a cold and a calculated decision. And it is not a decision that takes very long.

As I pointed out before, the jury instruction tells you, the law does not undertake to measure in units of time the degree of thought that goes into the thinking called premeditation and deliberation. And now you can see this is a perfect example of how such a decision can be made in mere moments. The defendant has Nicole Brown down, Ron Goldman comes walking up with the envelope, a witness, and the decision is made; that's all it takes. I can't leave him live. I can't let him stay alive.

Ladies and gentlemen, this is strong, and it's compelling evidence that proves that the murders of Ronald Goldman and Nicole Brown were premeditated and deliberate murders of the first degree.

. . .

Now, ladies and gentlemen, we've proven all of this evidence that I've reviewed with you easily beyond a reasonable doubt that the defendant committed the premeditated and deliberate murders of Ronald Goldman and Nicole Brown.

And I spoke to you before a little bit about direct and circumstantial evidence. This is what they call — this is a physical evidence case, obviously, and they call it circumstantial evidence.

Now that I have reviewed all of the evidence you can see what I am talking about when I say a circumstantial evidence case gives you much more assurance of the guilt of the defendant, and that is because of this, in a direct evidence case, you may have one eyewitness to tell you I saw it. That means you have one thing to rely on.

But in a circumstantial evidence case, especially this one, you have many things to rely on. You have the blood at Bundy, you have the blood of Nicole on his socks, you have his blood on the rear gate at the Bundy, you have Ronald Goldman's blood in his car, you have his hair on Ron Goldman's shirt, you have the fiber from his clothing on Ron Goldman's shirt, on his socks, on the Rockingham glove. You have the Bronco carpet fiber on the Rockingham glove, you have the Bronco carpet fiber on the knit ski cap. The wealth of evidence in this case is simply overwhelming.

And now let me summarize for you what we have proven. One piece of the puzzle, we have proven the opportunity to kill, we have given the time window in which he was able to kill because his whereabouts were unaccounted for during the time that we know the murders were occurring.

We have the hand injuries that were suffered on the night of his wife's murder to the left hand, as we know the killer was injured on his left hand. We have the post-homicidal conduct that I told you about, lying to Allan Park, making Allan Park wait outside, not letting Kato pick up that little dark bag, his reaction to Detective Phillips when he made notification, when Detective Phillips said to him, Nicole has been killed, instead of asking about a car accident, the defendant asks no questions.

We have the manner of killings, killings that indicate that it was a rage killing, that it was a fury killing, that it was not a professional hit, the manner of killing that indicates one person committed these murders, one person with the same style of killing.

We have the knit cap at Bundy, we have the evidence on Ron Goldman's shirt of the blue-black cotton fibers, the defendant's hair. We have the Bruno Magli shoeprints, size 12, all of them size 12, his size shoe, all of them consistent going down the Bundy walk.

We have the Bundy blood trail, his blood to the left of the bloody shoeprints. We have the blood in the Bronco, his and Ron Goldman's. We have the Rockingham blood trail up the driveway, in his bathroom, in the foyer.

We have the Rockingham glove with all of the evidence on it, Ron Goldman fibers from his shirt, Ronald Goldman's hair, Nicole's hair, the defendant's blood, Ron Goldman's blood, Nicole's blood, and the Bronco fiber and the blue-black cotton fibers.

We have the socks, and we have the blue-black cotton fibers on the sock. And we have Nicole Brown's blood on the socks. There he is.

I haven't seen spoken — you haven't even heard yet about the motive. You haven't even heard the why of it, the why he did it, and you know he did it.

Now, these murders did not occur in a vacuum, and it's very important evidence that you heard in the beginning of this case. They occurred in the context of a stormy relationship, a relationship that was scarred by violence and abuse, and this important evidence completes the picture of the defendant's guilt as it explains the motive for these murders and shows you what led this defendant to be sitting here in this courtroom today.

Thank you very much, ladies and gentlemen.

The Court: All right. Thank you, Ms. Clark. Mr. Darden, are you ready to proceed?

Mr. Darden: Well, there is no better time than right now, Your Honor. May I?

• • •

The Court: Thank you, sir. Proceed.

Mr. Darden: Okay. Good evening, ladies and gentlemen. They asked me to do the summation Marcia Clark just did but I told them no, it's too long, I am not the kind of person who likes to talk that long. And Marcia isn't, either, but she had to.

And I think that one of the things that you probably gathered from hearing her today is that this case really is a simple case in its essence. When you get down to the bottom line, this case really is a simple case.

All you have to do is use the tools God gave you, the tools he gave you to use and utilize whenever you are confronted with a problem or an issue.

All you have to do is use your common sense and the defense would have you believe that this is a complex series of facts and evidence and law and science and all of that. Not really. Not really.

You have to question or wonder how it is that a lawyer can summarize a case in eight hours when presenting the case took eight months. It's a simple case.

But there has been a lot of smoke, a lot of smoke screens, a lot of diversions, a lot of detractions, a lot of distractions, and in some respects, there has been an attempt to get you to lose focus of what the real issues are in this case. And that takes time.

If I could give you any advice, as jurors, any advice at all, I would say to you, use your common sense. When you get all of this evidence and go into the jury room and after you pick a foreperson, take that common sense that God gave you, take the evidence that the prosecution gave you, and the defense evidence, go into that jury room, sit down, spread it out, using that common sense, ask yourself a question, what does the evidence show? What does the evidence show?

And when you look at it in the simplest terms, what you are going to see is blood in the Bronco, a blood trail from Bundy, blood in his bathroom, blood on his socks. Simple evidence. You can look at it, try and see what the DNA results are.

It really, really won't be that difficult when you use your common sense and when you get down to the bottom line and when you put aside all the distractions and all of the smoke that has been blown throughout this courtroom and in your direction.

● ● ●

A trial is supposed to be a search for the truth. And sometimes the truth is uncovered or revealed at the end of a long road, at the end of a long journey. And this has been a long journey. But let me say this to you that today, tonight, the whole world is watching us tonight, they're watching me, and they have listened to the evidence and they have watched the witnesses testify here on television and they want to know what you're going to do. And we want to know what you're going to do.

So some people are supposed to think that justice in this case would be to just ignore the evidence, say he's not guilty. Some people think that justice in this case would be to just jump to some conclusion, some silly conclusion, some conclusion not based on the law and forget about the evidence.

Some people think that because the defendant in this case is a celebrity that perhaps he is somewhat above the law, that there ought to be special rules for him or that somehow he should be treated differently than any other defendant. But that's not justice. And there are some people that think that because Fuhrman is a racist that we ought to chuck the law out of the window, throw it out of the window and perhaps it shouldn't be applied in this case.

Well, that's wrong, and that's not why we're here because we don't ignore the law just because of the status of the defendant, because of who he is or because of who he knows. That isn't justice. You're here to ensure justice. I'm here to ensure justice. And we all know the rules.

And the rules say and the law says that he should not kill, that he should not have killed these two people. And the law says that if you believe that he killed these two people and if you believe that it has been proven to you beyond a reasonable doubt, that you should find him guilty.

You heard Marcia Clark and you heard the evidence and you've seen the evidence and you're reasonable people. And you know, we know, I mean, if we're honest with ourselves, we know. And it's unfortunate what we know. What we know is the truth. And the truth that we know is that he killed these two people.

• • •

This man, this defendant, we believe that given the state and equality of the evidence is guilty. And there's nothing wrong with voting guilty in this case given the state of the evidence and the quality of the evidence.

Now, a vote of guilty in this case isn't a vote for any interest group in particular or any interest group at all, it isn't a vote for the prosecution, for Marcia and I.

It certainly isn't a vote for the LAPD. And it's not a vote against anyone. It's not a vote against the defendant. It's not a vote for the victims or the victims' family.

When you go into that jury room open-minded and fairly and consciously consider this evidence and then cast a ballot, a vote for guilt or innocence based only on the evidence that you've seen in this case and only on the law given to you by Judge Ito, when you cast a vote on that basis, then you're voting for justice, you're voting for fairness. You're doing the right thing under the law. And that's what we're going to ask you to do.

They say that justice is supposed to be blind and all of that good stuff. I know you've heard all of that before, but we just have to believe, Marcia Clark and I, that justice is blind in this case. There have been lots of issues, lots of issues that came up in this trial. This trial has been an amazing experience, I'm sure you would agree.

But even though there are a lot of small issues, a lot of other issues, a lot of little distractions here and there. You're here to address a single issue. This is a single case, okay, one issue: Did the defendant kill these two people? One defendant: O.J. Simpson.

You heard from the defense in this case and they presented testimony about slurs, epithets, as they call them, a bunch of nasty, hateful low-down language used by Mark Fuhrman. And I'm not even going to call him Detective Fuhrman, if I can help it, because he doesn't deserve that title. He doesn't warrant that kind of respect, not from me.

But this isn't the case of Mark Fuhrman, this is the case of O.J. Simpson. And let me say this to you, if you will allow me to, and I don't mean to offend you or demean you and I hope that you don't feel that I am, but this is the case of O.J. Simpson, not Mark Fuhrman.

The case of Mark Fuhrman, if there is to be a case, that's a case for another forum, not necessarily a case for another day because today may be the day, but it is a case for another forum, another jury, perhaps.

This case is about this defendant, O.J. Simpson, and the M-word, murder. It's not about Mark Fuhrman and the N-word, and you know what that is. I'm going to ask you to consider the fact of his misstatements or lies or untruths, however you want to determine, of course, you have to consider that. That's the law.

You have to consider everything Fuhrman said on the witness stand, because that's the evidence in this case. And I want you to consider it. I want you to consider all the evidence. So don't think that I'm saying, hey, just overlook it, just overlook what he said, just overlook the fact that he lied about having used that slur in the past 10 years.

But I am asking you to put it in the proper perspective. You decide what it's worth. You decide what it means. If it helps you in assessing his credibility, and it should, or his lack of credibility, I don't know, then you use it.

But please just remember Fuhrman isn't the only issue in this case, and his use of that word is not the only issue in this case. And you have to be concerned about that. I have to be concerned, as a lawyer for the prosecution in this case, because it apparently was a very, very significant event for the defense, I mean, you saw all those people that came up to testify about Fuhrman's use of this word.

And then at one point you heard a tape of Fuhrman, and that was Fuhrman, by the way, okay, no doubt about that, using those slurs.

And you heard a tape of him using those slurs, and it had to make you angry to hear him say that, made us angry. But that wasn't enough, not only did you get to hear the words, you were given — the transcript was scrolled across the Elmo, remember?

So you could hear it and you could see it, but that wasn't enough, you had to have a transcript for some reason of the words, as well. A lot of emphasis on that. I don't know why, I know you do. But it's evidence, just like all the other evidence in this case. Attach whatever value you think is appropriate. I would.

I would say use it to assess his credibility. Any other use you want to put to it, look to the law, look to the instructions that the judge gives you. Ms. Clark mentioned to you that I was going to talk to you about domestic violence, and I'd like to do that right now, if I can, and I did that, I suppose, when I began back speaking with you back on January 24th.

• • •

That's a long time ago. You're probably like me, you didn't think it would ever go on this long. Well, you're almost there. It's almost over. We believe that this evidence of domestic violence is very important. It's important that you understand the nature of this man's relationship with one of the victims in this case. It's important because when you consider it, it may help explain to you or it may suggest to you his motive for killing Nicole Brown and perhaps his motive for killing Ron Goldman as well. And the law allows you to use this evidence as you attempt to determine whether or not there was a motive to kill.

• • •

Now, when I spoke to you back in January, I told you — I — I promised you, I think, that I would expose to you another side of this man, of this defendant. I promised you that I would expose to you the private side of him, that part of him, the side of him that's capable of extreme rage, jealousy, and violence. And I said to you back then, I said to you and I asked of you that you consider the nature of their relationship, his relationship with Nicole. Because to understand what happened at Bundy, you need to know what happened between them during the 17-year period that they were together off and on. Because when you look at that, you see a motive for killing.

Now, I'm sure the defense is going to get up here at some point and say, ah, that domestic violence evidence, it's irrelevant. And they may say to you that just because this defendant had some marital discord or violence in his marriage to Nicole Brown that it doesn't mean anything.

Well, this isn't a just-because issue. This is a because issue. Okay. It is because he hit her in the past. And because he slapped her and threw her out of the house and kicked her and punched her and grabbed her around the neck. It's because he did these things to her in the past that you ought to know about it and consider it. And it's because he used a baseball bat to break the windshield of her Mercedes back in 1985. And it's because he kicked her door down in 1993, you remember the Gretna Green incident? Remember the 911 call? It's because of a letter he wrote him — he wrote to Nicole, rather, around June the 6th talking about the IRS. It's because he stalked her. It's because he looked through her windows one night in April of 1992. They may say that, well, the defendant's just looking through a window late at night. We say that's stalking. It's because of all those things and because all of these things alongside the physical evidence at the scene — the bloody shoeprints in his size, the blood drops at Bundy, the blood on his sock, the blood trail to Rockingham.

It's because when you look at all of that, it all points to him [indicating Simpson]. See, I'm not afraid to point to him. Nobody's pointed him out and said he did it. I'll point to him. And why not? The evidence all points to him. And it's also because when you — when you look at the bloody ruthlessness — my mouth is getting dry — of these murders. And when you see as Ms. Clark pointed out that these killings were rage killings, rage, I mean you have say to yourself, well, who in the past has ever raised a hand to this woman? Who during the days and the hours leading to her death was upset with her? And as Ms. Clark alluded to earlier — you're too kind. And as Ms. Clark alluded to earlier the killing was personal, the way it was done. The way it was done, this is personal. Somebody had a score to settle. Who had a score to settle with Nicole?

When you look at all of that, when you look at the domestic violence, the manner of the killing, evidence, the physical evidence, the stalking, when you look at it, it all points to him, it all points to him.

• • •

You think about Denise Brown and what she had to say about the defendant. Remember that time at the Red Onion that he grabbed her by the crotch in front of a bar full of strangers and said, "This is where my babies come from. This is mine?" Remember that testimony?

This relationship between this man and Nicole, it's like a time bomb ticking away, just a matter of time, just a matter of time before something really bad happened.

You know, you meet people in life and there are people with short fuses, you know, they just go off, and there are others with longer fuses, you know, it takes them a little while longer to go off, and relationships are the same way sometimes, you know, especially violent, abusive relationships like this one.

This thing, this thing was like a fuse, it was a bomb with a long fuse, and there were incidents along the way, and along the way as each incident occurred, that fuse got shorter. If nothing else, that fuse was lit in 1985 that night when he took that baseball bat to her car, and we don't know the reason behind his decision to do that, we only know that he did.

But when you stop and you look at it and you consider the conduct, breaks the windshield, dents the car up. You saw the baseball bat. That's a pretty novel approach. The wife was sitting on top of the car crying, face covered, hair over her face.

If nothing else, look at it this way, what message does that send to Nicole? What are we going to do with this evidence? How do we evaluate this when a man takes a baseball bat to his wife's car and just beats the heck out of it?

If nothing else, it sends a message to her. It instills fear. Wouldn't you agree? And would you agree that it suggests to her that this can happen to you, that maybe you will be next? That fuse is burning. It's burning in 1985. It is burning in 1985, and 1985 was the year of their marriage. The fuse was lit, it's burning, but it's a slow burn.

We next go to 1989. You heard from Denise Brown, you know, she testified about 1989, Detective Edwards testified about 1989. I said before you got to go back, we have to go back and look at their relationship, you have to go back in the past and see how we got where we are today, because when you do, you see a pattern developing here.

You see that that fuse is lit in 1985 on New Year's night about 4 o'clock in the morning, and as I recall, we called to the witness stand a 911 operator and her name was Sharyn Gilbert. And that night, that morning, she received a call.

The caller never identified herself. The line was left open. The call came in, the line was left open. The 911 operator stayed on the line and listened in, and as she testified here at the trial, if you stay on long enough, if you are the 911 operator, you get a fix on the origin, the address from where the call is coming.

She stayed on the line, she determined that the call was coming from 360 North Rockingham, and she listened in for a few moments. You recall that tape? Can I play that for you? It only takes a couple seconds. And this is People's 1. This is the first Exhibit 1, marked for you in this case eight months ago.

The tape was played.

Mr. Darden: I stood before you back in January and I asked you, if you listen carefully to that tape and you have the tape in the jury room you put it in a tape recorder and you listen to it, listen carefully, because you can hear in the background the sound of someone being struck or slapped, and that's what the 911 operator heard and she told you on the witness stand, she heard that, she heard the sound, the noise of someone being beaten, and she put that out on the radio. Do you recall that? She put it out on the radio that there was a woman being beaten at 360 North Rockingham.

Now, they may say that this isn't important evidence. I say they are wrong. There is physical abuse here, wife beating here, spousal abuse, spousal battery going on, and this is an emergency situation.

• • •

And he also said she had a handprint, he saw a handprint, a handprint on the left side of her neck, on the left side of her throat, a handprint. Someone had grabbed at this woman, his wife, by the neck hard enough to leave an imprint around her neck, an imprint in the shape of his hand.

Well, let me say this to you: We submit to you that the hand that left that imprint five years ago is the same hand that cut that same throat, that same neck on June 12, 1994. It was the defendant. It was the defendant then, it's the defendant now.

• • •

And this defendant, he was jealous and he was out of control and he was consumed with passion for Nicole and he was obsessive because in April of 1992 he is peeping through windows. He has already beaten her, he has beaten up her car, and he has done some other things.

In 1988 and 1989 I told you already that the testimony — Denise Brown said he humiliated Nicole in public by grabbing her crotch in front of a bar full of strangers.

And what else had he done? What else had he done? He had thrown Nicole and Denise out of his house one night. Remember that night, that night that Denise said to him, "O.J., you take Nicole for granted," and he blew up.

Remember, he blew up and he said, "Hey, I do everything for her," and he became enraged back then and he picked Nicole up and he threw her against the wall and he threw her out of the house and he threw Denise out and he threw all of the clothes outside of the house, too.

Remember that testimony? This is the private side of him. This is the other side. This is the side of this man that you don't see in the commercial, he is out of control. He cannot handle it. And the fuse is burning.

A recess is called until the following morning.

Mr. Darden: But we talked about that yesterday and we talked about justice and we talked about what the real issue in this case was about. And I pointed the defendant out to you, and I told you he killed her and you've heard the evidence.

He killed Ron Goldman. O.J. Simpson is a murderer. That's what the evidence indicates. That is what the evidence indicates. That is what the evidence shows. It shows that he is not just a murderer, but he's a double murderer. That's unfortunate. It's unfortunate that I have to stand here and tell you this because I would rather be somewhere else. I'm sure you would rather be somewhere else. Who wants to really have to confront and deal with these issues but we have to, because we have a duty.

Marcia and I have a duty, and you have a duty as well. Your duty is to look at all the evidence, to be fair, be conscientious. Be objective.

Your duty is to look at all the evidence, the totality of circumstances. Everything. We don't want you to look at one piece. Don't just look at the prosecution's case, look at the entire case. Look at everything. Because when you do — when you do, hey, what can you say, except he did it. And we have proven it. And we have proven it beyond a reasonable doubt.

And we talked about the safe deposit box yesterday, and we talked about the fact that Nicole knew she was going to die, and we know she knew that because she told the police that in 1989. And we know she knew that because of what she saved for us, the road map she left for you in the safe deposit box: The letters, the photographs, the will. You recall that testimony.

• • •

But this morning, you know, I want to take things a step further, if I may, if you will allow me to. Let's just cut right to the chase.

Imagine the defendant in his Bronco. He is full of anger and he is full of rage. And it's nighttime, and he's driving that Bronco, and he is full of jealousy. And the fuse continues to burn, and the focus of his anger is Nicole.

For some reason, in his mind, she has done something that he can't ignore, something that has set him off. He is jealous, he is raging, he is raging, he is out of control and he is in that Bronco, and he is driving as fast as he can toward Nicole's house. It is about ten o'clock, and he is out of control, folks. He is completely out of control.

And when he gets to Nicole's place, he quickly parks the Bronco and he gets out. It's ten o'clock. He's in his Bronco. He's at Nicole's house. It's nighttime, but we're not even talking about June 12. We're not talking about June 12th, 1994. We're talking about October 25, 1993.

All along I have asked you to be open-minded, to be open-minded about this man and who he is. And we have suggested to you — and I think we have proven to you, that he is not the person that you see on those TV commercials and at half-time in those football games, that is his public persona. We all have one. We all have one.

· · ·

I want you to listen to a tape, a tape of an emergency call, and you will recall I played that tape for you months ago. You probably forgot about it. Up until yesterday, I hope. And I'm going to ask you to listen to that tape for just a moment.

And you know, some people say, well, how could — how could O.J. Simpson actually kill this woman, and Ron Goldman, when her kids are in the house? You know? You know what I mean. They say: Who would do something like that? Well, he would. Keep this in mind, if you will. If you think it's important.

In 1989 when he beat her, you will recall that when the police came and wanted to take her to Parker's Center to have photographs of her injuries taken, you will remember that she said: I don't want to go. I just want my kids. Just take me back home. Take me back home to my kids. My kids are at home. I want to be with my kids.

The night he beat her, his kids were in the house. When you listen to the tape from October 5, 1993, after the first couple of minutes you hear the defendant in the background, yelling and screaming and raging.

You hear that rage. And you will here Nicole on the telephone say, "The kids are upstairs." The fact that the kids are in the house means nothing to this man.

· · ·

Plays 911 tape

And I think you get you get the message, and you get the message straight out of his mouth. You hear this man in the background raging. He is raging about a picture, a picture of a man he saw at Nicole's house, a picture of a man she had apparently dated how many months before? How many months did Nicole say? About 18 months, or something like that. It's on the tape. And Nicole said on that tape, as well, that it always comes up. This man, that issue, always comes up.

· · ·

And you hear him back there yelling and screaming at Nicole, and you hear the language and you hear the things he is saying about her and you hear him in the background saying, "I don't give a shit anymore." That's what he said.

. . .

And it's October 25 of 1993 and Nicole doesn't know it at the time, she knows he is going to kill her at some point but she doesn't know at the time that she only has eight months to live.

. . .

And she tries to calm him and as she is trying to calm him she tries to calm him in a — by using a calm voice of her own. Get what I am saying? I mean, she says, "O.J., O.J."

Not three minutes before she was in tears on the phone calling the 911 operator, but when he comes near, he is enraged, she is trying to calm him down with a calm voice.

What does that mean? Is that helpful to you at all? Let me suggest to you that what that means is that she has been there before. She apparently feels as if she has a way, some tactic or some approach that might help calm him down. It's Nicole's approach to her problem when the defendant becomes enraged, a calm voice.

. . .

And perhaps what set him off was this four-minute phone call at two in the afternoon. Perhaps his inability to find Paula this afternoon. Set him off. Now, the fuse is really burning now, the fuse is getting shorter and there is going to be an explosion. There is going to be an explosion.

He arrives at the recital, sees Candace Garvey, literally ignores her. He's angry. He takes a seat in the auditorium. He sees the Brown family seated in the auditorium. Juditha Brown, Denise Brown, and her sisters. Nicole is seated near them or with them.

He goes over to the Brown family and greets everyone in the family. Every one of them. He greets everybody but Nicole. He doesn't address Nicole.

This is a family event, right? His daughter, Nicole's daughter, is at the recital dancing. But he didn't address her. Because he is angry. He is consumed with anger. His fuse is getting shorter.

He doesn't appear the O.J. they knew. The man they knew. Candace Garvey is frightened. He takes a seat around the family. There's no seats near the family. Nothing wrong with the fact he takes the seat.

But as Denise Brown told you on the witness stand after a few minutes he just abruptly got up and moved. He got up, took a chair, and in the dark, in this dark auditorium, because the program is going on, he takes that chair, and he moves it into the corner. And he sits in the corner of the auditorium.

Denise Brown told you that she could not understand — she did not understand why he did that. She told you on the witness stand that she didn't say anything to offend him. Nobody said anything to offend him. Why is he so angry? Who was he angry at?

Well, common sense will tell us he is angry at Nicole. Why? Because he didn't address her. But for another reason as well. As he sits there in the corner, in the dark, he isn't watching the program on the stage. He is watching Nicole. Candace Garvey told you this.

Denise Brown told you this as well: Whenever they looked over at the defendant, that he was not looking at the stage or the program on the stage or the kids dancing up on the stage. They told you that every time they looked over in the dark corner at the defendant, he was staring at Nicole. He was staring at Nicole, and had simmering anger that he had, feelings, he was about to lose control. The fuse was getting shorter. The fuse was getting shorter and there is about to be an explosion. He is about to loose control.

And he is about to lose control like he did on those earlier occasions also. And, sure, he didn't kill her in those earlier occasions in October of '93 or in 1989, but that was then. But that was then, and back then the fuse was a lot longer. But now, the fuse is way short, it's awfully short, and when the program was over, when the program was over, clearly you knew that the relationship was over. In the past he had done things to Nicole and she had come back, but not only that, the Brown family, he still had the Brown family.

But when you consider the evidence in this case, you see that after the recital, Nicole and the kids and the Brown family went to the Mezzaluna for dinner. They didn't invite him to go. He has been rejected, completely rejected. He has been rejected in public.

And this is how these things work, this is how these things go. You may sit here and think, oh, well, you know, this isn't such a big deal. Why, sure. Perhaps in your lives and in your relationship this wouldn't be such a big deal.

But you have to put it in the context of the relationship that they have had. This is a big deal. It is a big deal to him and he is rejected in public. They go off to dinner. He is left to go off to dinner with Kato Kaelin.

He isn't used to rejection. He is a celebrity. We talked about that earlier, celebrities get — you get the best tables, you always get everything you want, you get what you want. There are no rules for celebrities.

But on July 12th he isn't getting what he wants. And so he goes home. And the fuse is getting shorter. And it's getting shorter. And he talks to Kato Kaelin and he complains about the dress she wore, and the fuse is getting shorter.

A recess is taken.

When we left off, we were talking about the fuse, how short the fuse was getting and how the defendant was on his way to Bundy in that white Bronco.

The same Bronco he drove in October 1993 and he is on his way and he is panicked and he is out of control. And he is calling Paula and he can't find Paula. He calls her in L.A., he calls her in Florida, she's nowhere to be found. He can't find her. He has lost her. And he has lost Nicole.

And whose fault is this? It's Nicole's fault. He made a choice that day. He chose Nicole over Paula and he lost them both.

And so he arrives at Bundy and Ms. Clark discussed with you yesterday the details of the murder, of both murders. And I don't want to, you know, repeat all that she said, but one of the things that she said that I want to elaborate on just a little bit is his choice, his weapon choice, his use of a knife.

This is a rage killing and it is up front and it is personal and that is why you see all the brutality that you see. Common sense tells us that. I mean, we know that just from life experience and from living in L.A., we know what kind of killing this is. This is a rage killing. And he's using a knife because he is there to settle a personal score, a personal vendetta that he has.

He stabs this woman in the neck and he's right there, I mean, it's one-on-one. And the rage that he has, the anger, the hate that he has for her that night at that time, it's like it flows out of him into the knife and from the knife into her, into her.

And he kills Goldman and he kills her in this rage. And let me make it clear to you, he's in rage, but he has made a conscious decision, a premeditated decision, a deliberate decision to go there and do what he is about to do to this person.

Otherwise, why would he take a big knife with him, right? He killed her that way because he wanted to make a statement. He wanted to teach her a lesson. He wanted to let her know. He wanted her to be there face-to-face to know just who it was who was doing this to her.

With each thrust of that knife into her body and into Ron's body, there is a release, you know, a small release, it's like a tiny time capsule, you know, like Contact, there is a release, gradual release of that anger and that rage. And he stabs and he cuts and he slices until that rage is gone and until these people are dead.

And after that rage is gone, he's better. One of the most remarkable things about this case is that after this man, him, after he did this to these two people, he didn't run away, he didn't jog away. Apparently, he didn't limp away. You heard Agent Bodziak's testimony. He just walked away.

He had released all of that rage and that anger during this homicidal fit he was having and as he killed these two people. Now, I'm just a messenger, and I hate to be the one to stand here and tell you about these things, but, you know, this is a murder case. And this is what he did.

All these things we talked about, these are the things that he did. This is how he lived. This is his life, okay. And so I think we've come full circle at this point. We've shown you that he had the opportunity to kill.

We've shown you that he had the motive, that he had a motive to kill. We've shown you in this trial that he was physically capable of killing. We've shown you that he had a reason to kill. We've shown you that he would have killed, could have killed and did kill these two people.

He's a murderer. He was also one hell of a great football player. But he's still a murderer. And so we've come full circle. There was Ron and there was Nicole and, you know, Ron, he was just at the wrong place at the wrong time. Nicole, she was in the wrong place for a long time.

And there was this common factor, this common element between the two of them, and one thing they had in common was this man, this defendant, and so we began with them, two very much alive, vibrant human beings.

We went through 1989 and 1985, through the beating he inflicted on her. And we went from that in '85 into 1989 and we came to this point on June 12 at Bundy...

• • •

And so we've come full circle. And the only common element in all of this, and the only direction in which all of the evidence points, is to O.J. Simpson.

• • •

Let me say that what you do in this case is entirely up to you. I mean, you are the jury. When I sit down, I sit down. I'm done. I've completed my duty. I've done what the law requires me to do. I have lived up to the oath, my oath as a member of the District Attorney's office. And I have presented — we hope we have presented the best evidence we could. And if we didn't present the best evidence we could, don't hold that against us. I just want you to, you know, when the time comes, to go into the jury room. I want you to — somebody — somebody just say: "Let's calm down. Let's elect the foreperson. Let's read the law. Let's take a minute, and let's just look at the evidence."

And I would just like you to use your common sense when you do. When you do that, I mean, use your common sense, when you try to be objective, when you remove all the emotion from this case, when you remove all the sympathy and passion, and when you just look at the facts, the evidence as best you can, you will come up with the right decision.

The world's watching. Everybody wants to know what you are going to do. Marcia Clark and I know you are going to do the right thing under the law. Whatever you do, the decision is yours. I'm glad that it's not mine.

• • •

The Court: Thank you, Mr. Darden. ... All right. Ladies and gentlemen, that concludes the prosecution's opening argument to you. What is next is the defense argument. And what I'm going to do at this time is take a little break as far as you are concerned. As when the prosecution argument started, you noticed that they used some demonstrative boards for you that were not actually in evidence. And what I need to do now is to preview the ones that the defense is going to use to see if they are appropriate and acceptable for use during the course of the argument.

So that's what we'll be doing here in the courtroom for probably the next — probably take us about a half-hour or so to do that. I'm going let you go early for lunch. ... Have a nice lunch, and we'll start the defense argument at 1:30.

Chapter 7
The Closing Argument
of the Defense

Defense Attorney Johnnie Cochran puts on a knit cap for effect during closing arguments. Photo: Vince Bucci, Pool/AP/Wide World Photos.

THE DEFENSE SUMMATION

September 27, 1995

The Court: All right. The record should reflect we've been rejoined by all the members of our jury panel. Good afternoon, ladies and gentlemen.

The Jurors: Good afternoon.

The Court: And as I mentioned to you, we had some preliminary matters we had to take up out of your presence. We are now ready to proceed with the defense argument. Mr. Cochran, you may proceed.

Mr. Cochran: Thank you very kindly, Your Honor. Judge Ito, my colleagues on the defense, my colleagues on the prosecution, the Goldman family, the Brown family, and to the Simpson family. Good afternoon, ladies and gentlemen.

The Jurors: Good afternoon.

Mr. Cochran: The defendant, Mr. Orenthal James Simpson is now afforded an opportunity to argue the case, if you will, but I'm not going to argue with you, ladies and gentlemen. What I'm going to do is to try and discuss the reasonable inferences which I feel can be drawn from this evidence.

At the outset, let me join with the others in thanking you for the service that you have rendered. You are truly a marvelous jury, the longest-serving jury in Los Angeles County, perhaps the most patient and healthy jury we have ever seen. I hope that your health and your good health continues.

We met approximately one year and one day ago on September 26th, 1994. I guess we have been together longer than some relationships as it were. But we have had a unique relationship in this matter in that you have been the judges of the facts, we have been advocates on both sides, the judge has been the judge of the law. We all understand our various roles in this endeavor that I am going to call a journey toward justice. That's what we're going to be talking about this afternoon as I seek to address you.

The final test of your service as jurors will not lie in the fact that you have stayed here more than a year. It will lie in the quality of the verdict that you render, and whether or not that verdict bespeaks justice, as a move towards justice.

• • •

No one, no one, can tell you what the facts are: That's going to be your job to determine. It's not a question of age or experience. We talked about that. This is one of those jobs where you kind of learn on the job.

And so it's important that you fully understand that, and that's why *voir dire* was so very important, as we asked you all of those questions before you were sequestered and before you were actually picked. Now, each of you filled out the questionnaire, and you answered the questions honestly, I'm sure.

You know, Cicero said a long time ago that he who violates his oath profanes the divinity of faith itself. And, of course, both sides of this lawsuit have faith that you live up to your promises, and I'm sure you will do that.

And Abraham Lincoln said that jury service is the highest act of citizenship. So, if it's any consolation to you, you have been involved in that very highest act of citizenship. And so, again, we applaud you, and we thank you as we move toward justice.

• • •

In the course of this process where we're discussing the reasonable inferences of the evidence, I ask you to remember that we're all advocates. We are all officers of this court. I will recall the evidence and speak about the evidence. Should I misstate that evidence, please don't hold that against Mr. Simpson. I would never intentionally do that.

In fact, I think you will find that during my presentation, unlike my learned colleagues on the other side, I'm going to read you testimony of what the witnesses actually said so there will be no misunderstanding about what was said about certain key things. But remember that we're all advocates. And I think it was Ms. Clark who said: Saying it's so doesn't make it so.

I think that applies very much to their arguments. Ultimately, it's what you determine to be the facts is what's going to be important. And all of us will live with that. You are empowered to do justice. You are empowered to ensure that this great system of ours works.

Listen for a moment, if you will please, to one of my favorite people in history is the great Frederick Douglas. He said, shortly after the slaves were freed: In a composite nation like ours as before the law, there should be no rich, no poor, no high, no low, no white, no black, but common country, common citizenship, equal rights, and a common destiny.

This marvelous statement was made more than 100 years ago. It's an ideal worth striving for and one that we still strive for. We haven't reached this goal yet; but certainly, in this great country of ours, we're trying. With the jury such as this, we hope we can do that in this particular case.

Now, in this case, you are aware that we represent Mr. Orenthal James Simpson. The prosecution never calls him Mr. Orenthal James Simpson. They call him "defendant."

I want to tell you right at the outset that Orenthal James Simpson, like all defendants, is presumed to be innocent. He's entitled to the same dignity and respect as all the rest of us. As he sits over there now, he's cloaked in a presumption of innocence. You will determine the facts of whether or not he is set free to walk out those doors or whether he spends the rest of his life in prison.

But he's Orenthal James Simpson. He's not just "the defendant." And we on the defense are proud and consider it a privilege to have been part of representing him in this exercise and this journey toward justice. Make no mistake about it.

• • •

Finally, with regard to your responsibilities, we ask you at the very beginning to don't compromise. This is not a case for the timid or the weak of heart. This is not a case for the naive. This is a case for courageous citizens who believe in the constitution.

And while I am talking about the constitution, think with me for a moment, how many times I heard my lawyers, adversaries, say the defense didn't prove, the defense didn't do this, the defense didn't do that.

Remember, back in *voir dire*, what did the judge tell us? Judge Ito said the defense could sit here and do absolutely nothing. One of you is from Missouri, and he reminded you — who is from Missouri here? Said to the prosecution, you show us.

We didn't do that, but we don't have an obligation, as you will see, and you have heard from the jury instructions, and at the end I will show you some others. We don't have to do anything. We don't have to prove anything. This is the prosecution's burden. And we can't let them turn the constitution on its head. We can't let them get away from their burden.

My job, one of my jobs, is to remind you of that, and to remind them of that, that that's their burden. They must prove Mr. Simpson guilty beyond a reasonable doubt and to a moral certainty, and we will talk about what a reasonable doubt means.

And so now, as we have this opportunity to analyze the facts of the case, I agree with one thing that Mr. Darden said, to this task, I ask you to bring your common sense.

• • •

Let me ask each of you a question. Have you ever in your life been falsely accused of something? Have you ever been falsely accused? Have you ever had to sit there and take it and watch the proceedings and wait and wait and wait all the while knowing you didn't do it?

All you could do during such a process is to really maintain your dignity. Isn't that correct? Knowing that you were innocent. But maintaining your dignity and remembering always that all you are left with after a crisis is your conduct during it.

So that's another reason why we are proud to represent this man, who has maintained his innocence and has conducted himself with dignity throughout these proceedings.

Now, last night as I thought about the arguments of my colleagues, two words came to mind, and I want to — I asked my wife this morning to get the dictionary out and look up two words. The two words were speculative and cynical. Let me see if I can get those words that she got for me.

I asked her, as I was thinking about this case, to go to *Webster's*, and I want you to tell me, what does it mean to speculate? What does it mean to be cynical, as I thought about my colleagues' arguments and their approach to this case and their view of this case.

Cynical is described as contemptuously distrustful of human nature and motives; gloomy, distrustful view of life.

And to speculate, to speculate, to engage in conjecture and to surmise or — is to take to be the truth on the basis of insufficient evidence.

I mention those two definitions to you because I felt that much of what we heard yesterday and again this morning was mere speculation.

Understand this, ladies and gentlemen, that none of us in this courtroom were out at 875 Bundy on June 12th, 1994, after 10:30 or 10:45 in the evening. So that everything we say to you is our best effort to piece together what took place in this case.

When people theorize about things that may have been and talk to you about short fuses, you are going to see, that's just that, it's speculation. People see things that are totally cynical, maybe that's their view of the world. Not everybody shares that view.

Now, in this case, and this is a homicide case and a very, very, very serious case, and, of course, it's important for us to understand that. It is a sad fact that in American society a large number of people are murdered each year.

Violence, unfortunately, has become a way of life in America, and so when this sort of tragedy does, in fact, happen, it becomes the business of the police to step up and to step in and to take charge of the matter.

A good, efficient, competent, non-corrupt police department will carefully set about the business of investigating homicides. They won't rush to judgment. They won't be bound by an obsession to win at all costs. They will set about trying to comprehend the killer or killers and try to protect the innocent from suspicion.

In this case, the victims' families had an absolute right to demand exactly just that in this case. But it was clear, unfortunately, that in this case there was another agenda, from the very first orders issued by the LAPD so-called brass. They were more concerned with their own images, the publicity that might be generated from this case, than they were in doing professional police work.

That's why this case has become such a hallmark, and that's why Mr. Simpson is the one on trial. But your verdict in this case will go far beyond the walls of Department 103 because your verdict talks about justice in America and it talks about the police and whether they are above the law.

• • •

So it seems to us that the evidence shows that professional police work took a back seat right at the beginning. Untrained officers trampled — remember I used the word in opening statements they traipsed through the evidence.

• • •

They delayed unconsciously routine procedures and notifying the coroners. They didn't call the criminalists out on time. And yes, they allowed this investigation to be infected by a dishonest and corrupt detective. They did that in this case, and they may try to back away from it all they want, but that's very important, as you are going to see, to this case and the resolution of my client's innocence.

Because of their bumbling, they ignored obvious clues. They didn't pick up paper at the scene with prints on it. Because of their vanity, they very soon pretended to solve this crime and, we think, implicated an innocent man.

And they never, they never, ever looked for anyone else. We think if they'd done their job as we have done, Mr. Simpson would have been eliminated early on.

And so this case is not, let me say at the outset, is not about attacking the Los Angeles Police Department. We're not anti-police in making these statements. You're not anti-police. We all need the police. As I just said, we have so much crime in this country, we need the police.

But what we need and what we must demand, what all of us should have are honest, effective nonbiased police officers. Who could demand less? Can any of you say that's not what we should have?

And so let me tell you about how we're going to proceed here this afternoon. The defense has one opportunity, basically, to address you. This is after the prosecutors are finished. I will address you first.

And after I'm concluded — and I will talk generally about the lay witnesses and an overview of the evidence and what you've heard. I'll strive not to bore you. I'll strive to be honest in my discussions, to be relevant, to be concise in what we talk about here.

When I'm finished, Mr. Barry Scheck will come before you and address some of the forensic issues. And then finally after Mr. Scheck finishes, I will come back and conclude some concluding remarks regarding what you've heard over the course of the last two days at any rate.

Now, you understand that because the prosecution bears the burden in this case and in all cases, Ms. Clark will argue last, to seek to rebut that which we bring up. And presumably she won't be back up here talking about all kinds of new things; seek to rebut that which we bring up.

And let me tell you in front, if she brings up anything, we may be precluded from standing up and saying, wait a minute, your Honor, here's the answer to that. But you can then substitute your common sense and your judgment in that place. And that's required in this journey toward justice.

. . .

Everybody is entitled to dignity. That's what we fought for in this country. You don't treat witnesses who just come in here, they don't get paid to tell the truth like that, just purely and simply because they are not saying what you want them to say, in your contorted version of what the truth ought to be.

But you saw that yourself. I don't have to tell you about it. Interestingly enough, they chose not to mention even one of the defense witnesses in Ms. Clark's discussion of her timeline. The prosecutors noted that none of their timeline witnesses asked to be involved in this case. Well, none of the witnesses that we called asked to be involved in this case. They came forward. You saw how they were treated, but yet they told you what they observed.

But perhaps the most important thing about it is these aren't any family members, these aren't people who know O.J. Simpson, these are just people who happened to be out there that particular night.

And I think you can now see from their graphic, is how they and you passed by there. We tried to make it as clear as we could, it's common sense, it's common sense, just like he said. It becomes very, very clear right at the outset.

So if you accept the prosecution's scenario, there is not enough time for O.J. Simpson to have committed these murders, given the evidence that we understand.

. . .

Also, if the circumstantial evidence, as to any particular count, either one of these counts, is susceptible of two reasonable interpretations, one of which points to guilt, and the other which points to innocence, you as jurors, must adopt that interpretation which points to the defendant's innocence and reject that interpretation which points to his guilt.

If on the other hand one interpretation of such evidence appears to you to be reasonable and the other interpretation to be unreasonable, you must accept the reasonable interpretation and reject the unreasonable.

I put that up at this very moment because you've just seen the time line, which is circumstantial evidence of O.J. Simpson's innocence, because he couldn't have done the crime, given this time.

So under that scenario, even if the prosecution's time line was reasonable, if they're both reasonable, I think you must agree ours is reasonable, it becomes your duty to adopt that which points towards innocence.

But even further, if theirs is unreasonable and ours is reasonable, he's still entitled to an acquittal. The only way they're entitled to conviction is if ours is unreasonable and theirs is reasonable. And I think you can see and understand that's not true, that shouldn't happen, that's not the facts of this case.

So before I look at their time line, let me just see if I can summarize what I believe the prosecution has tried to tell you about their theory in this case.

And this is just kind of rough, but listening to them yesterday, they tried to tell you that an insanely jealous man stalks his ex-wife, stabs her and a male visitor in a murderous rage, leaves a trail of blood to his home, barely catches a plane for Chicago, in a rush to go there leaves one glove at the murder scene and one glove behind his house.

In the defense of this case, you have heard evidence about O.J. Simpson's great life. Not only did he have a great life, he had a great day that day, playing golf, comes back from being out of town all week long, comes back to go to his child's recital.

He goes to that recital, prepares in the evening, gets something to eat, a hamburger. By the way, I have to stop at this point. I'm glad Ms. Clark doesn't know this, but you know if you've ever been to McDonald's, they don't like you to bring a hundred dollar bill in there. You can't get one hundred dollars change there generally. Some of these things about common sense, your Honor, people don't know.

• • •

Use your common sense about fast food places. He then takes a shower, barely catches his plane to Chicago. Someone murders his wife and this male visitor for reasons unknown in this trial.

Others seek to implicate him as the most obvious suspect, the investigation becomes a tragic combination of sloppy errors and cover-ups to try and achieve his conviction. Those are going to be pretty much the hypothesis that you've heard and will be hearing in this case.

Under whatever scenario, based upon what I've already told you in this first hour of the argument, this man is entitled to an acquittal. But let's now turn briefly to the prosecution's time line scenario.

And you heard Ms. Clark yesterday talk about this time line and talk about these witnesses, and she relies very heavily on this Pablo Fenjves. You remember him, he's one of the early, early witnesses who started off, I think, talking about the plaintive wail of a dog at 10:30, got pushed back to 10:15.

Interesting because Darden, not Marcia Clark, has now come back and conceded, well, maybe it really was later, they did a pretty good job, you know, so he's saying that.

But Fenjves told us he was in that alleyway, down the alleyway and across from where Nicole Brown Simpson lives, 10:15, 10:30, whatever, 10:20.

Eva Stein next door was asleep, claims she was awakened. You ever wake up at night? You might see the time right, you might not. She says about 10:20 or so. She thinks she hears dogs barking.

Well, I presume the dogs bark throughout that neighborhood all the time. And we don't know. And that's the problem of trying to convict somebody or set the time of death by a dog barking.

Louis Karpf, her boyfriend, comes home sometime after 10:20. And then, of course, Ms. Elsie Tistaert, the lady from across the street doesn't know precisely when she heard the barks.

• • •

Ms. Clark does take some licenses regarding times. She says that Mr. Goldman leaves Mezzaluna. And she says about 9:50 p.m., says he goes home and changes clothes, that he talked to Stewart Tanner about getting together later that evening. Remember that?

Talked about going to Baja Cantina out at the Marina. You know, wouldn't you think it would be logical to expect, if you worked all day, when you went home to change clothes, you might have showered, you might have gotten something to eat.

Especially later on, when you hear Mr. Scheck, you look at the amount of food, undigested food in the stomach of these two victims.

But in a rush to judgment, in a rush to contort these facts, Ms. Clark tells you yesterday, let's give him 5 minutes, and he's been working all day, he's got to change clothes, he's got to come home, let's give him 5 minutes, 10 minutes, correct?

She says let's give him 10 minutes. That seems to me to be really, really fast. What it is, ladies and gentlemen, is more of that speculation. She doesn't know how long Mr. Goldman was there. None of us know that.

We know he changed clothes. She has absolutely no idea, but — so you understand that when you look at — when somebody says something like that to you.

And then as part of their timeline, she tells you yesterday that there is something sinister in Mr. Simpson seeking change to buy a Big Mac from McDonald's.

I suppose that if you are in this jealous rage, if the fuse is running so short, it's interesting — isn't it — to stop, go get a hamburger at McDonald's. Does that make any sense to any of you? Does it make any sense to you to drive to McDonald's.

There is no evidence that he tried to tell Kato Kaelin not to come. The evidence is that these two men got into the Bentley and went to McDonald's. The evidence is that while O.J. Simpson is in this murderous rage, he's worried about money to tip the skycaps at the airport because he has hundred dollar bills. So he gets twenty dollars from Kato Kaelin. What's unusual about that? Kato Kaelin is living there for free, so I suppose he could give him twenty dollars, and Kato Kaelin wanted to go get something to eat.

And Ms. Clark says they could have gone into a restaurant. Well, you could do anything, I suppose. But the facts are, they went to McDonald's to get a hamburger. O.J. Simpson ate the hamburger. Presumably he was hungry. Now, what's sinister about that unless you are cynical in your view totally of this case?

Kato Kaelin, their witness, they called him. They turned on him. You observed him. I ask you to hold him up to the same standards you do all the other witnesses. But I ask you, don't misquote him. Tell the truth about what he had to say. And so when he says 10:40 to 10:45, don't try to make it 10:52.

So if you believe in this prosecution's theory, there is this blood leading down to this rear walkway. And Ms. Clark told us yesterday, and unveiled her theory — here's what they ask you to believe: O.J. Simpson comes home from these brutal murders in a Bronco that he must be driving awfully fast to get back in this time frame, that he parks his Bronco out there at the Rockingham gate, somehow gets in the gate, gets down the side of his house, and — what does she tell you — he bumps into the air conditioning? Let's examine that for a minute.

The evidence is that O.J. Simpson has lived at this house for 17 years. Who do you think knows this place better or the best of all? This is his estate. This is where he lives. This is where he's raised his children. This is where he's been married. This is where he had two marriages. He knows this place.

So, as part of their fantasy, their theory, their speculation, they have O.J. Simpson walking down this walkway, running into an air conditioning.

Well, if he ran into the air conditioning, where is all the bruises that he got from running into the air conditioning? Where is the sound that he made? That doesn't make any sense.

You see, the reason why they come up with this running into the air conditioning, because they can't say he climbed over the fence. Because there is too much shrubbery there, and it's not broken. And they really don't know if he can climb over the fence with this arthritis, but they have him walking into the walkway, bumping into the air conditioning. And, ladies and gentlemen, we're talking about common sense here. Bumping into the air conditioning, and then he just leaves? Is that what happens?

• • •

Under this scenario, under their scenario, while Allan Park is out here somewhere looking over in this direction, they have O.J. Simpson rushing back, parking the Bronco out here, and some way or other he gets all the way down here.

Do you remember Fuhrman told you how far that was? He gets all the way down here where this air conditioning is out here by Kato Kaelin's room. You will see this right here. They have him running into his air conditioning; he doesn't know his own house? They have him all the way back here, and she says the reason he is back here, is he is going to bury the knife and the clothes. Isn't that something? How does she know that? Make that up out of whole cloth.

Do you believe that's reasonable? Is that reasonable to you? Does anybody on this jury believe that? That's what you were told yesterday. He runs into this air conditioning, and he just bumps into it, and he drops his glove. That's what she told you. Doesn't make any sense at all, does it, ladies and gentlemen? Doesn't make any sense at all.

No sound from Kato Kaelin. And what kind — the sound has always been very confusing — maybe not to you, but to me. When Kato Kaelin goes (*demonstrating three "thumps"*) it's more like a signal than anything else. Come out here or whatever.

But those are the facts of Kato Kaelin or what happened. And that's her theory. That's her reasonable, rational theory, that you have to buy into. Which I think that you will find to be totally ridiculous.

Now, remember, down this same way, there is a door into that side room there. If Mr. Simpson wanted to get in his house, what would stop him from going in the side door? Who knows this house better? If he wanted to not be seen. I suppose he would know better than anybody else. It doesn't make any sense. It doesn't make any sense at all what they are now trying to tell you.

Here's something else that's equally implausible. She tells you that the reason why Mr. Simpson couldn't stop and hide these clothes is because he's too famous and too well-known. Do you remember that?

She said O.J. Simpson is too famous and too well-known to stop and try to hide clothes or whatever of that nature.

Well, let's take that just a little bit further. Part of what makes their theory so ridiculous is O.J. Simpson going to get into a white Bronco that's well-known in Brentwood, drive over to his ex—wife's house, park the Bronco in this well-lit alleyway that you have just seen, leave the car there where everybody knows him, knows that car. That's equally preposterous. She can't have it both ways: He's too famous to stop and try to throw things in a dumpster, the way she put it; is he too famous to stop this car and go over these (inaudible). That is preposterous.

So if you believe the prosecution's theory, and they told you all this about the bloody trail; where's the blood back there?

Ladies and gentlemen, there is not one drop of blood. Where is the blood back there? Where is the trail that leads to that glove. And further, look at this — look at this, ladies and gentlemen; it's not something I'm making up.

You have seen this with your own eyes. Look at the glove. When that glove was picked up, do you see any blood on the ground — any blood on that shrubbery, any blood on anything there. Where is the blood?

Fuhrman and Vannatter — and we'll discuss them later — will say that when they get that glove after six o'clock in the morning, it's still moist and sticky. Do you remember that testimony? Where is the blood on the ground? Where is the blood on the leaves around there? Where is any of that? That glove looks as though it's been placed there. That glove looks as though it's been placed there. If you look at A, you will see how far it is out to the street.

So their theory doesn't hold water. It doesn't make sense. And so they get mad at Kato Kaelin, and they tell you why he's biased; he's just indebted to O.J. Simpson, so we just can't trust him. But yet they want you to trust him about the knocks on the wall, and he becomes part of their theory.

But their theory doesn't make sense. And when you were back there deliberating on this case, you are never going to be ever able to reconcile this time line. And the fact there is no blood back there, and that O.J. Simpson would run into an air conditioning on his own property. And then, under her scenario, he still has the knife and the clothes.

But what does she tell you yesterday? Well, he still has the knife. And he's in these bloody clothes and, presumably, in bloody shoes. And what does he do? He goes in the house.

Now, thank heaven Judge Ito took us on a jury view. You have seen this house. You have seen this carpet. If he went in that house with bloody shoes, with bloody clothes, with his bloody hands as they say, where is the blood on the doorknob? Where is the blood on the light switch? Where is the blood on the banister? Where is the blood on the carpet? It's like almost white carpet going up that stairs.

Where is all the blood trail they have been banning about in this mountain of evidence? You will see it's little more than a river or stream. They don't have any mountain or ocean of evidence. It's not so because they say so. That is just rhetoric.

We, this afternoon, are talking about the facts. So it doesn't make any sense. It just doesn't fit. If it doesn't fit, you must acquit.

So she has him then still with the knife, still with these bloody clothes. And then she does something very unusual again on the time. Do you remember she gave Mr. Goldman 10 minutes to get dressed and go over to Nicole Brown Simpson's house with this envelope? Mr. Simpson, she says, walked in this house, in the walkway, and by the way. They were wrong. She was wrong about something else, again, I would like to read you. She's wrong in her description of Allan Park — if I can locate it.

Allan Park says he saw this figure in the walkway only. And so that we're clear about that, let me just read it to you. I don't have to tell you just what I think it is; I'm going it read it to you. 20571 counsel. Line 17. "Yes, I saw a figure — well, not come down — but I saw a figure come into the entranceway of the house just about where the driveway starts." So he saw a figure come into the entranceway of the house just about where the driveway starts there (pointing).

Do you see that? Right there (indicating) is where the driveway was. That's what he said. Yesterday they tried to put it all down here and have him come in, because that was convenient to the theory. You look at the facts in this case and you will see. Not what they tell you.

Continuing on, there is absolutely no evidence at all that Mr. Simpson ever tried to hide a knife or clothes or anything else on his property. You recall that Fuhrman, and when I get to Fuhrman we will be spending some time on him, as you might imagine, but one of the things he said was that he encountered cobwebs further down that walkway indicating, if that part is true, and I don't vouch for him at all, there had been nobody down that pathway for quite some time.

And so she talks about O.J. being very, very recognizable. She talks about O.J. Simpson getting dressed up to go commit these murders. And just before we break for our break, I was thinking last night about this case and their theory and how it didn't make any sense and how it didn't fit and how something was wrong.

It occurred to me how they were going to come up here and tell you how O.J. Simpson was going to disguise himself, was going to put on a knit cap and some dark clothes and he was going to get in his white

Bronco, this recognizable person, and go over and kill his wife. That's what they want you to believe. That's how silly their argument is.

And I said to myself, maybe I can demonstrate this graphically. Let me show you something. This is a knit cap. Let me put this knit cap on. You have been seeing me for a year. If I put this knit cap on, who am I? I am still Johnny Cochran with a knit cap.

And have you looked at O.J. Simpson over there? And he has a rather large head. O.J. Simpson in a knit cap from two blocks away is still O.J. Simpson. It's no disguise, it's no disguise. It makes no sense. It doesn't fit. If it doesn't fit, you must acquit.

A luncheon recess was taken.

The Court: Let the record reflect we've been rejoined by all the members of our jury panel. Good afternoon, ladies and gentlemen again. And, Mr. Cochran, you may continue with your final argument.

Mr. Cochran: Thank you, Your Honor. Good afternoon, ladies and gentlemen.

The Jury: Good afternoon.

Mr. Cochran: Thank you for your patience thus far and we'll start up again and see if we can make it to dinner.

• • •

With regard to that walkway, lest I be totally clear to you, if O.J. Simpson had been the one, for whatever reason, to walk into that air conditioning, where is the hair and trace? Where is the fiber? Where is the blood?

They want to tell you about his hands and fingers bleeding one minute and it stops bleeding. And Ms. Clark's scenario, he bleeds, it coagulates, stops bleeding and starts bleeding again because that's convenient for her theory.

You know, as I listened to both of them, I wanted to call them Doctor, Dr. Clark, because Dr. Clark told you, well, gee, look at that blood drop. That cut wasn't big enough for that blood drop.

She's not any doctor. How does she know that? Dr. Darden, for the love and forlorn, he knows everything about relationships, and speculates on and on and on, has this great vivid imagination.

Only thing is, this is real life. This isn't anything for Murder She Wrote. If they tried to sell this story to Murder She Wrote, they'd send it back and say that's unbelievable.

And you're going to see that as we tie it together. It's nice to have vivid imaginations but not in this courtroom because here you are searching for truth on this journey for justice.

So we know that Kato had some concerns. He was looking around. We know that at some point Mr. Simpson comes down the stairs carrying the Louis Vuitton bag or whatever and that Mr. Simpson leaves about 11:00, 11:02 for the airport.

I think that's pretty clear, based upon the evidence. And you'll recall that Ms. Clark again gives Mr. Simpson five minutes to rush in.

According to her theory, he rushes in, changes clothes, disposes of all these clothes, showers, packs, does everything and comes downstairs and says composes himself.

Now, can you imagine that? Who do they think they're talking to? Five minutes he does all these things. And then they tell you, well, under this post homicidal way you act, you get yourself all composed and you just do this.

This is preposterous. They are not experts. They can't testify. Those are just their wildest, rankest theories. You use your common sense when they tell you things like that.

O.J. Simpson was O.J. Simpson, the way he always appeared by the people who knew him and talked to him. We'll talk more about that when we talk about demeanor.

But the reason they can't explain his demeanor and the way he acted like he always acts, they talk about, well, you can't tell who's a murderer. Those are all real convenient words, aren't they? But they fly in the face of reasonable activity by a reasonable man on that particular night.

So there is Allan Park. O.J. Simpson comes down within five minutes of the time that they believe he goes upstairs. No time to dispose of bloody clothes. What about blood on the carpet? What about dirt on this white carpet? How does he shower? How does he get dressed? I mean, it doesn't make any sense at all, does it?

• • •

Consider everything that Mr. Simpson would have had to have done in a very short time on their time line. He would have had to drive over to Bundy, as they have described, in this little limited time frame where there is not enough time to kill two athletic people in a struggle that takes 5 to 15 minutes, walk slowly from the scene, return to the scene, supposedly looking for a missing hat and glove and poking around, go back to this alley a second time, drive more than five minutes to Rockingham where nobody hears him or sees him, either stop along the way to hide these bloody clothes and knives, et cetera, or take them in the house with him where there it is still hoisted on their own petard because there is no blood, there is no trace, there is nothing.

• • •

Now, let's turn our attention for a moment and let's look at some other things that don't fit in this case. As I started to say before, perhaps the single most defining moment in this trial is the day they thought they would conduct this experiment on these gloves.

They had this big build-up with Mr. Rubin, who had been out of the business for five, six, seven, eight years. He had been in marketing even when he was there. But they were going to try to demonstrate to you that these were the killer's gloves and these gloves that fit Mr. Simpson.

You don't need any photographs to understand this. I suppose that vision is indelibly imprinted in each and every one of your minds of how Mr. Simpson walked over here and stood before you and you saw four simple words, the gloves didn't fit.

And all their strategy started changing after that. Rubin was called back here more than all their witnesses, four times, all together. Rubin testified more than the investigating officers in this case, because their case from that day forward was slipping away from them and they knew it and they could never, ever recapture it.

We may all live to be one hundred years old, and I hope we do. But you will always remember that those gloves, when Darden asked him to try them on, didn't fit.

They know they didn't fit, and no matter what they do, they can't make them fit. They can talk about latex gloves, doesn't make any difference. They can talk about shrinkage, but we did something better, even better.

• • •

You saw these pictures of the gloves. We had a couple of pairs of Aris Lite, and when you have gloves that don't fit, you can hardly do anything with them. It makes it very, very tough.

I will put on a pair of Aris Lite gloves that are real tight and you can see how tough it is to try to get these on my hands. But I will put them on anyway here. It's the same kind of gloves that Dr. MacDonell did his experiment with so there would be no mistake about the leather and all those things they like to talk about.

They are hard to get on. Not as hard as Mr. Simpson, but they are hard to get on. The reason I wanted you to see these gloves, because then I want to tell you that when you take off gloves, you take them off by this V portion. Remember this? Somebody testified.

You don't take off gloves that way. One of the People's witnesses said that. You don't take them off that way. So we are asked to believe that in this tremendous struggle that night in which Ron Goldman fought so valiantly that somehow or another in that struggle somebody took these gloves off — the way you took these gloves off, you pull them off like this, even Rubin knew this, gloves came off like this, not through any way like that.

So I think it's interesting when you look at these gloves and you look at what they are trying to have you believe. They talked a lot about in their rebuttal case about the glove pictures and the glove photographs. Remember that each of the gloves photographs were taken — or pictures of Mr. Simpson were taken in the winter.

You know the evidence. Mr. Simpson was living in New York, generally, from August through January when it was football season, working for NBC sports. Generally in Southern California you don't need or wear winter dress gloves in California. You don't go skiing in Aris Lite gloves.

And you remember that the police, in searching Mr. Simpson's house, remember Detective Lange? They searched O.J. Simpson's house for gloves, for shoes, for clothes. That one brown glove, I want you to look at it at some point, the brown glove. It looks very similar to the brown gloves that Mr. Simpson...

• • •

Compare the fact that he stopped looking after two with Agent Martz, who finds three of the four things you need to find EDTA on this sock and the back gate, and rather than looking carefully for the characteristic — the fourth one, he stopped searching, uses a far less discriminating test.

Consider the EAP-B found under Nicole Brown Simpson's fingernails where they try to come in and tell you it's a degraded BA and on cross-examination Bob Blasier got Matheson to admit there was no specific support in any of the literature for a BA degrading to a B, and this was, by all accounts, a double-banded B.

The reason they didn't want to pursue that, because she may have scratched somebody with the B type, but they never pursued those things.

The second hat at Bundy, at the Bundy location inside, when the defense investigator finds this hat, nobody wanted to collect it, they refused, in fact, to collect it.

When we — in this trial, before we discovered that evidence had been moved at Bundy and that a key piece of evidence, the piece of paper, had disappeared, they didn't do anything to find out about it that we know of. We are concerned about those kinds of things.

But it's important, and when you look at Rubin, because you put him along with the other prosecution witnesses and the things that they have had to say, they told you about the Bloomingdale's receipt, told you about when the shoe came in and Brenda Vemich, that was interesting, she was the lady who — that was the day — I won't forget that day probably ever because that was the day that — she is a pretty tough witness. I was just trying to talk about receipts and things. She is pretty tough.

. . .

Now, this is interesting because Mr. Darden started off by saying, well, you know, we're going to put together this other piece, it's not really one of the elements of the crime of murder, motive, but we're going to talk to you about motive now and we're going to tell you and convince you about the motive in this case.

And then he spent a long time trying to do that. And, as I say, he did a fine job to address the facts and conjure up a lot of emotion. But you notice how at the end he kind of petered out of steam there. And I'm sure he got tired, but he petered out because this fuse he kept talking about kept going out.

It never blew up. It never exploded. There was no triggering mechanism. There was nothing that would lead you to that. It was a nice analogy, almost like that baby analogy of the baby justice in the house of fire.

. . .

Somebody had to have some good sense in this courtroom. We had to bring this matter to a close. We did what we set out to do, to demonstrate to you reasonable doubt. We think we've done that.

We could call a lot more witnesses, as I talked to you about in opening statement, but I don't think that's necessary.

Another word about opening statement. In opening statement, I stood before you and I told you this is what we expect to show. This is not evidence. That was in January. This is what I would hope the evidence would show.

If there's a witness that I didn't feel was credible or we didn't feel was credible, I wouldn't call that witness. This was a witness that was not available, we couldn't call that witness. If we didn't feel a witness was not necessary, we wouldn't call that witness.

The defense doesn't have to prove anything. We've done that in this case, prove things, however, but we don't have to prove anything.

So the witness wasn't called. Don't hold that against O.J. Simpson. You hold that against me. And I don't think you can hold that against me because the defendant doesn't have to prove anything.

And, remember, the Judge has already instructed you as follows: Let me read it to you again so we make this clear, maybe Mr. Darden will remember this. "The prosecution has the burden of proving beyond a reasonable doubt each element of the crimes charged in the information. And that the defendant was a perpetrator of any such crimes, the defendant is not required to prove himself innocent or to prove that another person committed the crimes charged."

Now, that law is not just for O.J. Simpson. That's the law of the state of California for everyone. And they know it. I told you at the beginning in this search for truth, in your courage, we cannot let them turn the Constitution on its head. I am going to be your reminder of that.

• • •

O.J. Simpson didn't try to kill or didn't kill Nicole Brown Simpson when they got a divorce, when they went through whatever (inaudible) they went through when Faye Resnick moved in. Any of those things — none of these things happened. Because of their rush to judgment, they have to try to come up with some kind of a motive that doesn't make any sense.

• • •

This is a case about stealth. This is a case about somebody who, it seems to me, is a professional assassin who kills these two people. And the thing that is so outrageous for them to stand here and say that this is all about Nicole Brown Simpson. Have any of you thought during the last year what if the perpetrators were after Ron Goldman and that envelope that he had in his hand that Dr. Lee found that smear on? Who in this courtroom would know? The rest is speculation. This is their theory that they tried to come up with. We don't know.

This is a case of reasonable doubt. This is a case of an innocent man wrongfully accused. They can't answer those questions. No one can under these circumstances.

• • •

But there is something else, again. They want to tell you, and you will hear a lot about socks before we are finished, that these socks, these socks that all of a sudden appear in that video at the foot of his bed were being worn by Mr. O.J. Simpson.

Well, ladies and gentlemen, when you see these socks — what do you think the dirt and dust was on these socks? Now let's see if they can ever explain this. Where was the dirt that was thrown up and moved around on these socks? You are not going to see any. You are not going to see any dirt because those socks weren't there.

• • •

You remember this when you talk about this case and you wonder whether or not there is a reasonable doubt, whether or not this is an innocent man wrongfully accused. And so you look at this. When you expect common sense would tell you there would be bruises and nicks, being kicked, there would be marks on all the perpetrators, with the heavy foliage there, with the fence and the trees, you would expect scratches on everyone, whereas Mr. Goldman has more than 30 stab wounds, you would expect this struggle, 5 to 15 minutes, to have left that.

But there is nothing like that in this case, nothing like that on Mr. Simpson's body. And you have seen that before and you will see it again.

• • •

And so we did call — Bob Shapiro called Dr. Robert Huizenga as a witness in this case, and Dr. Huizenga, you will recall, Dr. Huizenga seemed to be a very honest witness in this case.

And what did he say? He said O.J. Simpson looks likes Tarzan but he walks more like Tarzan's grandfather. That's not to say O.J. Simpson wouldn't be capable of committing a crime. That's never what we were trying to say.

What we are trying to say is that see this man for who he is. See this man for the arthritis that he suffers. Everybody in his family suffers from arthritis. You saw his mother, you heard his sister. And you heard he has it worse than they have.

Now, he can still play golf, you can still do that, and some of you I hope don't, but if you have it in the early stages you know what it is, certainly on certain days.

What I think it means is you don't go out looking for anybody to be in an altercation with. O.J. Simpson, by all accounts, has trouble with lateral movement, moving from side to side, because you saw when I had him come over here, those knee operations that basically spelled NFL, National Football League, four or five times on the left knee, maybe a couple times on the right knee, that's the price that a running back pays.

And while I am talking about running backs, wasn't it interesting yesterday that Ms. Clark in his argument says O.J. Simpson was a football player and he has to run through the line and he has the killer instinct? Isn't that really stretching it, ladies and gentlemen?

A dinner recess is taken

Mr. Cochran: ... So now where were we when we left off?

• • •

You heard the testimony of Drs. Huizenga and Baden who said this is not consistent with a knife cut, it's consistent with some kind of glass cut because it's raggedy, it's jagged, you remember that, you remember the testimony, and we can prove it further by witnesses who saw him before he was in that room in Chicago and witnesses who saw him after, and we will talk about that.

So on the plane was Bingham and then we had the pilot on the plane. And the pilot who was flying the plane came back and asked Mr. Simpson to autograph the logbook, which he did, and I think we have a photograph of that.

Again, you saw pilot Stanfield, who described how Mr. Simpson was sitting there reading a book, a light shining down on him, not trying to hide from anybody, not anything, sitting there reading his book, looked up, talked to the pilot, gave his autograph, and they both continued on with their business.

Then he gets to Chicago and he lands and he deals with Jim Merrill, the Hertz driver, you will recall him, Hertz driver describes the number of bags that Mr. Simpson has, luggage when he lands, describes the garment bag, the garment bag with OJS, the golf bag, the Louis Vuitton bag. All those bags are described by Merrill.

And then, you remember we talked about the knapsack bag which we think logically had golf balls in it and was inside the golf bag.

So Merrill watched O.J. in the luggage area meet with some I think, say, 20 different fans while waiting for his luggage. Merrill says he was friendly, relaxed, and he saw no noticeable cuts on his hands. That's what Jim Merrill told us. That was his testimony, so we brought him here from Chicago to testify in that regard.

Now I want you to contrast Mr. Simpson's demeanor and behavior after he goes to this hotel room in Chicago. After he learns of his ex-wife's death, everybody is consistent, and again, these witnesses don't know this person. He was emotional, concerned, with a cut finger....

But Mr. Simpson gets the call, and here is what I want you to think with me for a moment. I want you to look at how he reacts to this information.

We have already covered how his daughter describes him, she has never heard him like this before. He immediately gets plane reservations to come back to Los Angeles. He is then trying to get back, frantically trying to leave this hotel. It's early in the morning. He is trying to get back to Los Angeles on the first thing flying. He is trying to get somebody to take him back to the airport. He is there to play in a golf tournament that day.

Obviously, that's never going to happen. So we know that Dave Kilduff, the Hertz manager, drove Mr. Simpson to the airport.

Remember how he describes — now this is the first witness — O.J. Simpson's finger is bleeding.

And this fishhook cut, this cut that he got in that room when that broken glass was there, but the prosecutors, again, with a cynical view say, well, that couldn't have happened, Dr. Baden said from talking with Mr. Simpson that he got this cut from the glass breaking into the sink. That's entirely consistent. Doctors deal with cuts and they said this is consistent with a glass cut.

Kilduff said that O.J. Simpson is crying and he is upset. He finally makes the plane, and I think it's important to note that when he makes the plane, he sits next to — I think in Seat 9 — to a lawyer by the name of Mark Partridge, just fortuitous, and I thought was very interesting about this man, Partridge. Remember, he is the man who was a patent lawyer who had gone to Harvard and he observed O.J. Simpson on this flight back.

He saw him make these phone calls. He saw his emotional state. He saw him trying to gather information. He saw his finger. He saw the Band-Aid he had had that came off, he saw that it was cut. You saw his testimony.

These were all citizen time line witnesses, like you or I, who are brought here pursuant to subpoena. They didn't ask to be here, they didn't volunteer, but they had relevant information about what had taken place and what had happened.

So it seems to me that we, in our search for justice and our journey toward the city of justice, must take these witnesses seriously.

But you understand, with the power of the State, the prosecution had an equal access to all these witnesses, but they didn't call them. They didn't call them because they didn't fit. They didn't fit and they didn't want to hear.

So the prosecutors decided to attack. And you will remember how these witnesses generally were treated. I thought Partridge was treated especially bad. Here is a man who was so concerned about no one stealing his notes, he wrote notes about what took place, not to publish them. He is a patent lawyer so he understood. He put his name in the side of the margin to write down his notes because he knew it would be important, and he said he knew this would be important.

And he sent those notes to the prosecution and to the defense, said I am just a witness here and this is what I saw. Can I be of some help? They chose not to call him. They chose to attack him as though he had like something to hide.

• • •

And then there was Ken Berris, the police officer in Chicago. Ms. Clark talked about him coming out here, but we brought him out here. We brought Ken Berris out here. He was the police officer who maybe three hours after O.J. Simpson left that room, went into that room at the O'Hare Plaza, was it? 11:00 or thereabouts I believe he said he went in the room.

He found the glass. He found the doily. He found the towel. He found the bedding. Because the maids had not done anything with regard to that room. Found this broken glass. And the evidence is contrary to what the prosecutor would try to tell you is that this glass was consistent with O.J. Simpson cutting his hand on it. And this is the cut, the fishhook cut.

• • •

Doesn't it strike you as strange that under her hypothesis, under her theory, he comes back home with these bloody shoes on, bloody clothes with his white carpet, goes upstairs.

There's no blood anywhere, just a little tiny spec in the pathway. Does that seem to you to be reasonable or rational or related to this case?

One thing about blood spots, you can never date them. You can never tell generally how old they are. Another thing that doesn't fit; the fingerprints. They didn't call them, but we called. Gilbert Augilar, you remember him, he's the fingerprint expert.

He examined and dusted and found 17 latent prints that he was able to lift at Bundy, the crime scene. The gate. The fence. The front door. He was able to identify eight of the prints after comparing the known exemplars of — the known ones being the police officers and people that you might expect around there.

But there were nine identifiable prints that were never identified. Remember I asked about these various systems that you can put the prints in. Doesn't work for palms, but it works for prints.

What efforts did you take to try to find out who do these 9 identifiable prints belong to? To this day, we don't know. Are those the prints of the real killers? We will never know. They have not found those prints.

• • •

The so-called trial of the century. This is how they conducted themselves. Then we come to those socks. Those socks. They just don't fit, they just don't fit, they just don't fit. Watch with me now with a video. I want you to watch the time counter in this time frame and you will understand how important this is.

The video was shown.

Now where it says 3:13 p.m. Mr. Willie Ford says — back it up, please. This is Mr. Willie Ford going up in the bedroom. It's 3:13, which he says it's 4:13 because it hadn't been changed. This is 4:13 p.m. on June 13th, 1994.

Okay. Thank you, Your Honor. Look at the foot of the bed there where the socks are supposed to be. You will see no socks in this video, and you will recall that Mr. Willie Ford testified about this.

And I asked him, well, where are the socks, Mr. Ford? I didn't see any socks. So now that's interesting, isn't it? At 4:13 on June 13th, 1994, these socks they supposedly recovered, these mysterious socks, these socks that no one sees any blood on until August 4th, all of a sudden these socks that are picked up, that Luper says he picks them up because they look out of place. I didn't have any reason to pick them up, I will just take these socks, they are out of place.

The only items that they took out of place on that day is Lange, Lange takes the Reebok tennis shoes, the ones he takes home, remember that, that's all they really take because come back on the 28th and get that one brown glove.

But these socks would be their undoing. It just doesn't fit. None of you can deny there are no socks in front of that bed at 4:13 p.m. Where are these socks? Where are these socks, that important piece of evidence?

Well, let me show you something. This board here was a board used by Dr. Henry Lee, and this is interesting. Bear with me for a moment as you look at this.

A photograph marked exhibit 1552 is displayed.

And this photograph here, the one on the left ... notice something, the socks are at the foot of the bed. If you look closely at this photograph you will see there is no little white card here. You know how they put these little evidence cards where they are going to collect something? No little white card on this photograph here.

And this is interesting because you see these straps on the bed? Now, Luper told us when he testified, these straps were like — he called them some kind of luggage straps and these luggage straps are down at this point. Aren't they? See how they are down and no evidence card and the socks are there?

And we come over to this photograph here, notice how the strap is now up on the bed. It's no longer hanging down anymore, it's been moved up. And Luper says that's when he looks under this bed and he sees that photograph.

By the way, how wrong can they continue to be? That's no wedding photograph, that's a photograph they took at some formal event. You look at that photograph and see. That's how they speculate, and most times they have been wrong.

But this is a — this is interesting. The strap is now up on the bed and you look at the socks. Now there is — it's been posed for you. Here is this number 13 out here with these socks. Now, you look back at that video and you will have it. You will notice that the video has the strap down so the video is at a time before this card is placed, before the strap is up, before this is about to be collected.

Isn't that strange? Because at 4:13 there are no socks there. How do we tie all this together? Remember Fung and Mazzola have a log, and on their log they tell when they collected things.

They tell us that they collected the blood in the foyer at 4:30, that they then come upstairs, that they collect — here it is as we speak... . They collected things sequentially and they kept this log, and I think that you will remember the testimony that at 4:30 they collected the blood in the foyer. Remember that?

Let me see if I can point that out for us. In foyer, red stain. And there is testimony. They testified 4:30 — 16:30 is 4:30. This is at least 17 minutes after Mr. Ford is up there with that camera where there are no socks. Right? So 16:30, right there, they are downstairs.

Then they say they go upstairs and they leave this time blank, but at 16:40 they go and they look at this little red spot in the bathroom. Remember that? And they say in their testimony that the socks are collected between 16:30 and 16:40. So let's give them the benefit of the doubt, 16:35.

How could the socks be there at 4:35 when you just saw they are not there at 4:13? Who is fooling whom here? They are setting this man up and you can see it with your own eyes. You are not naive. Nobody is foolish here.

• • •

Something is wrong in this case. It just doesn't fit. If it doesn't fit, you must acquit .... And then we have heard a lot about the so-called blood in the Bronco. And I want to tell you, I am not anything like a scientist. In fact, when my mother and my father wanted me to become a doctor I didn't because I wasn't that good at science, so I became a lawyer so I could talk.

But let me tell you something, even I know about amounts of blood, especially after this case. They tell you about all this blood in the Bronco. And you remember one of the early witnesses testified the total amount of blood on this console is .07 of a drop of blood.

• • •

Now, this is an amazing thing because you remember this is the vehicle, in tradition of everything they did in this case, that's picked up, is towed away from Rockingham, you have all seen that photograph, is taken over, and ultimately it ends up at Viertel's...

Everybody knew this was O.J. Simpson's vehicle and they were all looking in it, supposedly all this blood that was supposed to be in here.

And this killer must have been covered in blood. And they say he drove this Bronco, it would be covered with blood, wouldn't it? So everyone's looking for blood. So Meraz says he gets in the car and he didn't see any blood. Meraz says that. They maligned him and said, yeah, I did take those receipts out there that had — one had Mr. Simpson's name on it, one had Mrs. Simpson's name on it.

But he said he didn't see any blood in there. They never called anybody to contravene that. But we want to make sure you understood what was happening. So we called William Blasini, the man who works for Pick Your Part, as far as vehicles.

And he was a pretty good witness, wasn't he? He said, look, this is my business, looking in cars, because I go in and buy them. He says I got in that car on June 21. And first of all said, "I went looking for blood because I'd heard in the news there was going to be lots of blood in this car."

So I went and got in the Bronco. It was not secured, as usual. Bob Jones said, "There it is, go ahead and get in it. No holes in it, could be released to Hertz."

• • •

How does anyone drive away in that car with bloody clothes, with no blood there on the seats, no blood anyplace else? Every police officer came in, talked about how bloody the scene was. It doesn't make any sense. You can't explain it because Mr. Simpson was not in that car and didn't participate in these murders.

That's the reasonable and logical explanation. And none other will do. And it's too late for them to change now with these kind of shifting theories. So the prosecution then has no shoes, no weapon, no clothes. They don't have anything, except these socks, which appear all of the sudden under these circumstances.

• • •

There's some missing blood in this case. Where is it? Prosecution wants to explain that for you, too, make everything real easy for you. So what do they do? What do they do? Gonna talk about the police, but what do they do? Hank Goldberg — doesn't give us any notice — goes out there with the video camera with Oppler and this other lady,

Ms. Ramirez, and they take this bizarre home video of Peratis sitting there talking and mouthing words.

It's the most bizarre thing. I mean, as jurors, I'm sure you've seen some pretty high quality testimony here. But this was bizarre. He's sitting there talking about, well, you know, gee, I don't really remember how much I took and he's going through all these gyrations. It was sad. The depths to which they had sunk.

• • •

So Vannatter, the man who carries the blood, starts lying in this case at the very, very beginning, trying to cover-up for this rush to judgment. Those are the words. That's rhetoric. Let me prove it for you. He tells us — and this is a board. The board's entitled "Vannatter Big Lies, the man who carried the blood." He tells us, that O.J. Simpson is not a suspect. That's the biggest lie we have heard probably in this entire trial. O.J. Simpson is not a suspect. They handcuff him within 30 to 45 seconds of the time he gets back here. He lies about that.

• • •

But one thing they do, they decide that O.J. Simpson is a suspect in this case. And let me tell you why you are going to know that. They want to talk a lot about 1985, but he missed the whole point. In 1985 something interesting happened in this case. In 1985, Mark Fuhrman responded to a call on Rockingham.

Mark Fuhrman is a lying, perjuring, genocidal racist. And from that moment on, anytime he could get O.J. Simpson, he would do it. That's when it started, in '85, when Farrell asked all the officers at West L.A., or ten of them, do you know anything about this residence, only one steps forward. And what does he say? It's indelibly impressed in my mind that call back in '89, four years later, sits down and writes a report. Now, he knew what he knew, what he was going to do on this particular night. So O.J.'s not a suspect? Went to save lives. He wanted to get a search warrant. That's why they were lying.

• • •

Then to get that search warrant, he lies to a judge. He says in the search warrant that O.J. left unexpectedly from Chicago, and there is some writing on the search warrant. I think it's in evidence. And it's kind of interesting because everybody knew — Kato knew he was going to Chicago, everybody knew he was going to Chicago. It wasn't any unexpected trip. But, I suppose, it would help out.

In fact, if you think about it — Ms. Clark said this — well, that's why those socks were out there and everything, because he left in a hurry. Like he had one pair of socks. You know why those socks were out there? He left unexpectedly to try and do just what they were doing; it all comes back to Fuhrman when he says in that letter: If I see an interracial couple, I'll stop them; if I don't have a reason, I'll make up a reason. This man thinks he's above the law.

• • •

And so he lies to the judge. He lied to the judge. He's lied to you, his jurors. And he says that Arnelle and Kato said O.J. left unexpectedly. That's written in the warrant. Never said anything of the kind. Kato knew this was a planned trip to Chicago for Hertz. He talked to Cathy Randa.

In the search warrant he puts — this was confirmed — there was human blood on the door. That's never been tested even to this day. Another lie in the search warrant. He denies telling Thompson to handcuff O.J. Simpson; then he lies about O.J. Simpson's blood.

• • •

You think I am making this up? And who would know Mark Fuhrman better in this case, his lack of credibility, his lying, racist views, than Ron Phillips, his supervisor, who apparently chose to look the other way. And I am sure he is as embarrassed as anybody else by this disgrace, Fuhrman.

So it's important at the outset that we understand the role of Phillips as we need to understand the role of Vannatter. He was the one allegedly given this order by Bushey to go over and give the death notification. He didn't comply with it until much later.

And presumably, the reason they were going to go over was to give the notice to Mr. Simpson and Fuhrman was going because he was needed. Now, can you imagine this? Fuhrman, with his views, genocidal views, was going to go over to give notice to O.J. Simpson, to help O.J. Simpson, in his time of need. Can you imagine that? He is going over there to help him, help him with his kids? That is ludicrous.

So from Riske to Bushey, you have seen and are seeing a part of this code of silence, this cover-up, a cover-up that Laura McKinny talks about, where male officers get together and cover up for each other, don't tell the truth, hide, turn their head, cover. You can't trust this evidence. You can't trust the messenger. You can't trust the message.

• • •

And let me just take a moment. This whole thing about the police and what they have done in this case is extremely painful to us, and I think to all right-thinking citizens, because you see, we live in Los Angeles and we love this place, but all we want is a good and honest police force where people are treated fairly no matter what part of the city they are in. That's all you want.

So in talking to you about this, understand there is no personal pride, but I told you when we started, this is not for the weak or for the faint of heart.

. . .

But what I find particularly troubling is that they all knew about Mark Fuhrman and they weren't gonna tell you. They tried to ease him back. Of all the witnesses who have testified in this case, how many were taken up to the grand jury room where they have this prep session and ask him all these questions?

And Ms. Clark and I went back and I read again her introduction of Mark Fuhrman. How many witnesses did they do that with? Where they took him up there and they prepared him for this. Because, you see, they knew about the Kathleen Bell letter. But she didn't fit. She didn't fit.

And what they wanted — they didn't want her, they'd rather malign her and believe this lying police officer. So they knew. Make no mistake about it. And so when they try to prepare him and talk to him and get him ready and make him seem like a choir boy, make him come in here and raise his right hand, as though he's going to tell you the truth and give you a true story here, they knew he was a liar and a racist.

There's something about good versus evil, something about truth. Truth crushed to earth will rise again. You can always count on that.

. . .

Oh, well, it's just terrible all these bad things that happen to you, Detective Fuhrman.

You go back and look at your notes of how the testimony was, as they tried to bring him in here and pass him off. These things were all happening. The Kathleen Bell letter was in '85, '86, the same time he went out to O.J. Simpson's house in '85, that they want to talk so much about.

What they're talking about is not even relevant. What we're talking about now is what happened in this case. And so, after having made all these denials and been adopted and accepted by the prosecution and put him on the stand and, you saw it, you saw it. It was sickening.

And then my colleague, Lee Bailey, who can't be with us today, but God bless him, wherever he is, did his cross-examination of this individual. And he asked some interesting questions.

Some of you probably wondered why is he asking that? He asked this man whether or not he'd ever met Kathleen Bell. Of course he lied about that. Never met this woman. I don't recognize her. I don't know her. Gee, I don't know anything about that.

Boy, and he sounded really convincing, didn't he? He says, quote, I do not recognize this woman as anybody I have ever met. That's what he says.

Then Bailey says, have you used that word, referring to the N-word, in the past 10 years? Not that I recall, no. You mean if you called someone a nigger, you have forgotten it? I'm not sure I can answer the question the way it's phrased, sir.

And they go on. He said Bailey then pins him down. I want you to assume that perhaps at some time since 1985 or '86 you addressed a member of the African-American race as a nigger. Is it possible that you have forgotten that act on your part?

Answer, no. It is not possible. Are you, therefore, saying that you have not used that word in the past 10 years? Detective Fuhrman, answer, yes. That is what I'm saying.

Question, and you say under oath that you have not addressed any black person as a nigger or spoken about black people as niggers in the past 10 years, Detective Fuhrman?

That's what I'm saying, sir.

So that anyone who comes to this Court and quotes you as using that word in dealing with African-Americans would be a liar, would they not, Detective Fuhrman?

Yes, they would.

All of them, correct?

All of them.

That's what he told you under oath in this case. Did he lie? Did he lie? Did he lie under oath? Did this key prosecution witness lie under oath? And I'm going to end this part and resume with him tomorrow morning.

Did he lie? And when they try to tell you he's not important, let's remember this man. This is the man who was off this case shortly after 2:00 in the morning, right after he got on it.

This is the man who didn't want to be off this case. This is the man, when they're ringing the doorbell at Ashford, who goes for a walk and he describes how he's strolling.

Let me quote him for you. Here's what he says, "I was just strolling along, looking at the house, maybe I could see some movement inside. I was just walking while the other three detectives were down there."

That's when he walks down. He's the one who says the Bronco was parked askew and he sees some spot on the door. He makes all of the discoveries. It's got a be the big man, because he's had it in for O.J. because of his views since '85.

This is the man. He's the guy who climbs over the fence. He's the guy who goes in and talks to Kato Kaelin while the other detectives are talking to the family.

He's the guy who's shining a light in Kato Kaelin's eyes. He's the guy looking at shoes, looking for suspects. He's the guy doing these things. He's the guy who says I don't tell anybody about the thumps on the wall.

He's the guy who's off this case, who is supposedly there to help this man, our client, O.J. Simpson, who then goes out all by himself, all by himself.

Now, if he's worried about bodies or suspects or whatever, doesn't even take out his gun. He goes around the side of the house and lo and behold he claims he finds this glove. And he says the glove is still moist and sticky.

Now, under their theory at 10:40, 10:45, that glove is dropped. How many hours is that? It's now after 6:00. So what is that, seven and a half hours? What's the testimony about drying time around here? There's no dew point that night.

Why would it be moist and sticky, unless he brought it over there and planted it there to try to make this case. And there is a Caucasian hair on that glove. This man cannot be trusted. He is central to the prosecution.

• • •

The Court: Thank you. All right. Ladies and gentlemen, we're going to conclude our evening session at this time. Please remember all my admonitions to you. Do not discuss the case amongst yourselves, form any opinions about the case, conduct any deliberations until the matter has been submitted to you.

Do not allow anybody to communicate with you with regard to the case. We'll stand in recess until 9:00 a.m. tomorrow morning. All right. Thank you, Counsel. We're in recess.

September 28, 1995

The Court: And let the record reflect that we have now been rejoined by all the members of our jury panel. Good morning, ladies and gentlemen.

The Jury: Good morning.

The Court: We are in the midst of the final arguments. Mr. Cochran, you may continue with your argument, sir.

Mr. Cochran: Thank you very kindly, Your Honor. Good morning, Judge Ito. Good morning again, ladies and gentlemen.

The Jury: Good morning.

Mr. Cochran: When we concluded last night, ladies and gentlemen, we had discussed a number of things, and I am sure you have them very much in mind.

To summarize some of the things that we talked about and put it in perspective, we talked about a police department who from the very beginning was more interested in themselves and their image, and that carried through.

We talked about socks that appeared all of a sudden that weren't there, socks where evidence was planted on them. We talked about police officers who lie with impunity, where the oath doesn't mean anything to them.

We talked about messengers, where you couldn't trust the message. We talked about gloves that didn't fit, a knit cap that wouldn't make any difference, a prosecution scenario that is unbelievable and unreasonable.

In short, we talked about reasonable doubt. We talked about something that's made this country great, that you can be accused in this country of a crime, but that's just an accusation, and when you enter a not guilty plea since the beginning of the time of this country, since the time of the Magna Carta, that sets the forces in motion and you have a trial.

That's what this has been about. That's why we love what we do, an opportunity to come before people from the community, the consciences of the community. You are the consciences of this community. You set the standards. You tell us what's right and wrong. You set the standards. You use your common sense to do that.

Your verdict goes far beyond these doors of this courtroom. As Mr. Darden said, the whole world is watching and waiting for your decision in this case. That's not to put any pressure on you, just tell you what's really happening out there.

So we talked about all those things, hopefully, in a logical way. Hopefully, something I said made some sense to you. Hopefully, as an advocate, you know my zeal, you know the passion I feel for this. We have all got time invested in this case.

But it's just not about winning, it's about what's right, it's about a man's life at stake here. So in *voir dire* you promised to take the time that was necessary, and you have more than done that.

Remember, I asked you, though, that when you got down to the end of the case, when you kept all your promises about coming here every day and taking these notes and paying attention and, you know, listening to us drone on and on and on, that pretty soon it would be in your hands, and then you couldn't just rush through that, could you?

Now, we have tried to make it a little more simple with regard to the issues, but you still, you are going to have 12 minds coming together, 12 open minds, 12 unbiased minds, to come together on these issues and you will give it, I am sure, the importance to which it's entitled.

Please don't compromise your principles or your consciences in rendering this decision. Don't rush to judgment. Don't compound what they have already done in this case. Don't rush to judgment.

Have a judgment that is well-thought-out, one that you can believe in the morning after this verdict. I want you to place yourself the day after you render the verdict, when you get up and you look in the mirror and you are free, you are no longer sequestered, you will probably look for each other, but you will be happy to be home again.

But what's important is look in that mirror and say have I been true to my oath? Did I do the right thing? Was is I naive? Was I timid? Or was I courageous? Did I believe in the constitution? Did I believe in justice? Did I do my part for integrity and honesty? That's the mission you are on in this journey toward justice.

• • •

And the bottom line is the positive things in this man's [Simpson's] life. The good days far outweigh the bad days. And in your life, in all of our lives, we just hope at the end when we must ultimately meet our makers that the good days have outweighed the bad days.

And in this marriage, the lasting monuments and memorials to this marriage are these two beautiful children. They had more good days than bad days by all of the evidence. These two people loved their children. They may have gone separate ways, but they loved their children. That's why he was back in town to go to that recital, that recital where there's so many people where it's in this auditorium where Nicole Brown Simpson gets these tickets. You know that's why they're talking in the afternoon to make arrangements. And she is the one who holds a seat for him. This is what happened on that day. This isn't about any argument. This is a family thing. So Mr. Darden wants to make a big thing and says, well, he had to go out to dinner with Kato. He had to catch a plane.

See the evidence for what it is. Understand these things, put them in perspective. And so you can use your common sense. There is no fuse with regard to that. It's important for you to know that. Take a look at that video when you're back there. Take a look at all of the evidence.

. . .

Now, let's go back to where we were when we broke last night. We had started talking about the messengers in this case. We talked briefly about Vannatter and about all of his big lies. His lies become very important because he's the co-lead investigator in this case. From the very beginning he was lying to you. ... And you're smart, you know when somebody's lying and not telling you the truth. I mean I don't have to go into that. You don't need the jury instruction. You've got his reaction. You've got experiences in life. And you know somebody's lying.

And he said something really interesting. It's really preposterous when you think about it. He said, "Mr. Shapiro, Mr. O.J. Simpson was no more a suspect than you were." Now, who in here believed that? Did he really think he's going to come back in here, and we're going to believe that, that O.J. Simpson was no more a suspect than Robert Shapiro? That's what he told you. Big lies. You can't trust him. You can't believe anything that he says because it goes to the core of this case. When you're lying at the beginning, you'll be lying at the end. The Book of Luke talks about that, talks about if you're untruthful in small things, you should be disbelieved in big things.

. . .

So this man with his big lies. And then we have Fuhrman coming right on the heels, and the two of them need to be paired together because they are twins of deception. Fuhrman and Vannatter, twins of deception, who bring you a message that you cannot trust, that you cannot trust.

Let's continue to where we left off then with this man Fuhrman ... You recall that he was asked, as I read to you yesterday briefly the question well-phrased by Lee Bailey, have you ever used this N-word in ten years? Went right back to '85. And he picked that '85 date. You know why? Because of the Kathleen Bell letter, just like they knew about it. He picked that date because they knew he was lying, honed in on him. You know, liars can be tricky. And so he was at that point trying to pin it down for you, ten years, '85 to '95. This is like in February of this year.

. . .

So then why then is this big liar in the crime scene with access to the glove and the hat? Why is he down there pointing at this glove where he's walking in all — in the blood and everything, when he wants you to believe it's 7:00?

• • •

Well, now, let me tell you why this is important. You recognize Fuhrman, personification of evil. When he's doing that, he's trying to tell you this is some important piece of evidence here, and I just came back from Rockingham, this matches the glove found over there. That's what he tells you. But he's lying again. He's lying that's why he's central to this case, because he hadn't even been to Rockingham at that point, and he's tracking in that blood at that point.

And that becomes very important because remember he slips up and says "in the Bronco" at some point. Did he get in a Bronco. Did he put a bloody fingerprint in that Bronco. Are his shoes size 12?

• • •

This man who in '85 in his mind started this, this man who was asked to go over and help O.J. Simpson and notify and take care of the kids, this man, this perjurer, this racist, this genocidal racist. This is the man.

• • •

One of the things that has made this country so great is people's willingness to stand up and say: That's wrong; I'm not going to be part of it. I'm not going to be part of the cover-up.

That's what I'm asking you to do: Stop this cover-up. Stop this cover-up. If you don't stop it, then who? Do you think the police department is going to stop it? Do you think the DA's office is going to stop it? Do you think we can stop it by ourselves? It has to be stopped by you.

• • •

You learn early on in your life that you are not going to be naive that you love your country, but you know it's not perfect. So you understand that it's no surprise to me. But I don't take any pride in it.

But for some of you, you are finding out the other side of life. You are finding out that's why this case is so instructive. You are finding out about the other side of life. That things aren't always as they seem. It's not just rhetoric. It's the actions of people. It's the lack of courage and lack of integrity at high places; that's what we're talking about here.

• • •

And what becomes so important when we talk about these two twin demons of evil, Vannatter and Fuhrman, is the jury instruction which you know about now, and it says, essentially, that a witness willfully false ... in one material part of his or her testimony is to be distrusted in others. You may reject the whole testimony of a witness who willfully has testified falsely to a material point unless from all the evidence you believe the probability of truth favors his or her testimony in other particulars.

• • •

A witness who walks through those doors who raises his or her hand swears to tell the truth. You have heard lie after lie after lie that's been exposed.

And when a witness lies in a material part of his testimony, you can wipe out all of his testimony as a judge of the facts. That's your decision again. Nobody can tell you about that unless you feel that the greater probability of truth lies in something else they said. Wipe it out.

This applies not only to Fuhrman, it applies to Vannatter, and then you see what trouble their case is in. Because they lied to get in there to do these things, when Vannatter carries that blood, they can't explain to you why he did that, because they were setting this man up.

And that glove, anybody among you think that glove was just sitting there, just placed there, moist and sticky after six and a half hours. The testimony is that it would be dried in three or four hours, according to MacDonell.

We are not naive. You understand. There is no blood on anything else. There is no blood trail. There is no hair and fiber. And you get the ridiculous explanation that Mr. Simpson was running into an air conditioner on his own property.

• • •

So when they take the law into their own hands, they become worse than the people who break the law because they are the protectors of the law. Who, then, polices the police? You police the police. You police them by your verdict. You are the ones who send the message.

Nobody else is going to do it in this society. They don't have the courage. Nobody has the courage. You have a bunch of people running around with no courage to do what is right except individual citizens.

You are the ones in war. You are the ones who are on the front line. These people set policies, these people talk all this stuff. You implement it. You are the people. You are what makes America so great. And don't you forget it.

And so understand how this happened. It's part of a culture of getting away with things. It's part of a culture. Looking the other way.

If we determine the rules as we go along, nobody is going to question us. We are the LAPD.

And so you take these two twins of deception, and if, as you can, under this law, wipe out their testimony, the prosecutors realize their case, then, is in serious trouble.

• • •

But there is something else about this man, Fuhrman, that I have to say before I am going to terminate this part of my opening argument and relinquish the floor to my learned colleague, Mr. Barry Scheck, it's something that Fuhrman said, and I am going to ask Mr. Douglas and Mr. Harris to put up that Kathleen Bell letter.

• • •

But I want to tell you about what is troubling, what is frightening, what is chilling about that Kathleen Bell letter. Let's see if we can see part of it, and I think you will agree. So I want to put the focus back where it belongs on this letter, and its application to this case.

You will recall that God is good and he always brings you a way to see light when there is a lot of darkness around, and just through chance this lady had tried to reach Shapiro's office, couldn't reach it, and in July of 1994 she sent this fax to my office, and my good, loyal and wonderful staff got that letter to me early on, and this is one you just couldn't pass up.

You get a lot of letters, but you couldn't pass this one up because she said some interesting things. And she wasn't a fan of O.J. Simpson. So what did she say?

"I am writing to you in regards to a story I saw on the news last night. I thought it ridiculous that the Simpson defense team would even suggest that there might be racial motivation involved in the trial against Mr. Simpson."

Yes, there are a lot of people who thought that at that time, and, you know, you can't fault people for being naive, but once they know if they continue to be naive then you can fault them. That's what it is and that's why this case is important.

Don't ever say again in this county — or in this country that you don't know things like this exist. Don't pretend to be naive anymore. Don't turn your heads. Stand up. Show some integrity.

"So I then glanced up at the television and was quite shocked to see that Officer Fuhrman was a man that I had the misfortune of meeting. You may have received a message from your answering service last night that I called to say that Mr. Fuhrman may be more of a racist than you could even imagine."

I doubt that, but at any rate, it was something that got my attention. If he [Fuhrman] sees an African-American with a white woman, he would stop them. If he didn't have a reason, he'd find one or make up one. This man will lie to set you up...

He will do anything to set you up because of the hatred he has in his heart. A racist is somebody who has power over you, who can do something to you. People can have views if they keep them to themselves. But when they have power over you, that's when racism becomes insidious. That's what we're talking about here. He has power. A police officer in the street, a patrol officer, is the single-most powerful figure in the criminal justice system. He can take your life. Unlike the Supreme Court, you don't have to go through all these Appeals. He can do it right there and justify it. And that's why, that's why this has to be rooted out in the LAPD and every place else. Make up a reason because he made a judgment, that's what happened in this case.

They made a judgment. Everything else after that was going to point toward O.J. Simpson. They didn't want to look at anybody else.

• • •

But if that wasn't enough, if that wasn't enough, the thing that really gets you is she goes on to say, "Officer Fuhrman went on to say that he would like nothing more than to see all niggers gathered together and killed. He said something about burning them or bombing them. I was too shaken to remember the exact words he used. However, I do remember that what he said was probably the most horrible thing I had ever heard someone say. What frightened me even more was that he was a police officer sworn to uphold the law."

And now we have it. There was another man not too long ago in the world who had those same views who wanted to burn people who had racist views and ultimately had power over people in his country. People didn't care. People said he's just crazy. He's just a half-baked painter. And they didn't do anything about it. This man, this scourge became one of the worst people in this world, Adolph Hitler, because people didn't care, didn't try to stop him. He had the power over his racism and his anti-religion. Nobody wanted to stop him, and it ended up in World War II. The conduct of this man.

And so Fuhrman, Fuhrman wants to take all black people now and burn them or bomb them. That's genocidal racism. Is that ethnic purity? What is that? What is that? We're paying this man's salary to espouse these views. You think he only told Kathleen Bell whom he just had met? Do you think he talked to his partners about it? Do you think his commanders knew about it? Do you think everybody knew about it and turned their heads? Nobody did anything about it.

Things happen for a reason in your life. Maybe this is one of the reasons we're all gathered together here this day one year and two days after we met. Maybe there's a reason for your purpose. Maybe this is why you were selected. There's something in your background, in your character that helps you understand this is wrong. Maybe you're the right people at the right time at the right place to say no more. We're not going to have this. This is wrong. What they've done to our client is wrong.

This man, O.J. Simpson, is entitled to an acquittal. You cannot believe these people. You can't trust the message. You can't trust the messengers.

• • •

Thank you for your attention during this first part of my argument. I hope that during this phase of it I have demonstrated to you that this really is a case about a rush to judgment, an obsession to win at all costs, a willingness to distort, twist, theorize in any fashion to try to get you to vote guilty in this case where it is not warranted, that these metaphors about an ocean of evidence or mountain of evidence is little more than a tiny, tiny stream, if at all, that points equally towards innocence. That any mountain has long ago been reduced to little more than a mole hill under an avalanche of lies and complexity and conspiracy. This is what we have shown you.

And so as great as America is, we have not yet reached the point where there is equality and rights or equality of opportunity.

I started off talking to you a little bit about Frederick Douglas and what he said more than a hundred years ago, for there are still the Mark Fuhrmans in this world and in this country who hate and are yet embraced by people in power.

But you and I, fighting for freedom and ideals and for justice for all, must continue to fight to expose hate and genocidal racism and these tendencies. We then become the guardians of the constitution.

As I told you yesterday, for if we, as the people, don't continue to hold a mirror up to the face of America and say: This is what you promised; this is what you delivered.

If you don't speak out, if you don't stand up, if you don't do what's right, this kind of conduct will continue on forever, and we'll never have an ideal society, one that lives out the true meaning of the creed of the constitution of life, liberty, and justice for all.

I'm going to take my seat, but I get one last time to address you. As I said before: This is a case about an innocent man wrongfully accused.

The Court: All right. Ladies and gentlemen, we will take a 15-minute recess at this time. Remember all my admonitions to you. We will see you back here in 15 minutes. All right. We will stand in recess.

A brief recess was taken.

The Court: Ladies and gentlemen, please be seated. Let the record reflect that we have been rejoined by all the members of our jury panel. Good morning again, ladies and gentlemen. And Mr. Scheck, I understand that you are going to address the DNA issues, or physical evidence issues.

Mr. Scheck: I would say. Right, yes.

The Court: You may proceed.

Mr. Scheck: Ladies and gentlemen of the jury, good morning.

The Jury: Good morning.

Mr. Scheck: Let me join with everybody in thanking you for your service. I can — the frustration, the loneliness, the sacrifice you have made in this sequestration is something that we understand, or we are trying to understand.

As the judge has pointed out a number of times, my colleague, Mr. Neufeld and I, we are from New York City, more specifically, we are from Brooklyn, and we have been out here quite unexpectedly for a lot of months.

• • •

Now, you know, it's our job to make it simple, to make it cogent without sacrificing detail that was important, and sometimes we let you down. I know that. Some days when we were talking about some of this, it was hard and we came back to it again. And I think both sides tried to clarify the issues as much as we could.

But you never let us down because those were long days but you were more than fair with us. I know you followed and paid attention to this evidence.

So it is a privilege and honor to have presented that evidence to you, and I must also say that standing before you right now is a terrifying responsibility. It's a terrifying responsibility because we think the evidence shows that we represent an innocent man wrongly accused.

We represent — we think the prosecution hasn't come close to meeting its burden of proof in this case beyond a reasonable doubt, and we think that the integrity of this system ... is at stake. You cannot convict when the core of the prosecution's case is built on perjurious testimony of police officers, unreliable forensic evidence, and manufactured evidence.

It is a cancer at the heart of this case, and that's what this evidence shows when you go through it patiently, when you go through it carefully, when you go through it scientifically, logically, that's what the evidence shows.

And you cannot convict on that evidence. There are many, many reasonable doubts buried right in the heart of the scientific evidence in this case, and we have demonstrated them. And we don't have to prove them, but the evidence shows it.

So, in the words of Dr. Lee, something is wrong. Something is terribly wrong with the evidence in this case. You cannot trust it, it lacks integrity. It cannot be a basis for a verdict of beyond a reasonable doubt.

● ● ●

The testimony is clear in this case, they did not give their criminalists training in state-of-the-art techniques, in particular, of great relevance here, there was no DNA training for the evidence collectors. Now, that's got to be a significant point.

Ms. Clark told you in the opening statement that collecting, preserving blood stain evidence for purposes of DNA testing was as simple as going into your kitchen and cleaning up spillage. Now, we all know, we all know, that's not true, based on what we have heard in this case.

Can we have the next slide, please? Quality assurance. That's a term that's used in bureaucracies and hospitals and laboratories, anyplace where you are trying to deliver service with integrity.

What is going on here? There is a failure to document how you collect the evidence. A fundamental duty, as Dr. Lee showed you, remember with that chart, fundamental duty of a criminalist to document the evidence.

In other words, where it was picked up, how it was picked up, when it was picked up. And we have seen the problems in this case when you can't do that and you try to reconstruct it later when you memories are gone, and you can't do it. Well, that's not done. And failure to document testing is tolerated.

● ● ●

There was no serious supervision of these people. That's just clear, you saw it, this lab was not inspected. This lab is not accredited. This lab does not subject its — certainly the DNA to external/blind proficiency testing, which you know, which you know is what you need. Dr. Gerdes told you about that. Everyone talked about that.

This National Research Council report, DNA Technology in Forensic Science — Can we have the next slide? Now, this is critical. Chain of custody and security. There is absolutely nothing more fundamental to preserving integrity of forensic evidence in a chain of custody than having security. You have to know what you're picking up. You have to be able to document it, otherwise bad things can happen, and nobody can trace it.

In this case they did not count the swatches when they collected them. They did not count the swatches when they got back to the laboratory and put them in the tubes for drying. They did not count the swatches when they took them out of the tubes and put them in the bindles. We don't know how many swatches they started with. They didn't book the evidence in this case for three days. They kept it in the least secure facility, the evidence processing room, for three days, without being able to track the items.

The lead homicide detective in this case — and we've talked about it a little, and we'll talk about it some more — is walking around with an unsealed blood vial for three hours. It's unheard of.

The other lead detective in this case is taking shoes home right out of that — this could be critical evidence, the shoes that their suspect was wearing that night, taking it home.

Now, you know, it was amazing when Mr. Fung testified the extent to which, you know, they've lost all track of the rules. At one point I asked him, "Well, would it have been all right if they took the blood home?" And he said, "Sure, as long as you put it in the refrigerator overnight." Do you remember that answer? I mean there's — there's no sense of what has to be done in order to give you reliable evidence, none.

Think about the Bronco. They finished doing the collection in the Bronco, and then it's abandoned literally for two months. There's a box you're supposed to check off, give special care if you're going to collect for biological evidence, not checked off. It is sent to Viertel's. It is abandoned for two months. There are no records of who went in and out of that car. There was a theft. Anybody was allowed in there. And then on August 26th they're collecting evidence from it.

And then finally — and this is — could we have the next board? This is a critical point that I think demonstrates all you need to know about security and chain of custody in this laboratory, the missing lens, the missing lens. Now, this is very important evidence. This is the envelope that's found at the crime scene with the prescription glasses. If you were investigating a case, you're very concerned about this.

• • •

Now, we can tell, as Dr. Lee pointed out on this lens, there are smears of blood, trace evidence. There could have been fingerprints from the perpetrator who was going into that envelope.

On June 22nd Dr. Baden and Dr. Wolf got an opportunity just to look, just to look at the evidence, not touch or examine or test, just to look, and they saw two lenses there, made a note of it. February 16th, think about it, that's the first time we got a chance to inspect and just even handle the evidence. You were already sitting here, February 16th. There's something wrong. When we look at it, that lens is gone. There is no report, no record, no investigation of its disappearance. Nobody comes in and tells you what happened.

Now, that tells you a lot. Did somebody take this from the laboratory as a souvenir? Did somebody walk off with this? How can that be? This is critical evidence in a case. How can that be? It just vanished down this black hole?

Now, they're going to say we're Fort Knox, nobody could get to the evidence in this case with our evidence tracking system.

Now, I should just tell you in passing, I'm sure you caught it, that even when it's booked into the evidence control unit and it's supposedly being tracked, they didn't say their computer tracking system was a chain of custody system. It isn't. They have all the evidence items in boxes like the sock and the blood drops, and they will put them in the serology freezer, and they're in a box there. Then somebody will hit the computer, and they can go in, and then they can take any item they want out of that box. It's not tracked by specific items. There is no good security in this system. There's plenty of access if you want to tamper with evidence, if you're authorized personnel, if you are a lead detective, if you are somebody there. It can happen.

And the missing lens tells you all you need to know. What is going on here? And if they come back and say, well, maybe there is — maybe Dr. Baden and Wolf are wrong, there was no lens to begin with. Well, that's even weirder, isn't it? What kind of killer takes a souvenir like this? How does that fit in with their theory? The missing lens is a serious problem in this case.

Now, the black hole symbolizes something else. You know, science is no better than the methods employed and the people who employ them. DNA is a sophisticated technology. It is a wonderful technology. But there's a right way to do it and a wrong way to do it.

• • •

And you can have the most sophisticated technology in the world, and if you don't apply it correctly, you can't trust the results. There's no compliance with the NRC report. There's no compliance with the kind of standards that you would require in a life-and-death situation.

And this is a life-and-death situation. And that's what you have to demand of a laboratory.

You can't just say sloppy criminalists, sloppy coroner, big deal. She said, big deal. It insults your intelligence. DNA is used to identify the war dead; therefore, accept all the evidence in this case. That doesn't answer the question, does it?

As a matter of fact, the DNA test she is talking about is something they call mitochondrial DNA test that has nothing to do with the tests in thi, case. And the war-dead has nothing to do with what was going on in this case. Zero. It's not an answer. It's not this case. It's not the techniques.

They argue the defense has to prove exactly how, exactly where, exactly when tampering occurred with any of this evidence. That's not our burden.

They have to prove to you that this evidence has integrity beyond a reasonable doubt. And you know when people tamper with evidence, they don't do it on videotape. They try to do it with some stealth. They try to cover their tracks. And as Mr. Cochran has pointed out, and if you think about this evidence, it wouldn't take more than two bad police officers to do this and a lot of people to look the other way.

• • •

Now, we don't have to prove anything. And we don't have the burden of proof here. And I'm going to confront each and every one of these essential pieces of evidence in this case and raise a reasonable doubt about it — more than a reasonable doubt, many reasonable doubts. But if they fail in one of their essential facts, you have to acquit.

• • •

Ladies and gentlemen of the jury, I thank you very much for your patience. I have tried to reason through this evidence drawing the fair inferences as best we could, looking at the integrity of the evidence, and I just think there is very little question here, isn't there?

So much of the essential facts in this case are just shot through with reasonable doubt. There is something wrong. There is something terribly wrong about this evidence. Somebody manufactured evidence in this case.

• • •

There is missing blood, there is EDTA, there is questions, serious, deeply troubling questions. You must distrust it. You have to distrust it. You cannot render a verdict in this case of beyond a reasonable doubt on this kind of evidence because if you do, no one is safe, no one. The constitution means nothing. This cannot, will not, shall not happen in this country with you good people. It just won't. Thank you very much.

After Scheck concludes his comments on the DNA evidence, Johnnie Cochran concludes the closing arguments for the defense.

The Court: Please be seated ... Mr. Cochran, you may make your concluding remarks.

Mr. Cochran: Thank you, Your Honor, Judge Ito, again, to my colleagues. Good afternoon, again, ladies and gentlemen.

The Jury: Good afternoon.

Mr. Cochran: Seems like we did this yesterday, but I won't be nearly as long this time. I am back, as I promised you I would come back, to try and wrap up the defense discussion of the evidence with you.

You have heard what I believe was a remarkable discussion by Mr. Barry Scheck, an excellent lawyer. He may be from Brooklyn, but he has become a Californian, as far as we are concerned. He is a very valued member of our team of defense lawyers for Mr. O.J. Simpson, and you see why. He is, indeed, a very talented lawyer.

And so he shared with you a number of things which I will not be redundant about and you have them clear in mind, and if I were to go over anything else, there are many reasonable doubts in this case and O.J. Simpson is entitled to an acquittal based upon what we have told you.

This is my last chance, of course, to speak to you, and I want to take this time to tell you again that the prosecution, because they bare the burden of proving this case beyond a reasonable doubt, will have the opportunity to speak to you last.

We may not be here too late tonight because I am not going to be much longer, and I think that — more than likely, I think we can probably guarantee this case is going to get to you sometime tomorrow afternoon, so you can kind of sit back and relax.

It's been a long, long, long road to get to this point. It's been kind of like a relay race, hasn't it been, in many respects in this journey toward justice. The prosecution was first running with it, we then took the baton and we started running with it. We have run almost up to the jury box.

And soon we are going to pass the baton to you. This is how our system works, this is what makes it so great. We will pass the baton to you, and we will be glad. We can then sit back and watch you at work.

You have watched us for a year, two or three days. Now we get to watch you. It will be symbolically watching you because we won't see you back in that room, but you know we are going to be counting on you giving both sides the benefit of your individual opinion. Now it's your time to perform.

You know how you can think about us and those days when you want to criticize us. We are not going to criticize you, though, we are going to just watch you work, and watching you work is what makes this country so great, because it's 12 citizens good and true coming together from this community from disparate backgrounds, experience not required, citizenship, the only requirement, to do justice, to do right, to right some wrongs, to straighten this out.

That's what we are asking you to do, to follow the law, determine the facts and come to a well-reasoned decision. That's what's going to happen tomorrow afternoon for you.

Now, it may take one day or 100 days, but you have been committed. I know that you will stay the course, keep your eye on the prize and do the right thing.

Now, when I sit down this time, I won't get another chance to argue to you or discuss the inferences because it has to stop sometime, but Ms. Clark gets to talk to you later tonight or tomorrow, and I want you again to use your common sense.

And remember, if she raises some point, I may not be able to get up and respond, Mr. Scheck or I. If it's something that's not purely rebuttal, you may see more objections this time, because we got to keep it in line, but if it's a point that we can't respond to, you substitute your wisdom and common sense as to any point. I think you know, by this time we can answer anything that they would say.

So I am sure you will give her the same attention you have given us today, and I wish them good luck. In fact, let me say this. In this case, we have been advocates. We have fought hard, I hope, but it's not personal. What is personal in this case, what is personal, is our zeal and our desire that our client be acquitted. It's not personal against these prosecutors.

• • •

Mr. Darden asked the question, "Who did this? Who committed this crime?" Why would he ask you that when the judge just said the defendant doesn't have to show anything.

And we know in this case they rushed to judgment. They didn't look at anybody else. That's a question he should be asking these detectives, not us. We're the ones who wanted to bring on the experts who wanted to help out. They wouldn't accept them. How could he ask us that question? How could he ask us that question in good faith? So what the answer is, "You go ask your detectives," that's the answer.

Now, he asked another question. He said, "Well, where was O.J. Simpson?" And he says, "Well, you know, how does he account for his whereabouts after 10:00?" Let me just take a minute about this. He asked that question, so let me — let me answer it for you and for him. Some of you in your former life probably lived alone. If you lived alone, if something happened between 10:00 and 6:00 in the morning, it's real difficult if you live alone to prove where you were if nobody lives there with you; isn't that true? Is that common sense? Mr. Simpson lived alone.

And we've done more than that. We can, I think, establish where he was. He was at home. That Bronco was outside. He was packing and getting ready and rushing around at the last minute and coming outside to that Bronco, getting his phone, getting the paraphernalia for that phone; that's what he was doing. He was packing. He was getting the golf balls — golf bag out of his car that was seated out there. He was getting golf shoes and whatever goes with golf, if you're a golfer. That's what he was doing. He's getting his little knapsack out that has balls in it, and he was bringing another bag down, all of which were ready when Park and Kato were out there. And he comes down with the other bag carrying it. That's what he was doing, Mr. Darden, that's where he was. It's your speculation he's on the side of his house running into an air conditioner. That didn't happen, that's unreasonable. Nobody here believes it. It's not going to help save their case. They're speculating again, speculating, cynically speculating. And it's not going to work.

And so that brings me to this other instruction. It's called alibi. You remember during *voir dire* I asked you about this. I said that you won't place a bad connotation on the term alibi, if that's what the — the law calls it, alibi.

And it says as follows: That evidence has been received for the purpose of showing that the defendant was not present at the time and place of the commission of the alleged crime for which he is here on trial. If after a consideration of all the evidence, you have a reasonable doubt that the defendant was present at the time the crime was committed, you must find him not guilty. Can I repeat that last part for you? If after a consideration of all the evidence, you have a reasonable doubt that the defendant was present at the time the crime was committed, doesn't say you might find him not guilty, you might think about it, it says you must find him not guilty.

And so, you know, when you talk about this whole concept of reasonable doubt, and we'll talk a little bit more about that, it's how you feel inside about this evidence. It's how you feel inside about these messengers and their message. It's when you have that queasy feeling, you can't trust this evidence. Barry Scheck described it well as cancer. He talked about one cockroach. You don't need to see anymore because you know if you see one, there's a lot of them around. All you need is one, and that's going to make you go the other way. In this case, you get past the — You don't have to get past the socks, but then you get to the glove and the Bronco, and you get to all of it, none of which you can trust, and then how do you do it?

Do you get back there and say, well, I don't trust them on this, I think I can trust them on that? When this essential link in the chain is broken, you got reasonable doubt.

And so your job won't be quite as tough as you may have thought. Reasonable doubt in this case? The prosecution has not offered one coherent theory to explain how these deaths occurred.

• • •

So forgive me if I speak out for O.J. Simpson. If I'm so presumptuous as to believe that the Constitution means that you are presumed to be innocent until you make the decision. Nobody outside here has a vote. You have a vote. Thank heaven. These narrow-minded people. Thank heaven they don't have a vote. You will have the final say.

And so this concept then of reasonable doubt, what then does it mean? We have heard about it. We have talked about it. We have a chart now I'm going to ask Mr. Douglas to put over there.

Let's talk about this whole idea of burden of proof and reasonable doubt and what is reasonable doubt. Do you remember during *voir dire* I talked to you about this concept of reasonable doubt.

And before we go to that chart I mean: "That state of the case after the entire comparison and consideration of the evidence leaves the minds of the jury in that condition where they cannot say they feel an abiding conviction of the truth of the charge." That's what reasonable doubt is.   And let's go over it one more time because this is the cornerstone of every criminal case.

What it really is is a doubt based upon a reason. In this case, we have given you myriad reasons. There are many, many, many, many reasonable doubts — it's not just one — all of which lead you to one verdict in this case, and one verdict only, of not guilty. But let's go over it one last time together.

A defendant in the criminal case is presumed to be innocent until the contrary is proved, and in case of a reasonable doubt whether his guilt is satisfactorily shown you, he is entitled to a verdict of not guilty. This presumption places upon the People the burden of proving guilty beyond a reasonable doubt. You have heard a lot about that. That's what people need to learn and be reminded of in this country.

Reasonable doubt is defined as follows: "It is not a mere possible doubt" — we know that — "because everything relating to human affairs is open to some possible or imaginary doubt. It is that state of the case where after the entire comparison and consideration of all of the evidence, leaves the minds of the jurors in that condition that they cannot say they feel an abiding conviction of the truth of the charge."

That's reasonable doubt. It's not written just for O.J. Simpson. It's for (indicating) you. It's for (indicating) you. It's for (indicating) you. It's for all of us who are citizens. It is given in every criminal case. You have to give it. That's the burden.

You don't change it once the trial starts. That's the burden. Let's see how it works. In this whole idea of the burden of proof, we'll start down at the bottom and look at the burden that is placed upon the State and they should have a burden like this, when you are talking about taking somebody's freedom for the rest of their life or whatever.

There are a number of things that you might want to think, but in the case sometimes — sometimes in cases, you actually can prove the person charged not guilty. And in this case, at my 32 and-a-half years, this may be as close as any case where somebody has been proven not guilty.

Because if you look at these facts, you look at what we have shared with you over the course of the last two days, this man has been proven not guilty. But that's at the very bottom of the rung.

• • •

I don't trust the police. Fuhrman was central. I don't trust Vannatter; it's the messenger, it's their message. It just doesn't fit. Something is wrong. There is a cancer here. Possibly not? Guilty? Maybe not.

As Mr. Scheck said to you, "maybe not" is not good enough. If you are talking about somebody's freedom for the rest of their life, if you will, well, somebody may say perhaps — gee, I don't know; I suspect; I suspect that he might be. Maybe he's possibly guilty of something. Maybe he's probably guilty. Maybe guilt is likely. Maybe guilt may be highly likely. I don't think anybody is going to find in this case because I think we have shown, we have proven, he's not guilty.

But all of those levels from "proven not guilty" to the "guilt highly likely" is our interpretation of what you have to do before you get all the way up to "guilt beyond a reasonable doubt" so that you won't have that queasy feeling about this case, where you can believe to an abiding conviction of the truth of these charges.

Can you have that? I think not on this evidence. Not on this evidence. Not on this case. They have failed. You know, we asked you a question. Did you have the courage? Did you have the intestinal fortitude to walk back into this courtroom — if they failed to prove Mr.

Simpson guilty, did you have the courage to walk back in and say, "We find him not guilty?" And you said you could do that. That was part of your job. You said you could do that. I'm going to hold you to that, because that's what makes the system great. Your courage, your willingness to stand up for what is right.

And so, in this scenario, thinking about reasonable doubt even more, the prosecution had a puzzle. And it was interesting how they did this puzzle. Technology is wonderful. And you saw they kept under this puzzle putting on pieces and that sort of thing, and so we thought about that. I thought about this puzzle. Thought about what it meant in this particular case.

Then I got a call from a very, very wise, wise, wise lady who reminded me that if you have ever gone to the store and bought a puzzle, when you buy a puzzle, on the outside of the box of the puzzle there is a picture so you know what the puzzle looks like when it's finished.

Well, in this case, the prosecution took a photograph or picture of O.J. Simpson first. Then they took the pieces apart. If they really wanted to talk about reasonable doubt, you don't jump to conclusions at the beginning. You don't rush to judgment and then be concerned about an obsession to win. What you do is you take the pieces and put them together and then you come to conclusion. They got it all backwards.

It's like what they did with the Fourth Amendment. It's like asking us: Where is this witness? What did you prove? Solve this crime for us. They got it all backwards. Don't you see? And so that little example, a jigsaw puzzle, was clever. But really it trivializes a man's fight for his freedom who has always said that he was innocent from day one.

• • •

If you believe what the prosecutors want you to believe, you have to believe that O.J. Simpson who has a limo driver coming I guess around 10:30, 10:40, after he goes and gets a hamburger at McDonald's, after having been worried about change because he had hundred dollar bills, that he has already been packing because clothes are being brought down, and he's taking his golf clubs because he's going to be playing golf — because it's a pre-planned trip; he's off the road and then back on the road . That he is perhaps the most recognizable person present in Brentwood in that area where he lives for, we know, for 17 years, and he drives a white Bronco, that he decides to put on a knit cap — and you saw that exhibition yesterday of him or you or I in a knit cap — he decides he will put that on.

He changes out of his tennis shoes, his Reebok tennis shoes, and his sweat socks and put on some dress socks. And puts on some

Bruno-Magli shoes. And let me just stop right there and put a pin in that. The Bruno-Magli shoes, you heard all about Bruno-Magli shoes, and we searched all around the world and went to Bloomingdale's. And what did we find?

There is nobody who ever sold O.J. Simpson any Bruno Magli shoes. They searched, they tried, they never sold him any shoes. So they are talking about Bruno Magli shoes. There may be every other house in Brentwood, if somebody wanted to afford some Bruno Magli shoes, I guess they could.

Now, that's their case. There is no evidence that O.J. Simpson had any Bruno Magli shoes, ever. In fact, when Lange is looking for the clothes and O.J. Simpson says this is what I wore, here are the tennis shoes, he took only tennis shoes that night. There is no evidence that O.J. Simpson ever owned any Bruno Magli shoes, and please remember that.

So he gets — puts these Bruno Magli shoes on. He is trying to disguise himself, of course, he puts on a pair of gloves that don't fit and he gets in his car and he decides that what he will do is he will drive over to the alleyway behind Bundy where his wife lives in this big Bronco.

Now, while he is going to do that, he has been over there a number of times and you know they have already told you about Pablo Fenjves and these people who live over there. Remember when you were on that jury view that there are homes and windows and things that face down on that alley, and both sides, from I guess Gretna Green side and from the Bundy side. People are looking down in that alley. It's well-lit.

You saw the photograph yesterday of what Mark Storfer would have seen. He pulls into this alleyway in this Bronco, in this disguise, dressed the way they want to have him dressed, to come and kill his wife.

Now, somehow they are trying to say he killed his wife, or whatever, he doesn't kill her in the back, back there, where the car is, he goes and lures her to the front. Doesn't make any sense to lure her to the front gate.

And then he gets into a fight with somebody he doesn't even know. This fight goes on for 5 to 15 minutes. The fight is so fierce that a hat and a glove are torn off. That's how fierce this fight had to be.

The keys, the beeper, you saw how tough it is in any kind of an altercation for gloves to come off, for a hat to come off. There is kicking. There is all kind of fighting in this small, small area.

But that's what they want you to believe, and so we find the keys and the beeper and the gloves all — of course, we find, specifically, the cap and the gloves neatly packaged under the item there. Then he leaves this one glove behind and then just walks slowly out to the alleyway.

Now, the dog we heard so much about who he bought, who was his dog, doesn't go with him, he goes the other way, out the front to go down the other way. Kato, the dog. Under what they would have you believe.

And he has got these bloody clothes on and everything. Now he goes back out there where his car has been sitting 10, 15, 20 minutes right out there in the alleyway. Anybody could look, anybody coming home. People are driving up and down the street.

Gets back in his car, then, presumably, he races back home where the limousine driver who was there doesn't hear him come up, doesn't see him, doesn't do any of those things.

And we know from the time they see O.J. Simpson, within 5 minutes he is coming downstairs, packed, luggage is already down there, looking neat as a pin heading for the airport. Now, he was expecting this man, after he came back from the hamburger. This is what their case is. This is what they want you to believe. And just for good measure, it's not enough. That's not enough.

Under their scenario once he gets home after he is rushing, he has got enough time and he has got all these bloody clothes on, he runs down the side of his house where he has lived for 17 years and runs into the air conditioning and says, oops — no marks, of course, on his body, but while he is back there he drops a bloody glove to match the other glove found over at Bundy.

And just for good measure, so he will be sure they find it, he knocks on the wall, he doesn't run into the wall, he knocks on the wall. He says (indicating). Then he gives a signal. Then he comes in the house.

But nobody has him doing any of that. That's what they have you believe. That is the prosecution's case. We have been here one year, ladies and gentlemen, and two days to hear this is what they have told you. It just doesn't fit. If it doesn't fit, you must acquit.

Something is wrong with the prosecution's case and your common sense is never going to let you fall for it. So the other side, of course, we submit, in answering the questions, that O.J. Simpson is at home getting ready for his trip.

He had no problem with his ex-wife. He had gone to this concert. She had gotten the tickets for him. There is no argument. Nobody has come in here and said they had any argument that day. There is no fight.

They talked earlier, made arrangements for the tickets. He went to the concert. You saw him at the concert. You traced his steps that day and what he did. And then he went on to Chicago and came back immediately and everything he did was consistent with innocence.

This case is a tragedy for everybody. For certainly the victims and their families, for the Simpsons' family, they are victims, too, because they lost an ex-daughter-in-law, for the defendant, who has been in custody since June of 1994 for a crime that he didn't commit.

Someone has taken these children's mother. I certainly hope that your decision doesn't take their father and that justice is finally achieved in this case.

• • •

If, after hearing all of this evidence, you have a reasonable doubt, it is clear that O.J. Simpson is entitled to an acquittal, and whether it is O.J. or "no J.," the result would have to be the same. His status doesn't count. It's the evidence that counts. And what's been proven to you under these circumstances.

But he is a good and decent man who you have seen and observed every day we are in session since September 26th, 1994.

Now, as it comes time for me to conclude my remarks, I may never have an opportunity again to speak to you, certainly not in this setting, maybe when the case is over.

As you have been told many, many times, this is a very heavy burden placed upon the People, and for good reason, prove this case beyond a reasonable doubt.

As such, it is Ms. Clark's duty to answer for you, as best she can, any legitimate questions arising from the evidence which we believe casts doubt upon Mr. Simpson's guilt.

There may be 1,000 such questions in a case like this we'd put to her, but we intend no such exercise. I do intend, after careful deliberation, that it might be fair to suggest 15 questions, just 15 questions, which literally hang in the air in this courtroom at this moment, and as the time approaches for you to decide this case, for us to hand the baton to you.

I offer these questions now as a most important challenge to the prosecution. The prosecution, which claims that it's met its burden in this case, if that burden has, in fact, been met, you will be given logical, sensible, credible satisfying answers to each of these 15 questions.

If the questions are overwhelming and unanswerable, they will be ignored or you will be told that the prosecution has no obligation to answer the questions.

If you are given anything less than a complete, sensible and satisfactory response satisfying you beyond a reasonable doubt to these 15 questions, you will quickly realize that their case really is transparent and you will think about the scenario that I just went through for you. And that the term smoke and mirrors that you heard about doesn't apply to the defense. We proved real hard things for you, things that you can see, things you can take back in that jury room. And accordingly, you'd have to find Mr. Simpson not guilty.

When I'm concluded, for Ms. Clark's convenience, should you decide to deal with these very troublesome questions, I'm going to leave a written list of these questions here when I conclude.

Let me go over these 15 questions with you just briefly.

Why — and they're on the monitor — did the blood show up on the sock almost two months after a careful search for evidence? And why, as demonstrated by Dr. Lee and Professor MacDonell, was the blood applied when there was no foot in it? Think that's a fair question in this case? Let's see if she can answer that question.

Question number 2, why was Mark Fuhrman, a detective who had been pushed off the case, the person who went by himself to the Bronco, over the fence to interrogate Kato, to discover the glove in the thump, thump, thump area?

Number 3, why was the glove still moist when Fuhrman found it if Mr. Simpson had dropped it seven hours earlier? As Agent Bodziak told you, Professor MacDonell has told you, blood dries very rapidly.

Four, if Mark Fuhrman would speak to — openly about his intense, genocidal racism to a relative stranger such as Kathleen Bell, how many of his coworkers, the other detectives in this case, were also aware that he lied when he denied using the N-word, yet failed to come forward? Part of Barry Scheck's (inaudible) of continuing coverup.

Five, why did the prosecution not call a single police officer to rebut police photographer Rokahr's testimony that Detective Fuhrman was pointing at the glove before — before Fuhrman went to Rockingham; that is, around 4:30 in the morning.

Six, if the glove had been dropped on the walkway at Rockingham ten minutes after the murder, why is there no blood or fiber on that south walkway or on the leaves the glove was resting on? Why is there no blood in the 150 feet of narrow walkway on the stucco wall abutting it? And you've been back there.

Number 7, for what purpose was Vannatter carrying Mr. Simpson's blood in his pocket for three hours and a distance of 25 miles instead of booking it down the hall at Parker's Center?

Number 8, why did Deputy District Attorney Hank Goldberg in a desperate effort to coverup for the missing 1.5 milliliters of Mr. Simpson's blood secretly go out to the home of Police Nurse Thano Peratis without notice to the defense and get him to contradict his previous sworn testimony at both the grand jury and the preliminary hearing? Peratis was never sworn. We were never given notice.

Nine, why if, according to Ms. Clark, he walked into his own house wearing the murder clothes and shoes is there not any soil or so much as a smear or drop of blood associated with the victims on the floor, the white carpeting, the doorknobs, the light switches, and his bedding?

Ten, if Mr. Simpson had just killed Mr. Goldman in a bloody battle involving more than two dozen knife wounds where Mr. Goldman remained standing and struggling for several minutes, how come there is less than seven-tenths of one drop of blood consistent with Mr. Goldman found in the Bronco?

Number 11, why following a bitter struggle alleged with Mr. Goldman were there no bruises or marks on O.J. Simpson's body? And you'll have those photographs back in the jury room.

Number 12, why do bloodstains with the most DNA not show up until weeks after the murders? Those on the socks, those on the back gate, those on — those are the two major areas.

Number 13, why did Mark Fuhrman lie to us? Why did Phil Vannatter lie to us?

And, finally, 15, given Professor MacDonell's testimony that the gloves would not have shrunk no matter how much blood was smeared on them and given that they never shrank June 21, 1994, until now despite having been repeatedly frozen and thawed? How come the gloves just don't fit?

I'm going to leave those questions for Ms. Clark, and we'll see what she chooses to do with and about them. That will be her choice. But I think you have a right to demand answers. If you're going to do your job in this case, it seems to me you will need to have answers to those questions.

Now, there are many, many, many more. But as with everything in this case, there comes a time when you can only do so much. We took 15 as representatives, but I can tell you we had more than 50 questions, but 15 will be enough, don't you think? I think so.

In this case when we started out a long time ago, we talked a lot about truth. And I always think in a circular fashion that you kind of end up where you started out. The truth is a wonderful commodity in this society. Some people can't stand the truth. But you know what? That, notwithstanding, we still have to deal with truth in this society.

Carlyle said that "no lie can live forever." We've seen a number of big lies in this case in their so-called rush to judgment. We've seen lie after lie, so much so that at least two of the major witness, Vannatter and Lange — Vannatter and — strike that, and Fuhrman, their testimony by you may be totally disregarded, further dismantling the People's case. You have that right, you know, in this search for truth.

In times like these, we often turn to the Bible for some answer to try to figure out when you've got situations like this and you want to get an answer and you want to try to understand, I happen to really like the Book of Proverbs. And in Proverbs, it talks a lot about false witnesses. It says that, "A false witness shall not be unpunished. And he that speaketh lies shall not escape." That meant a lot to me in this case because there was Mark Fuhrman, acting like a choir boy, making you believe he was the best witness that walked in here, gently applauded for his wonderful performance. Turns out he was the biggest liar in this courtroom during this process. But the Bible had already told us the answer, that "a false witness shall not be unpunished. And he that speaketh lies shall not escape."

In that same book it tells us that "a faithful witness will not lie, but a false witness will utter lies."

And finally, in Proverbs, it says that, "He that speaketh truth showeth the forthrightfulness, but a false witness shows deceit." So when we're talking about truth, we're talking about truth and lies and conspiracies and coverups. I always think about one of my favorite poems which I think is so very appropriate in this case, you know, "When things are at the darkest, there is always light the next day." In your life, in all of our lives, you have the capacity to transform all Mr. Simpson's dark yesterdays into brighter tomorrows. You have that capacity. You have that power in your hands. And James Russell Lowell said it best about wrong and evil. He said that "Truth forever on the scaffold. Wrong forever on the throne. Yet that scaffold sways the future. And beyond the dimmer known standeth God within the shadows keeping watch above his own." You walk with that every day. You carry that with you. And things will come to you. And you'll be able to reveal people who come to you in uniforms in high positions who lie and are corrupt. That's what happened in this case.

And so the truth is now out. It's now up to you. We're going to pass this baton to you soon. You will do the right thing. You've made a commitment for justice. You'll do the right thing. I will some day go on to other cases no doubt, as will Ms. Clark and Mr. Darden. Judge Ito will try another case some day, I hope, but this is Mr. O.J. Simpson's one day in court.

By your decision, you control his very life in your hands. Treat it carefully. Treat it fairly. Be fair. Don't be part of this continuing coverup. Do the right thing, remembering that if it doesn't fit, you must acquit; that if these messengers have lied to you, you can't trust their message.

That this has been a search for truth that no matter how bad it looks, if truth is out there on a scaffold and wrong is in here on the throne, remember that the scaffold always sways the future. And beyond the dimmer knowns standeth the same God for all people keeping watch above his own. He watches all of us, and he'll watch you in your decision and thank you for your attention. God bless you.

The Court: Thank you very much, Mr. Cochran. All right. Let me see counsel over at the sidebar without the court reporter, please.

The Court: All right. Ladies and gentlemen, contrary to our previous schedule, I'm going to recess for the evening at this time. We will resume tomorrow morning at 9:00. And the lawyers have promised me that we will finish this case — One of the conditions that we go over until tomorrow morning is that we will finish tomorrow afternoon with the rebuttal arguments by the prosecution. I will instruct you. And the case will be yours tomorrow afternoon. And I hope — Hopefully we'll at least get it far enough to have you go in, select a foreperson to preside over your deliberations, and then Mrs. — Mrs. Robertson has a list of the exhibits and everything that will be presented to you, so you can get organized for the coming days.

All right. Having said that, please remember all my admonitions to you, don't discuss the case amongst yourselves, don't form any opinions about the case, don't discuss any deliberations until this matter has been submitted to you, don't allow anybody to communicate with you with regard to the case.

We'll see you tomorrow morning, 9:00 sharp.

All right. We'll be in recess.

REBUTTAL OF THE DEFENSE SUMMATION

September 29, 1995

Judge Ito: Good morning, ladies and gentlemen.

Jury: Good morning.

Judge Ito: All right, at this time the defense has concluded their summation and the prosecution now has the opportunity to offer their rebuttal to the defense summation, and Ms. Clark, the prosecution may proceed.

Marcia Clark: Thank you very much, Your Honor, Mr. Darden will begin our closing arguments.

Judge Ito: All right, thank you very much. Mr. Darden?

● ● ●

Christopher Darden: Well, we've come full circle, again, it seems. Here you are and here I am, and as Judge Ito just indicated, this is my last opportunity to speak with you, that is, until after you've rendered your verdict, if, at that time, you're kind enough to spare a few moments and allow me to thank you personally at that time, not only for your verdict, but for your service, as well.

You've got a tough job, very tough job. I don't envy you in that regard. But, let me tell you something, I've had a tough job, too. The law is a tough thing to enforce in this town. Not everybody, not everybody wants to live up to the law, to follow the law. Not everybody thinks that the law applies to them. I have been a prosecutor for almost 15 years, and if there is one rule that I have lived by, if there is one rule that means a lot to me, it's this one: no one's above the law. Not the police, not the rich, no one. And I hope you agree with that. I hope you agree with that rule. I hope you consider that model. O.J. Simpson isn't above the law.

You've heard a lot of argument over the past couple of days, and I know you listened to all of the attorneys in this case, intently, and I did, when I could. And I listened yesterday, and I had been anticipating yesterday's arguments from the defense. I knew that those arguments would be passionate. I knew they'd be loud, and I knew they'd be forceful, and I knew that they'd be provocative. And I wasn't disappointed. But, I also knew that they wouldn't talk much about the evidence. Well, Mr. Scheck did. But, that's OK. And I knew they'd want to deliver a message to you, and that's why, when I spoke to you the other day, I said to you, "Hey, you can't send a message to Fuhrman, you can't send a message to the LAPD, you can't eradicate racism within the LAPD or within the L.A. community, or within the nation as a whole, by delivering a verdict of not guilty in a case like this where it is clear and you know it's clear, you feel it." You know it, you know it in your heart, you know it. As you have sat here day after day listening to this testimony, you know it. Everybody knows it. Everybody knows he killed...

Johnnie Cochran: I object to the form of that argument, Your Honor.

Judge Ito: Overruled. Proceed.

Christopher Darden: Everybody knows.

Johnnie Cochran: Objection to that, Your Honor.

Judge Ito: Overruled. Proceed.

Christopher Darden: The evidence is there. You just have to find your way through the smoke. You just have to find your way through the smoke. You heard from Mr. Scheck yesterday. You heard him talk about our science. They have to attack our science because all the science points to O.J. Simpson, to this defendant. It all points to him as the killer. They have to attack that science. Not only does common sense dictate that he is guilty, and we have proven him guilty to a scientific certainty. We've proven him guilty beyond a reasonable doubt. They hoisted that chart up on the on the thing, there, yesterday, with "Reasonable Doubt." You remember that chart? It had "Reasonable Doubt" at the top, and below that it had "Highly Unlikely" and all this other stuff. They put it on this thing and then they hoisted it all the way up to the ceiling. That isn't reasonable doubt. That's not what I'm required to prove to you.

Mr. Cochran said to you, "Well, reasonable doubt is doubt with a reason." That's not reasonable doubt. When you look back at that instruction, when you look back at the reasonable doubt instruction, you'll see when it comes to human affairs, there's always some degree of doubt, no matter how small. The sun could explode tomorrow, it could explode today, but I doubt that that'll happen. I really have no reason to believe that's true. I have no reason to believe that the sun will explode today or tomorrow. When you read the reasonable doubt instruction, apply it to — read it, and apply it to your every day situation, your every day circumstances. What does it take what does it take you, as a human being, after hearing all the evidence and hearing the law that the judge gives you, what does it take for you to feel comfortable in your conclusion that he killed these people?

They said that you have to be able to wake up the next day and feel as if the day before — the day that you rendered your verdict — that you did the right thing, that you rendered a verdict that you can live with. Let me ask you this: if you were to acquit him, what explanation would you give the day after that acquittal, if someone said, "Why did you acquit him?" Would you say "racism." Would you say it's because there's racism in the LAPD? That's what they want you to say. That's what they want you to think. You heard all of that — all the speaking and the fiery rhetoric and the quotes from Proverbs, and the like. You heard all of that yesterday, all of that fiery rhetoric.

Well, let me tell you what Marcia Clark and I are. Let me tell you who we are. We are the voice, the voices of calm and reason in all of this. You just need to calm down, take that common sense God gave you, go back in the jury room, don't let these people get you all riled up and all fired up because Fuhrman is a racist. Racism blinds you. Those epithets, they blind you. You never heard me use that epithet in this courtroom, did you? I'm not going to put on that kind of show for "you know who" for people to watch. That's not where we're coming from. We want you to focus on the evidence. I am eternally grateful that Mr. Fuhrman was exposed to be what he is, 'cause I think we should know who those people are. I've said it once, I've said it before, we ought to put a big stamp, tattoo it on their forehead "Racist" so that when we see 'em we know who they are, so that there's no speculation, so that we don't have to guess.

But, what they want you to do, and what they've done in this case, is they've interjected this racism and now they want you to become impassioned, to be upset. And then they want you to make quantum leaps in logic and in judgment. They want you say "Fuhrman is a racist. He planted the glove." You can't get from point A to point B if you just sit down and use your common sense. If you're logical. If you're reasonable. You can't do that.

• • •

You can write the law, but if you're not willing to enforce the law, then what is it? What is it worth? You can write the law, you can pass a law, but if people aren't willing to follow the law then what good is it?

• • •

I looked back at the Constitution last night. I sent my clerk to go get it for me. And I looked through the Constitution and you know what I saw? I saw some stuff in the Constitution about Ron and about Nicole. And the Constitution said that Ron and Nicole had the right to liberty. It said that they had the right to life. It said that they had a right to the pursuit of happiness. It said that Nicole didn't have to stay with him if she didn't want to stay with him. That's what the Constitution said.

And I looked further and I looked in the Constitution to see if it said anything about O.J. Simpson and you know what it said? It said he doesn't have the right to take those lives. He did not have the right to do what he did. They talk about courage. Courage is what Marcia Clark and I do every day.

• • •

I was reading last night about how important it is to remain calm. And we heard a lot of quotations over the last couple of days. And I remembered a story that I had read once. And a lot of people quote Martin Luther King and the like and that's all fine. But you know I'm a student, I'm a student of that. I've studied him and studied him and studied him. And I recall that in 1961 there was an incident involving Dr. King and it might be helpful for you to recall this, as I'm sure you dc. But it was 1961 and he'd written a book and he was up in Harlem and there was a book signing. And he was seated there at the table. a line of people walking up to him asking him to sign their books, meeting him, saying "hello." And finally this one woman walked up to him and she said to him "Are you Martin Luther King?" And he said, "Well, ma'am yes I am." And she said "Well, I've been looking for you," and she reached into her purse and she pulled out an envelope opener and she plunged it into his chest. And the people in the store were horrified and everyone became panicked and people began running and screaming, "Oh my God. Dr. King has been stabbed. Oh my God. Dr. King has been stabbed." And he fell to the floor and he laid there. And one of his assistants ran over to him and saw this massive thing embedded in his chest and the assistant started to reach for it to pull it out and Dr. King calmly said "No. Don't touch it. Just get me to a hospital." Well, the assistant was — he was hysterical. "Doctor let me pull it out. Let me pull it out." Dr. King was calm. He lay there with this thing embedded in his chest and he said "No. Just don't touch it. I'll be all right. Just get me to the hospital."

And so the assistant did as he was told, as Dr. King instructed him to do. And he took him to the hospital and they rushed him into surgery and they operated on him for five hours. And they removed what for all intents and purposes was a knife out of his chest. And it was removed by a black doctor a black surgeon, I'm proud to say. And a few days later, the surgeon went to see Dr. King who was still resting and rehabilitating in the hospital and he went to see him. And the doctor said to Dr. King, he said "It's a good thing you were so calm, Dr. King. It's a good thing you were so calm about the whole thing. The point of that blade was touching your aorta. Had you moved suddenly, if you so much as sneezed, you would have died instantly. You would have drowned in your own blood." Some folks would like to get you all riled up and get you so upset that you move suddenly and that and so that you drown in the minutia, so that you choke on the smoke. Some people want to make you mad and angry and bitter. King once wrote that we should never succumb to the temptation of bitterness and that the one thing about bitterness is its blindness. So don't be blinded by all this. Just do your job. I know you know what your job is. I know you know what to do and I hope you don't mind too much that I keep reminding you of that job because this is important. This case is important. This is a murder case. There are two people that are dead.

• • •

See, now go back to Martin because I feel comfortable with Martin Luther King — after that some Malcolm X, but I'm not going to drop that today. I don't want to get that deep. For Martin Luther King, for Martin Luther King justice was a critical issue in his life, in his life, your Honor. And it was more than a legal issue. And it was more than a moral issue. It was a spiritual issue. Let me read to you what he said about justice. ... Read along with me what Martin Luther King said about justice. "Justice is the same for all issues. It cannot be categorized. It is not possible to be in favor of justice for some people and not be in favor of justice for all people. Justice cannot be divided. Justice is indivisible."

OK? We can't have a system of law, or a system of justice or concept of justice or a concept of law or a legal standard of burden of proof. We can't have reasonable doubt over here for everybody else and then have another reasonable doubt standard for a particular individual. That ain't justice. That's not justice. That's what he's talking about. That's what he's talking about. He's talking about a double standard of justice. We can't have that. Let me ask you to ask yourself something. Ask yourself this when you're in the jury room. As you go through all of that evidence — and I know you're going to critique each and every piece of it. I know you are. I can tell just by looking at you that you are. You're not going to let anything slip by you. You're not going to let anything get by you. You're going to take that evidence, you're going to take it apart, you're going to review it. Ask yourself something as you look at that evidence and assess how important or significant it is to you in this case, as you ask yourself whether it incriminates the defendant or not, as you ask yourself as they want you to ask yourself is it planted or not, ask yourself, hey, if this wasn't O.J. Simpson would I even be thinking that this might be planted? Would I even be thinking that he wasn't guilty? Am I applying a double standard? Just ask yourself that. Because if it was anybody else, same fine lawyers, the same defense, how would you view the case then?

• • •

Now, if I'm the messenger, you know I've delivered the message as best as I could. And the message is that he killed these two people. And that's what the evidence dictates. You know, they mess around with our science evidence and stuff and try to cause you to lose confidence in that evidence, but Marcia Clark will go back and go over some of the points we think you might be interested in hearing about to sort of straighten that out.

But I know that you're going to do a good job when you go into the jury room. All I could ever ask from you and all that I ask from you today is that you try and be as objective as you possibly can be, that you not allow any passion or emotion or any bias, any of that human feeling, those human feelings we all have, to interfere with the decision you have to make. When I stood before you back in January, I said there were many victims in this case. And there are many interests involved in this case. It's an important case to O.J. Simpson and it's an important case to the victims and the families. We just want you to be fair. I just want you to do the right thing. That means the right thing under the law. We believe we've proven this case beyond a reasonable doubt and it's unfortunate, it's unfortunate what jealousy does to you.

It's unfortunate that obsession — it's unfortunate that obsession can do these things to you. It is unfortunate that two innocent people are dead because they got in this man's way.

That's the message we wanted to deliver and I'm the messenger and I'm proud to have delivered it. And I thank you for your verdict in advance in the event I don't get a chance to talk to you then. All of us owe you a debt of gratitude. God bless you.

Judge Ito: Ms. Clark.

Marcia Clark: Thank you, Your Honor. Good morning. How are you? I'm not allowed to ask you that, I just realized. Excuse me. I know you're tired of hearing us talk. I'm going to get right into the evidence because I want to go through what they said. I want to show you how the evidence corrects that and I want to talk to you about logic. I want to talk to you about what makes sense, OK? Because you've been hearing a lot of stuff that really makes no sense. You've been hearing lawyers spin stories and spin yarns for you with no evidence to it. Not only does it have no evidence, but it has no logic. And in that specifically I'm talking about this story about Mark Fuhrman swiping a bloody glove inside the Bronco. That's quite a story. That's an interesting story but it has no substance. Not only does it have no proof to it, but it also has no logic to it and I'll show you why. And that's what I want to talk to you about now. Logic. What makes sense.

In this case, we have seen what the defense has done, and it's been a very contorted, very inconsistent thing. I'm going to point out the inconsistencies to you. But basically, they have jumped from we are stupid bumblers or we are brilliant conspirators. And he includes us in this. And I find that particularly painful, ladies and gentlemen particularly painful, because I've been doing this a lot of years. I didn't start here. I started on that side of counsel table. I was a defense attorney. I know what the ethical obligations are of a prosecutor. I took a cut in pay to join this office because I believe in this job. I believe in doing it fairly and doing it right. And I like the luxury of being a prosecutor because I have the luxury on any case of going to the judge and saying "Guess what, Your Honor? Dismiss it. It's not here." Ladies and gentlemen, I can come to you and I can say "Don't convict. It's not here."

• • •

I have that right. I have that luxury. This job gives me that luxury. It doesn't give me a lot of money, but it gives me that luxury. I can get up in the morning and look at myself in the mirror and say ``I tell you the truth." I will never ask for a conviction unless I should, unless the law says I must, unless he is proven guilty beyond a reasonable doubt on credible evidence that you can trust, that you can rely on. I can never do it otherwise. That's my obligation.

. . .

Prosecutor Clark concluded her final remarks, once again describing the frictions between O.J. Simpson and his former wife that may have led to murder. She also reminded jurors of the especially brutal nature of the killings. Clark used slides projected onto the wall of the courtroom, as one of Nicole's 911 calls placed in 1993 was played. The scrolling slides showed a bruised Nicole Brown Simpson, her battered face and swollen arm — but then switched to pictures of the evidence, including gruesome crime scene photographs, a black sock at the foot of Simpson's bed, and a bloody glove on the pathway at his Rockingham Avenue. Her concluding words:

Marcia Clark: What we have here is logic and evidence and common sense ... I don't have to say anything else ... Ladies and gentlemen, on behalf of the people of the state of California, because we have proven beyond a reasonable doubt, far beyond a reasonable doubt, that the defendant committed these murders, we ask you to find the defendant guilty of murder in the first degree of Ronald Goldman and Nicole Brown.

Chapter 8
Jury Deliberations, Verdict, and Epilogue

The Simpson jury. Cameras were not allowed to photograph members of the jury. Illustration by Bill Robles. Reprinted with permission.

JURY DELIBERATION BEGINS

September 29, 1995

Following Marcia Clark's closing comments, Judge Ito gave the jury some quick instructions, and ordered them to briefly meet for the purpose of choosing a foreperson. In cases where the evidence is either very clear or very weak, jury deliberations may be short, lasting only a matter of hours or even minutes. Some juries, however, deliberate days or sometimes weeks, carefully weighing all the nuances of the evidence they have seen and heard. Most experts expected that Simpson jurors would deliberate for weeks. Within only a few hours of beginning deliberations, however, the jury signaled that it had reached a verdict.

THE VERDICT

A **verdict** is a decision of a jury as to a defendant's guilt or innocence. In most jurisdictions — as in California — a jury verdict must be unanimously agreed upon by all members of the trial jury. In non-capital cases, however, the U.S. Supreme Court has ruled that unanimous verdicts are not required.[1] Even so, some juries are unable to agree upon any verdict. When a jury is **deadlocked**, it is said to be a **hung jury**. Where a unanimous decision is required, juries may be deadlocked by the strong opposition of only one member to a verdict agreed upon by all of the others.

A number of court-watchers expected the Simpson jury to be hung. However, in what was to be a surprise to almost everyone involved in the case, the jury signaled that it had reached a unanimous verdict after only 4 hours of deliberation. Although the announcement came late in the afternoon of Tuesday, October 2, 1995, Judge Ito delayed revealing what the verdict was until lawyers for both sides could have the opportunity to be present in the courtroom. He announced that the verdict would be read at 10 a.m. (PST) on October 3, 1995.

Judgment Day

October 3, 1995

Judge Ito: All right, back on the record in the Simpson matter. Mr. Simpson is again present before the court with his counsel, Mr. Shapiro, Mr. Cochran, Mr. Kardashian, Mr. Bailey, Mr. Blasier. The People are represented by Ms. Clark, Mr. Darden, and Mr. Hodgman. The jury is not present. Good morning, counsel.

All right, the record should reflect that earlier this morning, at nine o'clock, the court met informally with counsel here in the courtroom because there were too many lawyers to go into chambers this morning for the purposes of discussing notifications to the jurors regarding their rights of privacy and the interest of the news media to interview them or speak to them, following the delivery of the verdict in court here today. The court distributed to the parties copies of the questionnaire that has been distributed to the jurors, and also the notice to them regarding confidentiality under 237 of the code of civil procedure, and those two questionnaires have been returned by the jurors. They have uniformly indicated their desire that their public — excuse me — their private information remain confidential. They have also indicated to the court unanimously a desire not to speak to the attorneys after the conclusion of the trial and not to speak with the news media, either.

All right, counsel, is there anything else we need to take up before I invite the jurors to join us? All right, Deputy Trauer, let's have the jurors, please.

Judge Ito: And the record should reflect that we have now been rejoined by all the members of our jury panel and our alternates. Good morning again, ladies and gentlemen. All right, Mrs. Robertson, do you have the envelope with the sealed verdicts in those, please?

Mrs. Robertson (Court Clerk): Yes, Your Honor.

Judge Ito: All right, would you give those to Deputy Trauer? And would you return those to our foreperson, jury number one? All right, madam foreperson, would you please open the envelope and check the condition of the verdict forms? All right, madam foreperson, you've had the opportunity to review the verdict forms?

Madam Foreperson: Yes.

Judge Ito: Are they the same forms that you signed and are they in order?

Madam Foreperson: Yes, they are.

Judge Ito: All right, would you hand those, please, to Deputy Trauer? And you have signed and dated those verdict forms, indicating the jury's verdict?

Madam Foreperson: Yes.

Judge Ito: All right, thank you. All right, ladies and gentlemen, and the jury, I'm going to ask that you carefully listen to the verdicts as they are being read by the clerk, Mrs. Robertson, as after the verdicts have been read, you will be asked if these are your verdicts, and I would caution the audience during the course of the reading of these verdicts to remain calm, and if there is any disruption during the reading of the verdicts, the bailiffs will have the obligation to remove any persons disrupting these proceedings. All right, Mrs. Robertson? All right, Mr. Simpson, would you please stand and face the jury? Mrs. Robertson?

Mrs. Robertson: Superior Court of California, County of Los Angeles, in the matter of the People of the State of California *vs.* Orenthal James

Simpson, case number BA097211, we the jury in the above entitled action find the defendant, Orenthal James Simpson, not guilty of the crime of murder in violation of penal code section 187A, a felony, upon Nicole Brown Simpson, a human being, as charged in count one of the information.

Superior Court of the State of California, County of Los Angeles, in the matter of the People of the State of California *vs.* Orenthal James Simpson, we the jury, in the above entitled action, find the defendant, Orenthal James Simpson, not guilty of the crime of murder, in violation of penal code section 187A, a felony, upon Ronald Lyle Goldman, a human being, as charged in count two of the information.

We, the jury, in the above entitled action, further find the special circumstance that the defendant, Orenthal James Simpson, has in this case been convicted of at least one crime of murder of the first degree and one or more crimes of murder of the first or second degree to be not true. Signed, this second day of October, 1995. Jury 230.

Ladies and gentlemen of the jury, is this your verdict, say so you one, so say you all?

Jury: Yes.

Judge Ito: All right, counsel, Mr. Simpson, would you be seated, please? Let's have it quiet in the courtroom, please. All right, Mrs. Robertson, would you please poll the jurors?

The court clerk, Mrs. Robertson, then conducted a verbal poll of the jurors, asking each one whether they agreed with the verdicts; to which each responded, "yes."

Judge Ito: All right, the clerk is directed to record the verdicts as read. The parties agree to waive reading of the verdicts as recorded. Mr. Cochran, do you waive the reading of the verdict as recorded?

Johnnie Cochran: Yes, we do, Your Honor.

Judge Ito: Ms. Clark?

Marcia Clark: Yes, Your Honor.

Judge Ito: Thank you. All right, ladies and gentlemen, I want to, at this time, take this opportunity to publicly thank you for the service that you've given to us. The burdens that we've placed upon you were enormous, and I, of course, can't begin to express the debt that we owe to you for the time, the patience, and exertion that you've given to us during the course of this case. I will have the opportunity to meet with you privately later and I'll give you my private comments when we have a chance to meet.

I want to caution you at this time that there is, as you know, intense media interest in this case. The news media will probably seek you out at your home or at your place of business, and I would implore that the news media act responsibly to avoid harassing you or identifying you without your consent or otherwise causing you concern. Whether you wish to cooperate with the news media is, of course, entirely up to you. However, I must warn you to expect the worst as far as that is concerned ...

All right, ladies and gentlemen of the jury, I am now going to excuse you from further service on this case. As you know, this does absolve you from your vows of silence. You may take with you your jury notebooks, as you have requested, and we'll be chatting with you shortly. All right, thank you very much, and I'll see you all later.

Everybody have a seat please. All right, Miss Clark, Mr. Cochran, anything else we need to take up?

Johnnie Cochran: Your Honor, we'd like to thank the court. You've been [inaudible] throughout, your Honor. Thank you very, very kindly, sir.

Judge Ito: Miss Clark?

Marcia Clark: Thank you.

Judge Ito: All right. The defendant, having been acquitted of both charges, he is ordered transported to an appropriate sheriff's facility and released forthwith. All right, we'll stand in recess.

Bailiff: Please clear the courtroom.

At the close of court Simpson was immediately taken back to jail for out-processing, and released within half an hour of the verdict. A free man after 474 days spent in a jail cell, Simpson was cheered by jubilant well-wishers who followed his two-car motorcade as it made its way back to his Brentwood estate. There Simpson was greeted by family members and close friends, who had arranged a simple coming home party.

After a verdict has been returned, the judge must enter a judgment in the case. A **judgment** is a written record of the jury's findings plus — in cases where a guilty verdict has been returned — a record of the **sentence** imposed by the court.

REACTIONS TO THE VERDICT

Reproduced below are excerpts from statements made by family members, the defendant, and lawyers on both sides of the case in response to the "not guilty" verdicts.[2] Also included are quotations from a few observers of the national scene.

O. J. Simpson: I'm relieved that this part of the incredible nightmare that occurred on June 12, 1994, is over. My first obligation is to my young children, who will be raised the way that Nicole and I had always planned. My second obligation is to my family and to those friends who never wavered in their support. ... But when things have settled a bit, I will pursue as my primary goal in life the killer or killers who slaughtered Nicole and Mr. Goldman. They are out there somewhere. Whatever it takes to identify them and bring them in, I will provide somehow. ... I can only hope that someday, despite every prejudicial thing that has been said about me publicly, both in and out of the courtroom, people will come to understand and believe that I would not, could not and did not kill anyone.

Defense Attorney Johnnie Cochran, Jr.: On behalf of the entire team, I'd just like to say how grateful we are for this verdict. We think this verdict — to seek justice. We never wavered in our faith. We were always optimistic. That optimism's proved right.

Defense Attorney Johnnie Cochran, Jr.: If you watched the trial, if you watched the arguments, then you know that this idea of jury nullification — the idea that we didn't have any of the facts — is preposterous. The opening part of my argument, the strategy devised by Mr. Bailey — we said that if we could shatter the prosecution time line — that O.J. Simpson couldn't have committed this crime — then there would be a reasonable doubt. And that's even before we got the socks, the glove or anything else. These people that make those statements don't know what they're talking about. These pundits who make those statements don't know what they're talking about. They don't try cases, they don't know what they're talking about.

Defense Attorney Johnnie Cochran, Jr.: This is a case based upon the evidence. And so that's all we're saying, that there was a reasonable doubt. And when you see a trial that's lasted nine months, the way the jury takes this period of time, they have gone through what we've said. Look at that timeline. O.J. Simpson could not, did not and would not have committed this crime. I think that's become very clear.

Defense Attorney Robert Shapiro: My position was always the same, that race would not and should not be a part of this case. I was wrong. Not only did we play the race card, we dealt it from the bottom of the deck.

Los Angeles District Attorney Gil Garcetti: We are, all of us, profoundly disappointed with the verdict. We want to hear from the jurors before we make any other comments, concerning their decision today. But it was clear — at least it is to me and I think other members of the prosecution team — that this was an emotional trial. Apparently, their decision was based on emotion, that overcame their reason. Certainly, we have received calls and letters from all over the country praising the efforts of the prosecution ... We had many, many, women throughout the country call and thank us for the efforts, many in tears.

Los Angeles District Attorney Gil Garcetti: Our job is to seek justice. This case was fought as a battle for victims of domestic violence. We hope this verdict does not discourage the victims, who are out there throughout our communities, throughout this country, from seeking help. I know there are, women especially, who are right this very moment living in fear, living in violence. We're asking you to reach out for help. There is new help out there. Think of yourself and think of the children who are in the house too. Don't wait. If you wait it could be too late.

Los Angeles District Attorney Gil Garcetti: And of course, lastly, to Chris and to Marcia. None of you will ever know the personal sacrifices that everyone here made. None of you will know too, the sacrifices that the families of this team made. They didn't see their husbands and their wives, their fathers and their mothers, for 16 months. I think on behalf of every citizen who has been looking at this case in an objective way, I think they want me to say thank you and I am saying thank you, but let me end by saying, we deserve to be proud of the effort that we made in this case. I am very proud of the total effort made in this case. We stand here in front of you with our heads held high because we did everything professionally possible to seek justice in this case.

Prosecutor Marcia Clark: Please don't let this make you lose faith in our system. Everyone here has put in 110 percent, given their all for everyone, for justice.

Prosecutor Christopher Darden: I accept the verdict...(but) we came here in search of justice and you'll have to be the judge of whether or not we found it. I am not angry, I am not bitter, and I would like to thank members of the team...

Fred Goldman (Ronald Goldman's father): Last June 13th, '94, was the worst nightmare of my life. This is the second.

Fred Goldman (Ronald Goldman's father): This prosecution team didn't lose today. I deeply believe that this country lost today. Justice was not served. I and my family will do everything in our power to bring about the kind of change that won't allow what happened today to ever happen to another family again.

Eric Adams, chairman of the Grand Council of Guardians. (The Council is a group of black police officers based in New York City): At my precinct in New York after the verdict, the atmosphere was hostile. The white officers were angry. At the same time, you could see black cops quietly acknowledging to each other what was going on — O.J. became a symbol of attacking the system. When I go into work, white officers will hit the soda machine and get a free soda. When I hit the machine and get a soda, they say, "We need to fix that machine." When I heard the O.J. verdict, it was as if all of black America hit the soda machine. And now that we got our free soda, everybody wants to fix the machine.

Armstrong Williams (African-American syndicated columnist and radio talk-show host): This case was a travesty of justice, a miscarriage of justice. It has had me in a slump all week. It hurts me. When I saw the families crying, it broke me up inside because they thought the man who killed their family members had got away — and you know they are right! ... This has to do with America's racist past. America used to let its black sons and daughters get lynched and discriminated against. It wasn't until recently that the system became colorblind. [Still], blacks believe there is an elite system in place to oppress them. They are wrong.

THE VERDICT AND RACE

The Public View

The Simpson double-murder trial had been watched almost daily for a year throughout the world by millions on television, listened to on radio by countless millions more, and read about in newspapers and magazines by still others. The Simpson trial was truly the mega-media event of the late 20th century. It's sudden and dramatic close, with "not guilty" verdicts on October 3, 1995, sent social and political reverberations throughout the United States which are still being felt. In the trial's immediate wake, however, it was easy to discern a huge gap between the attitudes of white Americans and African-Americans toward the criminal justice system.

Many whites remained firmly convinced that Simpson was guilty and felt he should have been convicted. The "not guilty" verdicts and Simpson's subsequent release, some felt, were a travesty. This remark, which came across an on-line service shortly after the verdict was read, sums up what many whites were feeling at the time: "A sense of sadness overwhelms me. And I am not the only one. You can feel it all over the ... building where I work ... It just doesn't feel like justice." Some whites claimed that Simpson had been found "not guilty by reason of race."

A large portion of the nation's blacks, on the other hand, celebrated Simpson's acquittal — seeing in the verdicts a triumph over racism and a vindication of the deep distrust many in the black community feel toward the justice system in this country. Reflecting on the Simpson trial, one black man put it this way: "Whether he's innocent or guilty, let him go — I think that's the way a lot of black people are feeling..."[3]

Central to the controversy were strong feelings aroused in many black Americans by the charges of racism that had been leveled against key prosecution witness LAPD Detective Mark Fuhrman. As transcripts in an earlier chapter showed, Fuhrman, a white police investigator, had gathered much of the crucial evidence against Simpson — including a bloody glove collected from a walkway at Simpson's estate. Some commentators concluded that what may have decided the case was the defense's ability to show that Fuhrman had lied on the stand about having repeatedly referred to black people as "niggers" during the course of his police career. While many whites saw such a revelation as irrelevant to the facts of the case, it may have convinced the mostly black jury that a racist cop could not be trusted to testify truthfully about other matters. Once Fuhrman had been successfully portrayed as a racist, it became easy for black jurors to conclude that he might have planted evidence or lied about critical issues in a case involving a black man accused of murdering a white woman and a white man. It may have been all that was needed for a jury with 9 black members to return a "not guilty" verdict — regardless of the apparent strength of the evidence.

For many black people — not only those on the jury — once the specter of racial discrimination had been raised in the Simpson trial, the underlying issue became one of social justice, rather than criminal justice. As one writer put it, "The Fuhrman factor evoked a powerful story in the African-American experience: of the black man fighting a system that's rigged against him. So when blacks applauded the verdict, many were cheering less for the literal event than its allegorical significance — for a different ending to the story."[4]

When the Simpson defense played "the race card" during the trial, it built upon a distrust of the police and of the criminal justice system among African-Americans which runs deep. Recent surveys, for example, show that only 33% of black people in this country believe that police officers testify truthfully, and only 18% of blacks say they would believe a police officer over other witnesses in a criminal trial.[5] John Mack, the black President of the Los Angeles Urban League, explained that while many whites have "a user friendly relationship" with police, many black people — especially young ones — have come to distrust the police because law enforcement officers are prone to viewing them and their activities suspiciously.

Such distrust, it should be noted, can have a significant impact on the entire criminal justice process, wielding influence far beyond that of a single trial — even a highly publicized one like Simpson's. "Increasingly," observed a *Wall Street Journal* article[6] published shortly after the Simpson verdict, "jury watchers are concluding that ... race plays a far more significant role in jury verdicts than many people involved in the justice system prefer to acknowledge." "The willingness of many blacks ... to side with African-American defendants against a mostly white-dominated justice system is a relatively new phenomenon with specific roots and ramifications," said the Journal.

The tenacity of those roots, some say, are founded in a realistic distrust of the justice system ingrained into the subculture of black Americans by years of experience with a system which was often biased against them. Others say that such verdicts merely reflect informal social understandings within the black community. Some jurors, for example, may simply feel that there are already too many blacks in prison, while others may not believe that prison will do any good — even though they know a suspect is guilty. In the Bronx, a New York City borough, for example, where juries are often composed mostly of African-Americans, the acquittal rate for black defendants in felony cases is nearly three times greater than the national average.[7]

Unfortunately, the Simpson verdict and the black-white differences it revealed, may have fed a long-standing racial divide that many had thought was beginning to heal. Following the verdict, 53% of blacks and 77% of whites interviewed in a USA Today poll said that the Simpson trial had done more to hurt race relations than to help them. The consequences of the Simpson trial for the justice system, however, may ultimately transcend racial lines. A survey conducted after the trial found a large proportion of both blacks and whites reporting a heightened distrust of the justice system — and especially of police officers and defense attorneys. Echoing that feeling, a *Newsweek* article said that the problem in today's justice system is not differing attitudes among the races, but the uniquely American "license that we give lawyers to engage in truth-defeating distortion and trickery at trial."[8]

What lasting changes the Simpson trial may have wrought in American criminal justice are difficult to discern. However, as Georgetown University Law School professor Paul Rothstein put it, one thing is certain: "Whites have had an unrealistic view of how perfect things function. Minorities ... have had an unrealistic view of how badly they function."[9] The Simpson trial has probably made attitudes on both sides of the racial divide more realistic — and if it has done that it may serve us all well in the long run.

The Professional View

On the heels of the verdict in the Simpson trial, Fraternal Order of Police (FOP) President Gilbert Gallegos prepared a news release entitled "Commentary: Racism in Law Enforcement." Gallegos was concerned that media revelation of racist attitudes on the part of at least one member of the Los Angeles Police Department during the Simpson trial might have a negative impact on the public image of police officers everywhere. In the press release (printed below) Gallegos sought to assure the 270,000 members of his organization (the largest police organization in the world) that racism could be eliminated from police ranks.

Commentary: Racism in Law Enforcement
It's Our Duty to Clean Up Our Ranks

Mark Fuhrman — an enigma or the norm? During the past two months citizens and members of the media have asked that question of me often. My response has been that Fuhrman and others like him are not representative of the vast number of professional police officers that I know. He, and others like him, do not represent the spirit and dedication of the 270,000 members of the Fraternal Order of Police.

While the numbers of racist cops are minute among the more than 600,000 professionals throughout the country, those few cause problems for all of us. The vast majority of hard working officers are conscientious, fair minded and dedicated to the principles of justice and service to the community. After all, we live in the communities we serve.

I foresee a concerted effort by departments to purge the "misfits" from the law enforcement ranks. Who defines misfits? Are they going to be defined by the media, reactionary groups, politicians, or should we, the professionals, clean up our own ranks? I feel the job of cleaning up the ranks is our responsibility as law enforcement professionals and that we can do it better and more fairly than the other groups I mentioned.

I also predict that many departments, in their zeal to purge the ranks, will violate the rights of many police officers. While I do not condone racist cops, I do support the concept and right of due process for everyone. Police officers do not give up their constitutional rights when they take their oath of office and pin the badge to their uniforms. We dedicate our lives to the Constitution of the United States. Sometimes we sacrifice our lives for others, for justice, and for the Constitution.

Recently, a conservative radio host accused me of defending racist cops.... Quite the contrary. I and other FOP leaders do not defend racism in any form. We defend the constitutional right of due process and fair treatment.

While law enforcement has taken many hits during the past few months — Waco, Ruby Ridge, the O.J. trial — we cannot lower our heads in shame. We must lift our heads with pride because of the service we continue to provide to citizens despite race or creed, rich or poor. Our efforts should be to right the wrongs and to continue serving the public we swore to protect.

The media will not carry our positive messages of dedication and hard work. Those messages do not sell newspapers, magazines, nor do they grab attention during a 30 second sound bite. The responsibility to take positive messages to the American people is ours. Not in defense of our profession, but in a sense of showing the many fine deeds we perform. We must learn to blow our horn if we are to turn the tide of public mistrust.

I have spoken to officers who feel the tension and mistrust as they patrol their beats. They do not exchange words. However, the doubting stares of a child or an honest citizen sends a chilling message to beat officers.

During these difficult times, we, the thin blue line, must stand together shoulder to shoulder in support of each other. I have no fear that our deeds, our professional dedication, and our FOP members will turn the tide of adversity, mistrust and doubt.

PROBLEMS WITH THE JURY SYSTEM

In the wake of the Simpson trial the jury system was soundly criticized by a wide range of commentators, who cast it as an inefficient and outmoded method for determining guilt or innocence. Such criticisms, however, are not new.[10] Even before the Simpson trial, California legislators were considering changing state law to allow for non-unanimous verdicts (of at least 10 – 2) in non-capital cases — a movement which received added support in some quarters by the Simpson trial outcome.

Some argue that jurors cannot be expected to understand modern legal complexities and to appreciate all the nuances of trial court practice. In fact, many instructions to the jury are probably poorly understood and rarely observed by even the best-meaning jurors.[11] Likewise, many jurors probably find it difficult to separate emotions from fact. Jurors may also become confused over legal technicalities, suffer from inattention, or be unable to understand fully the testimony of expert witnesses or the significance of technical evidence. Studies show that during deliberation many juries are dominated by one or two forceful personalities, sometimes with private agendas, who may or may not focus on the evidence.

Historically speaking, the Simpson jury is not the only jury to have been criticized by court-watchers. Often cited in professional legal circles, for example, is the fact that one of the jurors in the trial of Lt. Colonel Oliver North for illegally selling arms to Iran, was selected for jury duty after she stated that she did not know who Ronald Reagan was.

Many jury-related problems became evident in the trial of Raymond Buckey and his mother, Peggy McMartin Buckey, who were tried in Los Angeles a decade ago for allegedly molesting dozens of children at their family-run preschool.[12] The trial, which involved 65 counts of child sexual molestation and conspiracy, and 61 witnesses, ran for more than three years. Many jurors were stressed to the breaking point by the length of time involved. Family relationships suffered as the trial droned on, and jurors were unable to accompany their spouses and children on vacation. Small-business owners, who were expected to continue paying salaries to employees serving as jurors, faced financial ruin and threatened their absent employees with termination. Careers were put on hold, and at least one juror had to be dismissed for becoming inattentive to testimony. The trial cost taxpayers more than $12 million, but was nearly negated as jury membership and the number of alternate jurors declined due to sickness and personal problems. Ultimately, the defendants were acquitted.

Another trial in which the defendants were similarly acquitted of the majority of charges against them involved state-level prosecution of the officers accused in the now-infamous Rodney King beating. Following the riots in Los Angeles and elsewhere which came on the heels of their verdict, jurors in the "Rodney King trial" reported being afraid for their lives. Some slept with weapons by their side, and others sent their children away to safe locales.[13] Because of the potential for harm jurors faced in the 1993 federal trial of the same officers, U.S. District Judge John G. Davies ruled that the names of jurors be forever kept secret. The secrecy order was called "an unprecedented infringement of the public's right of access to the justice system"[14] by members of the press. Similarly, in the 1993 trial of three black men charged with the beating of white truck driver Reginald Denny during the Los Angeles riots, Los Angeles Superior Court Judge John Ouderkirk ordered that the identities of jurors not be released.

Opponents of the jury system have argued that it should be replaced by a panel of judges (probably three in number) who would both render a verdict and impose sentence. Regardless of how well considered such a suggestion may be, however, such a change probably could not occur without modification of the Constitution's Sixth Amendment right to trial by jury.

An alternative (and constitutionally more sound) suggestion for improving the process of trial by jury has been the call for professional jurors. Professional jurors would be paid by the government, as are judges, prosecutors, and public defenders. Their job would be to sit on any jury, and they would be expected to have the expertise to do so. Professional jurors would be trained to listen objectively and would be schooled with the kinds of decision-making skills necessary to function effectively within an adversarial context. They could be expected to hear one case after another, perhaps moving between jurisdictions in cases of highly publicized crimes.

The advantages a professional jury system offers are:

- Dependability. Professional jurors could be expected to report to the courtroom in a timely fashion and to be good listeners, since both would be required by the nature of the job.

- Knowledge. Professional jurors would be trained in the law, would understand what a finding of guilt requires, and would know what to expect from other actors in the courtroom.

- Equity. Professional jurors would understand the requirements of due process and would be less likely to be swayed by the emotional content of a case, having been schooled in the need to separate matters of fact from personal feelings.

A professional jury system would not be without difficulties. Jurors under such a system might become jaded, deciding cases out of hand as routines lead to boredom and suspects are categorized according to whether they "fit the type" for guilt or innocence developed on the basis of previous experiences. Job requirements for professional jurors would be difficult to establish without infringing on the jurors' freedom to decide cases as they understand them. For the same reason, any evaluation of the job performance of professional jurors would be a difficult call. Finally, professional jurors might not truly be peer jurors, since their social characteristics might be skewed by education, residence, and politics.

EPILOGUE: CIVIL SUITS FACING O.J. SIMPSON

As this book goes to press the O.J. Simpson saga is far from over. The parents of Ronald Goldman, Fred Goldman and Sharon Rufo, have filed a civil suit against Simpson, asking for monetary damages in the death of their son. Louis Brown, Nicole Brown Simpson's father has filed a similar suit on behalf of his daughter's estate. Both hearings will be held before 12 member juries in Santa Monica, California, civil court.

A civil suit requires far less proof than a criminal case, although the plaintiffs in both cases will have available to them all the evidence gathered against Simpson by LAPD detectives and police investigators. While criminal charges must be proved beyond a reasonable doubt, a finding of liability in a civil action rests on what is called **a preponderance of the evidence**. The phrase "preponderance of the evidence" means that the plaintiffs' lawyers must only convince jurors that it is more likely than not that Simpson was responsible for the deaths of either of the victims. Moreover, while California law requires that jurors unanimously agree on a finding of guilt in a criminal case (a requirement which has come under debate in the California legislature following the Simpson trial), California civil suits may be won if only 9 of 12 jurors agree that the defendant is responsible for the harm in question.

Reproduced below is the civil complaint filed against O.J. Simpson by Louis Brown, father of Nicole Brown Simpson. Brown acted in his capacity as executor of his daughter's estate.

LOUIS H. BROWN, in Pro Per
Executor and Personal Representative
of the Estate of Nicole Brown Simpson
222 Monarch Bay
Dana Point, California 92629

JOHN QUINLAN KELLY - OF COUNSEL
Attorney at Law
330 Madison Avenue
New York, New York 10017
(212) 697-2700

SUPERIOR COURT OF THE STATE OF CALIFORNIA
FOR THE COUNTY OF LOS ANGELES

LOUIS H. BROWN as Executor and personal
representative of the Estate of NICOLE
BROWN SIMPSON, deceased, Plaintiff,

vs.

ORENTHAL JAMES SIMPSON,
Defendant

CASE NO: SC036876

COMPLAINT FOR DAMAGES-
SURVIVAL ACTION
(C.C.P. Section 377.30)

Plaintiff alleges:

FIRST CAUSE OF ACTION

1) On or about November 7, 1994, Louis H. Brown was appointed executor of
the Estate of Nicole Brown Simpson, deceased, by the Superior Court of
California County in Los Angeles, in Case No. SP002190. Testamentary letters
are attached hereto, marked Exhibit A and incorporated herein by this
reference.

2) Plaintiff is the Executor and personal representative of the Estate of Nicole
Brown Simpson.

3) That at all times herein mentioned, all acts occurred in the community of
Brentwood, County of Los Angeles, State of California.

4) Orenthal James Simpson is and was a resident of the County of Los Angeles.

5) At all times herein mentioned, decedent Nicole Brown Simpson was a
resident of the County of Los Angeles.

6) The true names or capacities, whether individual, corporate, associate or
otherwise of the defendants designated herein as Does 1 through 10, inclusive,
and each of them, are unknown to plaintiff, who therefore sues said defendants
by such fictitious names, and plaintiff will ask leave to amend this complaint at
such time as the true names and/or capacities are ascertained. Plaintiff is
informed and believes, and thereon alleges, that each defendant designated
herein as DOE is responsible in some manner for the events and happenings
herein referred to, and caused or contributed to the injuries and damages to
plaintiff as herein alleged.

7) On or about June 12, 1994, after the foregoing cause of action arose in her
favor, Nicole Brown Simpson, who would have been the plaintiff in this action if
she had lived, died as the legal result of the wrongful acts of Orenthal James
Simpson and Does 1 though 10.

8) On or about June 12, 1994, Orenthal James Simpson and Does 1 through
10, planned and prepared to assault, batter and murder Nicole Brown Simpson
and did thereafter brutally, and with malice aforethought, stalk, attack and
repeatedly stab and beat decedent, Nicole Brown Simpson. Defendants, and
each of them, left her on the walkway in front of her residence to die. Nicole

Brown Simpson survived the brutal attack for some unknown period of time and thereafter bled to death as a direct legal result of the wrongful and homicidal acts of Orenthal James Simpson and Does 1 through 10.

9) The attack was perpetrated by defendant Orenthal James Simpson and Does 1 through 10 with the full knowledge that the assault and battery upon decedent's body would lead to her death. Each of the acts alleged herein were done with a wanton, reckless disregard for the rights of the decedent and with the full knowledge that she would die as a result of said acts.

10) As a proximate result of the assault, battery and murder of Nicole Brown Simpson by defendants, and each of them decedent was required to and did employ physicians and surgeons to examine, treat and care for her and did incur medical and incidental expenses in an amount unknown at this time. The complaint will be amended according to proof when the amount becomes known.

11) On or about June 12, 1994, and immediately prior to decedent's death, personal property of decedent was destroyed as a legal result of defendants' wrongful acts. The amount of said property is unknown at present. Plaintiff will amend this complaint according to proof when said amount becomes known.

12) In doing the acts herein alleged, defendant, and each of them, acted with oppression, fraud and malice, and plaintiff is entitled to punitive and exemplary damages in an amount to be proven at the time of trial.

WHEREFOR, plaintiff prays judgment as follows:

1) For medical and related expenses according to proof.

2) For personal property according to proof.

3) For punitive and exemplary damages according to proof.

4) For costs of suit herein incurred.

5) For such other and further relief as the court may deem proper.

Dated: June 12, 1995.

By:

(Signed) Louis H. Brown
LOUIS H. BROWN, as Executor and personal representative
of the Estate of Nicole Brown Simpson, deceased, in Pro Per

Notes

1 See *Johnson* v. *Louisiana*, 406 U.S. 356 (1972), and *Apodaca* v. *Oregon*, 406 U.S. 404 (1972).

2 Some quotations are excerpted from the Court TV forum on America On Line, October 20, 1995.

3 "Nation Seeing Simpson Case in Black and White," The Associated Press, October 1, 1995.

4 Mark Whitaker, "Whites v. Blacks," *Newsweek*, October 16, 1995, p. 34.

5 Maria Puente, "Poll: Blacks' Confidence in Police Plummets," *USA Today*, March 21, 1995, p. 3A.

6 Benjamin A. Holden, Laurie P. Cohen, and Eleena de Lisser, "Color Blinded" Race Seems to Play An Increasing Role in Many Jury Verdicts," *The Wall Street Journal*, October 4, 1995, p. 1A.

7 Holden, "Color Blinded," p. 1A.

8 John H. Langbein, "Money Talks, Clients Walk," *Newsweek*, April 17, 1995, p. 32.

9 Joe Urschel, "74% Say O.J. Verdict Hurt Racial Ties," *USA Today*, October 9, 1995, p. 1A.

10 See, for example, John Baldwin and Michael McConville, "Criminal Juries," in Norval Morris and Michael Tonry, eds., *Crime and Justice*, Vol. 2 (Chicago: University of Chicago Press, 1980).

11 Amiram Elwork, Bruce D. Sales, and James Alfini, *Making Jury Instructions Understandable* (Charlottesville, VA: Michie, 1982).

12 "Juror Hardship Becomes Critical as McMartin Trial Enters Year 3," *Criminal Justice Newsletter*, Vol. 20 (May 15, 1989), pp. 6–7.

13 "King Jury Lives in Fear from Unpopular Verdict," *Fayetteville Observer-Times* (North Carolina), May 10, 1992, p. 7A.

14 "Los Angeles Trials Spark Debate over Anonymous Juries," *Criminal Justice Newsletter*, February 16, 1993, pp. 3–4.

Appendices

APPENDIX A: The Witness List

A complete list of prosecution witnesses, along with dates of their testimony, is provided below. A list of defense witnesses follows. All told, prosecutors called 58 witnesses to testify before the jury, and another 13 rebuttal witnesses near the close of trial. A total of 53 witnesses testified for the defense.

Witnesses for the Prosecution

January 31, 1995: Sharon Gilbert, Los Angeles Police Department (LAPD) 911 Dispatcher

January 31, 1995: Detective John Edwards, LAPD

January 31, 1995: Detective Mike Farrell, LPAD

February 1–2, 1995: Ron Shipp, friend of O.J. Simpson and Nicole Brown Simpson.

February 2, 1995: Investigator Mike Stevens, LAPD

February 2, 1995: Terri Moore, 911 Dispatcher

February 3, 1995: Sgt. Robert Lerner, Los Angeles Police Department

February 3, 1995: Catherine Boe, Nicole Brown Simpson's neighbor

February 3, 1995: Carl Colby, Nicole Brown Simpson's neighbor

February 3–6, 1995: Denise Brown, sister of Nicole Brown Simpson

February 6, 1995: Candace Garvey, friend of Nicole Brown Simpson

February 6, 1995: Cynthia Shahian, friend of Nicole Brown Simpson

February 7, 1995: Tia Gavin, waitress at Mezzaluna Restaurant

February 7, 1995: Stuart Tanner, bartender at Mezzaluna Restaurant

February 7, 1995: Karen Crawford, manager at Mezzaluna Restaurant

February 7, 1995: Karen Goldman, sister of Ronald Goldman

February 7, 1995: Pablo Fenjves, neighbor of Nicole Brown Simpson

February 8, 1995: Eva Stein, neighbor of Nicole Brown Simpson

February 8, 1995: Louis Karpf, neighbor of Nicole Brown Simpson

February 8, 1995: Steven Schwab, neighbor of Nicole Brown Simpson

February 8, 1995: Sukru Boztepe, neighbor of Nicole Brown Simpson

February 8, 1995: Elsie Tistaert, neighbor of Nicole Brown Simpson

February 9 & 14, 1995: Officer Robert Riske, LAPD

February 14 & 15, 1995: Sgt. David Rossi, LAPD

February 15–17, 1995: Detective Ronald Phillips, LAPD

February 17, 21–22 and March 6–9, 1995, Detective Tom Lange, LAPD

March 6, 1995: Mark Storfer, neighbor of Nicole Brown Simpson

March 9–10 and March 13–16, 1995: Detective Mark Fuhrman, LAPD

March 16, 1995: Lt. Frank Spangler, Los Angeles Police Department

March 16–17 & March 20–21, 1995, Detective Philip Vannatter, LAPD

March 9, 1995: Patti Goldman, Ronald Goldman's stepmother

March 16, 1995: Darryl Smith, *Inside Edition* news photographer

March 21–23 & March 27–28, 1995: Brian "Kato" Kaelin, Simpson houseguest

March 28, 1995: Rachel Ferrara, friend of Brian Kaelin

March 28–29, 1995: Allan Park, limousine driver

March 29, 1995: Judge Delbert Wong, Special Master

March 29, 1995: James Williams, skycap at Los Angeles Airport

March 30, 1995: Sue Silva, Westec Security Inc.

March 31, 1995: Charles Cale, neighbor of O.J. Simpson

April 3, 5, 11–14, and 17–18, 1995: Dennis Fung, LAPD criminalist

April 20 and 25–27, 1995: Andrea Mazzola, LAPD criminalist

May 1–5, 1995: Gregory Matheson, chief chemist, LAPD

May 8, 1995: Bernie Douroux, towtruck driver

May 8–15, 1995: Robin Cotton, laboratory director of Cellmark Diagnostics

May 16–22 & May 31 – June 1, 1995: Gary Sims, California Department of Justice

May 23–24, 1995: Renee Montgomery, criminalist, California Department of Justice

May 24–31, 1995: Collin Yamauchi, criminalist, Los Angeles Police Department

June 2–15, 1995: Dr. Lakshmanan Sathyavagiswaran, Los Angeles County Chief Medical Examiner

June 15, 1995: Brenda Vemich, merchandise buyer, Bloomingdale's

June 15–16, 1995: Richard Rubin, former executive, Aris Isotoner

June 19, 1995: William J. Bodziak, FBI shoe print expert

June 20, 1995: Samuel Poser, shoe department manager, Bloomingdale's

June 21, 1995: LuEllen Robertson, custodian of records, Airtouch Cellular Phones

June 21, 1995: Kathleen Delaney, Mirage Hotel

June 22–23, and 26, 1995: Bruce Weir, population geneticist

June 26–27, 1995: Denise Lewis, criminalist, LAPD

June 27–28, 1995: Susan Brockbank, criminalist, LAPD

June 29 – July 6, 1995: Douglas Deedrick, FBI Special Agent

Rebuttal Witnesses

September 11, 1995: Mark Krueger, photographed Simpson in 1990

September 11, 1995: Bill Renken, professional photographer

September 11, 1995: Kevin Schott, photography teacher

September 11, 1995: Stewart West, former professional photographer

September 11, 1995: Debra Guidera, photographed Simpson in December 1993

September 11, 1995: Michael Romano, professional photographer

September 12, 1995: Richard Rubin, former executive, Aris Isotoner

September 13, 1995: Gary Sims, senior criminalist, California Department of Justice

September 13, 1995: Stephen Oppler, investigator

September 13, 1995: Theresa Ramirez, photographed interview with Thano Peratis

September 14, 1995: Douglas Deedrick, FBI Special Agent

September 14–15 & 18, 1995: William Bodziak, FBI Special Agent

September 20, 1995: Keith Bushey, commander, Los Angeles Police Department

List of Defense Witnesses

July 10, 1995: Arnelle Simpson, O.J. Simpson's daughter from his first marriage

July 10, 1995: Carmelita Simpson-Durio, O.J. Simpson's sister

July 10, 1995: Eunice Simpson, O.J. Simpson's mother

July 10, 1995: Carol Conner, philanthropist and writer

July 10, 1995: Mary Collins, O.J. Simpson's longtime interior designer

July 11, 1995: Mattie Shirley Simpson Baker, O.J. Simpson's oldest sister

July 11, 1995: Jack McKay, CFO for the American Psychological Association, played golf with O.J. Simpson on June 8, 1994

July 11, 1995: Danny Mandel, walked with his date, Ellen Aaronson, near Nicole Brown Simpson's home at about 10:25 p.m. on night of murders

July 11, 1995: Ellen Aaronson, walked with date, Danny Mandel, near Nicole Brown Simpson's home at about 10:25 p.m. on the night of the murders

July 11, 1995: Denise Pilnak, lived on the 900 block of Bundy near Nicole Brown Simpson's condominium

July 11, 1995: Judy Telander, friend of Denise Pilnak and was with her on night of murders

July 11–12, 1995: Robert Heidstra, neighbor of Nicole Brown Simpson

July 12, 1995: Wayne Stanfield, American Airlines captain

July 12, 1995: Michael Norris, Los Angeles Airport delivery service employee

July 12, 1995: Michael Gladden, Los Angeles Airport delivery service employee

July 13, 1995: Howard Bingham, passenger on flight from Los Angeles to Chicago

July 13, 1995: Stephen Valerie, passenger on flight from Los Angeles to Chicago

July 13, 1995: Jim Merrill, Hertz employee who picked up Simpson at Chicago's O'Hare Airport

July 13, 1995: Dave Kilduff, Hertz employee who saw Simpson outside his hotel in Chicago

July 13, 1995: Mark Patridge, sat next to Simpson on flight from Chicago to Los Angeles

July 14, 17–18, 1995: Dr. Robert Huizenga, Beverly Hills private physician

July 18, 1995: Juanita Moore, O.J. Simpson's hairdresser

July 18, 1995: Detective Don Thompson, Los Angeles Police Department

July 19, 1995: John Meraz, Vietrel's employee who towed Ford Bronco

July 19, 1995: Richard Walsh, fitness trainer in exercise video

July 19–20, 1995: Willie Ford, Los Angeles Police Department videographer

July 20, 1995: Josephine "Gigi" Guarin, O.J. Simpson's housekeeper

July 20, 1995: Detective Kelly Mulldorfer, Los Angeles Police Department

July 20, 1995: Detective Alberto Luper, Los Angeles Police Department

July 24 and August 14, 1995: Dr. Fredric Rieders, forensic toxicologist

July 25-26, 1995: Roger Martz, FBI Special Agent

July 27, 31, and August 1, 1995: Herbert MacDonell, blood splatter expert

August 1, 1995: Thano Peratis, jail nurse (taped testimony)

August 2–4 & 7, 1995: John Gerdes, clinical director

August 7-8, 1995: Terrence Speed, statistics professor

August 10-11, 1995: Dr. Michael Baden, forensic pathologist

August 14–16, 1995: Michelle Kestler, director, LAPD crime lab

August 17, 1995: Gilbert Aguilar, LAPD fingerprint specialist

August 21, 1995: John Larry Ragle, former director, Orange County Crime Laboratory

August 22, 1995: Christian Reichardt, friend of O.J. Simpson and former boyfriend of Faye Resnick

August 22, 1995: Detective Kenneth Berris, Chicago Police Department

August 22–23, 25 & 28, 1995: Dr. Henry Lee, chief criminalist, state of Connecticut

September 5, 1995: Kathleen Bell, heard Mark Fuhrman utter racial slurs

September 5, 1995: Natalie Singer, heard Mark Fuhrman utter racial slurs

September 5, 1995: William Blasini, general manager, wholesale parts shop

September 5, 1995: Rolf Rokahr, Los Angeles Police Department photographer

September 5–6, 1995: Laura Hart McKinney, North Carolina professor and screenwriter

September 6, 1995: Roderic Hodge, individual arrested by Mark Fuhrman

September 20, 1995: Detective Philip Vannatter, Los Angeles Police Department

September 20, 1995: Michael Wacks, FBI Special Agent, overheard Vannatter conversation with Larry and Craig Fiato

September 20, 1995: Larry Fiato, organized crime informant who met with Detective Vannatter

September 20, 1995: Craig Fiato, brother of Larry Fiato, and another organized crime informant who met with Detective Vannatter

APPENDIX B: Letter Said to Be from Nicole to O.J.

On July 10, 1995 Simpson defense attorneys presented a five-page handwritten letter to Judge Ito, claiming that it was authored by Nicole Brown Simpson and sent to O.J. Simpson after the couple argued in March 1993. Defense attorneys wanted to introduce the letter into evidence in order to demonstrate its potential impact on O.J. Simpson's state of mind.   Although the judge ordered the letter marked as Defense Exhibit 1226 for identification purposes, and although the letter was widely published in the press, it was ruled inadmissible. The letter was not seen by jurors, and its authenticity remains debatable. A copy of the letter is reproduced below in an enhanced handwritten style.   Misspellings and grammatical errors appearing in the original letter have been retained.

Dear O.J.

I'd like to see you, to talk to you in person. But I know you can't do that. I've been attending these meetings to help me turn negatives into positives -- to help me turn get rid of my anger . . . I've learned to "let things go" (the most powerful, helpful thing I've ever learned). I've learned that all things that upset & bother me are just a mirror of what's going on in me. I always knew that what was going on with us was about me -- I just wasn't sure why it was about me -- So I just blamed you. I'm the one who was controlling. I wanted you to be faithful and be a perfect father. I was not accepting to who you are. Because I didn't like myself anymore. I'm not sure exactly what went on with me these last few years. I know New Year's Eve started it. I sank into a depression that I couldn't control. I also agree with you now -- that I went through some sort of mid life crisis -- "that 30's thing," you called it, my own self esteem . . . ect. I know it was a combination of all of these things. But mostly, due to all of these things, I know I gave up. I gave up treating you like I loved you. We started taking each other for granted -- and I didn't know how to put it all back together. I never stopped loving you -- I stopped liking myself and lost total confidence in any relationship with you.

I really needed this time in my life -- It's allowed me to get to know and like myself (again). It's given me a chance to go from a non-person, (the past 3 years) to a whole person.

There's so much I want to say to you. It's very hard to express myself in this letter. I wish we could be taking a walk around the block like we used to. It would be so much easier to speak to you face to face.

I want to put our family back together! I want our kids to grow up with their parents. I thought I'd be happy raising Sydney & Justin by myself -- since we didn't see too much of you anyway. But, now, I [missing text].

I want to be with you! I want to love you and cherish you, and make you smile. I want to wake up with you in the mornings and hold you at night. I want to hug and kiss you everyday. I want us to be the way we used to be. There was no couple like us. I don't know what I went through . . . . I didn't believe you loved me anymore -- and I couldn't handle it. But for the past month I've been looking at our wedding tape and our family movies -- and I can see that we truly loved each other. A love I've never seen in any of our friends. Please look at the 2 tapes I'm sending over with this letter. Watch them along & with your phone turned off -- they're really fun to watch.

O.J., I want to come home -- I want us all to be together again -- We can move wherever you want -- we can stay here -- I just never want to leave your side again.

I've almost come home 20 times since I left -- but I was never totally sure about us until now. I know I love *you and know I'm in love with you and know I want to [missing text] and be with you forever.*

Please watch the tapes -- I know you have major anger against me -- but you owe it to your kids and to us. I had that same anger . . . I'd never let this happen to us again. Without this year, without this growth, I don't think we'd have had a chance together -- We let it die. And through death . . . something new always grows. I agree with what you said 6 or 8 months ago. The next time around will be the best. I totally feel that now. We want to come home -- we'd be there tomorrow if you'd let us. I'm not embarrassed about anything -- I don't give a hoot what anybody thinks. I only know I love you and our kids would be the happiest kids in the world.

If you're totally happy with your life now -- I'll understand -- especially if you're truly in love and know that's going to work. Then, I can't mess with that. If I don't hear from you soon -- then I'll assume that's the case and I'll never bother you or ask you to have [missing text] way to find out -- I had to ask.

O.J. You'll be my one and only "true love." I'm sorry for the pain I've caused you and I'm sorry we let it die. Please let us be a family again, and let me love you -- better than I ever have before.

I'll love you forever and always . . .

Me

A drawing of a "smiley face" was included at the bottom of the letter.

APPENDIX C: O.J. Simpson's "Suicide" Letter

On June 17, 1994, as the deadline for O.J. Simpson's arranged surrender to police passed, defense attorney Robert Shapiro appeared before media cameras to announce that Simpson had been at the San Fernando Valley home of his friend and personal lawyer Robert Kardashian. Although Shapiro said he did not then know of Simpson's whereabouts, he told reporters that Simpson had wanted to be with his lawyer to dictate a new provision to his will. When that had been done, Shapiro said, Simpson wrote three letters. One was to his children, another to his mother, and a third (addressed to "whom it may concern"), was for the public. Kardashian then read Simpson's "public letter" to reporters — who quickly dubbed it a "suicide note" (others called it a "goodbye letter"). The text of that letter, including misspellings and grammatical mistakes, is reproduced below:

To whom it may concern,

First, everyone understand, I had nothing to do with Nicole's murder. I love her. Always have and always will. If we had a problem, it's because I love her so much. Recently, we came to the understanding that for now we were not right for each other. At least for now. Despite our love, we were different and that's why we mutually agreed to go our seperate ways. It was tough splitting for a second time, but we both knew it was for the best. Inside, I had no doubt that in the future we would be close friends or more. Unlike what has been written in the press, Nicole and I had a great relationship for most of our lives together. Like all longterm relationships, we had a few ups and downs. I took the heat New Year's 1989 because that's what I was supposed to do. I did not plead 'no contest' for any other reason than to protect our privacy and was advised it would end the press hype. I don't want to belabor knocking the press but I can't believe what is being said. Most of it is totally made up.

I know you have a job to do, but as a last wish, please, please, please leave my children in peace. Their lives will be tough enough. I want to send my love and thanks to all my friends. I'm sorry I can't name everyone of you. Especially A.C. man, thanks for being in my life. The support and friendship I received from so many: Wayne Hughes, Lewis Marks, Frank Olson, Mark Packer, Bender, Bobby Kardashian. I wish we had spent more time together in recent years. My golfing buddies: Hoss, Allen Austin, Mike Craig, Bender, Wyler, Sandy, Jay, Donnie. Thanks for the fun. All my teammates over the years: Reggie - you were the soul of my professional career. Ahmad, I never stopped being proud of you. Marcus, you got a great lady in Katherine. Don't mess it up. Bobby Chandler, thanks for always being there. Skip and Kathy, I love you guys. Without you I never would have made it through this far. Margarite, thanks for the early years. We had som fun. Paula, what can I say? You're special. I'm sorry we're not going to have our chance. God brought you to me, I now see. As I leave, you'll be in my thoughts. I think of my life and feel I've done most of the right things, so why do I end up like this? I can't go on. No matter what the outcome, people will look and point. I can't take that. I can't subject my children to that.

This way they can move on and go on with their lives. Please, if I've done anything worthwhile in my life, let my kids live in peace from you, the press. I've had a good life. I'm proud of how I've lived. My mama taught me to do unto others. I treated people the way I wanted to be treated. I've always tried to be up and helpful, so why is this happening? I'm sorry for the Goldman family. I know how much it hurts.

    Nicole and I had a good life together. All this press talk about a rocky relationship was no more than what every longterm relationship experiences. All her friends will confirm that I have been totally loving and understanding of what she has been going through. At times I have felt like a battered husband or boyfriend, but I loved her. Make that clear to everyone. And I would take whatever it took to make it work.

    Don't feel sorry for me. I've had a great life. Great friends. Please think of the real OJ and not this lost person. Thanks for making my life special. I hope I helped yours.

Peace and love,

OJ

Although the letter was widely published, it was never read in open court, nor shared with the jury.

APPENDIX D: The Text Of Nicole's 911 Call On January 1, 1992

Reproduced below are transcripts of two 911 calls Nicole Brown Simpson made to police on Oct. 25, 1993, from her townhome on Gretna Green Way. The first call began at 21:43:42 and lasted one minute and four seconds. A few minutes later Nicole called back. The second call lasted 13 minutes and 34 seconds. Police released transcripts of the calls to the press on June 22, 1994.

Nicole: Can you send someone to my house?

Dispatcher: What's the problem there?

Nicole: My ex-husband or my husband has just broken into my house and he's ranting and raving. Now he's just walked out in the front yard.

Dispatcher: Has he been drinking or anything?

Nicole: No. But he's crazy.

Dispatcher: Is he a black, white, or Hispanic?

Nicole: Black.

Dispatcher: What's he wearing?

Nicole: Black pants and a golf shirt

Dispatcher: What color shirt?

Nicole: I think it's black and white.

Dispatcher: And you said he hasn't been drinking?

Nicole: No.

Dispatcher: Did he hit you?

Nicole: No.

Dispatcher: Do you have a restraining order against him?

Nicole: No.

Dispatcher: What's your name?

Nicole: Nicole Simpson.

Dispatcher: And your address?

Nicole: 325 Gretna Green Way.

Dispatcher: Is that a house or an apartment?

Nicole: It's a house.

Dispatcher: Okay, we'll send the police out.

Nicole: Thank you.

Dispatcher: Uh-huh.

The dispatcher sends out a domestic violence call for any car patrolling the area to respond to Nicole Brown Simpson's address at Gretna Green. At 21:53:58, Nicole Simpson called back. Here is how Nicole's second conversation with the dispatcher went:

Nicole: Could you get somebody over here now, to ... Gretna Green. He's back. Please?

Dispatcher: What does he look like?

Nicole: He's O.J. Simpson. I think you know his record. Could you just send somebody over here?

Dispatcher: What is he doing there?

Nicole: He just drove up again. (She begins to cry) Could you just send somebody over?

Dispatcher: Wait a minute. What kind of car is he in?

Nicole: He's in a white Bronco, but first of all he broke the back door down to get in.

Dispatcher: Wait a minute. What's your name?

Nicole: Nicole Simpson.

Dispatcher: OK, is he the sports caster or whatever?

Nicole: Yeah. Thank you.

Dispatcher: Wait a minute, we're sending police. What is he doing? Is he threatening you?

Nicole: He's f___ing going nuts. (sobs)

Dispatcher: Has he threatened you in any way or is he just harassing you?

Nicole: (Sighs) You're going to hear him in a minute. He's about to come in again.

Dispatcher: OK, just stay on the line...

Nicole: I don't want to stay on the line. He's going to beat the s--- out of me.

Dispatcher: Wait a minute, just stay on the line so we can know what's going on until the police get there, OK? OK, Nicole?

Nicole: Uh-huh.

Dispatcher: Just a moment. Does he have any weapons?

Nicole: I don't know (exasperated). He went home and he came back. The kids are up there sleeping and I don't want anything to happen.

Dispatcher: OK, just a moment. Is he on drugs or anything?

Nicole: No.

Dispatcher: Just stay on the line. Just in case he comes in I need to hear what's going on, all right?

Nicole: Can you hear him outside?

Dispatcher: Is he yelling?

Nicole: Yep.

Dispatcher: OK. Has he been drinking?

Nicole: No.

Dispatcher: OK. (speaking over radio to police units) ... All units: additional on domestic violence, 325 South Gretna Green Way, the suspect has returned in a white Bronco. Monitor comments. Incident 48221.

Dispatcher: OK, Nicole?

Nicole: Uh-huh.

Dispatcher: Is he outdoors?

Nicole: Uh-huh, he's in the back yard.

Dispatcher: He's in the back yard?

Nicole: Screaming at my roommate about me and at me here.

Dispatcher: OK. What is he saying?

Nicole: Oh, something about some guy I know and hookers and Keith and I started this s--- before and ...

Dispatcher: Um-hum.

Nicole: And it's all my fault and "Now what am I going to do." "Get the police in this" and the whole thing. It's all my fault, I started this before. (sigh) brother. (inaudible)

Dispatcher: OK, has he hit you today or...?

Nicole: No.

Dispatcher: OK, you don't need any paramedics or anything.

Nicole: Uh-uh

Dispatcher: OK, you just want him to leave?

Nicole: My door. He broke the whole back door in.

Dispatcher: And then he left and he came back?

Nicole: Then he came and he practically knocked my upstairs door down but he pounded it and he screamed and hollered and I tried to get him out of the bedroom because the kids are sleeping in there.

Dispatcher: Um-hum. OK.

Nicole: And then he wanted somebody's phone number and I gave him my phone book or I put my phone book down to write down the phone number that he wanted and then he took my phone book with all my stuff in it.

Dispatcher: OK. So basically you guys have just been arguing?

O.J.: O.J. works his ass off for this family. For Keith. A drug addict whose f__ing girlfriend is a Heidi Fleiss girl. For Keith. (inaudible)

Dispatcher: Is he inside right now.

Nicole: Yeah.

Dispatcher: OK, just a moment.

O.J.: Do you understand me? (inaudible) Keith is a nothing. A skunk, and he still calls me. (inaudible). So I told him, "Look, you don't want that s__." (inaudible)

Dispatcher: Is he talking to you?

Nicole: Yeah.

Dispatcher: Are you locked in a room or something?

Nicole: No. He can some right in. I'm not going where the kids are because the kids (voice trails off).

Dispatcher: Do you think he's going to hit you?

Nicole: I don't know.

Dispatcher: Stay on the line. Don't hang it up, OK?

Nicole: OK.

(inaudible)

Dispatcher: What is he saying?
Nicole: What?
Dispatcher: What is he saying?
Nicole: (Sighs) What else?
O.J.: ...(inaudible)...you like a ___damn queen bee. I asked you
  tonight...(inaudible)...I come in this f___ing house
  tonight...(inaudible).

(Sound of police radio traffic)

Nicole: O.J. O.J. The kids are sleeping.
O.J.: You didn't give a s___ about the ___damn kids when you were
  s___ing his d___ in the living room. They were here. Did you care
  about the kids then? Oh, it's different now. I'm talking, and you're
  doing fine. You go and shake your head. You're doing fine, Nicole.
Dispatcher: He's still yelling at you?
O.J.: (inaudible)
Nicole: (sobbing into telephone)
Dispatcher: Just stay on the line, OK?

(More yelling)

Dispatcher: Is he upset with something that you did?
Nicole: (Sobs) A long time ago. It always comes back.

(More yelling)

Dispatcher: Is your roommate talking to him?
Nicole: No, who can talk? Listen to him.
Dispatcher: I know. Does he have any weapons with him right now?
Nicole: No, uh-uh
Dispatcher: OK. Where is he standing?
Nicole: In the back doorway, in the house.
Dispatcher: OK.
O.J.: ... I don't give a s___ anymore.... That wife of his, she took so much
  for this mother_____ (inaudible)
Nicole: Would you just please, O.J., O.J., O.J., O.J., could you please
  (inaudible) Please leave.
O.J.: I'm leaving with my two f___ing fists is when I'm leaving. You ain't
  got to worry about me any more.
Nicole: Please leave. O.J. Please, the kids, the kids (inaudible) please.

Dispatcher: Is he leaving?
Nicole: No.
Dispatcher: Does he know you're on the phone with police?
Nicole: No.
Dispatcher: OK. Where are the kids at right now?
Nicole: Up in my room.
Dispatcher: Can they hear him yelling?
Nicole: I don't know. The room's the only one that's quiet.
Dispatcher: Is there someone up there with the kids?
Nicole: No.

(Yelling continues in the background.)

Dispatcher: What is he saying now? Nicole? You still on the line?
Nicole: Yeah.
Dispatcher: You think he's still going to hit you?
O.J.: Keith.
Nicole: I don't know. He's going to leave. He just said that. He just said he ain't leaving.
O.J.: You're not leaving when I'm gone. Hey! I have to read this bull____ all week in the National Enquirer. Her words exactly. What, who got that, who? (inaudible)
Dispatcher: Are you the only one in there with him?
Nicole: Right now, yeah.
Dispatcher: And he's talking to you?
Nicole: Yeah, and he's also talking to my, the guy who lives out back is just standing there. He just came home.
Dispatcher: Is he arguing with him, too?
Nicole: No. Absolutely not.
Dispatcher: Oh, OK.
Nicole: Nobody's arguing.
Dispatcher: Yeah. Has this happened before or no?
Nicole: Many times.
Dispatcher: OK. The police should be on the way it just seems like a long time because it's kind of busy in that division right now. (Yelling continues)
Dispatcher, to police: Regarding Gretna Green Way, the suspect is still there and yelling very loudly.
Police Officer on radio: (inaudible)
Dispatcher: Is he still arguing?

(Knock at the door.)

Dispatcher: Was someone knocking on your door?
Nicole: It was him.

Dispatcher: He was knocking on your door?

Nicole: There's a locked bedroom and he's wondering why.

Dispatcher: Oh. He's knocking on the locked door?

Nicole: Yeah. You know what, O.J.? That window above you is also open. Could you just go, please? Can I get off the phone?

Dispatcher: You want, you feel safe hanging up?

Nicole: Well, you're right

Dispatcher: You want to wait until the police get there?

Nicole: Yeah.

Dispatcher: Nicole?

Nicole: Um-hmm.

Dispatcher: Is he still arguing with you?

Nicole: Um-hum.

Dispatcher: He's moved a little?

Nicole: But I'm just ignoring him.

Dispatcher: Okay. But he doesn't know you're...

Nicole: It works best.

Dispatcher: Okay. Are the kids are still asleep?

Nicole: Yes. They're like rocks.

Dispatcher: What part of the house is he in right now?

Nicole: Downstairs.

Dispatcher: Downstairs?

Nicole: Yes.

Dispatcher: And you're upstairs?

Nicole: No, I'm downstairs in the kitchen.

O.J.: (inaudible) I tried my ___damn best. I ain't putting up with no f___ing...(inaudible)

Dispatcher: Do you see the police, Nicole?

Nicole: No, but I will go out there right now.

Dispatcher: OK, you want to go out there?

Nicole: Yeah.

Dispatcher: OK.

Nicole: I'm going to hang up.

Dispatcher: OK.

APPENDIX E: Official Autopsy Report on Nicole Brown Simpson

AUTOPSY REPORT   94-05136

I performed an autopsy on the body of BROWN-SIMPSON, NICOLE at the DEPARTMENT OF CORONER Los Angeles, California on June 14, 1994 @ 0730 HOURS.

From the anatomic findings and pertinent history, I ascribe the death to: MULTIPLE SHARP FORCE INJURIES.

Due To Or As a Consequence of:

_____

Anatomical Summary:

I. Incised wound of neck:

    A. Transection of left and right common carotid arteries.

    B. Incisions, left and right internal jugular veins

    C. Transection of thyrohyoid membrane, epiglottis, and hypopharynx.

    D. Incision into cervical spine, C3.

II. Multiple stab wound of neck and scalp (total of seven).

III. Multiple injuries of hands, including incised wound, ring finger of right hand (defense wound).

IV. Scalp bruise, right parietal.

NOTES AND PROCEDURES

1. The body is described in the Standard Anatomical Position. Reference is to this position only.

2. Where necessary, injuries are numbered for reference. This is arbitrary and does not correspond to any order in which they may have been incurred. All the injuries are antemortem, unless otherwise specified.

3. The term "anatomic" is used as a specification to indicate correspondence with the description as set forth in the textbooks of Gross Anatomy. It denotes freedom from significant, visible or morbid alteration.

EXTERNAL EXAMINATION:

The body is that of a well-developed, well-nourished Caucasian female stated to be 35 years old. The body weighs 129 pounds and measures 65 inches from crown to sole. The hair on the scalp is brown. The irides are brown with the pupils fixed and dilated. The sclerae and conjunctive are unremarkable, without evidence of petechial hemorrhages on either. Both upper and lower teeth are natural, without evidence of injury to the cheeks, lips or gums.

There are no tattoos, deformities or amputations. Two linear surgical scars are found beneath each breast, transversely oriented and measuring 2 inches in length.

Rigor mortis is fixed at the time of autopsy examination (please see form 1).

The body appears to the examiner as stated above. Identification is by toe-tag and the autopsy is not material to identification. The body is not embalmed.

The head is normocephalic and there is external evidence of antemortem injury to be described below. Otherwise, the external auditory canals, eyes, nose and mouth are not remarkable. The neck shows sharp force injury to be described below, and the larynx is visible through the gaping wound.

No recent traumatic injuries are noted on the chest or abdomen; tan lines are seen on the lower abdomen (bathing suit). The genitalia are that of adult female with no gross evidence of injuries. Examination of the posterior surface at the trunk shows some excoriations compatible with postmortem injuries on the upper back, right side, on the medial aspect of the right scapula and on the lateral aspect of the right scapula (compatible with ant to insect bites). An abrasion above the left scapula measures 3/4 x 1/2 inch and is red-brown in color and appears antemortem. Otherwise, the lower back and remainder of the posterior aspect of the body shows no evidence of recent injuries.

Refer to available photographs and diagrams and the specific documentation of the autopsy protocol.

CLOTHING:

The decedent was wearing a short black dress, blood stained. Also, she was wearing a pair of black panties. To the unaided eye examination there was no evidence of cut or tear.

EVIDENCE OF INJURY:

DESCRIPTION OF INCISED WOUND OF NECK:

The incised wound of the neck is gaping and exposes the larynx and cervical vertebral column. It measures 5 1/2 x 2 1/2 inches in length and is found at the level of the superior border of the larynx.

After approximation of the edges, it is seen to be diagonally oriented on the right side and transversely oriented from the midline to the left side. On the right side it is upwardly angulated toward the right earlobe and extends for 4 inches from the midline. On the left side it is transversely oriented and extends 2 1/2 inches to the anterior border of the left sternocleidomastoid muscle. The edges of the wound are smooth, with subcutaneous and intramuscular hemorrhage, fresh, dark red purple, is evident.

On the right side the upwardly angulated wound passes through the skin, the subcutaneous tissue, the platysma, passing under the ramus of the right mandible and upward as it passes through the strap muscles on the right, towards the digastric muscle on the right, and through the thyrohyoid membrane and ligament. Further dissection discloses that it passes posteriorly and transects the distal one-third of the epiglottis, the hypo-pharynx, and passes into the body of the 3rd cervical vertebra where a transversely oriented 3/4 inch incised wound is seen in the bone, extending it for a depth of 1/4 inch into the bone. The spinal canal and cord are not entered.

On the right side superiorly the wound passes towards the insertion of the sternocleidomastoid muscle, and then becomes more superficial and tapers as it terminates in the skin below the right earlobe.

On the left side the wound is transversely oriented and extends for 2 1/2 inches where the wound path intersects the stab wounds on the left side of the neck to be described below.

Dissection discloses that the right common carotid artery is transected with hemorrhage in the surrounding carotid sheath and there is a 1/4 incised wound or nick in the right internal jugular vein with surrounding soft tissue hemorrhage.

On the left side the left common carotid artery is transected with hemorrhage in the surrounding carotid sheath and the left internal jugular vein is subtotally transected with only a thin strand of tissue remaining posteriorly with surrounding soft tissue hemorrhage. The injuries on the left side of the neck intersect and the pathways of the stab wounds on the left side to be described below.

There is fresh hemorrhage and bruising noted along the entire incised wound path.

Depth of penetration is not given because the neck can be either flexed or extended, and the length of the wound is greater than the depth.

Opinion: This is a fatal incised wound or sharp force injury, associated with transection of the left and right carotid arteries and incisions of the left and right internal jugular veins with exsanguinating hemorrhage.

DESCRIPTION OF MULTIPLE STAB WOUNDS

There are four stab wounds on the left side of the neck over the left sternocledomastoid muscle; they extend to 3 inches below the external auditory canal.

1. This stab wound overlaps that of the incised wound of the neck described above. The wound measures 5/8 inch in length, is vertically oriented, and has a squared-off end inferiorly approximately 1/32 inch and a pointed end superiorly. The minimal depth of the penetration, from left to right, is 1 1/2 to 2 inches where it intersects the incised wound. Penetration is through the skin, subcutaneous tissue and muscle, and injury to the internal jugular vein or common carotid artery cannot be excluded.

2. Stab wound of left side of neck: This is a 1/8 inch superficial slit-like incision into the skin and dermis; no squared-off or dull end is evident.

Opinion: This is a superficial slit-like wound of the skin, non-fatal.

3. Stab wound on left side of neck: This is a diagonally oriented stab wound measuring 1/2 inch in length; there is a pointed end on the posterior aspect and a squared-off end anterior less than 1/32 inch in length. The edges are smooth, and dissection disposes a depth of penetration for 1 1/2 to 2 inches where the stab wound intersects that of the incised wound of the neck; the stab wounds are approximately 1 inch from the left lateral termination of the incised wound. Fresh hemorrhage is noted along the wound path which goes through the skin, subcutaneous tissue and muscle.

Opinion: This stab wound cannot be distinguished from injuries caused by the incised wound of the neck and may have injured the left common carotid artery and/or the left internal jugular vein.

4. Stab wound of the left side of neck: This is a diagonally oriented stab wound measuring 7/8 inch in length; on the posterior aspect there is a pointed end and on the anterior aspect a squared-off or dull end approximately 1/32 inch in width; otherwise the edges are smooth. Subsequent dissection discloses the wound path through the skin, subcutaneous tissue and muscle where it intersects the incised wound of the neck. Depth of penetration is 1 1/2 inches.

Opinion: This stab wound may have injured the left common carotid artery and/or the left internal jugular vein as described above.

5. Stab wound of scalp, left parietal: This diagonally oriented stab wound is located on the left parietal scalp, which is shaved postmortem for visualization. It measures 1/2 inch in length and no definite squared-off or dull end is evident, both ends appearing to be rounded. Depth of penetration is through the scalp, to the galea, approximately 3/8 - 1/2 inch. There is deep scalp hemorrhage and a subgaleal bruise, measuring 1 1/2 x 1 1/2 inches; there is no cutting wound or injury to the skull and there is no penetration into the cranium.

Opinion: This is a superficial stab wound or cutting wound of the scalp, non-fatal.

6. Stab wound or cutting wound of scalp: This is transversely oriented and is found in the right posterior parietal-occipital region. The transversely oriented wound measures 1 1/2 inches in length and has a pointed end to the left and a fork or split into the right. Depth of penetration is 3/8 – 1 1/2 inches with fresh deep scalp bruising.

Opinion: This is a non-fatal, stabbing or cutting wound of the scalp.

7. Stab wound or cutting wound of the scalp, right parietal-occipital: This is vertically oriented, measures 3/16 inch in length and involves the skin only. No squared-off or dull end is evident, both ends or aspects being pointed or tapered. There is a small amount of deep scalp hemorrhage or bruising, no subgaleal hemorrhage.

Opinion: This is a non-fatal superficial stabbing or cutting wound of the scalp.

8. Blunt force injury to head: On the right side of the scalp, 4 inches above the right external auditory canal there is a scalp bruise; this is revealed after postmortem shaving of the scalp. It measures 1 x 1 inches and is red-violet or purple in color. The skin is smooth, non-abraded or lacerated. Subsequent autopsy discloses fresh deep scalp hemorrhage and fresh dark red-purple subgaleal hemorrhage or bruising measuring 2 x 1 1/4 inches. Inferiorly the bruise extends to the superficial right temporal muscle. There is no associated skull fracture.

INJURIES TO HANDS:

Right hand: There is a 5/8 incised wound of the volar surface of the right index finger at the distal knuckle. This 5/8 inch incised wound is tangentially oriented or cut through the skin and dermis with the avulsed skin inferiorly indicating that the direction is from distal to proximal.

Further examination discloses that there is a split or forked end on the ulnar aspect and pointed end on the radial aspect. There is a small amount of dermal hemorrhage.

On the dorsal surface of the right hand, at the base of the ring finger, there is a 1/16 inch punctate abrasion.

Left hand: On the dorsal surface of the left hand, there is a punctate abrasion, red-brown in color at the base of the ring finger.

There is a 1/2 inch superficial incised skin cut, 1/2 inch in length, diagonally oriented, on the top of the left hand, midportion.

INTERNAL EXAMINATION

The body is opened with the usual Y-shaped thoracoabdominal incision revealing the abdominal wall adipose tissue to measure 1/4 – 3/8 inch in thickness. The anterior abdominal wall has its normal muscular components and there is no evidence of abdominal wall injury. Exposure of the body cavities shows the contained organs in their usual anatomic locations with their usual anatomic relationships. No free fluid or blood is found within the pleural, pericardial, or the peritoneal cavities. The serosal surfaces are smooth, thin, and glistening and there are no intra-abdominal adhesions.

INTERNAL EVIDENCE OF INJURIES:

There are no internal traumatic injuries involving the thorax or thoracic viscera, abdomen or abdominal viscera.

SYSTEMIC AND ORGAN REVIEW:

Autopsy findings, or the lack of them, are considered apart from those already stated. The following observations pertain to findings other than the injuries and changes that are described above.

MUSCULOSKELETAL SYSTEM—SUBCUTANEOUS TISSUE—SKIN

Examination of the breasts reveals bilateral silastic implants that are intact. Otherwise, no other significant changes are noted in the breasts. The remainder of the musculoskeletal system and subcutaneous tissue are anatomic.

HEAD—CENTRAL NERVOUS SYSTEM

The external injuries to the scalp have been described. A small abrasion, red-brown in color, measuring 3/8 x 1/4 inch and appearing to be antemortem is found lateral-posterior to the right eyebrow and this is a non-patterned superficial abrasion.

The hemorrhage beneath the scalp, due to the sharp force injuries have been described. There is no hemorrhage deep into the temporal muscles.

There are no tears of the dura mater and no recent epidural, subdural, or subarachnoid hemorrhage.

The dura is stripped to reveal no fractures of the bones of the calvarium or base of the skull.

The pituitary gland is normally situated in the sella turcica and is not enlarged.

The cranial nerves are enumerated and they are intact, symmetrical and anatomic in size, location and course.

The component vessels of the circle of Willis are identified. They are anatomic in size, course, configuration and distribution. The blood vessels are intact, free of aneurysms or other anomaly, and non-occluded and show no significant atherosclerosis.

Examination of the non-formalin fixed, fresh brain shows: The cerebral hemispheres, cerebellum, brainstem, pons and medulla to show their normal anatomical structures. The cerebellar, the pontine and medullary surfaces present no lesions. Multiple sections reveal an anatomic appearing cortex, white matter, ventricular system and basal ganglia. There is no evidence of hemorrhage, cyst or neoplasm involving the brain substance.

The spinal chord, in the vicinity of the cervical incised wound is dissected; there is no evidence or intraspinal hemorrhage and no evidence of sharp force injury to the spinal chord.

ORGANS OF SPECIAL SENSES:

Not dissected.

RESPIRATORY SYSTEM—THROAT STRUCTURES:

The oral cavity, viewed from below, is anatomic. The teeth are examined and there is no evidence of injury and there is no evidence of injury to the cheeks, lips, gums, or tongue. No blood is present.

Injuries to the upper airway including the incised wound of the hypopharynx and epiglottis have been described. Otherwise, the mucosa of the larynx, piriform sinuses, trachea and major bronchi are anatomic. No mucosal lesions are evident and no blood is present.
The hyoid bone and thyroid cartilages are intact, inasmuch as the incised wound passes through the thyrohyoid membrane and ligament and both greater

cornuas of the thyroid cartilage are intact. Hemorrhage is present in the tissue adjacent to the neck organs due to the incised would as described above. There is no hemorrhage into the substance of the thyroid gland which anatomic in size and location. The parathyroid glands are not identified.

Lungs: Right lung weighs 330 grams; left lung 300 grams. The external appearance and that of the sectioned surface of the lungs show minimal congestion and otherwise no injuries or lesions. No foreign material, infarction, or neoplasm is encountered. The pulmonary arteries are free of thromboemboli.

CARDIOVASCULAR SYSTEM:

The heart weighs 280 grams, and is anatomic in size and configuration. The chambers, valves and myocardium are anatomic, and a minimal amount of liquid blood is found within the cardiac chambers. No focal endocardial, valvular, or myocardial lesions are seen. There are no congenital anomalies.

Multiple transverse sections of the left and right coronary arteries reveal them to be thin-walled and patent throughout with no significant atherosclerosis. The aorta and major branches are anatomic and show only minimal lipid streaking of the intima. The portal and caval veins and the major branches are anatomic.

Note: The injuries of the common carotid arteries and internal jugular veins have been described above.

GASTROINTESTINAL SYSTEM:

The mucosa and wall of the esophagus are intact and gray-pink and no lesions or injuries are evident.

The gastric mucosa is intact and pink. No mucosal lesions are evident and there are no residuals of medication or blood.

Examination of the gastric contents reveals approximately 500 ml. of chewed semisolid food in the stomach. Recognizable food particles are identified as follows: pieces of pasta appearing to be rigatoni, fragments of apparent spinach leaves; and the remainder, chewed, partially digested non-recognizable food material.

The mucosa of the duodenum, jejunum, ileum, colon and rectum are intact. The lumen is patent. No mucosal lesions are evident, and no blood is present. The fecal content is usual in appearance.

HEPATOBILIARY SYSTEM—PANCREAS:

The liver weighs 1370 grams. The capsular surface is intact. The subcapsular and the cut surface of the liver are uniformly brown-red in color, and free of nodularity and are usual in appearance. The biliary duct system, including the gallbladder, are free of anomaly and no lesions are evident. The mucosa is intact and bile stained. The lumen are patent and no calculi are present.

The pancreas is anatomic both externally and on cut surface.

HEMOLYMPHATIC SYSTEM—ADRENAL GLAND:

The spleen weighs 90 grams and has an intact capsule. Cut surface shows the usual dark red-purple parenchyma which is firm and no lesions are evident.

The blood, the bone marrow and the usually-named aggregates of lymph nodes do not appear to be significantly altered.

The thymus gland is not identifiable.

The adrenal glands are their usual size and location and cut surface presents no lesions.

URINARY SYSTEM:

Each kidney weighs 100 grams. The kidneys are anatomic in size, location and configuration. The capsules are stripped to show a pale brown surface. On section the cut surface shows no abnormalities of the cortex and medulla.

The calyces, pelves, ureters and urinary bladder are unaltered in appearance. The mucosa is gray-pink, no calculi are present and no blood is present.

The urinary bladder contains a few ml. of clear urine.

GENITAL SYSTEM (female):

The uterus, tubes, and adnexa are anatomic. Cut surface of the uterus shows no lesions and a thin light brown endometrium. The vagina has its normal mucosal surface and no lesions or injuries are evident.

HISTOLOGY:

Representative portions of the various organs, including the larynx and hyoid, are preserved in 10% formaldehyde and placed in a single storage container.

TOXICOLOGY:

A sample of cardiac chamber blood and urine are submitted for toxicologic analysis.

SEROLOGY:

A sample of intracardiac blood is submitted in an EDTA tube,

RADIOLOGY:

None.

PHOTOGRAPHY:

In addition to the routine identification photographs, pertinent photographs are taken of the external injury.

WITNESSES:

Detective Vannatter and Lange, Los Angeles Police Department, Robbery-Homicide, were present during the autopsy.

DIAGRAMS USED:

Forms 16, 20, 20D, 20F, 20G, 20H, 22, 23, 24 and 29 were utilized during the performance of the autopsy.

OPINION:

Death is attributed to multiple sharp force injuries, including a deep incised wound of the neck and multiple stab wounds of the neck.

The sharp force injuries led to transection of the left and right common carotid arteries, and incisions of the left and right internal jugular vein causing fatal exsanguinating hemorrhage. The sharp force injury to the scalp were superficial, non-fatal.

Injuries present on the hands, including the incised wound of the right hand are compatible so-called defense wounds.

Routine toxicologic studies were ordered.

(Signed) Irwin L. Golden M.D.
IRWIN L. GOLDEN
DEPUTY MEDICAL EXAMINER

June 16, 1994
Date

APPENDIX F: Official Autopsy Report on Ronald Goldman

AUTOPSY REPORT   94-05135

I performed an autopsy on the body of GOLDMAN, RONALD at the
DEPARTMENT OF CORONER Los Angeles, California on June 14, 1994
@ 1030 HOURS

From the anatomic findings and pertinent history, I ascribe the death to:
MULTIPLE SHARP FORCE INJURIES.

Due To Or As a Consequence of:

_____

Anatomical Summary:

1. Sharp force wound of neck, left side, with transection of left internal jugular
vein.

2. Multiple stab wounds of chest, abdomen, and left thigh: Penetrating stab
wounds of chest and abdomen with right hemothorax and hemoperitoneum.

3. Multiple incised wounds of scalp, face, neck, chest and left hand (defense
wound).

4. Multiple abrasions upper extremities and hands (defense wounds).

NOTES AND PROCEDURES:

1. The body is described in the Standard Anatomical Position. Reference is to
this position only.

2. Where necessary, injuries are numbered for reference. This is arbitrary and
does not correspond to any order in which they may have been incurred. All the
injuries are antemortem, unless otherwise specified.

3. The term "anatomic" is used as a specification to indicate correspondence
with the description as set forth in the textbooks of Gross Anatomy. It denotes
freedom from significant, visible or morbid alteration.

EXTERNAL EXAMINATION:

The body is that of a well developed, well nourished Caucasian male stated to
be 25 years old. The body weighs 171 pounds, measuring 69 inches from crown

to sole. The hair on the scalp is brown and straight. The irides appear hazel with the pupils fixed and dilated. The sclerae and conjunctive are unremarkable, with no evidence of petechial hemorrhages on either. Both upper and lower teeth are natural, and there are no injuries of the gums, cheeks, or lips.

There is a picture-type tattoo on the lateral aspect of the left upper arm. There are no deformities, old surgical scars or amputations.

Rigor mortis is fixed (see Form 1 of autopsy report).

The body appears to the Examiner as stated above. Identification is by toe tag and the autopsy is not material to identification. The body is not embalmed.

The head is normocephalic, and there is extensive evidence of external traumatic injury, to be described below. Otherwise, the eyes, nose and mouth are not remarkable. The neck shows sharp force injuries to be described below. The front of the chest and abdomen likewise show injuries to be described below. The genitalia are that of an adult male, with the penis circumcised, and no evidence of injury.

Examination of the posterior surface of the trunk reveals no antemortem traumatic injuries.

Refer to available photographs and diagrams and to the specific documentation of the autopsy protocol.

CLOTHING:

The clothes were examined both before and after removal from the body. The decedent was wearing a long-sleeved type of shirt/sweater; it was extensively bloodstained.

On the front, lower right side, there was a 1 1/2 inch long slit-like tear. Also on the lower right sleeve there was a 1 inch slit-like tear. On the back there was a 1/2 inch slit-like tear on the right lower side.

Decedent was wearing a pair of Levi jeans bloodstained. On the outside of the left hip region there was a 1 1/2 inch long slit-like tear. The decedent also was wearing 2 canvas type boots and 2 sweat socks.

EVIDENCE OF THERAPEUTIC INTERVENTION:

None.

EVIDENCE OF INJURY:

SHARP FORCE INJURIES OF NECK:

1. Sharp force injury of neck, left side, transecting left internal jugular vein. This sharp force injury is complex, and appears to be a combination of a stabbing and cutting wound. It begins on the left side of the neck, at the level of the midlarynx, over the left sternocleidomastoid muscle; it is gaping, measuring 3 inches in length with smooth edges. It tapers superiorly to 1 inch in length cut skin. Dissection discloses that the wound path is through the skin, the subcutaneous tissue, and the sternocleidomastoid muscle with hemorrhage along the wound path and transection of the left internal jugular vein, with dark red-purple hemorrhage in the adjacent subcutaneous tissue and fascia. The direction of the pathway is upward and slightly front to back for a distance of approximately 4 inches where it exits, post-auricular, in a 2 inch in length gaping stab/incised wound which has undulating or wavy borders, but not serrated. Intersecting the wound at right angle superior inferior is a 2 inch in length interrupted superficial, linear incised wound involving only the skin. Also, intervening between the 2 gaping stab-incised wounds is a horizontally oriented 3 1/2 inch in length interrupted superficial, linear incised wound of the skin only.

In addition, there is a 1/2 inch long, linear-triangular in size wound of the inferior portion of the left earlobe.

The direction of the sharp force injury is upward (rostral), and slightly front to back with no significant angulation or deviation. The total length of the wound path is approximately 4 inches. However, there is a 3/4 inch in length, linear, cutting or incised wound of the top or superior aspect of the pinna of the left ear; a straight metallic probe placed through the major sharp force injury shows that the injury of the superior part of the ear can be aligned with the straight metallic rod, suggesting that the 3 injuries are related; in this instance the total length of the wound path is approximately 6 inches. Also, in the left postauricular region, transversely oriented, extending from the auricular attachment laterally to the scalp is a 1 1/8 inch in length linear superficial incised skin wound.

Opinion: This sharp force injury of the neck is fatal, associated with transection of the left internal jugular vein.

2. Sharp force wound of the right side of neck. This is a complex injury, appearing to be a combination stabbing and cutting wound. The initial wound is present on the right side of the neck, over the sternocleidomastoid muscle, 3 inches directly below the right external auditory canal. It is diagonally oriented, and after approximation of the edges measures 5/8 inch in length; there is a pointed or tapered end inferiorly and a split or forked end superiorly approximately 1/16 inch in maximal width. Subsequent autopsy shows that the wound path is through the skin and subcutaneous tissue, without penetration of injury of a major artery or vein; the direction is front to back and upward for a

total wound path length of 2 inches and the wound exits on the right side of the back of the neck, posterior to the right sternocleidomastoid muscle where a 2 inch long gaping incised/stab wound is evident on the skin; both ends are tapered; superiorly there is a 1 inch long superficial incised wounds extension on the skin to the back of the head; inferiorly there is a 2 inch long incised superficial skin extension, extending inferiorly towards the back of the neck.

There is fresh hemorrhage and bruising along the wound path; the direction, as stated, is upward and slightly front to back.

Opinion: This is a nonfatal sharp force injury, with no injury or major artery or vein.

3. At the level of the superior border of the larynx there is a transversely oriented, superficial incised wound of the neck, extending from 3 inches to the left of the anterior midline; it is 3 inches in length and involves the skin only; a small amount of cutaneous hemorrhage is evident.

Opinion: This is a nonfatal superficial incised wound.

4. Immediately inferior and adjacent to incised wound #3 is a transversely oriented, superficial incised wound involving the skin and subcutaneous tissue; there is a small amount of dermal hemorrhage.

Opinion: This is a nonfatal superficial incised wound.

SHARP FORCE INJURIES OF FACE:

1. There is a stab wound, involving the right earlobe; it is vertically oriented, and after approximation of the edges measures 1 inch in length with forked or split ends superiorly and inferiorly approximately 1/16 inch in total width both superior and inferior. Subsequent dissection discloses that the wound path is from right to left, in the horizontal plane for approximately 1 1/4 inches; there is fresh hemorrhage along the wound path; the wound path terminates in the left temporal bone and does not penetrate the cranial cavity.

Opinion: This is a nonfatal stab wound.

2. There is a group of 5 superficial incised or cutting wounds on the right side of the face, involving the right cheek and the right side of the jaw. They are varied in orientation both diagonal and horizontal; the smallest is 1/4 inch in length; the largest 5/8 inch in length. They are superficial, involving the skin only, associated with a small amount of cutaneous hemorrhage.

3. On the back of the neck, right side, posterior to the ear and posterior border of the right sternocleidomastoid muscle there is vertically oriented superficial incised skin wound, measuring 3/4 inch in length.

4. There are numerous superficial incised wounds or cuts, varied in orientation, involving the skin of the right cheek, intersection and mingled with the various superficial incised wounds described above.
The longest is a 3 inch long diagonally oriented superficial incised wound extending from the right side of the forehead to the cheek; various other superficial wound vary from 1/2 to 1 inch.

5. On the right side of the cheek, adjacent to the ramus of the mandible, right, there is a 1-1/2 x 3/4 inch superficial nonpatterned red-brown abrasion with irregular border, extending superiorly towards the angle of the jaw where there are poorly defined and circumscribed abrasions adjacent to the superficial cuts or abrasions described above. It should be noted that the 5th superficial incised wound of the right side of the mandible which measures 5/8 inch in length is tapered on the posterior aspect and forked on the anterior aspect where it has a width of 1/32 inch.

6. On the left ear, there is a superficial incised wound measuring 1/4 inch, adjacent to the posterior border of the pinna. Just below this on the inferior pinna, extending to the earlobe, there is an interrupted superficial linear abrasion measuring 1 inch in length.

SHARP FORCE INJURIES OF SCALP:

1. The scalp is shaved postmortem for visualization. On the right posterior parietal region of the scalp there is a sharp force wound, diagonally oriented, and after approximation of the edges it measures 5/8 inch in length with a perpendicularly oriented skin cut at the midpoint.

Depth of penetration is approximately 1/4 to 3/8 inch into the scalp, with associated deep scalp hemorrhage and a subgaleal hemorrhage beneath the wound measuring 2 x 2 inches in transverse diameter. There is no underlying fracture of the skull or penetration of the cranium.

Opinion: This is a sharp force wound that may represent either a cutting wound of a superficial stab wound; nonfatal.

2. On the posterior parietal region, midline, to the left of the wound described above there is a 1/4 inch superficial incised wound or skin cut measuring 1/4 inch in length; both ends are pointed or tapered; extension is 1/4 inch into the scalp with a small amount of deep scalp hemorrhage but no subgaleal hemorrhage.

3. On the left posterior parietal region there is an injury that is an abrasion, 1/4 x 1/8 inch in maximal diameter and an ovoid in configuration; it is red-brown with a small amount of superficial skin bruising.

Opinion: This is a skin abrasion-bruise, noncharacteristic.

DESCRIPTION OF MULTIPLE STAB WOUNDS:

On the right side of the chest adjacent to the stab wound there are multiple, irregular, brown abrasions consistent with ant bites.

1. Stab wound of right side of chest.

The stab wound is located on the right side of the chest, 22 inches below the top of the head and 5 inches from the back of the body; it is vertically oriented and after approximation of the edges it measures 5/8 inch in length. Inferiorly there is a squared off or dull end approximately 1/32 in length; superiorly the wound is tapered.

Subsequent autopsy shows that the pathway is through the skin, the subcutaneous tissue, and through the right 7th rib at the approximately midaxillary line where the rib is totally incised. Thereafter, it enters the right pleural cavity which at the time of autopsy contains approximately 100-200 ml of predominantly liquid blood. The path is through the lateral base of the border of the right lower lobe as the path is through the pleura and the immediately subjacent pulmonary parenchyma which is hemorrhagic; the pleural wounds are approximately 1/2–3/4 inch in length; thereafter the pathway is from right to left and back to front and through the pleural cavity where the wound path terminates on the anterior rib cage where a 3/4 cutting wound is found on the posterior aspect of the right 4th rib anteriorly at the approximate midclavicular line; there is overlying bruising in the adjacent intercostal musculature. Estimated length of the total wound path is 4 inches and as stated the direction is right to left and back to front with no other angulation measurable.

Opinion: This is a fatal wound associated with perforation of the right lung and a hemothorax.

2. Stab wound of right side of chest.

This wound is located on the right side of the chest, 21 inches below the top of the head and 2 inches from the back of the body. After approximation of the edges it measures 1 1/2 inches in length and is diagonally oriented; the posterior aspect is dull or flat, measuring 1/32 inch and the anterior aspect is pointed or tapered.

Subsequent autopsy shows that the wound is through the skin, the subcutaneous tissue, and the intercostal musculature and it penetrates into the pleural cavity through the 8th right intercostal space without striking rib. Thereafter the pathway is similar to stab wound #1 as it passes obliquely through the pleura and subjacent hemorrhagic parenchyma at the base of the right lower lobe; 1/2 inch and 3/4 inch pleural cuts are evident both posteriorly and anteriorly. No other terminating point is evident.

There is fresh hemorrhage and bruising noted along the wound path as well as the hemothorax described above.

The direction is right to left with no other angulation or deviation determined because of absence of fixed reference points. Estimated minimum total depth of penetration is 2–3 inches.

Opinion: This is a fatal stab wound associated with perforation of the lung and hemothorax.

3. Stab wound of right flank.

This is a diagonally oriented wound, on the right flank, 29 inches below the top of the head and 3 1/2 inches to the back of the body. It measures 3/8 inch in length and involves the skin and subcutaneous tissue without penetrating the chest wall or abdominal wall. No square or dull edges are evident. Both ends are rounded or tapered.

Opinion: This is a superficial cutting wound, representing either a superficial stab wound or an incised wound.

4. Stab wound of left thigh.

This is a transversely oriented stab wound on the lateral left thigh, 33 inches above the left heel and 4 inches from the back of the thigh. After approximation of the edges it measures 2 1/8 inches in length and posteriorly there is a dull or flat end 1/32 inch and anteriorly a pointed or tapered end.

Subsequent autopsy shows that the wound path is through the skin, the subcutaneous tissue, and the muscle without striking bone. There is fresh hemorrhage along the wound path. The depth of penetration is 3 to 3 1/2 inches from left to right without angulation or deviation.

Opinion: This is a stab wound of the soft tissue and muscle of the left thigh, nonfatal.

5. Stab wound of left side of abdomen.

This is a transversely oriented stab wound on the left side of the abdomen, located 45 inches above the left heel. After approximation of the edges it measures 3/4 inch in length with the anterior end pointed or tapered and the posterior end forked or split.

Subsequent autopsy shows that the wound passes through the skin, the subcutaneous tissue, and through the retroperitoneal tissue which is hemorrhagic; the pathway is through the left ilio-psoas muscle associated with fresh hemorrhage and bruising. The path is from left to right and slightly back to front; the wound path terminates in the abdominal aorta approximately 1 1/4 inches proximal to the bifurcation. Two perforating 1/2 inch wounds are seen in the wall of the aorta with surrounding para-aortic hemorrhage. In addition to the retroperitoneal hemorrhage, including hemorrhage into the mesocolon, approximately 100 ml of liquid blood is found free within the peritoneal cavity.

In addition to the fresh bruising and hemorrhage along the wound path the entire length of the wound path is approximately 5 1/2 inches.

The direction is left to right, and a slightly back to front direction with no other angulation or deviation evident.

Opinion: This is a fatal stab wound associated with perforation of the abdominal aorta with retroperitoneal and intra-abdominal hemorrhage.

6. Stab wound of the right upper chest, lateral border of right clavicle.

This vertically oriented superficial stab wound or incised wound is located on the lateral border of the right clavicle, is vertically oriented, and measures 1/2 inch in length; involves the skin and subcutaneous tissue; inferiorly the wound is split or forked and superiorly it is tapered or pointed. It should be noted that all of the split or forked ends of the previously mentioned stab wounds overall measure approximately 1/16 to 1/8 inch in overall width. There is a small amount of fresh cutaneous hemorrhage.

No direction can be evident except for front to back, inasmuch as it is superficial.

Opinion: This is a nonfatal superficial stab wound or cutting wound.

SHARP FORCE INJURIES OF HANDS:

1. On the palmar surface of the right hand, at the base of the index finger, there is a cutting or incised wound, 3/4 inch in length and 1/2 inch deep involving the skin and subcutaneous tissue with hemorrhage in the margins. Both ends are rounded or tapered.

Opinion: This is compatible with a defense wound.

2. On the palmar surface of the right hand, just proximal to the web of the thumb, there is a triangular or Y-shaped cutting wound measuring 1/2 inch in length maximally and 1/4 inch deep with hemorrhage at the margins.

Opinion: This is compatible with a defense wound.

3. On the palmar surface of the left hand at the web of the thumb, there is a 3/4 inch in size or cutting wound involving the skin, and subcutaneous tissue; it is

approximately 1/4 inch deep with hemorrhage at the margins. Both ends are tapered or pointed with smooth edges similar to the 2 wounds described above.

Opinion: This is compatible with a defense wound.

OTHER INJURIES TO HANDS AND UPPER EXTREMITIES:

1. On the lateral aspect of the right distal forearm, adjacent to the wrist, there is a 3/4 x 1/2 inch abrasion on the ulnar surface, red-brown in color, nonpatterned.

2. On the lateral or outer aspect of the left forearm there are multiple abrasions both linear and one that is approximately triangular measuring 3/4 x 1/2 inch; they are all brown to red-brown in color and antemortem; the longest linear abrasion is 3/4 inch in length.

3. On the dorsal surface of the right hand there are fresh bruises (red-purple in color) and fresh red-brown abrasions. On the proximal knuckle of the right middle finger a 1 x 3/4 inch bruise with no overlying abrasion. On the middle knuckle of the index finger a 1/2 x 1/2 inch bruise surrounding a 1/8 nondescript abrasion; just distal on the middle phalanx of the middle finger a 1/8 nondescript abrasion. On the proximal knuckle of the right index finer there is a 1/2 x 1/2 inch fresh bruise surrounding a linear diagonally oriented 1/2 inch red-brown abrasion.

There is a 1/2 x 1/2 inch fresh bruise on the middle of the right ring finger surrounding 2 punctate abrasions approximately 1/8 inch in maximal diameter; on the middle knuckle of the right 5th finger there is a 1/16 inch punctate nondescript abrasion.

4. On the dorsal side of the left hand there are multiple red-brown abrasions irregular in configuration and border, involving the 3 knuckles of the left index finger; maximal dimension 1/4 x 3/8 inch, all red-brown in color.

There is an irregularly configured abrasion on the proximal knuckle of the left middle finger consisting of an apparent 3 linear 1/2 inch abrasions converging at the center having a somewhat configuration of the letter W. These are all superficial skin abrasions. On the dorsal side of the left hand adjacent to the web of the thumb there is a linear, 3/4 inch long skin abrasion terminating in a 1/8 inch nondescript punctate abrasion near the base of the thumb.

There is a fresh bruise, 1 1/4 x 1 1/2 inch on the dorsal surface of the left hand adjacent to the wrist surrounding a punctate abrasion.

5. There are 2 fresh bruises on the ulnar surface of the left wrist, nonabraded, measuring respectively 3/8 x 3/8 inch and 1/2 x 1/2 inch, with the bruising involving the skin and dermis.

INTERNAL EXAMINATION:

The body is opened with the usual Y-shaped thoracoabdominal incision revealing the abdominal adipose tissue to measure 1/2 to 3/4 inch in thickness. The anterior abdominal wall has its normal muscular components and no blunt force injuries are evident. Exposure of the body cavities shows the contained organs in their usual anatomic locations with their usual anatomic relationships. The serosal surfaces are smooth, thin, and glistening and the free blood within the peritoneal cavity due to the stab wound as previously described; this also includes the left retroperitoneal hemorrhage, hemorrhage into the left ilio-psoas muscle, and the mesocolon.

INTERNAL EVIDENCE OF INJURY:

Aside from the stab wounds of the chest and abdomen, there are no other internal traumatic injuries involving the thoracic or abdominal viscera.

SYSTEMIC AND ORGAN REVIEW:

Autopsy findings, or lack of them, considered apart from those already stated. The following observations pertain to findings other than the injuries and changes that are described above.

MUSCULOSKELETAL SYSTEM—SUBCUTANEOUS TISSUE-SKIN:

Anatomic except as otherwise stated or implied.

HEAD—CENTRAL NERVOUS SYSTEM:

The brain weighs 1,400 grams. The external indications of injury as well as the deep scalp and subgaleal hemorrhage have been described above. There is no hemorrhage into the temporal muscle or the orbits.

There are no tears of the dura mater and no recent epidural, subdural, or subarachnoid hemorrhage. The dura is stripped revealing no fractures of the bones of the calvarium or base of the skull.

The pituitary gland is normally situated in the sella turcica and is not enlarged.

The cranial nerves are enumerated and they are intact, symmetrical and anatomic in size, location and course.

The component vessels of the circle of Willis are identified and they are anatomic in size, course and configuration. The blood vessels are intact, free of aneurysm or other anomaly, are non-occluded, and show no significant atherosclerosis.

Multiple coronal sections of the non-formalin-fixed, fresh brain shows: The cerebral hemispheres, cerebellum, brain stem, pons and medulla to show their normal anatomical structures. The cerebellar, the pontine and the medullary surfaces present no lesions. The cerebral cortex, the white matter, the ventricular system and basal ganglia are anatomic. There is no evidence of hemorrhage, cysts or neoplasm involving the brain substance.

The spinal chord is not dissected.

ORGANS OF SPECIAL SENSES:

Not dissected.

RESPIRATORY SYSTEM—THROAT STRUCTURES:

The oral cavity, viewed from below, is anatomic and no lesions are seen. The mucosa is intact and there are no injuries to the lips, teeth or gums.

There is no obstruction of the airway. The injury to the left internal jugular vein has been previously described. The mucosa of the epiglottis, glottis, piriform sinuses, trachea and major bronchi are anatomic. No injuries are seen and there are no mucosal lesions.

The hyoid bone, the thyroid, and the cricoid cartilages are intact. No hemorrhage is present in the tissues adjacent to the throat organs nor is there hemorrhage into the substance of the anatomic appearing thyroid gland. The parathyroid glands are not identified.

Lungs: The lungs weight: Right, 420 grams; left 320 grams. The external appearance and that of the sectioned surface of the left lung shows a pink external surface without evidence of injuries. There is minimal congestion, otherwise not remarkable. No foreign substance, infarction or neoplasm is encountered.

The right lung shows basilar atelectasis due to the hemothorax caused by the stab wound to the right lower lobe described above. Otherwise the external appearance of the sectioned surface shows no focal lesion; there is no evidence of foreign material, infarction or neoplasm.

CARDIOVASCULAR SYSTEM:

The heart weighs 290 grams, and has a normal size and configuration. The chambers, valves, and the myocardium are anatomic. There are no focal endocardial, valvular or myocardial lesion and no congenital anomalies.

Multiple transverse sections of the left and right coronary arteries reveal them to be thin-walled and patent throughout with no significant atherosclerosis. The aorta and its branches are anatomic; the perforating stab wound injury of the distal abdominal aorta has been previously described.

The portal and caval veins and the major branches are anatomic.

GASTROINTESTINAL SYSTEM:

The mucosa and wall of the esophagus are intact and gray-pink, without lesions or injuries.

The gastric mucosa is intact and pink without injury. There are no focal lesions, no residual medications, and no swallowed blood is present. Approximately 200 ml of partially digested semisolid food is found in the stomach with the presence of fragments of green leafy vegetable material compatible with spinach.

The mucosa of the duodenum, jejunum, ileum, colon and rectum are intact. The lumen is patent. There are no mucosal lesions or injuries and no blood is present. The fecal content is usual in appearance.

The vermiform appendix is present.

HEPATOBILIARY SYSTEM—PANCREAS:

The liver weighs 1,360 grams and is normal size and configuration. The subcapsular and the cut surfaces of the liver are uniformly brown-red in color, free of nodularity, and usual in appearance. The biliary duct system, including the gallbladder, is free of anomaly and no lesions are seen. The mucosa is intact and bile stained. The lumina are patent and no calculi are present.

The pancreas is anatomic both externally and on cut surface.

HEMOLYMPHATIC SYSTEM—ADRENAL GLAND:

The spleen weighs 210 grams and has an intact capsule. Cut surface shows a normal coloration with a firm red-purple parenchyma and no focal lesions.

The blood, the bone marrow and the usually-named aggregates of lymph nodes do not appear to be significantly altered.

The thymus gland is not identified.

The adrenal glands are usual in size and location and the cut surface presents no lesions or injuries. However, there is a small amount of left periadrenal hemorrhage due to the retro-peritoneal hemorrhage caused by the stab wound.

URINARY SYSTEM:

The kidneys weigh: Left, 150 grams; right, 140 grams. The kidneys are anatomic in size, shape and location. The capsules are stripped to show a smooth, pale brown surface. On section the cortex and medulla are anatomic without lesions.

The calyces, the pelves, the ureters and urinary-bladder are unaltered in appearance. The mucosa is gray-pink. No calculi are present, and no blood is present.

The urinary bladder contains no measurable urine.

MALE GENITAL SYSTEM:

The testicles, the penis, the prostate gland are anatomic to dissection.

HISTOLOGY:

Representatives portions of the various organs, including the larynx, are preserved in 10% formaldehyde and placed in a single storage container.

TOXICOLOGY:

A sample of right pleural blood as well as bile are submitted for toxicologic analysis. Stomach contents are saved.

SEROLOGY:

A sample of right pleural blood is submitted in the EDTA tube.

RADIOLOGY:

None.

PHOTOGRAPHY:

In addition to the routine identification photographs; pertinent photographs are taken of the external injuries.

WITNESSES:

Detectives Vannatter and Lange, LAPD, Robbery Homicide Division, were present during the autopsy.

DIAGRAMS USED:

Form 42, 16, 20F, 20H, 21 and 24 were utilized during the performance of the autopsy.

OPINION:

The decedent sustained multiple sharp force injuries, including multiple stab wounds involving the chest and abdomen; multiple incised-stab wounds of the neck; and multiple incised or cutting wounds. Fatal wounds were identified involving the neck where there was transection of the left internal jugular vein and stab wounds of the chest and abdomen causing intrathoracic and intraabdominal hemorrhage.

Of note the cutting wounds of the left and right hands, compatible with defensive wounds. In addition there were a number of blunt force injuries to the upper extremities and hands, likewise compatible with defensive wounds. The remainder of the autopsy revealed a normal, healthy adult male with no congenital anomalies. Routine toxicologic studies were ordered.

(Signed) IRWIN L. GOLDEN, M.D.
DEPUTY MEDICAL EXAMINER

June 17, 1994
DATE

APPENDIX G: List of Evidence Taken from O.J. Simpson's Estate

Police investigators seized more than 100 pieces of physical evidence from O.J. Simpson's estate. The evidence list, provided below, describes each items of evidence and indicates the place from which it was gathered. Judge Ito admitted all items into evidence except for: 1.) a video of Simpson's playing professional football, 2.) post-it notes, and 3.) legal documents deemed to be unrelated to the case. Many other items of evidence were gathered from the crime scene, and are not shown here.

1. Swatch (of blood) - Rockingham driveway
2. Swatch (of blood) - Rockingham driveway
3. Swatch (of blood) - Rockingham driveway
4. Swatch (of blood) - Rockingham driveway
5. Swatch (of blood) - Rockingham driveway
6. Glove; right-handed - Rockingham walkway
7. Blue plastic bag - Rockingham walkway
8. Swatch (of blood) - Rockingham walkway
9. Swatch (of blood) - Rockingham foyer
10. Socks - Rockingham bedroom
11. Swatch (of blood) - Rockingham bathroom
12. Airline ticket receipt - Rockingham bathroom
13. Baggage tag - Rockingham bathroom
14. Reebok shoes - no location cited
15. Hair and fibers from right glove
16. Swatch (of blood) - Bronco passenger door
17. Swatch (of blood) - Bronco driver door
18. Swatch (of blood) - Bronco driver door
19. Swatch (of blood) - Bronco instrument panel
20. Fibers - Bronco carpet
21. Swatch (of blood) - Bronco driver floor
22. Cap - Bronco driver floor
23. Swatch (of blood) - Bronco steering wheel
24. Swatch (of blood) - Bronco console
25. Swatch (of blood) - Bronco console
26. Swatch (of blood) - Bronco passenger backrest
27. Carpet - Bronco driver floor
28. Swatch (of blood) - Bronco driver wall
29. Hair - Rockingham driveway
30. White towel - Bronco cargo
31. Shovel - Bronco cargo
32. Plastic sheet - Bronco cargo
33. Glove; left-handed - Rockingham bedroom
34. Watch cap - Rockingham bedroom
35. Scarf - Rockingham bedroom
36. Shirt - Rockingham bedroom
37. Watch cap - Rockingham bedroom
38. Gloves - Rockingham bedroom
39. Gloves - Rockingham bedroom
40. Shirt - Rockingham bedroom
41. Shirt - Rockingham bedroom
42. Video - Rockingham home
43. Script and schedule - Rockingham
44. Notepad - Rockingham
45. Call sheet - Rockingham
46. Videos (2) - Rockingham home
47. Videos (2) - Rockingham home
48. Papers - Rockingham office
49. Hair and fibers from right glove
50. Hair and fibers from cap
51. Hair and fibers from white towel
52. Hair and fibers from plastic sheet
53. Hair and fibers from watch cap
54. Hair and fibers from shovel
55. Package - Bentley rear floor
56. Flyer - Bentley front console
57. Receipt - Bentley left front door
58. Parking citation - Bentley front console
59. Business card - Bentley front console
60. Paper - Bentley front console
61. Paper - Bentley front console
62. Paper - Bentley front console
63. Paper - Bentley front console
64. Tape cloth - Bentley front console
65. Cassette - Bentley front console
66. Business card - Bentley sun visor
67. Card - Bentley trunk
68. Folder - Bentley
69. Notepad - Bronco
70. Packing list - Bronco glove box
71. Garage door opener - Bronco glove box
72. Business cards - Bronco glove box
73. Note - Bronco center seat console
74. Note - Bronco center seat console
75. Business card - Bronco center seat console
76. Cassette Tape - Bronco center seat console
77. Illegal parking notice - Bronco center seat console
78. Cassette tape - Bronco front passenger door pocket
79. Note - Bronco center seat console
80. Call sheet - Bronco center seat console
81. Post it note - Bronco center seat console
82. Parking permit - Bronco center seat console
83. Post it note - Bronco center seat console
84. Post it note - Bronco center seat console
85. Page fax - Bronco center seat console
86. Photo - Bronco center seat console
87. Post it note - Bronco center seat console

88. Card - Bronco sun visor
89. Post it note - Bronco under driver seat
90. Card - Bronco rear seat
91. Card - Bronco rear cargo
92. Golf shoes - Bronco rear cargo
93. Paper bag - Bronco rear cargo
94. Picture frame - Bronco rear cargo
95. Newspaper - Bronco center rear console
96. Coat hanger - Bronco rear seat
97. Pyramid - Bronco rear floor
98. Golf shoe box - Bronco rear cargo
99. Brake pad - Bronco
100. Brake pad - Bronco
101. Accelerator pad - Bronco
102. Fibers - Bronco driver floor
103. Fibers - Bronco left rear floor
104. Fibers - Bronco front hump
105. Fibers - Bronco right front door
106. Fibers - Bronco passenger door
107. Fibers - Bronco right rear floor
108. Fibers - Bronco cargo
109. Fibers - Bronco back rear seat
110. Fibers - Bronco rear door interior
111. Debris - Bronco driver seat